ELUSIVE VICTORIES

To Andrew (great name!)

with my best wishes.

[signature]

ELUSIVE VICTORIES

THE AMERICAN PRESIDENCY AT WAR

ANDREW J. POLSKY

OXFORD
UNIVERSITY PRESS

OXFORD
UNIVERSITY PRESS

Oxford University Press, Inc., publishes works that further
Oxford University's objective of excellence
in research, scholarship, and education.

Oxford   New York
Auckland   Cape Town   Dar es Salaam   Hong Kong   Karachi
Kuala Lumpur   Madrid   Melbourne   Mexico City   Nairobi
New Delhi   Shanghai   Taipei   Toronto

With offices in
Argentina   Austria   Brazil   Chile   Czech Republic   France   Greece
Guatemala   Hungary   Italy   Japan   Poland   Portugal   Singapore
South Korea   Switzerland   Thailand   Turkey   Ukraine   Vietnam

Published by Oxford University Press, Inc.
198 Madison Avenue, New York, New York 10016

www.oup.com

Oxford is a registered trademark of Oxford University Press

Library of Congress Cataloging-in-Publication Data
Polsky, Andrew Joseph.
Elusive victories : the American presidency at war / Andrew J. Polsky.
p.   cm.
ISBN 978-0-19-986093-7 (acid-free paper) 1. Presidents—United States—History.
2. War and emergency powers—United States—History. 3. War and emergency
powers—United States—Case studies. I. Title.
JK558.P65   2012
352.23'5—dc23   2011041946

1 3 5 7 9 8 6 4 2

Printed in the United States of America
on acid-free paper

To Beth, Sara, and Alex, my kitchen cabinet

CONTENTS

Introduction   3

1. Lincoln's Shadow   31

2. Waging War to Transform the World: Woodrow Wilson   83

3. Freedom of Action: Franklin Roosevelt   133

4. Staying the Course: Johnson and Nixon   202

5. The Perils of Optimism: George W. Bush   273

6. Inheriting a Bad Hand: Barack Obama   326

Conclusion: Past and Future   340

Afterword   361

Acknowledgments   365

Notes   369

Index   427

ELUSIVE VICTORIES

Introduction

A Tale of Two Invasions

A convoy of ships approached the coast of Cuba near Daiquiri in June 1898, bearing almost 17,000 American troops. They belonged to a U.S. Army that had been created virtually overnight—veteran regulars combined with National Guard regiments and new, barely trained units, such as the celebrated 1st U.S. Volunteer Cavalry, the Rough Riders. With ships of the U.S. Navy bottling up a Spanish fleet in Santiago, the convoy faced no real danger on its voyage. The problem was what to do next. Because the army lacked a general staff of the kind contemporary European militaries had developed, senior officers had pieced together the invasion plan on the fly, repeatedly changing the landing site and target date. After boarding chartered cargo vessels in Tampa, the troops had no good way to land in Cuba. The army had had to borrow steam lighters from the navy to tow longboats filled with soldiers to the beach, while horses and mules were thrown into the water to swim to shore. Amid the din of naval gunfire, some of the animals became confused, turned out to sea, and drowned. Heavy guns that might be needed for a siege of Santiago had to be left on board because there were neither vessels nor facilities to get them ashore.[1]

3

Things improved little once the army reached land. Senior officers, with no experience commanding large military formations, misjudged the difficulties of moving through swamps; men sweated in heavy flannel and wool uniforms designed for fighting Indians on the Western plains; and some soldiers carried old rifles that fired black-powder cartridges, the telltale smoke revealing their positions to the enemy.[2] Despite the difficulties, the army managed to defeat the smaller Spanish forces at El Caney and San Juan Hill in costly attacks on July 1, 1898, and placed Santiago under siege.

At that point, nature intervened: the Americans were decimated by yellow fever and malaria. The medical services, unprepared for tropical conditions, were overwhelmed. Ships laden with supplies could not offload at the primitive docking facilities at Daiquiri and nearby Siboney, and men in the trenches went hungry. So desperate were the conditions that the American commanders asked Washington to accept terms that would allow the trapped Spanish troops to march unhindered to Havana rather than surrender.[3]

Now to another invasion by American military forces, this one in early 2003 and marked by the rapid but meticulously organized deployment of more than 150,000 troops to the other side of the world.[4] The assault on Iraq was conducted soon after another major military operation in Afghanistan, with substantial forces still committed there.[5] For the Iraq campaign, American defense staffers had devised a clear plan for the advance on Baghdad, one that incorporated several operational alternatives (one or two lines of attack, depending on political circumstances).[6] The American force assembled was the best-equipped military in world, highly trained and experienced. It enjoyed a vast technological edge over its Iraqi adversaries. So superior was the American advantage that Secretary of Defense Donald Rumsfeld scaled back the initial deployment plans.

Despite the striking differences between the two invasions, one important similarity bears noting: in both instances, the president of the United States had established the broad political goals that military intervention was designed to secure. William McKinley had been reluctant to go to war with Spain over Cuba, where violent unrest had plagued the island for years. Once he decided that war could no longer be avoided, however, he resolved to liberate Cuba from Spanish control.

He also intended to displace the Spanish empire from its remaining outposts in the Western Hemisphere and the Pacific.[7] George W. Bush had weighed the possibility of military action against Iraq since the September 11, 2001, terrorist attacks.[8] When he approved the invasion in 2003, Bush sought to end any threat that Iraq might use or share weapons of mass destruction (WMD) with extremist organizations, to remove Saddam Hussein and his regime, and to establish a functioning democracy in the heart of the Arab world that would serve as a model for other nations across the region.

A historical irony jumps out at us. McKinley, with the very modest and ill-prepared forces at his disposal, achieved his war goals quickly and completely. American forces did encounter a nasty insurgency in the Philippines, but this largely collapsed by 1901.[9] McKinley was rewarded with reelection in 1900 and his party retained control over the White House during the next two elections.

By contrast, despite a far greater military advantage over the enemy, Bush was unable to accomplish the larger political goal he defined for the Iraq War. Iraq did not become a beacon of democracy. Instead, the United States was dragged into a protracted conflict with competing sectarian factions, some aided by militants from abroad and foreign governments. The ongoing low-intensity combat and American losses contributed to Republican defeat in the 2006 congressional elections and to Bush's low approval ratings in his last two years in office. Not until 2008 did violence begin to abate in Iraq, and fighting there continued into the presidency of Bush's successor, Barack Obama. The last American combat units were withdrawn in August 2010, making the conflict one of the longest in American history. Iraq's political future remains very much in doubt.

In this book I examine the tasks that presidents must undertake in wartime and explain why they usually fail to accomplish at least some of them. The Constitution establishes the president as the "Commander in Chief of the Army and Navy of the United States, and of the Militia of the several States, when called into the actual Service of the United States." In that role, presidents face recurring challenges as they lead the nation into armed conflict. They must decide whether to go to war, prepare for it, define and pursue national political objectives through military operations, direct military operations to achieve those objectives, prepare for the peace that will follow the fighting, engage in diplomacy to secure and retain allies and undercut support for adversaries, and sustain political support at home. The list is daunting. Because every task demands its own time, moreover, the president also must wrestle with their relative importance. None can be ignored, lest he fail to achieve the goals he has established in taking the nation to war in the first place.

As I will show, presidents have struggled to manage their wartime leadership challenges, especially preparing for peace and the postwar order. Moreover, their performance appears to be worsening over time. Despite the enormous military resources at their disposal, modern American presidents have often failed in their military ventures. Results from recent wars range from prolonged stalemates (Vietnam in the 1960s and 1970s) to incomplete victory (the Persian Gulf in 1991) to initial triumph giving way to protracted violence (Iraq and Afghanistan). The repeated failures in wartime presidential leadership beg for explanation.

Debates and Puzzles

Writing on wartime leadership is as old as the study of history itself. Texts by Thucydides and Sun Tzu, and later volumes by Niccolo Machiavelli and Carl von Clausewitz mix analysis and prescription. In the fifth century B.C. Thucydides chronicled the Peloponnesian Wars in part to instruct subsequent generations of statesmen in how to avoid the errors made by his contemporaries.[10] When Thucydides writes, "It is a common mistake in going to war to begin at the wrong end, to act first, and wait for disaster to discuss the matter,"[11] his warning carries across the centuries to American policy makers who dismissed the prospects of sectarian strife in the aftermath of the 2003 Iraq invasion. In the wake of the Napoleonic Wars, Clausewitz developed a theory of war that famously treats it as an extension of policy or statecraft "by other means."[12] His implication is clear: a leader must never lose sight of his political objectives.

Debate over American presidential wartime leadership heightens when the wars themselves or the actions of presidents during them become controversial. The assertion of extraordinary executive authority, especially as it encroaches upon venerated civil liberties, has prompted many lawyers and academics to repudiate the exercise of unilateral presidential power. Bush administration decisions to detain suspected terrorists, al-Qaeda operatives, and captured non-Afghan Taliban fighters without trial at Guantánamo provoked widespread domestic and international condemnation. Controversy also swirled around other administration policies, such as extraordinary rendition, the practice of sending certain terror suspects to other countries where they might be subjected to extreme methods of interrogation and brutal incarceration. The disputes over post-9/11 presidential power recall those of the Vietnam era, when critics took issue with many presidential actions, including the secret bombing of Cambodia and increased domestic surveillance of antiwar activists during the Nixon administration. But presidents have their defenders, too, who insist that emergencies force presidents to extend their reach to keep the nation safe, and that their actions are therefore constitutional.[13]

For the most part, these debates address the legitimacy of presidential action. Lost in their heat is the first puzzle of wartime presidential leadership: in a constitutional system designed to check the unilateral exercise of power, how is it that presidents have been able to send American armed forces into battle nearly anywhere in the world with no effective political restraint?

Other arguments have raged over not whether but how a president should exercise wartime leadership. Contemporary views divide into two broad schools. One side follows the work of Samuel Huntington, who explored the relationship between politicians and the military in his influential post–World War II study, *The Soldier and the State*. The advent of military professionalism in the later nineteenth century, he suggests, allowed a division of responsibility in wartime between political and military leaders that would make best use of their respective expertise. Huntington endorses a system he terms "objective control": civilians should establish broad national goals and guide the allocation of resources, while military commanders should be given full control over the execution of strategy. When soldiers are encouraged to make political decisions, he cautions, mistakes occur. Mistakes also may happen when civilian leaders abdicate their responsibilities or trespass on matters more properly seen as military.[14] At certain times, Huntington's model has found favor, most notably in the wake of the Vietnam War, which was marked by interference by the White House in detailed planning of air operations against North Vietnam. Senior officers and politicians responded by urging adherence to the notion that the military side of fighting wars should be left to the military.

In reaction to the objective-control school, another has emerged, asserting that political leaders need to be involved in wartime command decisions—right down to the operational and even tactical level.[15] This camp argues that if war is an extension of policy, no separation exists between politics and combat. Rather, to make certain that military decisions conform to and help secure political objectives, civilian leaders must maintain close oversight of their field commanders. Eliot A. Cohen, a leading proponent of a hands-on or what I call "active direction" model, notes that a political leader in wartime must perform certain tasks—selecting commanders from among unproven generals, managing alliances, restructuring the military, setting operational priorities, and making sure military subordinates pursue their assignments vigorously—that go well beyond what "objective control" prescribes.[16] From this perspective, the problems in Vietnam stemmed not from too much political oversight but too little: Lyndon Johnson failed to exercise control over the ground war or to question the optimistic reports of his field commander General William Westmoreland. Cohen adds that the error of inadequate oversight was repeated in the 1991 Persian Gulf War, when President George H.W. Bush permitted the senior military officer on the scene, General Norman Schwarzkopf, to decide when to end the ground campaign and to set the terms of a cease-fire. By halting the fighting before the destruction of Saddam Hussein's Republican Guard, letting it escape, and allowing the Iraqi military to continue to fly helicopter missions, Cohen contends, Schwarzkopf made it possible for the Iraqi dictator to suppress internal uprisings and remain in power. Thus the field commander thwarted achievement of the president's most important war goal—eliminating Hussein as a threat to regional stability.[17]

Neither school, however, solves the problem of how a president should exercise command during wartime. Both objective control and active direction yield uneven results. Presidents have adhered to each approach and succeeded. But they have also pursued each and failed to achieve their larger political goals. Lyndon Johnson, for one, demonstrates the problems with both schools. He meddled in some military operations (the air campaign against North Vietnam) while he kept his distance from others, and achieved dismal results in both cases. This leads us to a second puzzle of wartime presidential leadership: Why do presidents, in their role as commander in chief, still struggle to find an effective approach to achieve the national objectives they have established in going to war?

Besides yielding no clear answer, the debate between the two camps is too narrow. No matter how large the conflict or how many demands it makes on them, wartime presidents are never *only* the commander in chief of the armed forces. Their domain encompasses American foreign policy writ large, with objectives that transcend the battlefield. Presidents also play a critical role in sustaining broad popular support for the war effort and securing the resources needed to bring the war to a successful conclusion—responsibilities that get brushed aside in the argument over whether a president should let military professionals run things.

Yet presidents often fall short in meeting their other wartime challenges, a failing that clouds the prospects for victory and undermines their capacity to fashion the kind of peace that gives it meaning.[18] Abraham Lincoln did little to prepare for Reconstruction; Lyndon Johnson futilely attempted to stem the collapse of popular support for the Vietnam War, which in turn put a halt to his vision for a Great Society at home. Their failures point us to a third puzzle: Why do wartime presidents regularly struggle to meet their non-military challenges, especially planning for the aftermath of the conflict?

Wars also do not put a stop to domestic politics. After winning the White House behind promises of sweeping domestic policy initiatives, several presidents—Woodrow Wilson, Franklin Roosevelt, and Lyndon Johnson—became wartime leaders. They all claimed strong popular mandates to pursue ambitious agendas, and all three introduced major domestic initiatives either before the war or in its midst. Their supporters wanted social reform to continue, yet these domestic projects collapsed amid the war, separating the president from some of his key constituencies. War per se does not necessarily doom social reform—witness the World War II Beveridge Report in Great Britain that led to the creation of its National Health Service. From the demise of presidents' domestic programs and the schisms that grow among presidents' supporters, a fourth puzzle emerges: Why do wartime presidents, even those elected by huge margins, suffer the defeat of their domestic agenda and the undoing of their reform aspirations?

At first glance wars appear to bestow on presidents dramatic freedom of action and broad discretion over the use of force. They decide whether to command in a hands-on manner or to delegate authority, and they establish national objectives and peace-building goals. Presidents seem to enjoy the kind of strategic flexibility that scholars see as a cornerstone of presidential success. For instance, Richard Neustadt emphasizes the value of flexibility and urges presidents to take particular care to think strategically, preserve their options, and safeguard their power prospects.[19] Presidents retain wide freedom of action when it comes to the use of force abroad. Indeed, this may be one reason that presidents in certain political situations tend to choose military intervention—they see it as a way to sustain their political coalition.[20] At least where "small wars" (the kind the United States has fought since 1945) are concerned, presidents anticipate positive results when they exercise their war powers: effective military intervention abroad will yield maximum political advantage at home.

Recent history argues otherwise. No president since the end of World War II has achieved all of the political objectives he has identified in going to war. (I do not include brief campaigns conducted with modest forces, as in Grenada in 1983 or Panama in 1989.) Worse, in several cases the United States has become bogged down, despite its vast conventional military superiority. Presidents mired in stalemates have been unable either to escalate their military commitment or to extricate the nation from the conflict. Wars that drag on without victory or exit have helped to unravel several presidencies, including those of Harry Truman, Lyndon Johnson, and, as noted at the outset, George W. Bush. Each has suffered from sharply declining approval ratings and watched his party lose the next presidential election.

In short, something about presidential war powers transforms their wielder from muscular to muscle-bound. This presidential frustration brings us to the fifth puzzle of wartime leadership: Despite broad flexibility to deploy coercion abroad against much weaker enemies, why do presidents find themselves bereft of strategic options, with little latitude to alter the course of the war they initiated?

The Constitutional Framework

To begin to address these puzzles, we should consider first the broader contexts of wartime presidential leadership. One is a constant: for more than two centuries, the Constitution has invested presidents with a broad warrant to act on matters of national security. The document's ambiguities and silences have enticed presidents to expand their capacity to undertake military operations on their own initiative. Situations often arise in which "strict construction"—a literal reading of the wording—cannot fix the extent of presidential authority. Politicians and scholars have argued heatedly about the proper limits of presidential war powers. Without question, however, the underlying logic of the constitutional system endows presidents with the means to win that argument when they think the nation faces a threat to its security.

The authors of the Constitution sought to divide war-making authority and the power to direct war. Article II, which most directly defines the role and powers of the chief executive, unifies military direction in the hands of the president. The first power listed is to serve as the commander in chief of the nation's armed forces, including the militia when called into national service. During the Revolution the new nation had barely survived the inefficiency of congressional direction of military affairs, which brought Washington's army to the brink of starvation more than once. Military operations also had been hampered by uncertainty about whether states would release their own troops for duty in other states facing a direct British military threat. The Framers remembered and chose to make plain that the chain of command leads directly to the president. In a constitutional system otherwise characterized by elaborate institutional checks, the president may act as commander in chief without securing approval from any other branch.

Congress is given the power to create and regulate the nation's military capacity, as well as to declare war. Under Article I, Congress gains clear authority to establish and finance the nation's armed forces, to summon state militia into service to repel foreign attack and put down domestic insurrections, and to impose standards upon the state militia. The article prohibits the use of any army appropriation for longer than two years, a legacy of colonial mistrust of standing armies. In giving Congress the power to declare war, the Framers recognized that such a step should be taken only after careful consideration. This reflects the broader spirit of a constitutional design that views debate and deliberation as offering the best path to the common good of the nation.

The Constitution's spare language leaves unresolved much about the allocation of authority over national security. For example, Article IV states, "The United States shall guarantee to every State in the Union a republican form of government, and shall protect each of them against invasion." Although the wording commits the national government to act, it does not specify which branch is responsible. The president as commander in chief may order an immediate military response, but only Congress may call state forces into national service. Nor does the Constitution define "invasion." Could the term be construed to include not just a massive attack across the borders of the United States but also more modest incursions or raids, possibly by irregular forces operating without the approval of any government? Perhaps most important, the Framers understood the difference between armed conflict and a formal state of war. They purposefully decided to grant Congress the power to *declare* war, not the power to *make* war.[21] But it is not clear what they intended to accomplish by establishing that distinction.

Constitutional ambiguity has fueled the recurrent debate about the scope of presidential war-making authority. On one side are those who contend that the Framers invested the president with broad authority to preserve the national security. In choosing to limit Congress to the power to declare war, they recognized that protecting the nation might require what Alexander Hamilton referred to as "energy," the capacity for urgent action that is not the strong suit of a deliberative legislature. They also appreciated that situations might arise in which the use of force would be appropriate without recourse to a formal declaration of war. From what I would call the *presidentialist* viewpoint, Congress can restrain such operations only by resorting to its explicit power to withhold funds from the armed forces, thereby compelling the president to bring the troops home.[22]

The opposing view—that Congress has the authority to make most decisions to employ military force—has been asserted by those I would label *congressionalists*. According to this school, the Framers expected Congress to restrain the president's use of force. Because military action can have far-reaching and unforeseeable consequences, the decision to take it ought to be made after the careful deliberation that only a legislative body offers. That presidents have repeatedly employed the military without legislative sanction, the noted congressionalist Louis Fisher insists, does not legitimize the practice.[23]

Both sides, though, recognize an enduring reality of the constitutional structure: the president is in a strong position to assert control, perhaps even supremacy, in national security matters. Intentionally or not, by creating a unitary executive, the Framers gave the president a decisive edge over Congress in situations involving prompt action.[24] Consider again the Article IV mandate to repel an invasion. The president may define what constitutes an invasion and deploy any available military forces. Once the United States finds itself engaged in a conflict, political pressures—to support our troops, for example—are certain to make it impossible for Congress to assert its powers. In theory, the legislature could refuse to continue appropriations for a conflict of which members strongly disapprove; in practice, Congress would not deny funds to embattled American forces lest it be accused of failing its patriotic duty.[25]

The combination of unchecked command authority and the ability to act with dispatch has allowed presidents to respond first to national security crises and has reduced Congress to a reactive role. Presidents can manipulate circumstances by ordering American troops into situations in which hostilities are likely to erupt, leaving lawmakers little choice but to acquiesce. In 1846, James K. Polk dispatched troops into the disputed Texas border region between the Nueces River (which Polk's predecessors regarded as the true southern border of Texas) and the Rio Grande, hoping to provoke a Mexican attack and create a casus belli. When the Mexicans obliged by ambushing an American cavalry detachment, Polk asked Congress to recognize that a state of war existed, brought on by Mexico's "aggression." Legislative opposition to Polk's expansionist agenda collapsed.[26] Simply put, by controlling the placement of American forces, the president can all but determine when and where the nation will go to war. Deployment is destiny.

Greater Military Means, Fewer Restraints, and the Wrong Kinds of Wars

The Constitution has remained a constant in presidential war-making, but nothing else has stood still. One change involves the dramatic increase in the military means at a president's disposal. Although the Polk example demonstrates that presidents have always exercised latitude in deploying force at their own behest, only when the United States became a superpower was presidential initiative matched by a standing military capacity to support a worldwide military reach. Superpower status also altered the popular mind-set about threats to our national security. These are now seen to arise in the most distant corners of the globe. Meanwhile, the institutional and political constraints on presidential use of force have weakened significantly in the period since the Second World War. On the other hand, the kinds of full-scale wars in which the American military might be used effectively to achieve national objectives have largely disappeared. Recent conflicts have assumed a character that neutralizes American military advantages, and presidents have discovered that the means at their disposal often do not match the challenges they face.

Expanding the President's Capacity to Wage War. Before the Second World War, the United States maintained a small standing army in peacetime. The nation had to start from scratch to create a suitable military force for every significant military conflict. Substantial armies were established either mere months before the shooting started (the War of 1812, the Spanish-American War, World War I, and World War II) or, in some cases, after the war had begun (the Mexican War and the Civil War). After the Civil War, a number of political and military leaders saw the need to alter this pattern. Their efforts yielded oddly mismatched outcomes. Advocates of army reform were thwarted in their quest to establish an expandable army and extend national control over state militia; yet proponents of a modern navy mounted a brilliant public relations campaign in favor of battleship construction in the early 1890s and made significant headway.[27] That was why President McKinley could call upon an updated fleet in 1898 even as he repeated the struggle of his predecessors to put a trained army in the field quickly.

The presidents who would face two world wars still depended on legislative action to bring the armed forces to a war footing. Apart from the U.S. Navy, the resources at the disposal of a commander in chief remained modest. When Woodrow Wilson asked Congress to declare war on Germany in April 1917, as I explain in Chapter 2, the United States could contribute no troops. Mobilization eventually put a sizable American army into the field in the final months of the conflict, giving Wilson the place at the peace table he sought. What had been created in a mad rush was then dismantled almost as quickly, much as after previous wars.

Frantic mobilization became necessary again a generation later, at the outset of the Second World War. As before, the nation scrambled to build a huge army for global conflict and to expand the navy so that it could wage full-scale war in two oceans. As warfare had become more complex, however, the time needed to train and equip militaries had increased. The United States required two years to mobilize fully, a delay that postponed the decisive Allied invasion of Europe until 1944, resulted in untold additional military and especially civilian deaths, and allowed the victorious Soviet army to advance deep into Central Europe.

Yet even that sobering experience, joined to the postwar threat posed by an increasingly hostile Soviet Union, did not entirely uproot the old habit of shrinking the military in peacetime. Weary of wartime sacrifices, Americans demanded the quick return and discharge of the troops.[28] Confidence that peace would become the norm extended all the way to the White House: after World War II ended, Harry S. Truman approved a redesign of the presidential seal in which the eagle's head was turned toward the olive branch as a symbol of the new era. The outbreak of war in Korea in June 1950 caught the U.S. Army once more at a low level of readiness.

Nonetheless, important changes had already occurred that marked the birth of a new era in American security policy. Americans drew a lesson from Pearl Harbor and Hiroshima: lost forever was the luxury of time and distance that had permitted the United States to arm itself at leisure when a threat loomed. American leaders now spoke of national security as a constant concern. Further, the vast "military-industrial complex"—as Eisenhower later termed it—spawned by the Second

World War had generated powerful political sponsors eager for ongoing defense contracts to sustain business and employment.[29] Last but not least, the emergence of the Soviet Union as a rival superpower and the spread of communism in Eastern Europe and Asia, coupled with the recognition that other nations such as Great Britain and France could no longer afford to take the lead in a major conflict, convinced American policy makers to accept a stronger standing military.[30] Force reductions after the Second World War, then, were not as severe as those following previous conflicts. The years immediately after the war saw the beginning of the modern national security state: the American embrace of collective security through establishment of the United Nations and NATO; passage of the 1948 National Security Act, which created the Department of Defense, the Central Intelligence Agency, and the National Security Council; and the adoption of a broad commitment to resist the spread of communism.[31]

From that time forward, the president has been able to call upon a permanent apparatus that can rapidly plan and execute large-scale military deployments. No longer does the president have to await the organizing, equipping, and training of an army before embarking on a military venture. The United States has maintained for decades a military that dwarfs any of the nation's pre-twentieth-century wartime forces. Even the end of the Cold War did not lead to dramatic reductions in the size of the U.S. military.[32] And the difference is not merely one of numbers; American armed forces in the postwar era stand apart from the peacetime military of the past by such other measures as professionalism, proficiency, and speed. Recall the contrast I described in the opening pages between the clumsy, poorly provisioned assault on Cuba in 1898 and the 2003 invasion of Iraq. American conventional military capacity is sufficient today to wage major wars in Iraq and Afghanistan without recourse to conscription or mandatory economic mobilization.

Greater military resources, though, tell only part of the story of how presidents have expanded their means to initiate and wage war. The vulnerability to distant threats that Americans felt at the end of the Second World War has surged and ebbed, but it has never fully subsided. Partly this is a function of the United States as a global superpower, first contending with the Soviet Union and later reigning as the sole state upholding the established international order. Any rebellion, coup, or war might shift the prevailing balance of power to American disadvantage.

More fundamentally, however, Americans have not felt themselves secure, except during brief interludes such as that in the immediate aftermath of the Cold War.[33] For more than four decades after World War II, the threat had a specific name—communism—and a specific home—the Soviet Union (sometimes grouped together with the People's Republic of China to cover much of the Eurasian land mass in menacing red, the color of warning, on our maps). Today the danger has taken on shapeless form. Terrorism claims no home but may strike nearly anywhere. A populace that sees itself at risk of attack, or endangered by turmoil and violence in faraway places, will be more receptive to presidential warnings of looming threats to its security.

Layered atop this deep-rooted sense of vulnerability is a more recent predisposition to celebrate the U.S. military. In response to a loss of confidence and public esteem caused by the Vietnam debacle, military leaders in the late 1970s and 1980s embarked on a campaign to restore the prestige of the armed forces. The glittering triumph of American arms in the 1991 Gulf War bolstered the public's confidence in the nation's military and what it could accomplish. As Andrew Bacevich puts it, Americans see military power as the measure of greatness and harbor "outsized expectations regarding the efficacy of force."[34] At the same time, with the end of conscription, the military has become more separate from the larger society, reflecting the decline of the earlier tradition of the citizen-soldier taking up arms at a moment of national emergency. Bacevich adds that Americans see fighting as the task of elite professionals making use of the most advanced technology.[35]

Possibly the costly conflicts in Iraq and Afghanistan, in which enemies with improvised explosive devices (IEDs) inflicted grievous losses on American forces, will temper this credence in high-tech warfare. Yet the confidence that American technology can solve military problems, even those posed by modern low-intensity warfare against shadowy insurgents, seems not to have diminished much. Witness the popular fascination with the pilotless Predator drone as an alternative to troops on the ground in the deadly cat-and-mouse struggle with the Taliban and al-Qaeda along the Afghanistan-Pakistan border.[36]

Weakened Constraints on Presidential War-Making. The demise of the classical legal step for going to war has nullified a key tool at the disposal of Congress to block presidential war-making. The formal declaration of war has become a constitutional anachronism. Since the United States last formally declared war on an adversary in 1941, the nation has found itself in major conflicts in Korea, Vietnam, the Persian Gulf, Iraq, and Afghanistan.[37] To legitimize military intervention, a president can draw upon extra-constitutional legal authority, including the UN Charter and security treaties that bind the United States to fight on behalf of other countries.

Although Congress occasionally has sought to reclaim the power to decide matters of war and peace, presidents have deftly sidestepped such legislative inhibition. Indeed, they even have turned the principle of legislative authorization for military action against its architects. The War Powers Resolution, passed over President Nixon's veto in 1973, was intended to restore a measure of congressional control. Yet the statute has failed to give Congress a real voice when presidents decide to commit troops. Chief executives have deemed it politically prudent to seek Congress's endorsement before commencing large-scale military operations but timed their requests strategically, seeking a vote either just prior to hostilities (the 1991 Gulf War) or on the eve of an election (in late October 2002, to authorize the use of force against Iraq).[38]

The judiciary has influenced the exercise of presidential war powers only at the margins. The Supreme Court has helped legitimize broad presidential authority in foreign affairs that exceeds any literal reading of the Constitution. In 1936, for example, the Court considered a case arising from an action by Franklin Roosevelt to bar arm sales to Bolivia during a conflict in which the United States was neutral. Going beyond the issue before it (whether the president had exceeded his authority under existing law), the court declared the president to be the sole organ of the nation in foreign policy.[39] Given that the Constitution explicitly grants Congress power over commerce with foreign nations and splits authority over treaties between the president and the Senate, the decision represented an extraordinary affirmation of executive discretion. High court decisions bolstered Lincoln's exercise of broad prerogative powers during the Civil War, Wilson's suppression of dissent during World War I, and FDR's internment of Japanese Americans during World War II. Supportive though the Court was in such cases, it either ratified actions presidents had already taken and would continue no matter how the Court ruled (Lincoln),[40] or dealt with matters peripheral to core presidential war powers (Wilson and Roosevelt).

On rare occasions judicial intervention has curbed war-related executive authority. For example, responding to President Bush's post-9/11 military and antiterrorist campaigns, the courts have upheld certain due process rights of persons classified by the administration as enemy combatants or suspected terrorists. But these decisions have not addressed the core war-making powers of the chief executive.

Another potential informal restraint on a president is the military establishment itself, which at times has been in a position to exercise considerable sway. By the end of the Vietnam War, American military commanders had come to believe that civilians could not be trusted with decisions about whether and how to fight a war. As Bacevich recounts, the self-confidence of the military revived after its Vietnam-era nadir, aided by the one-sided triumph over Saddam Hussein's overmatched legions in the Gulf War. That victory brought new prestige to military commanders, particularly to General Colin Powell, chairman of the Joint Chiefs of Staff. In the years after the 1991 war, he espoused his own doctrine on the conditions for military action, calling for a commitment to overwhelming force and a clear exit strategy from any conflict.[41] But as I discuss in Chapter 5, subsequent events showed the ascendance of the military to be short-lived. Under George W. Bush and Secretary of Defense Donald Rumsfeld—who marginalized Army Chief of Staff General Eric Shinseki after he questioned the administration's Iraq "cakewalk" expectations in the run-up to invasion—the voice of the uniformed leadership was curbed sharply.

The absence of effective institutional checks within the government on presidential military initiative leads us to look outside for possible constraints. When contemplating major military operations, presidents always consider how the public will react. Popular dissent has been recurrent in many American wars. As a conflict continues with no victory in sight and as casualties mount, the political risk to the president and his party increases. Stalemates in Korea and Vietnam helped the opposition win the White House in 1952 and 1968, respectively. Even military triumph carries no assurance of future political success, as George H.W. Bush learned after his overwhelming triumph in the 1991 Gulf War could not be translated into reelection a year later.

Still, the prospect of a popular backlash has not prevented presidents from committing the United States to armed conflict. Presidents rarely expect war to be long and costly (with the exception of the two world wars). Especially in the 1980s and 1990s, as the margin of American military superiority over potential adversaries widened and the United States fought brief, seemingly effective campaigns with low casualties in Grenada, Panama, the Persian Gulf, Bosnia, and Kosovo, it became easier for presidents to conclude that the vast American technological advantage had reduced the political downside of using force. The United States fought in six significant conflicts between 1945 and 1989; the number rose to nine between 1989 and 2003.[42] No conflict seemed likely to last long enough for political opposition to coalesce.

It is also less likely today that presidents will be deterred from military action by other countries. In the aftermath of World War II, when the United States faced a hostile Soviet Union, presidents had to consider that any large-scale military action in one theater might leave America and its allies dangerously vulnerable elsewhere. Presidents also calculated that a limited war might become a global conflagration should intervention go beyond what the Soviets were prepared to tolerate. Thus Harry Truman refused to widen the Korean conflict, despite the importuning of his battlefield commander, General Douglas MacArthur, and pressure from conservatives at home. The end of the Cold War and the collapse of the Soviet Union in 1991 put an end to such concerns.

From Wars between States to Asymmetric Warfare. The United States emerged as the world's foremost military power at a time when warfare assumed a particular form—immensely destructive contests between industrialized states. To achieve their political goals through military conflicts, such states would mobilize their economic resources, field mass armies and equip them with heavy armaments, and seek to smash completely their enemies' capability to wage war on the same terms. Although rarely admitted, civilians, essential cogs in the enemies' production processes, were treated as targets, and noncombatant losses became a necessary evil. For the United States, the Civil War was the first conflict to take on the characteristics of modern industrial warfare, which reached its apogee in the world wars of the twentieth century. After the Second World War, conventional conflict between mechanized armies became less common and usually did not involve the major powers.[43] The reason is simple: with the advent of nuclear weapons, full-scale warfare could have no victor.

Conventional industrial warfare played to the strengths of the United States as the most advanced industrialized economy, an edge that the American military has widened over time. In World War II, victory owed more to the ability of the United States economy to outproduce its German and Japanese counterparts than to any other single factor. The efforts of the inefficient Soviet military-industrial complex to keep pace with American advances in military technology during the Cold War helped bring on the collapse of the Soviet state. As the American economy entered the post-industrial information age, moreover, the Pentagon quickly incorporated into its arsenal weapons systems that made use of advances in computers, lasers, stealth technology, precision guidance systems, and more. The 1991 Gulf War demonstrated that technology gave the U.S. military an advantage in conventional warfare that no potential adversary could match. American military planners talked of a new "revolution in military affairs"—based on the capacity of information technology to get inside an enemy's command-decision processes, target precisely his command-and-control capabilities, and leave him directionless—that would make the heavy industrial armies of even the recent past obsolete.[44]

Yet even as the United States asserted its supremacy in conventional military hardware, the conflicts in which the American military fought increasingly assumed a different form. Wars after 1945 more often saw irregular forces engage the troops of established regimes, the latter often backed externally by one of the superpowers. The first such conflicts were triggered by anticolonial movements, typically with communist support, as in Vietnam; subsequently, ethnic separatists, radical Islamists, and others have adopted similar approaches. Unable to match the firepower of an established army, adversaries have submerged themselves within the population for protection. Irregulars have combined a political strategy intended to delegitimize the regime with military tactics designed to neutralize the government's greater means of violence, while inducing that government to turn those means against its own people. Commonly called asymmetric warfare, it may be more apt to refer to this form of conflict as "war amongst the people," a phrase coined by British General Rupert Smith.[45]

Much of the contemporary American arsenal is ill-suited for asymmetric conflicts. High-technology weaponry can inflict devastating damage on identifiable hard economic and military targets, but these are rare when guerilla forces conceal themselves among the people. Further, when American attacks cause collateral civilian damage, especially casualties among noncombatants, popular anger against the United States directly undermines a key political objective—boosting support for the local regime—that a president seeks. The strikes by Predator drones against suspected Taliban and al-Qaeda leaders in Pakistan and Afghanistan have provoked a backlash in both countries, weakening the legitimacy of the governments backed by the United States. Technology may have ignited a revolution in the way the U.S. military uses force, but thus far the application to asymmetric wars suggests the change may be counterproductive.

The Recurring Challenges of Wartime Presidential Leadership

Within these contexts of continuity (the constitutional system) and change (expanded presidential war-making capacity and the shift in the nature of armed conflict), wartime presidents face a recurring set of challenges.[46] The first is to decide whether to go to war or to accept that one is inevitable. For a political leader, no decision has greater consequences. All wars impose costs and carry risks. Presidents must take care, then, that they enter, provoke, or initiate war only when vital national interests are at stake and other means for securing them have been exhausted.[47] Sometimes the case for war is quite clear. Apart from unconditional pacifists or a few revisionists whose view was warped by anti-Roosevelt animus, the geopolitical and moral imperative for United States participation in World War II lies beyond question, even prior to the Japanese attack on Pearl Harbor. In other instances presidents have chosen war under much less compelling circumstances.

As a president considers whether to go to war, a second task arises: to lay the foundation to wage war successfully. When conflict approaches or erupts, he needs to set in place the appropriate means, create the most favorable international circumstances, and generate public support for military action. Persuading the public that war is necessary can present a major political test for a president. Franklin Roosevelt struggled to overcome strong isolationist sentiment up to the Japanese attack on Pearl Harbor; George W. Bush found it necessary to exaggerate connections between the 9/11 terrorists and Saddam Hussein to pump up public support for the 2003 invasion of Iraq.

Once a president chooses war, he faces the third challenge of a wartime political leader: to identify clearly the nation's political objectives. To recall von Clausewitz, leaders must always bear in mind that wars serve political ends. American presidents have waged war to achieve a variety of purposes, including preserving the nation, expanding its territory, and resisting aggression that posed a direct or indirect threat to American security or interests. Victory must be understood to mean the accomplishment of the identified goals. In addition to the immediate aims the nation pursues in a conflict, a leader may also see it as a vehicle for achieving other long-term political goals, in particular to eliminate the circumstances that led to the war. Wilson and Roosevelt alike looked to establish a new postwar order that would rely on collective security to deter would-be aggressors. I will refer to the achievement of these broader aims as "peace-building," without which military victory may be barren. Over the course of a conflict, as circumstances change, a president reassesses whether the objectives he set initially are still attainable. It may be necessary to develop military and diplomatic strategies for less than optimal outcomes to avoid stalemate or defeat.

From the responsibility that a president faces to define war aims follows a fourth task: to assure that the military pursues a strategy appropriate to the nation's political objectives. As Civil War historian James McPherson puts it, wartime leadership requires reconciling the nation's military strategy with its political goals. The president must find the military means to realize larger political ends. Indeed, this is his central task as commander in chief of the armed forces. If the nature of the war changes, McPherson adds, a president may need to adjust the military strategy accordingly.[48] To put a strategy into effect, a president must choose the military commanders who will conduct operations, ensure that their approach on the battlefield is consistent with the larger war goals he has established, and remain vigilant that how the military fights the war advances goals rather than undermining them.

The president also acts as the nation's diplomatic leader. Wars test presidential diplomacy. Military conflicts occur in an international system that contains other states and (increasingly, as I've pointed out) non-state actors. For both military and political reasons, presidents may seek military allies or coalition partners. In the confrontation over Kuwait in 1990–1991, George H.W. Bush enlisted the participation of several Arab nations in the UN coalition to neutralize the perception in the Middle East that the West was waging a war on Islam. Even when presidents have not sought international help in a conflict, they need to attend to diplomacy, especially to inhibit other states from intervening when the United States prefers to resolve a conflict on its own. Hence, a fifth task for a president at war: to pursue diplomacy that advances his political goals. The diplomatic side gains importance in conflicts in which the United States operates within (and, as a rule, dominates) a coalition structure.

Leading a nation at war also poses political challenges at home. The military chain of command leads directly from the president through senior uniformed officers to the lowest-ranking soldier or sailor. When necessary, a president can issue an order.[49] Not so on the domestic or civilian side; there, the president must pursue wartime goals in the framework of wartime politics. Despite presidential calls for unity and pledges of support from other political actors at the outset of a conflict, wars do not stop political strife. The opposite has often proven to be the case. Many wars, from the War of 1812 to the Iraq War, have provoked strident opposition. Add to this the stubborn reality that conventional politics continues, if temporarily (and usually briefly) submerged beneath a rhetoric of common purpose. A president may wish to be seen as leader of a nation at arms, but he is also the head of a political party, and that involves a range of interests and demands. Further, wars unleash or accelerate economic changes, enrich some while possibly impoverishing others, uproot people, and unsettle social roles. Simply put, wars remake politics. What Americans debate at the end of a war often is quite different from what stirred them when it began. After the Civil War, the country argued about civil rights, protective tariffs, and currency issues; World War I generated controversies over the enforcement of Prohibition and agricultural price supports (prompted by the collapse of farm prices when wartime demand subsided); and the Second World War put civil rights back on the agenda, along with national health insurance.[50]

Within this political environment, a president must address the sixth key task: to sustain political support for the war effort. The erosion or even collapse of popular backing for a war can doom the prospects for victory and peace-building. Public disillusionment may sap military morale and almost certainly will encourage an adversary. If the president has set ambitious postwar objectives, in the way Wilson did during World War I, the challenge is more daunting. The sacrifices imposed by the war may drain, even exhaust, public support and yield a strong craving for a return to the routine concerns of peace. Fortunately for a president who must boost public confidence in the war effort, he does not need to do it entirely on his own. His political allies, whose fortunes are tied to his and thus to success in the war, can be counted on to offer steadfast backing, both in the halls of government and with the public. Even as violence worsened in Iraq prior to the 2006 midterm election, most Republicans in Congress stood behind President Bush. Yet much will depend upon a president's ability to communicate effectively with the citizenry and upon the course of war events, over which he exercises only limited control.

Why Presidents Struggle at War

A wartime president's vast resources are not enough to overcome all the leadership challenges he must address. At the outset he can count on support from Congress, issue orders through the military chain of command and expect obedience, gain access to the airwaves to state the case for war, and offer inducements to other nations to join the United States in a military coalition. Above all, economic and technological might assure that a powerful military establishment will be at a president's disposal. But, as I've suggested, American military capabilities may not be appropriate for certain wars, especially ones that involve irregular adversaries who fight on terms that neutralize American advantages and exploit their own. (Time usually favors the weaker side in asymmetric conflicts.)[51] The resources presidents find most readily available, moreover, prove to be of limited value for meeting certain tasks. Again, peace-building comes immediately to mind. When postwar goals require new habits of voluntary cooperation among erstwhile enemies, it does not matter that the United States has more aircraft carrier groups.

The ruthless logic of wartime leadership is quite simple: a president's ability to shape outcomes or alter policy declines inexorably over the course of a war. In the lead-up to the outbreak of fighting and in its initial phases, a president demonstrates control or agency in dramatic ways. He pushes Congress to expand the size of the military, deploys troops in a manner that might invite an enemy attack or make it hard to back down from an armed confrontation, sends aid to an embattled ally so as to make American intervention more likely, enlists allies in a coalition to add to the legitimacy of a military solution, guides or orders military staff in planning the opening campaign(s), asserts emergency powers to overcome real or presumed obstacles and threats, and determines how many troops to commit. He also explains to the American people and a global audience the purposes for which the United States has decided to fight.

Key choices that a president makes at the outset, though, constrain what he can do later. For example, unless he has committed the nation to total war and full-scale mobilization, the resources for prosecuting the war will be limited. Yet if he defines the struggle as indispensable to national security, one in which defeat would imperil the American way of life, he also removes disengagement from being one of the possible options should things go badly. Other elements serve to tie a president's hands, including the course of the war itself and the desire of the public to return to domestic concerns once the enemy is defeated. We should note that the decline of presidential agency is not neatly linear. Wars can also create opportunities or generate possibilities not present at the outset. (Thus the counterinsurgency warfare methods used as the basis for the 2007 troop surge in Iraq had been rediscovered over the previous three-plus years.) But nothing can reverse or long forestall the larger trajectory of reduced presidential flexibility and control over events.

Diminishing freedom of action shapes how well presidents accomplish the six core tasks of wartime political leadership. With great latitude in determining whether to go to war, presidents have been extremely effective in exploiting circumstances to make armed conflict seem inevitable. They have also used their symbolic position as head of state to generate initial public and congressional backing for their decision to go to war.[52] Put another way, no president who has concluded that military action is necessary has been checked by Congress, the public, or other nations. Presidents have also succeeded in laying the diplomatic foundation for most wars, though in 2002–2003 the Bush administration stumbled in its attempts to forge a broad coalition in favor of military action in Iraq (the so-called Coalition of the Willing). In military terms, recent presidents have faced every national security crisis confident (sometimes overly so) that the military might at their fingertips would be equal to or greater than that of any potential foe.

Once they have settled upon the necessity of military action, most presidents have met the third challenge: they have identified national objectives clearly, including the articulation of ambitious peace-building goals that go beyond victory in the narrow sense. Since Wilson, wartime presidents rarely confine themselves to defeating the adversary. They envision military action as a vehicle to establish a more stable and harmonious international order, conducive to American security, economic interests, and values. On the other hand, presidents find it more difficult when circumstances force them to adjust their objectives as a war progresses. A president may have promised too much, misread the will or nature of his adversaries, or underestimated the cost of his goals.

In reconciling national goals and military strategy, the fourth challenge, presidents have compiled a mixed record. I will argue that the debate between advocates of hands-on political leadership and those who think that fighting a war should be left to military professionals largely misses the point. Both approaches can claim success—and both should own up to failures. A president who deploys the wrong kind of force or misunderstands the relationship between those means and the political goals he has identified (Johnson in Vietnam, as I explain in Chapter 4) will fail, whether he directs the troops closely or leaves military matters to his uniformed commanders. Lost in the argument is a larger point: presidents accomplish narrow politico-military objectives more effectively than peace-building, resulting in barren triumphs.

Other scholars have sought to explain the disappointing record of presidents in achieving their broader goals. In his recent book on the outcomes of America's wars, Gideon Rose emphasizes how presidents and their advisors have been constrained by the international environment and by the lessons they glean from previous wars.[53] I will focus instead on the impact of time: absent swift victory, a president loses strategic flexibility. Operating within an ever-diminishing space in which choice is possible, he struggles to remain the master of his circumstances. Ambitious postwar goals that depend on continued presidential flexibility, discretion, and broad authority up to and beyond the cessation of hostilities remain unfulfilled.

Presidents have fared better in mastering the diplomatic challenge, at least until the shooting stops. In the period before the United States emerged as the dominant global power, presidents worried that other nations might interfere in American conflicts and discouraged third-party intervention. Since the First World War, the United States has fought most often as part of an alliance or coalition and usually has led these multinational efforts. Concessions have always been part of the price paid to partner nations for their cooperation. Presidents have managed the business of alliance/coalition politics effectively, retaining control over the definition of war aims and broad military strategy. Problems may surface if a war stalls short of victory, however, as coalition partners, sensitive to their own domestic political pressures, withdraw. The modest coalition that supported the invasion of Iraq became smaller during the subsequent insurgency as participants recoiled from the cost, which included terrorist attacks within their own cities. Even successful military alliances can yield diplomatic complications. Once peace is imminent or the enemy lays down his arms, the glue of necessity ceases to bind the United States to its partners; they instead pursue their respective national interests. At the end of the Second World War, Stalin's determination to establish a Soviet sphere of influence in Eastern Europe precipitated decades of Cold War. Back home, too, presidents discover that enthusiasm for ongoing international engagement has declined, so they have fewer resources with which to entice erstwhile fellow combatant nations to continue to participate in collective security projects. Again, the impact is most evident on a president's capacity to attain his vision of a new postwar order.

Of the six core leadership challenges war poses, presidents have struggled most with the task of maintaining popular support. Americans continued to back the Second World War to its conclusion, but the years of sacrifice took their toll, replacing the gung-ho patriotism that followed Pearl Harbor with a grudging recognition that crushing Germany and Japan was a nasty job that had to be done. Short wars (American involvement in the First World War lasted just over eighteen months, with serious fighting by U.S. forces limited to the last five) never tested public commitment. In all other conflicts, presidents have grappled in vain to overcome rising public disillusionment and discontent.

The mismatch between American military means and the demands of asymmetric war has undercut popular support at home: the domestic audience sees not stirring images of tanks advancing in triumph across an empty desert landscape but endless small skirmishes with an elusive foe against a dreary backdrop of physical wreckage and civilian casualties. If early battlefield triumphs do not yield victory and the safe homecoming of the troops (see Korea or Iraq), the disappointment becomes especially bitter to swallow. Presidents have also sacrificed popular domestic initiatives as a trade-off for even limited military commitments. Accordingly, they have little with which to reward their political supporters.

Overview: Five Wars, Six Presidents

I support my argument about why presidents struggle as wartime leaders through six case studies that cover seven presidents. I begin with Abraham Lincoln and the Civil War. Lincoln wrestled with the full set of tasks that confront a wartime leader in a democratic society, and he did so under daunting circumstances. In many ways he established the template for his successors, though each would copy only parts of his approach. Much has been made of Lincoln's genius as a wartime leader, and rightfully so. But we should also learn from his mistakes and shortcomings.

The other cases involve modern presidents: Woodrow Wilson (First World War), Franklin D. Roosevelt (Second World War), Lyndon Johnson/Richard Nixon (Vietnam), George W. Bush (Iraq), and Barack Obama (Afghanistan). This is an incomplete list of wartime presidents, of course. But through my choices we can consider leadership problems that seem likely to arise again in the future, including the risks of overly ambitious goals, the complexities of relations with allies and client regimes, and the obstacles in maintaining popular support. These presidents make it possible to assess how the changing nature of war, especially the shift from large-scale industrial warfare to low-intensity "war amongst the people," has affected presidential effectiveness. Presidents sometimes inherit ongoing wars, and the selection of Vietnam and Afghanistan allows for an examination of what happens when responsibility for a war changes hands. In each case, I explore how well the president met the core challenges of wartime leadership and explain why he could not accomplish certain tasks.

From these examples we can account for the patterns of presidential success and, more important, failure. Presidents across time have fumbled key challenges. They have been overambitious in their war goals, misunderstood their allies, oversold their wars to the American people, overstated the risks of not going to war or ending a military intervention, and neglected to plan realistically for peace. All wartime presidents have seen their initiative and freedom of action slip from their grasp, usually without realizing it. In the end, presidents become the victims of the forces they set in motion, sometimes before the first shot is fired.

I

Lincoln's Shadow

ABRAHAM LINCOLN WAS AN EXTRAORDINARY wartime leader. He led the country through its most trying ordeal, a civil war that spanned nearly his entire presidency and took a greater toll in American lives than all the other conflicts with which this book will deal put together. At several points during the struggle, he faced the prospect of both military and electoral defeat, either of which would have spelled the end of the nation. His decisions and determination led to a triumph that also ended the brutal system of chattel slavery. The republic took the first tentative steps toward the "new birth of freedom" that he articulated as the ultimate goal of the terrible sacrifices the war imposed.[1] Our martyred sixteenth president accordingly, and appropriately, has been elevated to a kind of secular sainthood.

Lincoln's performance still calls for critical reappraisal. Even his admirers acknowledge its flaws.[2] This should be no surprise: Lincoln may have been extraordinary, but even he could not escape the impossible leadership demands and inherent conflicts that all wartime presidents face. It is unreasonable to hold them to a standard of perfection. We should instead weigh their full record, recognizing the challenges they met as they guided a nation through military conflict, challenges that grew in magnitude with the scale of the war.

Lincoln struggled to master the multiple responsibilities of the political leader of a nation at war. As James McPherson, Eric Foner, and other historians have observed, Lincoln's political objectives evolved over the course of the Civil War as the nature of the conflict changed, and one of his signature achievements was to reshape political goals accordingly.[3] Lincoln chose to play a hands-on role in directing the war. Eliot Cohen, unsurprisingly, depicts him as the paragon of effective wartime political leadership, the model to which any president commanding a conflict should aspire.[4] But there is more to the story. Lincoln established an overall strategy for pursuing victory and kept his military subordinates focused on that strategy. In the end, victory depended less on his active direction than on the strategic course he established when he embraced emancipation. Moreover, he took a back seat during the final campaigns. It is not clear, then, that he can serve Cohen's prescriptive purpose. Interestingly, the Civil War provides us with a second example of an active politico-military chief executive, Lincoln's Confederate counterpart, Jefferson Davis. A comparison of the two presidents is revealing: Davis demonstrated that a political leader's close involvement in military matters is no guarantee of success.

Further, wartime political leadership involves more than military matters, and we therefore need to extend analysis of Lincoln beyond the military realm. Two other leadership tasks stand out: maintaining popular support for the war effort and planning for peace. Both require as much active direction as military affairs. Here Lincoln's record is mixed. He did well in meeting the political challenge of keeping up Union morale, which was severely tested time and again. Given the depth of partisan strife in the North, this was an impressive achievement, though I will show that he was aided not just by his own skills but by the resources of the Republican Party. By contrast, Lincoln was far less successful at defining, early on, the postwar settlement in the South. After making the destruction of chattel slavery a central war goal, he invested little attention in explaining how race relations might be reconfigured when peace was restored. At the time of his assassination he had not articulated a coherent vision for Reconstruction, and had he lived he would likely have struggled to retain control over policy against resurgent congressional power.

One other aspect of Lincoln's wartime leadership rewards scrutiny. Faced with a truly existential threat to the nation, he chose to act unilaterally in ways that forever altered the powers of his office. In the first days of the war, he ordered measures he deemed essential to national survival, admitting that some violated the letter of the Constitution. He later extended curbs on civil liberties across the North, moves that sparked sharp opposition. To his credit, he offered forthright explanations for his actions, and the number of arrests (outside of the Border States) was small. But while Lincoln exercised emergency powers with a fair degree of restraint, he opened the door for later presidents to inflate the claim of necessity with no effective check.

From One War to Another

Within weeks of his election in 1860, Abraham Lincoln confronted the challenge of secession and the looming threat of civil war. South Carolina seceded in December 1860, quickly followed by six other states in the Deep South. Almost immediately they began to seize federal property, including arsenals, while the outgoing Buchanan administration insisted it could do nothing. The rebellious states met in Montgomery, Alabama, in February 1861 to form a united confederacy.[5] Most federal civil officials in the seceded states promptly switched allegiance to the Confederate States of America.[6] In a few places across the South, U.S. Army posts and forts held out, most famously at Fort Sumter in Charleston Harbor. Other southern states teetered on the brink of secession, waiting to see how the incoming Lincoln administration responded while warning against the use of force to suppress the rebellion. Northern citizens watched anxiously, fearful of secession and war alike, distressed as the economy sagged amid uncertainty and the loss of southern commerce. Lincoln tried to hold open options that might avoid violent conflict. He made several private offers to trade withdrawal from Fort Sumter for a promise from Virginia to disband a secession convention without a vote.[7] In his March 4, 1861, inaugural address, with its reference to the "mystic chords of memory" that bound all Americans, he went so far as to offer to support a constitutional amendment that would bar the national government from ever interfering with slavery where it existed.[8]

The decision to embark on war—or pursue a path that will inevitably lead to armed conflict—is one of the weightiest ones any national leader faces, so it is fair to ask whether Lincoln might have avoided recourse to arms in early 1861. Our assessment today, of course, is colored by our knowledge of the consequences of his actions—a violent struggle that cost more lives than any other war in American history yet resulted in the end of slavery and the restoration of a single, united nation.

That the price would be so high and the effects so far-reaching were not even dimly suspected by Lincoln or perhaps anyone else at the time. Instead he had to weigh the likely effects of the two primary courses of action available to him, neither promising. On one side, he could choose to let secession stand. To do so would spell political disaster for the young and fragile Republican Party that he led by virtue of his position. More than that, one act of secession would likely precipitate others, resulting in the complete dismembering of the United States and the end of the great experiment in republican government on a continental scale.[9] In his inaugural speech, Lincoln warned that the logic of secession knew no end point, that the southern states would disagree among themselves and fragment yet again. But his words applied with equal force to the North, where different regions had distinct economic interests that could easily drive them apart. In short, the conditions necessary to avoid bloodshed would spell the end of the Union. Lincoln concluded within weeks of his election that he could not countenance disunion without violating his fundamental responsibility to uphold the Constitution and preserve the nation.[10]

On the other side, the new president could act to retain federal installations in the South, Fort Sumter in particular, and to restore the authority of the national government. This choice, too, was unattractive, so much so that at first it was opposed by most members of the cabinet. To insist upon holding Sumter would almost surely bring on a violent confrontation. And the balance of forces was less favorable than might appear at first glance. States in the upper South had threatened to resist federal authority, too, if Washington sought to "coerce" their rebellious brethren back into the Union. Further, the military resources available to Lincoln were meager: the U.S. Army consisted of 16,000 troops, most scattered in distant posts across the Far West, and many senior officers with southern backgrounds had resigned or would follow their states out of the Union. General Winfield Scott, the army's venerable commanding officer, estimated it would take some six months just to prepare a sufficient force to relieve Fort Sumter. Lincoln would also have to deal with a northern public sharply divided over the question of slavery. War would provoke demands from abolitionists to confront slavery head-on while northern conservatives (and some in Lincoln's own party) would repudiate any war that aimed to destroy lawful property rights. Adding weight on the conservative side, the Border States that Lincoln needed to keep in the Union fold all embraced slavery.

On the day after his inauguration, Lincoln received word from the commander at Fort Sumter that its supplies would be exhausted within six weeks. Recognizing that war could not be avoided except at a cost he would not pay, he instead sought to bring about conflict on terms that might check additional secession by wavering southern and Border States. He began to maneuver events so as to force the South to commence hostilities.[11] (Eighty years later Franklin D. Roosevelt would take a similar approach toward Japan—with the attack on Pearl Harbor as the result.) Fully aware that any attempt to relieve or reinforce the garrison would provoke a violent response from the surrounding southern state troops, he ordered a supply ship to Charleston and so informed the South Carolina government. The rebel commander, General P. G. T. Beauregard, in turn ordered his guns to fire on the fort on April 12, 1861.

As with many of Lincoln's decisions over the next four years, this initial one yielded mixed results. Across the North, popular support for military action against the rebellion was robust. Much of this reflected a burst of genuine patriotism, although there is reason to believe that many young men were drawn to the colors by the poor economic conditions.[12] But the outbreak of hostilities pushed several additional southern states (Arkansas, Virginia, North Carolina, and Tennessee) over the edge, as they also voted to secede from the Union. The timing of the Fort Sumter bombardment was particularly unfortunate in the case of Virginia, where a convention to consider secession was in progress. Although a majority had opposed secession before the first shots were fired, the mood immediately shifted and the body voted for disunion. (Delegates from the western part of the state never agreed, resulting in the breakaway of that region and eventual formation of a separate state.)[13] Virginia's decision placed Washington, D.C., at immediate risk, a situation made more precarious by uncertainty over the course that Maryland, another slave state, would pursue.

Lincoln first established national preservation as the goal for which the North would fight, putting aside the question of slavery. In doing so, he chose the approach that plainly commanded the broadest public support. Even abolitionists at the outset of the war rallied behind the narrow cause of restoring the Union. At the other end of the political spectrum, Democrats embraced the idea that the war would be waged to compel the rebellious South to return to the fold even as they rejected any attempt to interfere with southern property rights (read: slavery).[14] McPherson terms Lincoln's initial approach a commitment to a "limited war," likening it to other armed conflicts in which a nation seeks objectives short of the complete destruction of the political system of the enemy state. (By comparison, in the Second World War the United States fought for the unconditional surrender of Germany and Japan, a clear marker of a total war.)[15] Labels fit awkwardly in the case of the Civil War, because Lincoln and the North made clear from the first that they would never settle for anything less than full submission of secessionist states to the authority of the United States government—that is, the Confederate States of America as a political entity would cease to exist, an outcome associated with total war. However, Lincoln promised in the beginning to leave untouched the social structure of the South, to restore the status quo ante bellum. Besides commanding the broadest support within the North, noninterference with slavery would reassure southern Unionists, whom he and some other key northern leaders thought constituted the true majority in the Confederacy.[16] Were the South to be defeated on those terms, then, it would be as though secession had never happened.

Although Lincoln made the prudent choice at the start, he faced a far more difficult task in reevaluating war aims as the conflict progressed. Consensus over war goals in the North barely lasted through the initial battles in the summer months of 1861. By autumn 1861 abolitionists were clamoring that the president widen the purpose of the Union struggle to include the destruction of slavery.[17] War Democrats warned against any move to use secession as an excuse to free the slaves. By late spring 1862, emancipation of slaves was clearly on the agenda, though many Democrats adamantly resisted. Lincoln faced the real possibility that his endorsement of emancipation could split the North.

Several factors drove the president to reconsider a limited war. First, whatever Lincoln and political and military leaders in the North may have thought about keeping the question of slavery out of the war, the slaves themselves would have it otherwise. At all points of contact between Union forces and the South, slaves sought the freedom they believed the northern soldiers would bestow. As runaway slaves started to make their way to Union lines, local commanders faced the delicate task of deciding what to do with them. General Benjamin Butler, at Fort Monroe in tidewater Virginia, declared the slaves who came across the lines to be "contraband of war" and insisted that they not be returned to their owners. The term "contraband" soon came into wide use to describe all slaves who fled to Union control. Against Democratic and border state opposition, Congress ratified Butler's ad hoc approach as official policy by passing the 1861 Confiscation Act.[18] Another senior officer, Major General John C. Frémont, placed in command of Missouri early in the war, decided to pressure the rebel sympathizers in that critical border state by declaring that their property would be confiscated and their slaves freed. After Lincoln ordered the general to soften his policy, the president drew both praise and intense criticism, an indication of how fragile the consensus was in support of a war that did not confront slavery.[19]

Second, it became increasingly evident during the first year of the war that slaves were a vital economic and, indirectly, military resource to the South. Slave labor sustained the southern economy, replacing white men who had gone off to the Confederate armies. Without the contributions from its African American subject population, the South would have been hard-pressed to feed itself, grow cotton to trade abroad for essential goods, or produce munitions for its troops. More directly, slave labor was put to use in constructing fortifications and repairing the transportation infrastructure upon which the Confederacy relied to move its armies. Union officers and their men recognized the vital role of the slaves in the southern war effort and started to wonder whether a hands-off approach toward the "peculiar institution" was self-defeating.[20]

These concerns soon found voice among northern politicians and the press.

Third, the human cost of the war hardened northern attitudes toward the enemy. By summer 1862, the toll in casualties had reached horrific proportions, far beyond what anyone could have imagined in the first days of the conflict when new recruits marched off to the sounds of bands and patriotic speeches. The two-day battle at Shiloh in April 1862 resulted in more casualties than had been incurred in all previous wars fought by the United States combined. And that was just the beginning, as later contests, such as the Seven Days and Second Bull Run (Manassas), added to the ever-longer list of dead and wounded. The carnage culminated at Antietam on September 17, 1862, where the 23,000 casualties made it the bloodiest one-day battle in American history. Because regiments were recruited from a single location, moreover, one severe fight could devastate a community. To this could be added the mounting death toll from illness, a bigger killer in the Civil War than combat, plus the ever-increasing cost of raising and maintaining vast armies. It is not surprising, then, that as the price of defeating the South rose, more and more northerners concluded that a "soft peace," one that left the social order of the rebel states intact, would be unacceptable.

Lincoln grasped the shifting mood in mid-1862 and began to consider widening the Union objective to encompass the destruction of slavery. He first broached the idea with members of his inner political circle early in the summer.[21]

Emancipation posed both benefits and risks. On the positive side, expanding the conflict to include freedom for those held in bondage would elevate the moral appeal of the struggle at home and abroad, while in practical terms it would encourage slaves to flee their owners and seriously disrupt the southern economy, potentially diverting manpower from Confederate armies. But Lincoln also appreciated the dangers, political and military. Northern Democrats in large numbers might turn against the war, complicating all aspects of the Union war effort.[22] For the South, the threat of emancipation would raise the stakes in the contest, encouraging the rebels to fight harder because the consequences of defeat would be so much more sweeping. There was also the matter of timing to consider. In the summer of 1862,

Union war fortunes were at low ebb, following the defeat of General George B. McClellan on the Peninsula and General John Pope at Second Bull Run.

The president wanted emancipation to appear to be a necessary war measure, required by circumstances, not an act of desperation by a government that seemed on the verge of losing. Therefore, having drafted a preliminary emancipation proclamation, Lincoln decided to await some kind of battlefield success before making it public. Antietam, though a victory of a dubious sort (McClellan wasted a chance to inflict a crippling defeat on Robert E. Lee's Army of Northern Virginia), gave Lincoln the opening he sought. That it was McClellan's quasi-triumph that provided the moment for emancipation was no small irony, because he was deeply hostile to abolitionism and closely connected to the Democratic opposition. On September 22, 1862, Lincoln published the preliminary proclamation, due to go into effect on January 1, 1863, which declared free all persons held in servitude in those places then in rebellion against the United States government. In literal terms, of course, the proclamation freed no one, for it applied only where it could not be enforced. But as Union armies advanced across the South, the proclamation would take effect.

The immediate repercussions of Lincoln's announcement followed predictable lines, but what was most important was that the northern public did not repudiate the policy change. Several generals who disagreed with the president, notably McClellan, were dismissed in the weeks that followed.[23] Northern reaction split by party—Democrats denounced emancipation while Republicans endorsed it as an essential measure if the war were to be fought to a successful conclusion. In the fall 1862 congressional elections the Republicans lost seats, but the losses were mild in comparison to typical off-year elections in the middle of the nineteenth century. Lincoln had weighed the public mood correctly: by not prematurely embracing emancipation, he had sustained public support for the war through a difficult period when morale on the home front sagged. It was an outstanding example of artful wartime political direction.

But the matter does not end there. Having moved from a limited conflict with a narrow political goal to a "remorseless revolutionary conflict," in words Lincoln used earlier to describe the kind of war he hoped to avoid,[24] he could never turn back. The commitment to the total destruction of the centuries-old social foundation of the South now drove policy and opened new challenges. Once the slaves were freed, they became an obvious military resource, and after some hesitation Lincoln approved the organization of black regiments by the army.[25] In turn, this further stiffened southern resolve to fight to the bitter end.[26] What to do with the former slaves also became a major challenge for postwar planning. The broadened war goals, moreover, contributed to a shift in the character of military operations, which had initially been conducted with careful attention to the personal and property rights of the southern white population. As the war progressed, Union commanders began to think in terms of breaking the will of southerners to resist, which implied a much more aggressive and destructive approach. With slavery and southern social and economic institutions now a target of Union war policy, this kind of "hard war" gained legitimacy in the eyes of northern troops and the broader northern public.

Finally, in a war for total objectives, few terms remained upon which peace might be negotiated. Through 1862, the South might have rejoined the Union by disavowing secession, with no changes in the region's underlying racial hierarchy. Northern opinion would not have countenanced the return to servitude of the limited numbers of slaves who had sought protection from the Union armies, but that problem could have been finessed through compensated emancipation. Once the Emancipation Proclamation went into effect at the start of 1863, by contrast, reunification of the nation could not be achieved on the same forgiving terms. Lincoln never declined to consider peace overtures from any quarter. But southern initiatives late in the war, even up to its final weeks, always presupposed that the proclamation would be withdrawn or negated. Having cast the die for a different kind of struggle, the president could not possibly accept anything less than a peace that included an end to chattel slavery, regardless of the human cost.

Lincoln captured the non-negotiable character that the conflict had assumed—with his deliberate endorsement—in his second inaugural address in March 1865, when he said of the war, "Yet, if God wills that it continue, until all the wealth piled by the bond-man's two hundred and fifty years of unrequited toil shall be sunk, and until every drop of blood drawn with the lash, shall be paid by another drawn with the sword, as was said three thousand years ago, so still it must be said 'the judgments of the Lord, are true and righteous altogether.'"[27] Divine judgment leaves no room for compromise.

Lincoln as a Military Leader

Lincoln really had no choice but to assert active direction over the war. The Union had no professional military organization capable of planning campaigns, training troops, coordinating the acquisition of military means, and more. Such organizations scarcely existed in the mid-nineteenth century—Prussia under Bismarck might be the sole exception[28]—and certainly the United States Army at the time of Fort Sumter would not qualify. Although the venerable Winfield Scott provided useful strategic guidance, he was too infirm to assume active command, and the rest of the army was devoid of high-level experience. As an organization, the army had no capacity to wage war on a continental scale against a well-armed adversary with significant geo-strategic advantages for conducting a defensive war. The national state as a whole was ill-equipped to mobilize the resources needed to defeat the Confederacy, which forced Lincoln to turn to the state governors to raise the needed troops. Especially in the early months of the war, then, the president would have to assume much responsibility or face the likelihood that things simply would not get done.

As a military leader, Lincoln faced several critical tasks. To begin with, he had to create an army capable of waging war across a continent, from the eastern seaboard to the trans-Mississippi West, and from the Border States to the Gulf of Mexico. He also needed to identify the men who would lead these forces. All this would have to be done with an eye toward sustaining popular support for the war; that is, the military effort could not be conducted without regard to politics. To use this new military instrument effectively, Lincoln would have to define a strategy for subduing the South. He would then have to make sure that his military subordinates pursued the strategy effectively and did so in a manner consistent with the aims he identified and adjusted.

The Union Army was assembled, equipped, and trained with great rapidity, but sustaining the necessary manpower became a persistent challenge for the Lincoln administration. Immediately after the attack on Fort Sumter, Lincoln on his own authority called for 75,000 three-month militia volunteers, then summoned an additional 300,000 men to serve for three years while also authorizing an expansion of the regular army.[29] (The assertion of emergency powers reflected in these actions, which had little or no legal basis, will be examined later.) Patriotism and a sluggish economy made it easy for northern governors to meet and then exceed their state quotas. Thus, despite the refusal of some Border States to cooperate, the ranks of the Union armies were soon filled, and by April 1862 some 637,000 men were in uniform,[30] most classified as U.S. Volunteers with specified terms of enlistment. Once the serious fighting began in 1862 and the appalling casualty lists appeared in hometown newspapers, however, the eagerness to join waned. Governors had to resort to such measures as enlistment bonuses to entice new recruits, and by 1863 Congress would be forced to pass the unpopular Conscription Act.[31] As an added complication, enlistment terms for two-year and three-year volunteers would expire in the same season each year (in summer 1863 and summer 1864, respectively), depriving the armies of many of their most experienced veterans in the middle of major campaigns.

With the establishment of a mass military came the need to find officers to command it. For units up to regimental size, officers were either elected by their men or appointed by state governors. The president selected general officers, though their commissions required congressional approval and many were recommended by lawmakers. To Lincoln, too, fell the vital task of assigning senior commanders of armies and military departments (effectively, geographic areas), choices requiring special care because they had both military and political implications. Often far removed from immediate political oversight, these senior commanders faced delicate questions involving the preservation of property, treatment of fugitive slaves, and management of political dissent.[32]

Several factors complicated the selection of senior military leaders. First, neither the president nor anyone else had a basis upon which to assess the fitness for command of the many candidates, a common problem at the outset of a war.[33] The United States Army had last fought a major war in 1846—the Mexican War (as it was then known)—and the officers who would lead the Union Army now had been mere captains or lieutenants then. In the intervening years, some had gained experience in small-scale actions against Indian tribes in the West, but this told little about whether they could manage armies of 100,000 men or more. Second, some Republicans mistrusted the regular army officer corps, especially those members who had trained at West Point, seeing that institution as infected by pro-southern sympathies and pro-Democratic leanings. They wondered whether commanders with close friends among their Confederate counterparts would be prepared to press the fight against the enemy, especially if and when the war turned into a contest to destroy slavery. Although the Republicans' concern about the partisan tilt of the officer corps was misplaced (because more were appointed to West Point by Whigs and Republicans than by Democrats),[34] they made their view known to the president. Third, political considerations weighed heavily on command choices, pulling Lincoln in different directions.

The influence of politics merits elaboration. As James McPherson points out, Lincoln understood that it was essential to preserve broad support for the war effort among different political factions, geographic regions, and key ethnic constituencies, such as Irish and German immigrants. Commissions for generals with clear political appeal or support contributed to sustaining the popular perception of a national war and helped raise troops among their constituencies.[35] Within the memory of Lincoln and his peers was the contrary example provided by James K. Polk during the war with Mexico: Polk had used general officer commissions as a form of patronage for his own Democratic Party, and Whigs had resented his partisan handling of the conflict.[36] Nonetheless, these political generals had a keen appreciation of the political dimensions of the war, including the impact of the electoral clock on the timing of military operations.[37]

Politics also led the president to share the task of selecting generals. Although the initiative for appointing generals rested with the president by custom and statute, Lincoln did not exercise this power unilaterally, particularly at the start of the war. Rather, to enhance his power within his own party coalition, he deemed it prudent to permit congressional Republicans to choose some generals. In this manner, for example, Elihu

Washburne, the ranking Republican in the House of Representatives and an influential moderate, put forward Ulysses S. Grant for a brigadier general commission despite Grant's checkered background.[38]

Another kind of politics, the organizational kind, would make these initial choices consequential for the entire war. Within the military of the Civil War era, a strong seniority convention held sway: where two officers shared the same rank, command devolved upon the one who held the earlier commission. Attempts to circumvent seniority, by violating protocol, generated ill feelings, intense bickering, and resignations by officers passed over for command. (For example, in 1864 Joseph Hooker asked to be relieved of duty when the less-senior Oliver Otis Howard was named to command the Army of the Tennessee following the death of James B. McPherson.)[39] Not surprisingly, then, the list of notable Union commanders throughout the conflict is dominated by the 1861 first-wave generals.

Apart from influencing the commissioning of generals, politics also shaped Lincoln's decisions about command appointments. In the early months of the war, when Lincoln was determined to prevent any premature moves to widen war aims, he could count on the conservative tendencies of generals closely linked to the Democratic opposition. The highest ranks of the Union Army command structure were more likely to be filled by generals with known political ties than was the general officer pool as a whole. Some two-thirds of the early-war army commanders and those in charge of politically sensitive departments (13 out of 20) had identifiable partisan backgrounds. Of these, eight were Democrats, a pattern that reflected the president's determination to contain the war and make it politically inclusive.[40] The single most important command, that of the Army of the Potomac, went to George McClellan, a Democrat with obvious political ambitions and an expressed commitment to leave slavery undisturbed.[41]

Over the course of the war, as the president redefined war goals and reconsidered how best to keep up political support for the war, he also weighed his commanders according to this new calculus. Lincoln's decision to embrace emancipation and the destruction of the southern racial order based upon slavery spelled the end of conservative Democratic backing for his war policy. Because McClellan had been outspoken in favor of a limited war, he was, as we've seen, jettisoned shortly before the 1862 midterm elections. (His removal was made easier by his record—mediocre at best—as a battlefield commander.) Major General Don Carlos Buell, a close McClellan associate, commander of the Army of the Ohio, and a foe of the "hard war" approach toward southern civilians, was let go at about the same time.[42] By the end of the war, Democrats had largely disappeared from the ranks of senior Union command, and the handful who remained had exceptional combat records.[43] The officers who led the Union Army to victory in 1864–1865 shared Lincoln's conception of the kind of war that had to be fought. Generals such as William Tecumseh Sherman and Phil Sheridan may have detested partisan politics, but they made themselves eager instruments of the president's commitment to destroy slavery by breaking utterly the will of the southern white population to continue the conflict.[44]

The Union needed a strategy that would let it use the army to defeat the Confederacy. To define that strategy, Lincoln made himself a student of military affairs. Historians praise him for the speed with which he mastered strategic principles. Learning both from officers such as Scott and McClellan and through books borrowed from the Library of Congress, Lincoln became an insightful military planner within the first year of the war. Although sometimes derided by the professional soldiers whom he commanded for his schemes, he soon demonstrated a superior grasp of the core strategic challenges the Union would face.[45] It may have helped that Lincoln came to the study of war without preconceptions, because the Civil War would be fought in the midst of dramatic technological innovations that would reshape military affairs. His open-minded approach made him highly receptive to the use of new weapons and alert to the possibilities inherent in the widespread use of railroads and telegraph communications.[46]

The fundamental military task, as Lincoln appreciated, was how to best use the Union's advantages to offset those enjoyed by its formidable adversary. In terms of such key resources as population and industrial capacity, the North far outstripped the Confederacy. The white population of the Union in 1861 numbered some 22 million, while there were only about 5 million whites in the South.

(At the start of the war, the Lincoln administration refused to enlist black soldiers; for the South, arming the slave population was not on the table until the last days of the war.) Northern industrial output was nine times that of the South, though the latter did have arms manufacturing factories that provided a measure of self-sufficiency.[47]

What the South had going for it was geography: the Confederacy encompassed a vast territory (800,000 square miles, roughly the size of France and Germany combined), only some of it accessible by rivers, good roads, and/or railroads. To conquer such a foe, Union armies would need to advance deep into hostile territory, with long and exposed lines of communication. A further Confederate advantage lay in the shorter distances southern troops would have to travel to reinforce threatened points, a situation known in military parlance as "interior lines."[48] Moreover, the southern coastline was extensive, with many ports and other points where ships might shelter. Given world demand for cotton and other raw materials, the South could readily buy on world markets anything its domestic industry could not supply. Closing off southern commerce via a blockade would require an enormous fleet, and the United States Navy in 1861 was no more up to its assignment than was the U.S. Army. Finally, the Confederacy controlled the vital egress from the Mississippi River, through which many products from the old Northwest reached the outside world.

At the beginning of the war, Winfield Scott outlined a strategy for defeating the South that would serve as a rough blueprint for what followed. Known as the Anaconda Plan, Scott's approach called for slowly cutting off the Confederacy from the outside world and strangling it (much as the giant snake squeezes to death its victims). In specific terms, this meant a thorough blockade of the southern coastline from Texas to Virginia, a movement down the Mississippi to isolate the western rebel states, and threats by northern armies on the Confederate perimeter that would force the South to maintain large and costly field armies. Scott assumed the cumulative pressure on the South would wear down the will of its people to resist and lead them to accept federal authority on the generous terms Lincoln initially offered.[49]

Framed to achieve the initial goal of restoring the Union, Anaconda did not envision a war that would seek to destroy the foundations of the South's slave-based political economy. Scott, a native Virginian, was appalled at that prospect. Still, the strategy could be adapted for another kind of war, one aimed at the thorough destruction of the slave economy and requiring much greater suffering in the rebel states to secure their acquiescence. In broad terms, this is just how Lincoln chose to proceed: he sought to isolate the South and divide it at the Mississippi, and then to drive the Union armies into the Confederacy in simultaneous advances that would capitalize on the North's numerical advantages to overwhelm the rebel forces. Putting this strategy into practice, though, proved daunting, and the effort severely tested the patience of the president and the resolve of the northern people before victory was achieved.

Geography shaped the war, dividing it into multiple theaters at the operational level (see map 1.1). One set of campaigns would be waged along the southern coasts, with a naval blockade and a series of small-scale amphibious operations. Although some ports (such as Wilmington, North Carolina) proved stubborn obstacles, this part of the war played to the Union advantages because the sheer length of seacoast meant it must be thinly garrisoned, assuring that the North's military could concentrate superior forces at any point it chose. On land, the terrain divided along the Appalachian spine: to the east, the war would be fought on the limited ground in Virginia; in the much vaster spaces to the west, campaigns ranged from eastern Tennessee to the Mississippi and beyond. The trans-Mississippi remained peripheral to the outcome of the war—neither side could win decisively in that sparsely settled region, although that did not prevent significant bloodshed and an ugly guerilla conflict in Missouri. On the other hand, the Mississippi River mattered greatly to the North, especially for the unimpeded shipment of goods from the Northwest. Yet opening the great river would not doom the rebellion—witness the continuation of the war for nearly two years after the surrender of Vicksburg. Rather, Tennessee and states to its south and southeast (Mississippi, Alabama, and Georgia) held the key, for Union campaigns through this region would expose the Carolinas to attack, deprive the Confederate government of vital resources, and make plain that it could not protect most of its citizens.[50]

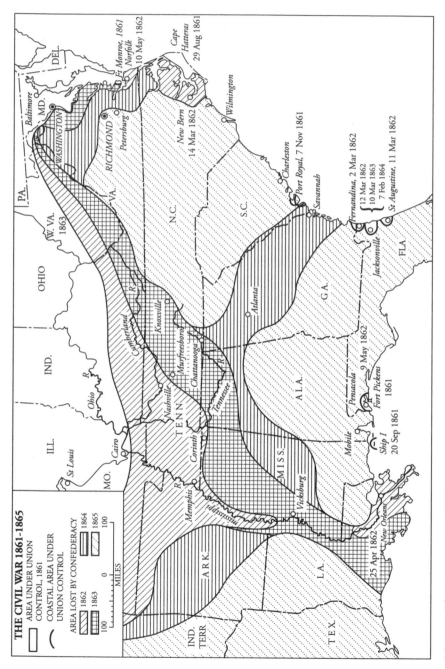

Map 1.1 The American Civil War

But politics imposed a second geographic logic on the war and on Lincoln's strategy. With Washington and Richmond, the Confederate capital, separated by a mere one hundred miles, most attention would focus on Virginia, especially the northeastern part of the state. Union victory here might not end the rebellion, since the Confederacy could opt for a defense in depth and force northern armies into long campaigns with severe logistical demands. But the North could lose the war in the eastern theater. Virginia was close to vital population centers such as Baltimore and Philadelphia, which might be endangered by southern raids or invasions. And the concentration of the press and politicians on what happened in Virginia meant that the outcome of battles fought there would reverberate across the North.[51] Above all, Washington, D.C., itself lay adjacent to Virginia, and the loss of the national capital would be a humiliation that might spell the end of the Lincoln administration and its war. Confederate leaders fully appreciated Lincoln's sensitivity to the vulnerability of the city and preyed upon it repeatedly (in General Stonewall Jackson's Shenandoah Valley campaign in spring 1862, Robert E. Lee's advances into Maryland later that year and into Pennsylvania in summer 1863, and finally Jubal Early's march to the very outskirts of the capital in summer 1864). To be fair, Confederate leaders were also guilty of a parochial fixation on Virginia and the East. Thus General Lee successfully resisted calls that he dispatch troops to Tennessee and Mississippi during the pivotal Vicksburg campaign or that later he himself assume command in the West.[52]

Reflecting the spatial and political geography of the conflict, Lincoln pursued Union military strategy through two primary military forces, each with its own characteristics, capabilities, and tasks. In the East, the Virginia campaign was led by the Army of the Potomac, seconded by various smaller forces tasked with protecting Washington. The Army of the Potomac vexed Lincoln like no other. Organized by McClellan and commanded mostly by officers he installed, it reflected his personal qualities—though well-trained and disciplined, it was accustomed to elaborate logistical support, deliberate in its movements, and suffused with a peculiar inferiority complex. When up against Lee's Army of Northern Virginia, the officers and soldiers in the Army of the Potomac seemed fatalistic, as though they knew they would be out-generaled.

For more than two years Lincoln searched for a commander who could use this army effectively, discarding one after another (McClellan twice, Burnside, Hooker, and Meade).[53] Eventually U. S. Grant, the most accomplished general on the Union side, came east to oversee the Army of the Potomac (Meade retained formal command), but even he could not make it more agile. He prevailed in the end because he was able to pin Lee's army in a siege at Petersburg while other Union forces swept through the South and wore down and defeated the other rebel armies.

In the West, the Union forces were divided into two main armies, the Army of the Tennessee and the Army of the Ohio/Cumberland,[54] which sometimes operated in coordination and under unified direction but also pursued separate campaigns. In central Tennessee, Buell's Army of the Ohio had many of the sluggish traits exhibited by his friend McClellan's eastern formation. When Buell was ousted in 1862, his successor, William Rosecrans, persisted in the habit of insisting that every supply deficiency be corrected before he began a campaign. Much quicker to move and less demanding of logistical fulfillment before it did so was Grant's Army of the Tennessee, in which Sherman emerged as his close deputy.[55] First in Tennessee and later in Mississippi, Grant showed relentless determination as his troops penetrated deeply into the South, mostly using rivers as highways. But once these campaigns shifted to land, they also pointed up the vulnerability of long supply lines in hostile territory. For example, when Vicksburg and the opening of the Mississippi seemed within Grant's reach in late 1862, a devastating raid on his main supply base at Holly Springs, Mississippi, and cavalry raids on his line of communications forced him to backtrack to Memphis and added months to the campaign.[56]

It was in the western theater that Union armies learned how to live off the land, thereby depriving the Confederates of essential local supplies while also delivering to the civilian population the painful lesson that the price of rebellion was economic ruin and social upheaval. And northern commanders in the West discovered that a lean force that brought with it enough to fight several engagements could survive occasional disruptions in its line of communications by Confederate cavalry raids.[57] The practice of stripping bare farms and towns along the line of march, moreover, fit well with the turn to the hard war that the Lincoln administration embraced when it chose to broaden war goals to include emancipation. Applied broadly by Sherman in his Atlanta campaign and the subsequent march across Georgia in 1864 (when Sherman simply abandoned his communications and vanished with his army until emerging on the Atlantic coast at Savannah), this would ultimately prove a key to the Union triumph.

Lincoln tried repeatedly to coordinate the movements of the Union armies to prevent the concentration of rebel forces against any single thrust, but his generals, fretting over their specific logistical problems, lacked his larger strategic vision. Typically they responded to his urging and even his direct orders by pointing out their difficulties with insufficient munitions, too few wagons and horses, and other shortcomings. Their professional mind-set and conventional training gave them a special appreciation of the demands of a tough campaign in enemy country; careful preparation now would prevent disaster later. Lincoln saw the bigger picture. If multiple armies attacked in unison, the Confederates could not concentrate against any one of them, and each Union force would enjoy a local advantage.[58] Both sides had a point, of course, and the tension between them could not be resolved so long as the war was limited in scope.

Not until 1864 did all the elements come together in a way that put Lincoln and his generals on the same page. I have noted some of these pieces—the widening of war objectives to encompass the elimination of slavery, the concomitant recognition that the will of white southerners to resist would have to be crushed, and the discovery by Grant around Vicksburg that depriving the population of what it needed to survive had both military and psychological benefits. To this we can add the emergence of Union military leaders in the West, Grant and Sherman, who were prepared to continue campaigns despite heavy casualties because they realized the enemy was less able to make good his losses. Lincoln recognized by the third winter of the war that vastly more soldiers died of disease in camps than in even the bloodiest engagements, so nothing was to be gained by suspending operations. The implication: once a campaign started, it must continue until brought to a successful conclusion.

In 1864, the Civil War assumed "modern" form, more closely resembling the bloodletting of the Western Front in 1917 than the episodic engagements common in the first two years of the conflict. Once Grant embarked on his "Overland Campaign" in Virginia in May 1864, the Army of the Potomac would be in constant contact with Lee's Army of Northern Virginia nearly every day for eleven months, until the latter's surrender at Appomattox in April 1865. The new nature of the violence is best reflected in a single sobering statistic: for the first month of the campaign, Grant's troops averaged 2,000 casualties *per day.*

Interestingly, in this final and most brutal phase of the war, the president became much less involved in directing military operations. Having found commanders, especially Grant, who shared his strategic vision and cold-blooded determination, Lincoln saw no need to manage things as he had earlier. Such was his confidence in Grant that he did not even ask for the details of campaign plans. Put another way, the Lincoln of the late-war period was much less the hands-on political leader that Cohen praises and better resembles Huntington's modern archetype—the leader who establishes war goals and entrusts the military effort to military professionals. It is no coincidence that the proportion of non-partisan professional soldiers holding senior command positions at the end of the war was substantially greater than at the start. The professionals had shown themselves to be the most reliable agents of their political masters.

Lincoln still made his presence felt at times. But he did so when he concluded that political considerations must outweigh purely military calculations. So it was in summer 1864, after Jubal Early's small rebel army threatened Washington and then drew back into the Shenandoah Valley, that the president insisted Grant put an end to such threats once and for all. The administration simply could not afford another embarrassment on the eve of the presidential election. Grant dispatched Phil Sheridan, a western general who exemplified the total war approach, to lay waste the Valley, so that no Confederate army could sustain itself there, a task Sheridan took to with evident glee.

Any depiction of Lincoln as the paradigmatic hands-on wartime political leader is not so much wrong as misleading and incomplete. Lincoln's active direction of the Union war effort was a necessary condition for victory, but not a sufficient one. He demonstrated remarkable strategic vision for someone as unschooled in military matters as he was at the start of the war. And most of his generals would never have displayed the energy, drive, and determination required to defeat a foe

with the resources and geographic advantages of the Confederacy had
he not prodded them. But the Union triumph required far more than
finding the right general, as one narrative line about the Civil War tells
it,[59] or even closely monitoring him (that is, Grant) once he was placed
in charge. Rather, a number of factors came together in the latter half
of the war, beginning with Lincoln's decision to embrace the total war
objective of destroying the racial economy of slavery. From that point
forward, it became clear that campaigns would assume a more merciless
and destructive form, to be sustained without interruption and
regardless of combat losses by generals of unbending will. Once the war
took on this new character, Lincoln stepped back from his efforts to
manage military affairs and largely left it to the professionals to
complete the job. His sporadic late-war interventions were usually
intended to remind commanders of the political dimensions of the
war.[60] The key point is this: absent the elements that came together
beginning in 1863, no degree of intervention by the president would
have sufficed to yield a Union victory.

Two Leaders and Their Mistakes

Any fair account of Lincoln as a military leader also has to reckon with
his mistakes. With the advantage of hindsight, of course, a later observer
can easily spot the ill-considered decisions. We need to judge decisions
in their context, that is, against the information available to the actors
at the time. Even from this perspective, Lincoln made errors: he pushed
for military initiatives that reflected his own political assumptions,
which were not always correct; he attempted to micromanage military
operations; and his distance from conditions on the ground gave rise to
unrealistic expectations about what his generals could accomplish. Yet
his military direction of the Union war effort should not be assessed in
isolation. A more balanced appreciation can be generated through a
brief comparison between Lincoln and his Confederate opposite,
Jefferson Davis. Lincoln emerges as the far more effective leader, possibly with decisive effects for the outcome of the conflict.

Lincoln was not immune to the temptation to see things as he
wished them to be rather than as they were.[61] Early in the Civil War, he
persuaded himself that the majority of southerners opposed secession

and would force their leaders to return to the Union after the first Confederate setbacks.[62] Rebel resilience in the wake of a series of defeats in the first months of 1862 finally disabused him of this misguided confidence. Still, he persisted in the notion that at least some parts of the South were ripe to defect back to the Union. That the western part of Virginia did so in 1861 (eventuating in the creation of West Virginia as a separate state in 1863) only served to fuel his conviction.

He focused in particular on East Tennessee, a mountainous region nearly inaccessible from the North by river or railroad. Even the roads from Kentucky could not be traversed by armies in poor weather conditions, something that became evident by the end of 1861, when a first Union campaign (under the extremely competent George H. Thomas) simply bogged down in the deep mud.[63] Repeatedly Lincoln called upon his western generals to liberate the region, adding as a sweetener the strategic rationale that a successful campaign would sever the most direct railroad link between Virginia and the western Confederacy. But by any measure East Tennessee was a distraction: the absence of transportation meant a Union army could not launch campaigns from there into the Deep South; freeing loyalist citizens from Confederate control would add few troops to the North; the impoverished region provided no important resources for the southern war economy; and disruption in east-west Confederate rail connections would merely hamper enemy transportation arrangements, as the rebels showed when they successfully reinforced their principal western army prior to its great victory at Chickamauga in September 1863 *after* the direct rail line through Knoxville had been severed by a Union force.

Concern for foreign policy could also lead Lincoln to insist upon ill-conceived military ventures. With the United States government preoccupied by the rebellion, France under Napoleon III found a pretext to move into Mexico and establish a puppet regime. Lincoln worried that if French control reached the Texas border, resources might flow across it into the Confederacy, undermining the blockade. He plainly overestimated the danger. Even had the French wanted to assist the South through Mexico, poor transportation and Union control of the Mississippi would have precluded significant help.

Compounding the error, Lincoln chose an ill-considered military response. After the capture of Vicksburg and Port Hudson restored

Union control over the Mississippi in summer 1863, Grant and other generals wanted to use the available forces to attack Mobile, Alabama, and open another front into the Confederate heartland. Lincoln instead demanded that General Nathaniel Banks, commanding in New Orleans and occupied Louisiana, launch an attack toward Texas via the Red River in northwestern Louisiana. Lincoln wanted to show the flag as close to the French occupation as possible, yet a move into distant East Texas made little geopolitical sense. In any event, Banks botched the campaign, small Union landings along the Texas coast were poorly handled and failed to impress the French, and as a result the more important Mobile campaign did not get under way until mid-1864.[64]

At times, Lincoln strayed into the direct management of military operations, with unfortunate results. In spring 1862, the redoubtable Confederate commander Stonewall Jackson led a small army down the Shenandoah Valley, posing a possible threat to Washington.[65] Total Union forces in the area far outnumbered Jackson's men, but the northern troops were divided into at least three separate commands. As a further complication, the Union troops approached the Valley from different directions and had poor direct communications with each other, while Jackson had the advantages of interior lines and intimate acquaintance with the terrain. Rather than appoint a single overall field commander and combine the Union detachments into a single powerful army, Lincoln and Secretary of War Edwin Stanton tried to direct their movements via telegraph in a vain attempt to trap Jackson between them. He proved far too adroit, defeating each opposing force in turn. The effects were far-reaching: troops that might have reinforced McClellan on the main drive up the Peninsula were instead directed to the Valley, while Jackson himself slipped away to join Lee outside Richmond where together they threw back McClellan's hosts. Although Lincoln learned from the experience that he could not manage field campaigns from the capital, he still intervened occasionally to push generals to launch attacks that would have been foolhardy.

What looked simple on a map at the White House was far more difficult and perhaps impossible for the soldiers actually doing the fighting. Both the East Tennessee expedition in 1861 and the attempt to synchronize the movement of widely separated units during the 1862 Valley campaign foundered in mud that made movement of large bodies of troops and their heavy equipment slow at best. In the latter instance, Lincoln and Stanton fell prey to a technological illusion—the notion that the speed of the telegraph allowed distant observers to exercise real-time command over units on the battlefield. The fragmentary information available via wire communication was an insufficient basis upon which to base tactical decisions and simply left officers in the field and their political superiors frustrated with each other.

Sometimes what Lincoln asked of his generals verged on the reckless. After the Army of the Potomac under General George Meade won its famous victory at Gettysburg, Pennsylvania, in early July 1863, the Army of Northern Virginia under Lee retreated, seeking to re-cross the Potomac. To Lincoln, it appeared that Meade had a golden opportunity to pin Lee's force against the river and annihilate it. Such a triumph, coupled with the surrender of Vicksburg to Grant, might have brought the war to a close. The president urged Meade to strike. But in reality his army had been hurt almost as badly at Gettysburg as its adversary. And Lee was prepared for such an attack, on ground suited for defense, so the result almost certainly would have been a crushing setback for Meade's troops that would have undone their recent triumph. Lincoln knew full well that weapons technology in the Civil War era favored the defensive side. The president also forgot on this occasion—as he did every time a Confederate forced raided the North—that armies had shown themselves too resilient to be destroyed in a single battle of annihilation.[66]

As we weigh Lincoln's mistakes, though, two considerations must be entered in his favor. First, he learned the limits of what he could do to influence the outcome of campaigns, so his intervention was episodic rather than constant. Second, in a war, the outcome depends on the decisions made by political principals on both sides. The Civil War involved two opposing leaders operating under broadly similar political arrangements with comparable powers as commander in chief. Whatever errors Lincoln made as a military leader, they pale in comparison to those of Jefferson Davis.[67] On the surface, Davis seemed to have all the attributes one might want in a wartime commander in chief: a professional military education, a record of distinguished combat leadership as a regimental commander in the war against Mexico, and an effective stint as secretary of war during the Pierce administration. Yet the very conventionality of his background proved his undoing, for in situations that required imaginative approaches he remained wedded to orthodoxy.

To secure its independence, the Confederacy might have pursued several paths, each implying a particular military strategy. First, the South might have induced outside powers, specifically Britain and France, to break the blockade, grant diplomatic recognition, or impose a peace agreement on the North. To do that, the Confederacy would have had to have shown that the blockade was ineffective and demonstrated that it could defend its territory successfully. Davis wanted the British to declare that southern ports were open, but he never pursued a naval campaign to demonstrate that the Union had failed to meet what London had long held to be the legal standard for a blockade.[68] Second, the South could have sought outright military victory and compelled the Lincoln administration to sue for peace on southern terms. Yet triumph through arms seemed unlikely, since the Union could replenish its losses much more readily than could the Confederacy. Third, as the lesser side in an asymmetric war, the Confederacy might have outlasted its foe, extending the struggle until a war-weary North demanded that its leaders accept southern independence. Here the South could have capitalized on its enormous territory, trading space for time, disrupting the lines of communication of invading Union armies, and harassing occupying forces until the North concluded that conquest was too costly.

Davis never considered this third course. To the observer today, in an era when non-state insurgencies have become commonplace, it seems an obvious option. But to suggest that Davis might have considered it is not just a modern conceit. Harassment by irregular forces had been familiar in the Civil War era, too. The term "guerilla" originated during the French efforts to subdue Spain and Portugal during the Napoleonic period, as Spanish irregulars conducted effective attacks on the extended French communications while French armies tried to bring Wellington's smaller British-Portuguese force to bay.[69] More to the point, the American South had a historical legacy of insurgent warfare dating to the American Revolution. After the defeat of regular American forces in 1780 in South Carolina, local resistance took the form of raids by irregular troops led by the likes of Francis Marion (renowned as the

Swamp Fox). During the Civil War, Confederate irregular operations and cavalry raids behind Union lines gave northern commanders fits, as shown by the raids that drove Grant into retreat in his first effort to take Vicksburg.

Davis persuaded himself that the Confederacy was too fragile to base its strategy on defense in depth and harassing operations. He believed that any territory left to the enemy would defect. As evidence, he could point to increasing desertion by soldiers whose homes had fallen under Union control.[70] Yet he clearly underestimated what carefully planned and organized guerilla-style activity might accomplish, as well as the dedication of Confederate supporters to the cause of southern independence. Even after the trans-Mississippi South (Arkansas, Texas, Missouri, and part of Louisiana) was cut off following Grant's capture of Vicksburg in July 1863, the region remained loyal to the Richmond government.[71] Davis worried, too, that loss of political control would encourage slaves to flee or rebel, one reason that owners of twenty or more slaves were exempt from conscription.[72] Here again he misjudged the potential of unconventional forces. As postwar depredations against freedmen in the South would show, violence by irregulars could serve as a powerful instrument for continuing racial intimidation. Davis left himself with no alternative, then, but to pursue conventional warfare against an adversary of far greater means.

Even on the terms he chose, Davis proved himself to be a poor leader. Although he recognized that the Confederacy could not hope to hold its entire 1,000-mile frontier with the Union, he devised no coherent strategic response. Initially, he acquiesced as General Albert Sidney Johnston in Tennessee adopted a cordon (linear) defense, which collapsed quickly when pierced by Union advances in early 1862.[73] Davis understood that his commanders would need to join forces to defeat larger enemy armies, but he never ordered them to do so or grouped them under a single general. Rather, he merely urged them to cooperate for the common good, failing to recognize that each one would perceive that good from his own particular perspective.[74] Time and again, whether in Kentucky in summer 1862 or at Vicksburg in 1863, Confederate generals refused to work together. They thus surrendered the key geographic advantage of interior lines that might have let them fight particular Union armies on equal or better terms and instead allowed themselves to be defeated in detail. Davis also refused to abandon any territory willingly—a reflection of his conviction that Confederate nationalism was too weak—making strategic concentration impossible.[75]

Compounding the strategic problem were Davis's abysmal choices of field commanders. Here his conventionality often asserted itself, as he remained wedded to the principle of seniority long after it outlived its usefulness.[76] Having selected a handful of high-ranking generals in 1861, he continued to rely upon the same small group of officers, regardless of their performance. (I noted earlier that seniority mattered in the Union Army, too, but the pool of generals holding equal rank and even common date of appointment was much larger.) Thus he repeatedly restored General Joseph E. Johnston to critical commands despite a virtually unbroken record of caution and indecision.[77] Davis also let himself be guided by his perception of particular officers dating back to his earlier career in the military or his tenure as secretary of war. Sometimes, as in the case of Sidney Johnston or John C. Pemberton (the ill-fated commander at Vicksburg), Davis's assessment had no foundation in the officer's prewar career performance.[78]

To the Confederate president, moreover, fidelity to the cause of southern independence mattered greatly, and he had no patience with those who seemed more concerned with their own reputation or advancement.[79] Contrast this attitude with Lincoln's tolerance for common emotions such as ambition. In one famous case, Lincoln selected Joseph Hooker to command the Army of the Potomac even after hearing that the general believed a dictator should seize power in Washington. Bring us victory, Lincoln wrote to Hooker, and I will accept the risk of dictatorship.[80] Most fatally, Davis retained in command certain officers long after it became clear that they could not lead effectively. In the Army of Tennessee, the principal western field force, most of the senior officers turned against Lieutenant General Braxton Bragg by late 1862, even refusing to obey his orders during battles. Yet Davis kept him in place through the disastrous Confederate defeat at Chattanooga in November 1863.[81]

In the end, the Confederacy probably came closest to victory when it pursued defense in depth in 1864 not by Davis's design so much as in spite of it. Union war weariness mounted that summer in the face of staggering casualty figures from Grant's Overland campaign and Sherman's inability to take Atlanta directly, necessitating a siege. The siege came about after Joe Johnston retreated before a frustrated Sherman, despite Davis's expressed preference that the former act boldly by striking the much larger Union army.[82] To the northern public, it seemed that the Union armies were simply stalled outside of Richmond and Atlanta, victory nowhere in sight. Had the situation remained static through the election, Lincoln was convinced he would be defeated at the polls, resulting in a negotiated peace and southern independence.[83]

Then Davis made a command decision that transformed the Atlanta siege and soon radically altered the political equation in the North. He replaced Johnston with the impulsive John Bell Hood, who followed his president's wishes by launching several foolish assaults against Sherman, and thereby so depleted the Confederate forces defending Atlanta that Hood had no choice but to abandon the city.[84] Sherman marched in, which, coupled with Union victories at Mobile, Alabama, and in the Shenandoah Valley, abruptly lifted morale across the North and propelled Lincoln and the Republicans to sweeping victory in the elections. From that point forward, final Union triumph was merely a matter of months, with the Confederate collapse complete by spring 1865.

Leading a People's (and a Party's) War

Abraham Lincoln appreciated—indeed, he would be reminded repeatedly—that the war was fought in a partisan context. He made military strategy and operational decisions with a keen awareness of their political implications. I have remarked on some of the ways in which politics framed his actions as a military leader, including his selection of generals to appeal to certain political constituencies and his acute sensitivity to the defense of Washington, D.C. More than that, Lincoln realized he was directing a people's war. Both the future of the nation and his own political fate depended on sustaining broad popular support for the Union war effort. Lincoln called upon his rich political gifts, particularly a rare talent for expressing his goals and principles in language that evoked a powerful popular response and a sense of timing that kept him in step with the public mood. He also had at his disposal an elaborate party organization and partisan press to help him shape public opinion and intimidate opponents. It helped, too, that the Republican Party could deliver non-military benefits to key constituencies. In this respect, Lincoln stands apart from other wartime presidents, whose domestic agendas have been derailed by their military commitments.

Several factors severely tested Lincoln's ability to maintain support for the war. First and foremost was the sheer cost of the conflict in human and financial terms, beyond anything Americans had experienced, almost beyond comprehension. Sustaining support was a daunting challenge in the face of heavy losses and battlefield setbacks. Morale slumped in the wake of defeats, as in the late summer of 1862, after the Second Battle of Bull Run, or the perception that even staggering casualties yielded no real gain, as happened two years later. Had voters gone to the polls in August 1864, Lincoln and everyone else was convinced he and his party would have suffered a crushing defeat.[85] Second, due to the frequency of elections, including important spring contests, electoral considerations could never be put off; the administration had no grace period in which bad news might be absorbed by the public before people voted again. Even elections for state offices were perceived by all as referendums on the war. Third, disagreement over war aims persisted in the North throughout the war. Opposition to the war rose from late 1862 (following the announcement of emancipation) through the 1864 elections, sometimes finding violent expression, as in the July 1863 New York City anti-draft riots that "degenerated into a virtual racial pogrom."[86] Last, antiwar sentiment claimed an organizational home in the Democratic Party, particularly after publication of the Preliminary Emancipation Proclamation in September 1862. Although Jefferson Davis faced significant discontent as Confederate president, it never coalesced into a political organization that could compete for power at the polls.[87] The Democratic Party in the North, by contrast, became the center of opposition, even resistance, to the war, its papers virulent in their condemnation of emancipation and eager to feed defeatism for partisan electoral advantage.

While Lincoln wrestled with how to maintain popular backing for the war, he also faced challenges from within his own political party.

He had wrested the presidential nomination in 1860 from more prominent party leaders, such as William Seward and Salmon Chase. Despite his efforts to mend fences and neutralize them by bringing them into his cabinet, they remained potential (and, in the case of Chase, actual) political competitors.[88] Key Republicans in Congress refused to recognize the president as their leader and took his flexibility as a sign of weakness.[89] Lincoln realized, too, that his renomination by his party was problematic. No president had been elected to a second term since Andrew Jackson. Further, as the lineal descendant of the Whig Party, the Republican Party had inherited the Whig skepticism toward executive authority.[90] During the Civil War, this skepticism assumed concrete form when congressional Republicans established the Joint Committee on the Conduct of the War. The committee annoyed and irritated the president; though it could not compel him to change course, he could not afford to ignore it. The Whig tradition also stressed the merits of rotation in office, which Lincoln had experienced when he was replaced after a single term in the House of Representatives in the 1840s.

He was reminded of this when bad news from the battlefield shook Republican support for the president and his war policy. In the bleak summer of 1864, Lincoln faced calls from fellow Republicans to consider abandoning emancipation as an objective to make possible negotiations for restoring the Union on prewar terms, an idea he briefly entertained before reaffirming there could be no turning back on the decision to destroy slavery.[91] Some Republicans, convinced that Lincoln at the top of the ticket meant disaster at the polls in the fall, cast about for another candidate in 1864. Although the president had been renominated by party convention in May 1864, the following two months saw efforts to call a new convention that would pick another candidate.[92] Only Sherman's victory at Atlanta and Sheridan's in the Shenandoah Valley put an end to talk of a different party standard bearer.

Abraham Lincoln's best resource for influencing popular opinion may well have been Abraham Lincoln. He possessed almost unparalleled rhetorical talents that he used to good effect, especially in published letters. (The president gave few speeches during the war and never addressed Congress.)[93] His words could soar, reaching for the higher aspirations that might ennoble sacrifice—"so that government of the people, by the people, and for the people shall not perish from the earth."[94] But he could also write plainly, in homespun language that would resonate with any American who had been raised on a farm and had sent a son or husband off to the war. Lincoln demonstrated a special genius for the use of metaphors to express complex ideas or abstract principles in everyday terms.

Consider as an example how he justified his emergency executive actions, including issuing the Emancipation Proclamation, on the grounds of absolute necessity. Although as a general principle a president must fulfill his oath to uphold the Constitution, Lincoln said, he would violate the essence of that oath were he to act in a way that sacrificed the nation for the sake of literal fidelity to the Constitution. And then the telling metaphor: "often a limb must be amputated to save a life, but a life is never wisely given to save a limb."[95] To an audience that by 1864 had become very familiar with the sight of men returning from battle missing an arm or a leg, Lincoln's words struck a responsive chord.

The president put his political and rhetorical skills to good use when he decided to embrace emancipation in 1862. To make such a move without laying the groundwork in the court of public opinion would have been dangerous. Emancipation could not be seen as a response to abolitionist pressures lest Republican conservatives and War Democrats turn against the administration. Lincoln chose a clever path—he set the stage for emancipation in a letter that seemed to *repudiate* abolitionist demands. Emancipation, he said, had to be subordinated to the proper objective of the war, to restore the Union. Were it possible to win the war without freeing any slaves, he would do so; if victory required freeing all of them, he would pursue that course; and if it meant freeing some while leaving others in bondage, he would choose such a policy.[96] Necessity, not ideology, would govern his actions, a stance that commanded far wider support than abolitionism even in the second year of the war.[97] By distancing himself from the radicals' cause, Lincoln gave himself the political space he needed to endorse their fundamental goal.

As he sought to sustain popular support for the war, Lincoln could call upon one critical political asset, his party organization. The party apparatus functioned first as a means by which the president and other

Republican leaders could gather information about the public mood. Long before public opinion polls offered politicians accurate feedback, parties had developed elaborate mechanisms for reporting popular attitudes down to the grassroots level.[98] That parties took pains to track opinion reflected a concern for their self-interest: to lose touch with the people was an invitation to electoral defeat. Lincoln realized that he could not afford to get out of step with the center of northern public opinion, all the more because he faced pressures from radicals and conservatives claiming to speak for the citizenry. So the president attended to communication from party officials at all levels and editorials from influential newspapers, especially those known to speak for particular Republican factions. (The press in the mid-nineteenth century was usually associated with a political party and often subsidized by it through government printing contracts.)[99] When popular discouragement surged in the wake of defeat or heavy casualties, word quickly reached the White House. Likewise, the administration heard promptly of significant attacks on its policies by opposition figures.

The party and its press also became instruments through which Lincoln and his fellow Republican leaders could shape public views of the war and foster popular support. In an early and important step, Republicans sought to incorporate pro-war Democrats into a mass political organization that would back administration priorities, mirroring the appointment of Democrats as generals. Republicans reached out to draw opposition party leaders who supported the war into an umbrella political coalition, usually called the Union Party. The move helped mask Republican weaknesses in the Border States and gave political cover to War Democrats unwilling to take the extreme step of switching parties. Yet the Union Party remained Republican at its core, notwithstanding the visible role it awarded to some Democrats (including the unfortunate nomination of Andrew Johnson for vice president in 1864).[100]

The administration's war policies were aided more directly by Republican control over state governments. Republican governors actively recruited troops, though they struggled as the casualty figures cooled the patriotic ardor of 1861.[101] Two Republican governors, Richard Yates in Illinois and Oliver P. Morton in Indiana, effectively eliminated partisan competition by dissolving their legislatures once Democrats won control, governing instead through their expanded executive authority.[102] Further, the Republican press became a major propaganda instrument, supporting administration policy and giving wide circulation to its views. Some Republican newspapers expressed criticism of the administration in the run-up to the 1862 elections, which contributed to the party's losses. The president and other party leaders responded by using their control over printing contracts to rein in the dissenting Republican editors.[103] From that point forward, the administration made certain its message was heard. When Lincoln wrote letters in 1863 and 1864 defending his controversial actions, such as emancipation, conscription, and suspending the writ of habeas corpus, his missives received wide circulation, first in party newspapers and then in pamphlets printed by the party.[104]

The Republican organization could also turn public skepticism about partisanship during wartime into a club with which to batter foes of the war. As Mark E. Neely Jr. observes, many northerners thought partisan competition should be suspended for the duration of the conflict. In their outlook, the idea of "loyal opposition" had no clearly defined place; if a party stood against the war, that stance seemed more like sedition than legitimate policy disagreement in a healthy political system.[105] Nor had American parties made a habit of cultivating moderation or political civility. "Carelessly pressing charges of treason and tyranny," Neely comments, "was the way the system worked at election time and had for years."[106]

Given the dominant role that the South had played in the Democratic Party, Republicans found it easy to associate antiwar Democrats with secession. Republican newspapers then stoked fears of Democratic betrayal and conspiracy. Disappointing results from the front and the dogged resistance of the Confederacy were depicted by Republicans as the result of evil political designs in the North: the "Slave Power" received aid and comfort from Democratic politicians, including Representative Clement Vallandigham of Ohio and Democrat-supported secret societies that hatched plans for the Northwest to break away from the Union and reach a separate peace with the South.[107] With his partisan allies so willing to smear the opposition, Lincoln himself did not need to engage in the attacks or accuse war critics of disloyalty.

In one other vital area, the Republican Party helped the president keep up popular support. The North was so wealthy that it could generate sufficient resources to both sustain a major war and promote economic expansion.[108] Accordingly, although at times financing the war presented a challenge to the administration, congressional Republicans moved ahead with programs that promised benefits to key backers. Lincoln had limited involvement in these actions, reflecting his Whig roots and the conviction that the legislature should take the lead in shaping policy other than that implicated in a national emergency.[109] Only on a few key measures, such as the bill to establish a new national banking system to help finance the war, did Lincoln intervene directly to pressure lawmakers.[110] Usually his aid was unnecessary. Before secession, southern lawmakers had blocked federal initiatives to promote industrial development and agricultural settlement by free labor. With the resignation of most southern members of Congress, though, Republicans moved quickly to push through major legislation. This included steep protective tariffs that generated significant revenues while boosting domestic manufacturing in sectors such as iron and steel. Meanwhile, a homesteading law encouraged westward migration to settle new land, long a popular idea among northern voters, while subsidies for railroad construction drew significant support in the Border States. Perhaps the best measure of how much largesse the Union government could support was its decision to charter a transcontinental railroad, a move that could not possibly yield significant benefits to the government for years.[111]

Later wars would demonstrate just how fortunate Lincoln and the Republicans were to be able to wage a war and pursue a bold program of domestic reform. Most wartime presidents and their parties, as we will see, have been forced to abandon popular domestic initiatives. Partly this has been dictated by the economics of financing a war, with higher defense outlays crowding out social expenditures while the need for increased revenues has compelled the federal government to adopt unpopular tax increases. The Lincoln administration did have to step up tax collections,[112] but a good deal of revenue came from hidden taxes, as when northern consumers paid more for imports whose price reflected high tariff duties.

Also, wartime presidents usually have had to deal with significant partisan opposition in Congress, which may demand fiscal prudence as the price of cooperation in financing the conflict. The Democrats during the Civil War, however, could not pose an effective legislative check on Republican programs. It helped, too, that key Republican initiatives either involved no direct revenue loss (homestead acreage was carved out of public lands that would not otherwise generate revenue) or contributed to revenue collection (protective tariffs). In sum, a peculiar set of circumstances placed the president's governing coalition in that rarest of wartime positions: it could afford both guns and butter, a situation that let it buy political support.

Toward Reconstruction

Planning for peace is very much a part of a nation's war policy. Fundamental war goals will shape the tasks a nation will face once the fighting concludes or winds down. In wars with sweeping goals that result in profound political, economic, and social disruption, the postwar project is very demanding. New political and social institutions have to be created, potentially requiring a long-term commitment to a politico-military occupation by the victor and substantial postwar expenditures. Institution-building will be impeded if elements among the defeated side refuse to accept their loss and turn to protracted resistance, including violent insurgency.

Vital though preparing for the aftermath of a conflict might be, political leaders may be tempted to avoid the task or minimize its hazards. They have what appears to be a more urgent matter on their plate—the need to bring the war to a swift and successful conclusion. With their limited time and waning reserves of energy, they are prone to devote themselves to the immediate problems of directing the war effort, sustaining popular morale, and providing the resources to win on the battlefield. Peace also spells the end of whatever unity the commitment to victory inspired among various political actors and social groups. In the United States, moreover, postwar planning may provoke conflicts between the White House and Congress that were tamped down by the need for cooperation during the war. The return of peace alters dramatically the institutional equation for a president and leaves him with reduced capacity to determine the national agenda.

A president planning for postwar needs to have a realistic appreciation of the scale of the challenges the nation will face. As the end of the war approaches, moreover, he should shift his attention from military matters to political ones. Finally, because postwar operations involve ongoing commitments and costs, a president needs to invest in forging a public consensus around his peace-building agenda. By these standards, Lincoln does not score well. At certain moments, he voiced an expansive vision of a more inclusive social order. But he did little while the fighting raged to lay the necessary groundwork. This highlights a sobering truth: even the most able commanders in chief stumble when it comes to peace.

As the Civil War moved from its initial limited character to a total struggle, the postwar challenge assumed a far more complex and demanding form. When the North sought merely to force the rebel states to rejoin the Union with their social institutions intact, the postwar challenge seemed straightforward: once a seceded state accepted federal authority, it would be welcomed back. The Republican program explicitly blocked any extension of slavery into new territories, but early on Lincoln had made plain he did not intend to interfere with it where it existed. Emancipation transformed the terms for a postwar settlement. From the moment the president made slavery itself a major focus of military operations, a Union victory would fundamentally revolutionize social relations across the South. The potential for far-reaching upheaval was magnified by the decision to muster into the ranks of the Union armies freedmen by the tens of thousands. What to do with the free black population—a problem that had vexed observers of slavery since the American Revolution first placed its future on the national agenda—would move from the realm of abstract speculation to urgent priority.

Lincoln himself had grappled with the question at least since the late 1850s. Although he loathed slavery as a violation of everything the nation represented and had argued steadfastly for the rights of all persons, regardless of color, to control the fruits of their own labor, he recognized the deep-seated obstacles to racial equality and social integration. Whites would not acknowledge Negro equality, Lincoln had observed in his first debate with Stephen A. Douglas in 1858, and policy had to take this sentiment into account. As Lincoln put it, "A universal feeling, whether well or ill-founded, cannot be safely disregarded."[113] He had suggested it might be better if blacks were not permitted to enter the newly opened western territories. Yet Lincoln had also confessed then that he had no clear idea of what to do with former slaves once they were freed. Returning them to Africa, a scheme that enjoyed some support across racial lines, did not seem a practical alternative in the short run.[114]

With war and then his emancipation policy, the president now confronted the enormous challenge of defining a future without slavery in which its victims would need to survive and stand on their own. War between free and slave states, he perceived, did not ease the underlying prejudice against African Americans, which may have been as deep-seated in the North as below the Mason-Dixon Line. In 1862 Lincoln met at the White House with a delegation of free blacks and insisted physical separation was in the best interest of both races. He urged them to consider leading an expedition to settle former slaves in Central America, and charged that it would be selfish of them to decline.[115]

That Lincoln could for a moment entertain the hope that the problems of 4 million African American former slaves could be solved through a new exodus of biblical proportions says much about his pessimism that emancipation alone could resolve the intractable dilemma of race. For a short time after he endorsed emancipation, the president still hoped exile for the freedmen might obviate the need to find an answer within the United States. It was a mark of desperation that he signed an agreement in December 1862 to transport 5,000 blacks to an island off Haiti.[116] Once the Emancipation Proclamation went into effect at the start of the New Year, however, he dropped all talk of colonization as a solution. Lincoln's decision to support black enlistment for military service marked an implicit recognition that colonization had ceased to be an option.[117] Answers to the problems posed by the newly freed black population would have to be found in the United States.

To the formidable challenges posed by race relations, we must add another: the tension between Lincoln's immediate objectives and the long-term rehabilitation of the South. His proximate goal was clear—to win the war. As he saw it, the Union's approach to Reconstruction ought to be designed to induce southerners to lay down their arms. Were it possible to convince some to abandon the Confederacy in exchange for generous terms that let them retain most of their prerogatives, the enemy would be weakened and southern defeat hastened.[118] Yet wartime leniency might subvert long-term plans to remake the social order in the South in ways vital to protect the possibility that the former slaves might achieve economic independence and social dignity. If we understand war to be a means for achieving political goals, then these goals rather than military victory become a statesman's primary responsibility. Amid the carnage, though, a political leader faces constant demands to find the quickest path to a successful military outcome. Lincoln resolved the tension by choosing to focus on the immediate military objective at the expense of the future.

The advance of Union armies beginning in the earliest months of the conflict compelled the administration and the army to begin to address how best to assist southern blacks abruptly freed from slavery. In the Sea Islands of South Carolina (1861), the parts of Louisiana near New Orleans (1862), and the Mississippi Valley after the capture of Vicksburg (1863), the national government effectively initiated a great social experiment, guiding the transition from racial subordination to a new order of legal emancipation. Army commanders in different places adopted different approaches, ranging from efforts by a small legion of northern reformers on the Sea Islands to educate blacks and foster some measure of self-sufficiency to mandated annual labor contracts that returned erstwhile bondsmen to their plantations under conditions scarcely better than those under chattel slavery. The harsher approaches sparked opposition from their black subjects, who demanded stronger legal protections and then called for the right to vote to better secure their legal and economic status. Their cause found a warm reception among Radicals in Congress, eager to make certain that the old southern planter aristocracy would never regain power and to lay a foundation for lasting Republican Party influence in the region.[119]

Although Lincoln's views on the long-term restructuring of southern society were ambiguous and in flux, his proximate objective pushed him in a more conservative direction. From the outset of the war, he believed that a lenient approach might encourage southern whites to lay down their arms.[120] Accordingly, under his own authority as commander in chief, in 1862 he established a policy that would permit the restoration of state government as soon as 10 percent of the total of the 1860 electorate took an oath of loyalty, with only senior Confederate civil and military officials excluded from the terms. Those who swore the oath received presidential pardons. On these generous terms, Reconstruction governments were organized in Tennessee, Arkansas, and Louisiana. With only a narrow majority in Congress in December 1862, Republicans agreed to seat the Louisiana delegation.[121] Emancipation in 1863 did not alter Lincoln's basic approach, but he added the condition that the restored state governments agree to abolish slavery, a move that met with public and Republican Party approval.[122] Still, even the new qualification implied nothing about the rights or status of former slaves; for the president, such matters were better addressed later, after the return of peace.

Lincoln's Reconstruction formula set him on a collision course with many in his own party who viewed the 10 percent threshold as an invitation to restore not merely a state government but the system of privilege and racial subordination that was the root cause of the rebellion. Committed now to the president's hard war, his Radical foes were unwilling to countenance a soft peace. They were spurred especially by mounting complaints from blacks in and around New Orleans, where the local Union commander, General Nathaniel Banks, had imposed a harsh regimen on former slaves that forced them to sign annual labor contracts with their former masters that provided low wages and gave the workers no protections.[123] Radicals and some Republican moderates coalesced in 1864 behind the Wade-Davis Bill, which set the bar for the restoration of state government at 50 percent of the prewar electorate.[124] Such a figure could be achieved only if a significant number of former slaves were allowed to vote.

Although Radicals accepted black suffrage, the president did not, at least at that point. The Wade-Davis Bill passed in Congress in the waning days of the session, but Lincoln declined to sign it and the measure died.[125] Politics guided his handling of the Wade-Davis challenge. In summer 1864, with an uphill battle for reelection looming, the president was not prepared to go before the northern electorate as an advocate of extending the franchise to former slaves. Given that some influential Republicans in this dark period of military stalemate advised him to forsake emancipation, Lincoln's caution seems justified.

His refusal to move more boldly after his overwhelming reelection, however, cannot be so easily rationalized. With his victory Lincoln stood as the uncontested head of his party. The Radicals were in retreat, as demonstrated by the defeat of Wade-Davis when put before the lame duck 38th Congress again in December, and the removal of Radical-backed generals, such as Benjamin Butler, from senior command. Lincoln had been given political capital, as we now call it, and he used some of it that December to secure congressional approval of the Thirteenth Amendment, which banned slavery.[126]

But he certainly could have done more. He might have used his popularity with voters and his dominant political position to begin to shape public opinion in favor of black suffrage and commence serious planning for Reconstruction. Further, the end of the war was plainly in sight: Sherman's army moved at will through the southern interior and Lee's army, trapped by Grant's at Petersburg, suffered from rising desertions. The 10-percent formula thus had outlived whatever usefulness it might have once had as a device for driving a wedge between southerners. Yet, presented with a golden opportunity to shape the postwar South at the very peak of his political power, Lincoln failed to seize the moment. He spoke movingly at his second inauguration of the need to bind the nation's wounds and show "malice toward none,"[127] but noble-sounding generalities do not a policy make. Quietly he started to acknowledge that at least some freedmen should be enfranchised, but he did not take the case to the northern people.[128] That it would be necessary to lay a foundation in public opinion for black suffrage Lincoln certainly understood, for he had often observed that race policy had to accommodate racial attitudes.

As the South collapsed in April 1865, the administration had barely begun to prepare for peace, and it is not clear what Lincoln could have done to forestall the disaster that Reconstruction became. His assassination deprived the nation of its most credible leader (and elevated in his place a deeply polarizing one, Andrew Johnson). Yet even had Lincoln lived, he would have faced multiple obstacles to successful peace-building and would have found himself with little time to overcome them—contrary to his wartime assumption that the best alternatives for Reconstruction could be sorted out when the guns fell silent.

To begin with, he would have had few resources for coping with a devastated South and the particular crisis faced by the former slaves. The federal government had little organizational capacity for meeting their needs. Although Congress established the Freedman's Bureau under the War Department in early 1865 as a stop-gap entity for resettling blacks on abandoned land, the Bureau had no firm legal basis for transferring title to them.[129] Here was another example of how the lack of planning and preparation invited confusion rather than constructive solutions. In turn, the insufficiency of preparation for addressing the urgent needs of destitute and uprooted freedmen—despite abundant warnings about their plight in the last two years of the war—suggests that Lincoln had badly underestimated the magnitude of the problems that Reconstruction would face.

Add next the institutional dynamic that peace sets in motion: power swings back to the legislative branch. Lincoln knew this, since he had witnessed what happened to James Polk after the war with Mexico. Polk achieved all of his territorial ambitions in the conflict, only to lose control over the postwar debate when an obscure Pennsylvania representative, David Wilmot, offered his proviso to ban slavery from all of the newly acquired lands. Congress already had made plain that it would no longer accept Lincoln's Reconstruction formula: in December 1864 lawmakers declined to count Louisiana's electoral votes in the presidential election and refused to seat the Arkansas delegation.[130] When the new 39th Congress finally met a year later, it would surely have insisted on establishing the terms for readmitting states to the Union, even if the president had been Abraham Lincoln rather than Andrew Johnson. Lincoln paid heavily, then, for his success in prolonging presidential Reconstruction by turning back any congressional alternative in December 1864. For a few additional months of exclusive control, he sacrificed the broader legitimacy and shared institutional commitment that results when a policy is jointly "owned" by Congress and the White House.

Finally, divisive political forces were unleashed with the Union victory, and these would have entangled any president. The war had set the stage for a deep split within the Republican coalition.[131] On one side, Republican Radicals wanted to ensure the thorough destruction of the antebellum southern economic system through a strongly statist approach in which the national government remade the South from the bottom up, creating real opportunities for the advance of freedmen. But this agenda would require extended military occupation, a costly proposition. A conservative alternative envisioned rapid withdrawal of most occupying military forces and their demobilization, followed by the quick return of southern states to the Union and an end to national oversight over their internal affairs. Northern financiers, eager to see the reduction of expenditures and the repayment of war debts, backed the conservative option, and they had gained considerable standing in the Republican Party through their vital efforts to raise money for the Union war effort.[132] The two sides began a contest for control from the moment the South surrendered, and Lincoln would have been caught in the crossfire. In sum, even a victorious and popular president has less time than he imagines when a war ends.

How Many Limbs Must Be Amputated?

Lincoln's expansion of presidential power was controversial at the time and remains a subject of debate, one that sharpens whenever a president asserts broad claims to unilateral authority. In the opening moments of the conflict, Lincoln acted on his own initiative to set in motion the Union war effort and secure control over wavering Border States, effectively inventing a new conception of presidential wartime emergency power. He continued throughout the war to exercise powers not explicitly given in the Constitution to the president. Among the measures he ordered were several that imposed significant limitations on traditional civil liberties. Critics accused him of acting as a dictator, but they surely overstated the matter. Certainly despots do not go to the lengths that Lincoln did to explain and justify their actions or commute the sentence of their fiercest critic, as he did with the outspoken Clement Vallandigham.[133] But if Lincoln exercised emergency power with moderation, he established a rationale for assertion of presidential power during wartime that could be taken up by successors who might not be so restrained.

Following the rebel bombardment of Fort Sumter, Lincoln took measures to deal with the widening crisis. As I noted earlier, he called for short-term militia forces from the states, followed soon thereafter with an appeal for volunteers to serve for three years; he declared a blockade of Confederate ports; and he expanded the regular army and navy. Some of these steps preempted powers explicitly granted to Congress under the Constitution.[134] Lincoln chose not to call Congress into session immediately, preferring to wait until July to convene a special session. He believed he had all necessary authority to act under what he termed the "war power of the government," a concept with no historical precedent. Congress did approve of Lincoln's initiatives as soon as it met, conferring upon them a form of post hoc legitimacy that helped them later withstand judicial scrutiny.[135] Whether Lincoln had to act without Congress is another matter, however. Spring congressional elections were still under way as of April 1861, but this does not seem to be a compelling justification for the delay.[136]

In the opening months of the war, moreover, Lincoln insisted that the emergency gave him the authority to suspend civil liberties in the Border States. Maryland appeared ready to secede, and arriving northern troops were attacked in Baltimore. Lincoln authorized the local commander to take preemptive measures to thwart secessionist moves. However, although the president knew of strong secessionist sympathies in the state legislature, he directed military officials not to prevent it from convening. Instead, he imposed martial law in Maryland, under which secessionist sympathizers were arrested and held without trial. This sparked Lincoln's famous confrontation with Chief Justice Roger Taney, in which Lincoln refused to comply with a writ of habeas corpus when Taney ordered the release of a rebel suspect.[137] It was the first of several contested actions Lincoln took during the war that violated established civil liberties. As a point of comparison, Jefferson Davis did not invoke the power to suspend habeas corpus until the Confederate Congress gave its explicit authorization.[138]

Lincoln would later extend his suspension of habeas corpus to cover the entire North in September 1862, at which point he also authorized martial law and military trials of all rebels, draft resisters, those discouraging volunteer enlistments, and anyone guilty of disloyal practices or of giving aid and comfort to the rebels. Most of the 13,000 civilians detained without trial lived in Border States and might have had some connection to Confederate irregular military operations. But the proclamation was also used, more controversially, against opponents of the war in the North, especially when the unpopularity of conscription in 1863 spurred advocacy of regional secession and a separate peace with the South.[139]

Opponents of the war such as Vallandigham urged soldiers to return home to force the administration to come to terms with the Confederacy. When he was placed under arrest by a military commander without administration approval, Lincoln felt he had to support the move. (Vallandigham was later deported to the Confederacy, then made his way to Canada and ran in 1864 for governor of Ohio, only to be soundly whipped at the polls.)[140] Determined to defend the encroachment on free speech, Lincoln again displayed his rhetorical gifts, explaining that it violated common sense to shoot the "simple-minded soldier" who deserted while leaving untouched the "wily agitator" who had induced him.[141] By some accounts, this image of brave but innocent youth led astray by cowardly and disloyal foes of the war helped turn the 1863 election decisively in favor of the Republicans.[142] The president also secured congressional ratification for his actions, which enhanced their popular legitimacy and shifted some responsibility from his shoulders.[143]

Behind Lincoln's assertion of extraordinary powers lay a bold new theory of the legitimate scope of presidential power in a national emergency. He contended that as commander in chief in wartime—at least in a war in which the survival of the nation hung in the balance—he could do things that lay outside the powers of the office during peace. Emancipation illustrates how he used his authority over military matters to stretch presidential power. At his First Inauguration, he avowed that as president he had no power to interfere with slavery where it existed. But as it became clear that slavery was facilitating the South's capacity to wage war, Lincoln became more receptive to arguments that as the nation's military commander he could assert any power needed to secure victory. Certainly property used by the enemy to support his war effort was fair game. On military grounds, then, he might declare free all slaves who assisted the rebellion.[144] Although this left unresolved questions about slaves living within the Union and whether slavery could be reestablished after the war, the president appreciated that he had likely dealt a death blow to the South's peculiar institution. He also maintained that his emergency authority extended beyond that of Congress: where a commander in chief could emancipate slaves as a war measure, he defended the pocket-veto of the Wade-Davis Bill on constitutional grounds, insisting that Congress overstepped its bounds by including language that made emancipation a part of Reconstruction.[145]

In sum, Lincoln adopted an expansive reading of wartime presidential power that served his immediate purposes, while recognizing the political dangers inherent in such an interpretation. By his reading of the Constitution, the president had a broad warrant to act during a war in ways that would otherwise be illegitimate. The indispensable character of unconstitutional measures made them lawful.[146] He thus was able to reconcile his actions with his underlying Whig beliefs in a limited executive and legislative supremacy. By implication, for Lincoln the expansion of presidential power represented but a temporary shift in balance among institutions, something to be remedied as soon as peace returned.

At the same time, though, he had the political wisdom to appreciate that wielding excessive power could undermine the war effort. Suspending habeas corpus was an unpopular measure, and not just among Democrats opposed to the war. Arrests of dissidents sat poorly with a public that valued its freedoms, even if, as I have observed, it was unsure about where loyal opposition left off and treason began. To avoid offending the sensibilities of too many northerners, especially those who backed the war, Lincoln sought to limit the exercise of military authority against antiwar elements. He was condemned by some of them as a despot. But by exercising emergency powers circumspectly, he helped to deprive such an accusation of the traction it might otherwise have had with the broader public.

Not that Lincoln sought to minimize or conceal his incursions on treasured civil liberties. To the contrary, he offered direct and compelling defenses for his action. Recall first the "wily agitator" who hid behind the shield of free expression while letting gullible soldiers pay the price for desertion. (As an aside, Lincoln had a soft spot for soldiers charged with desertion and often commuted their sentence, especially when the request came from a politician who might then owe the president a favor.)[147] The second justification was his comparison of the nation and its Constitution to the wounded patient and his limb. In the latter example, habeas corpus served as the infected appendage that needed to be excised so that the patient/nation might survive. Lincoln asserted that those who dwelled upon his initial suspension of habeas corpus in 1861 at a time when secessionist plots had already gone far toward dismembering the Union failed to appreciate that with its demise the Constitution and the liberties it protected would also cease to exist.

Yet, irrefutable though Lincoln's logic was, it begged other questions. How many limbs should be sacrificed to save a life? And at what point should the surgeon stop cutting, wipe clean the blade, and give the patient a chance to recover? After the indispensable "procedure" to rescue the Union in 1861, in other words, the second or third ones in subsequent years might not have been necessary. The suspension of habeas corpus nationally and the extension of martial law and military tribunals were drastic measures, even if applied with a relatively light hand. Moreover, as Lincoln demonstrated by the impact of his letters answering his detractors, well-crafted words explaining war policies such as emancipation and conscription proved to be highly effective in rallying support for those policies. Persecution of war foes before military tribunals, especially from 1863 onward, seems to have represented a largely gratuitous exercise of executive power—that is, the surgeon could have put down his knife sooner, at no risk to the patient.

One additional query suggests itself in response to Lincoln's medical metaphor, inspired by the modern era of medical review boards and malpractice claims. To whom is the surgeon accountable for his decision to operate? The assertion of extra-constitutional emergency powers by a president will only be legitimated by the acquiescence of other political institutions and actors. During the Civil War, Congress repeatedly granted ex post facto approval to Lincoln's actions, including both his assumption of war powers assigned to the legislative branch under the Constitution and his orders that curtailed civil liberties. The Supreme Court, its standing weakened by the unpopular 1857 *Dred Scott* decision, avoided confrontation with the president after his 1861 refusal to obey Taney's order. When Lincoln extended the suspension of habeas corpus across the nation in 1862 on the thin pretext that the entire country was a war zone, the Court never ruled on his action.[148]

The cooperation of or submission by other governing institutions left only the press and opposition parties as organized vehicles that might force the president to answer for his claim of extraordinary wartime authority. They performed this function effectively. By calling out Lincoln for stepping beyond the established limits of his office, his political foes and press critics (including some Republican editors) pressured him to explain himself to the American people. But their experience, which included charges of disloyalty and varying levels of harassment and persecution, demonstrates that questioning executive emergency powers during a war carries a serious penalty.

Reconsidering the Lincoln Legacy

On March 4, 1865, Abraham Lincoln delivered his Second Inaugural Address, perhaps the most haunting speech ever given by a president of the United States. Although victory was in sight (Lee would surrender at Appomattox less than six weeks later), his words contain no hint of triumphalism. The war's cost instead weighed heavily on Lincoln. Some 600,000 soldiers had perished on both sides, an unknown number of civilians had died, and hundreds of thousands had fled or been driven from their homes. If most of the destruction had occurred in the South, he took no satisfaction from that fact, for he had always regarded the people there as his own countrymen. The president had never shielded himself from the suffering, either, frequently visiting wounded troops and reading many letters from those who had lost loved ones. Lincoln used the occasion to express the deeper meaning of the war. He saw in it a divine judgment about the price Americans had to pay for tolerating slavery in their midst. Before reaching that point, he recounted the origins of the conflict, speaking in broad terms of how "both parties," North and South, were too committed to their ideals to avoid war. "And the war came."[149] It is an oddly passive phrase because, by implying that impersonal forces drove events toward an outcome no one preferred, it brushed past another truth: Lincoln's own decisions brought on the conflict. For a president, there is always choice, and with it responsibility.

On balance, Lincoln exercised his responsibility as a war leader with distinction, setting a very high standard for all later wartime commanders in chief. He understood how the war evolved, moving from a limited struggle to reestablish the old Union to a more radical and total conflict that would eliminate slavery. Lacking a military background, he assembled an army, chose commanders to lead it, established a strategy and pushed those commanders to pursue it or replaced them with others who would, and adjusted strategy when his expanded war goals dictated that it change. His hands-on engagement extended beyond military affairs to other pivotal realms of wartime presidential leadership. Boosting popular morale and securing the resources needed to defeat the enemy are vital for a nation at war, and Lincoln played a key role in both. He took control of a range of political matters vital to a successful war effort. Of special note, a president must resist the temptation to retreat into a defensive shell in the White House when public discontent rises over the lack of military progress and the heavy human price. Lincoln had deep reserves of willpower that allowed him to weather reverses and withstand attacks.

No president leads alone in wartime, and Lincoln's effectiveness depended a great deal on others. Some of his cabinet members, such as Secretary of War Stanton, assumed critical duties, and Lincoln received prudent advice from his cabinet as well as from important Republican Party politicians and editors. Within the general scheme of American government, war empowers the presidency, and I observed how Lincoln expanded presidential authority at the expense of other institutions. Nevertheless, these remained active and provided important help to the president. Congress bestowed legitimacy on some of Lincoln's questionable moves.

A kind word should be spared, too, for the Joint Committee on the Conduct of the War, often maligned by both contemporaries and historians. Unfortunately, through its members' lack of understanding about the nature of warfare in the age of the rifled musket, the Joint Committee gave congressional oversight a poor reputation that persisted long after the Civil War. On the other hand, as Lincoln showed, a hands-on president who tries to direct a war can make mistakes. So there is much to be said for an institutional mechanism to ask hard questions about the assumptions behind strategy, whether war goals are appropriate and can be achieved, how much progress has been made, and more.

If Lincoln's overall performance merits high praise, he still falls short on certain dimensions of wartime leadership. He did too little and waited too long to lay a foundation for Reconstruction. In contrast to politicians who fear and defer to public opinion, Lincoln at times chose to defend unpopular actions, and he demonstrated some capacity to persuade doubters that he was correct. (Absent reliable data of the sort that we now get from opinion polls, such judgments must remain provisional. But historical accounts credit Lincoln's letters with great impact.) On the matter of race, though, he shied away from efforts to influence white Americans, even at the peak of his popularity. To the very end of the war, he approached Reconstruction entirely as a tool for dividing southern whites to expedite the defeat of the Confederacy. His narrow approach suggests that a preoccupation with military victory will lead any president to devote too little attention to postwar planning. If that is a consequence of taking direct charge of all things military, then we may have additional grounds for reconsidering the ideal of the hands-on supreme commander. Lincoln's failure to plan for peace, moreover, raises the troubling possibility that wartime political leadership, with its multiple, demanding challenges, exceeds the capacity of any person.

We also need to interrogate other aspects of Lincoln's legacy, all the more so since, as we shall see, later wartime leaders have drawn heavily on his example. Presidents during wars always believe they are pursuing the national interest. From their perspective, opposition to their war policy is problematic, for critics appear to stand against the nation itself. Yet in a healthy democratic society, people should ask sharp questions about the grave matters of war and peace. Such challenges remain a vital part of presidential accountability, especially if other political institutions fail to assert themselves. Lincoln was a better leader *because* his critics forced him to explain his policies to the American people.

Expansive claims to emergency powers represent Lincoln's most dubious contribution to wartime presidential leadership. Once we accept his premise that the Union had to be preserved, we cannot doubt that immediate action was needed to respond to secession and prevent other Border States from leaving the Union. He offered a persuasive case, too, that under the circumstances he faced in summer 1861, the civil liberties "limb" of habeas corpus should not be exalted over the "life" of the nation. In addition, to Lincoln's credit, he sought congressional ratification of most of his emergency orders. Just the same, the negative side weighs heavily. Lincoln preferred to act without Congress, rather than wait for it to return or call it back into session early. In so doing, he established a precedent for broad unilateral presidential action in wartime. And though he may have exercised emergency authority with some restraint, nothing assured that his successors would follow his lead.

2

Waging War to Transform the World

Woodrow Wilson

WOODROW WILSON REMAINS A CONTROVERSIAL wartime leader. Nearly a century after the First World War, his performance still divides, even polarizes, historians. Some praise him for his clarity of purpose and vision while others dismiss him as a "misfit in office."[1] Much of the debate surrounds his character—self-confident to the point of arrogance (French Premier George Clemenceau suspected Wilson fancied himself the new Messiah),[2] intolerant of dissent, driven by self-righteous convictions.

Viewed through my perspective, his personal attributes matter only insofar as they influenced his ability to accomplish the tasks that face every wartime president. An analysis of Wilson as a wartime president needs to go beyond his character to consider the other factors that shaped his effectiveness—the role of other political actors at home and abroad, the relationship between president and Congress, his administration's efforts to mobilize public opinion in the United States and overseas, and more.

As a wartime commander in chief, Wilson represents a mix of both impressive success and epic failure. From the outbreak of war in Europe in August 1914 to the point at which America entered the conflict in 1917, Wilson sought to secure American interests, broker a negotiated settlement, and lay the groundwork for a new kind of postwar order. His determination to assure that American businesses would continue to trade abroad and maintain the rights of neutral powers during wartime provoked conflicts with both sides. Most critically, the president allowed the choice of whether the United States would be drawn into the war to slip from his hands. The German decision to commence unrestricted submarine attacks in early 1917 forced him to ask Congress for a declaration of war. Wilson proclaimed a lofty set of goals designed to do nothing less than make the world, as he put it, "safe for democracy." Because the objectives required support from domestic and foreign political actors over whom he exercised limited influence, it proved a riskier approach to a core leadership task than he realized.

Once the United States entered the war, Wilson faced other key tasks, tasks of a magnitude comparable to that which confronted Lincoln in 1861: creating the military force needed to secure the war aims he established and selecting its senior commanders, organizing the economy to produce the means this force would need to fight, defining the military strategy that would accomplish his war aims, making certain that military operations were properly directed to accomplish his objectives, and managing relations with allies. On the whole the president and his administration addressed the challenges effectively. The United States achieved an impressive mobilization of resources, both human and economic, within a brief time; a substantial American army was in the field in about fifteen months, though barely in time to influence the outcome. As a military commander in chief, too, Wilson accomplished exactly what he set out to do, using military force to secure an end to the fighting on his terms and positioning himself to play a key role in the postwar peace conference.

Wilson's effort to maintain public support for the war and for his broader objectives yielded more mixed results. To promote popular enthusiasm, the administration mounted a broad publicity campaign that included establishing the first official wartime propaganda organ. But faced with significant criticism of mobilization efforts and with opposition to the war, Wilson became defensive. He turned the war into a partisan issue in the 1918 congressional elections, alienating Republicans. His administration also launched a sweeping assault on the civil liberties of groups and individuals who opposed the war that eclipsed anything done by the Lincoln administration.

With battlefield triumph in hand, Wilson faced the final key task of wartime leadership: peace-building. Lincoln had accomplished his central goals by defeating the Confederacy and destroying slavery in the process. Not so with Wilson and Armistice in November 1918. That did no more than open the door for what the president insisted must follow—a just postwar order that would be generous to the enemy, assure that emerging peoples could choose their own form of government, and protect smaller states from aggression by larger ones. And here his grand design collapsed. Allied leaders frustrated the president at the peace conference, while domestic opponents thwarted his bold effort to engage America in a system of collective security to guarantee the peace.

His failure resulted from both the circumstances specific to his situation and factors that recur across wars. Historians have tended to focus more on the former, in particular Wilson's personality attributes and his failing health. But we should attend, too, to the elements that any wartime president is likely to encounter when the guns fall silent. Presidential power, especially leverage over other political actors and a dominant voice in shaping public opinion, begins to ebb immediately. Thus Wilson discovered that he could not impose his will on other Allied leaders, on distant armies contesting the borders of newly emerging countries, or on the United States Senate. His struggles with the Senate also demonstrate that peace brings into play another political force—a resurgent legislative branch—that can thwart the presidential postwar agenda. His own mistakes and the general decline in presidential capacity following a war, then, combined to prevent him from delivering the kind of peace he had promised.

The Perils of Neutrality

When Europe stumbled into war in August 1914, the belligerents recognized that the United States could have a decisive impact on the outcome. Industrial expansion had propelled the United States to the forefront of the world economy, while American agricultural exports also boomed. Warring nations, especially the Entente or Allies (Great

Britain, France, and Russia), looked across the Atlantic to purchase munitions for their military forces and food for their hungry people. The Central Powers (Germany and Austria-Hungary, soon joined by the Ottoman Empire) likewise valued American exports, though the volume of trade was significantly less.[3]

American military power, though a mixed bag, also influenced both sides. Following the striking success of the U.S. Navy in the war against Spain in 1898, the service continued to expand, particularly during the presidency of Theodore Roosevelt. At the outset of the war, the United States possessed one of the world's more formidable battleship fleets, though a number of its ships were already outdated by the advent of modern dreadnought-class vessels.[4] If the country entered the conflict, its ships might tip the balance at sea decisively. (Only as the war progressed would it become evident that the naval war hinged on submarines and the measures to counter them.) The U.S. Army, by contrast, frightened no one, its modest numbers making it insignificant in the scale of warfare that would be waged in Europe. Appreciating both the importance of American resources and the potential impact of the American fleet, the combatants hesitated to antagonize the United States.

The United States had much at stake in the war, but it is not clear that Woodrow Wilson appreciated this at the outset. As the leading economic power, America most needed a stable world order in which nations could trade securely. The country had benefited greatly from decades of free security provided by the Royal Navy and from the peace that had prevailed in Europe for most of the previous century.[5] However, the German decision to challenge British naval supremacy posed a threat to stability and represented a risk to American trade. During the previous twenty years, the British government had bent over backward to avoid conflicts with the United States, effectively ceding naval control in the Western Hemisphere to Washington (and doing likewise in the Pacific to Tokyo) as it prepared for the expected showdown with Germany. The latter, by contrast, seemed eager to confront the United States; witness a series of disputes ranging from Samoa to the Philippines.[6] Wilson admired aspects of both British and German culture, and he was deeply shocked when war erupted. (He was also distracted from the European crisis by the death of his first wife.)[7] Possibly the president recognized the long-term danger posed by a German drive for global hegemony,[8] but he did not respond to it in August 1914. Instead, while urging Americans to remain neutral in thought as well as deed, Wilson announced that the government would refrain from favoring either side. He shared the common belief that the conflict would end quickly—nations simply could not sustain the cost of modern warfare for any length of time.[9]

Most Americans initially accepted Wilson's call for neutrality. The war was too distant, separated by a vast ocean from American shores. Of course, many immigrants had arrived from nations on both sides of the conflict, and these newcomers certainly tended to favor their homelands.[10] The Allies worked hard to shape American attitudes and succeeded in stirring fears in elite circles about what a German victory might mean.[11] Much of the American heartland, though, was unmoved by Allied propaganda and steadfastly resisted the idea that America had a real stake in the outcome of the conflict. There were also pro-German voices, especially Americans of German descent who objected when ostensibly neutral policy (e.g., the refusal to ban the sale of arms to belligerents) in practice favored the Allies. Unfortunately for German sympathizers, their appeals were nullified when the Wilson administration revealed clumsy German propaganda campaigns or plotting by German and Austro-Hungarian diplomats to subvert American neutrality.[12]

Whatever Wilson may have thought about the long-term implications of the war, he realized that it posed immediate risks to American commercial interests. Trade with Europe was an important element in domestic prosperity. Cotton prices collapsed almost overnight with the outbreak of war, for example, an alarming development to a Democratic president whose political base was the old Confederacy, while the corresponding decline in customs revenues left the federal government facing an unexpected deficit.[13] But history suggested the effort to preserve trade might drag the United States into the war. A century earlier, as the Napoleonic Wars raged across Europe, the young United States had faced pressure from both England and France to suspend commerce with the other. Impressment of American sailors by the Royal Navy had helped propel the United States into war with Great Britain. Popular opinion in the United States, moreover, would tolerate only limited interference with American sovereign rights.[14] With London determined to curb trade with the Central Powers, Wilson had reason to anticipate difficulties with the British again. At the same time, any accommodation with the British might be perceived as a pro-Entente policy by their foes.[15] Germany also would not stand by idly while American goods sustained the Allied war effort.

The president did have options that would have allowed the country to avoid the complications inherent to wartime trade, but he was loath to sidestep what he saw as a matter of principle. The administration might have adopted the prudent recommendation by Secretary of State William Jennings Bryan that the small American merchant fleet be kept in port. Bryan suggested that the combatants be allowed to buy American goods but required to transport them in their own hulls, certainly no real hardship for Great Britain.[16] But Wilson stubbornly insisted that warring nations respect the rights of neutrals under international law. The president always sought to identify core principles and proceed from there, and for Wilson "neutral rights" was the key issue.[17] If American ships plied European waters, confrontations with the belligerents would be inevitable. Both the Entente and the Central Powers were determined to prevent the Americans from providing decisive aid to their adversaries, and both declared blockades of enemy ports, subsequently extended to any neutral ports through which goods could be shipped to their foes.

Although the Royal Navy provoked American ire, just as it had one hundred years earlier, several elements worked to contain British-American tensions. The British blockade operated in a traditional manner, with surface ships intercepting merchant vessels and searching them for contraband. This approach posed little threat to civilian passengers. At times the British tightened the definition of contraband to include American raw materials, a stance that could harm the U.S. economy,[18] but London also understood how vital American exports were to the Allies and preferred not to alienate the Wilson administration to the point at which it might rupture relations. Thus, when London in 1915 declared all raw cotton to be contraband, British purchasing agents also arranged to buy enough to sustain the price for American growers.[19]

It helped the British, too, that some of Wilson's senior advisors favored the Allied cause, though they had to tread carefully around their leader. One key actor with strong pro-British leanings was State Department Counselor Robert Lansing. Because Wilson kept such a tight leash on foreign policy, none of his diplomats could exercise much discretion. Still, Lansing made or influenced several minor decisions early in the war that the Germans viewed as pro-British, such as relaxing a ban on loans to belligerent powers that facilitated Allied purchases of American products. American popular opinion also backed trade with the Allies, while there was little direct commerce with Germany.[20]

For Germany to enforce its blockade, on the other hand, its navy would need to resort to unorthodox techniques. Most of the German surface fleet remained anchored at its main base. To halt ships from reaching Allied ports, then, the Germans would have to rely on its modest fleet of submarines (popularly called U-boats). But submarines could only give warnings to merchant and commercial traffic by inter-cepting ships while surfaced, which made them vulnerable if the other vessels were armed. Surfacing also deprived the U-boats of the key advantage of surprise. Wilson, refusing to see that established interna-tional law governing blockades worked to British advantage, expected German submarines to conform to traditional practice.[21] In February 1915 the Imperial German government announced a new policy under which its U-boats would attack without warning Allied ships as well as neutral ships because Allied vessels often flew under neutral flags. Wilson responded that the United States would hold Germany strictly accountable for American loss of life or property, a stance that implied war if the Germans made good on their threat.[22]

Despite several attacks on American ships with loss of lives and published warnings in newspapers, American civilians continued to sail aboard ships bearing Allied flags. The sinking of the liner *Lusitania* (with a cargo that included munitions) on May 7, 1915, resulted in more than one hundred American deaths. Additional ship losses and casu-alties over the summer precipitated a diplomatic crisis between Germany and the United States that brought the two nations to the brink of war.[23] Unwilling at that point to provoke the United States to join its enemies, the German government under Chancellor Theobald von Bethmann Hollweg decided to back down, in part because it had too few U-boats to make the blockade fully effective. It suspended submarine attacks, handing Wilson what appeared to be a major diplomatic victory.

Yet the terms under which the president resolved the immediate crisis shifted the initiative to German hands. Wilson warned that if Germany resumed submarine warfare on American vessels, the United States would be forced to declare war. This left the policy decision to the German government—it might choose to resume the attacks at a moment when these would be of greatest advantage. Still worse, the United States might be propelled into the war by the unsanctioned decision of a random U-boat commander who decided to fire his torpedoes at a passing merchant ship caught in the crosshairs of his periscope. As Wilson himself put it, "Any little German lieutenant can put us into the war at any time by some calculated outrage."[24] This prospect sufficiently alarmed Secretary of State Bryan that he resigned from the cabinet (to be replaced by Lansing, who was of course anything but neutral).[25] Events would show that the Germans realized the discretion Wilson had given them. German civilian and military leaders argued over whether the benefits of unrestricted submarine attacks outweighed the risks, with the former initially persuading the Kaiser that the danger from provoking the United States to enter the war was too great.[26] But his decision could be reversed if the players in Berlin and/or their calculations changed.

Even as Wilson sought to safeguard American economic interests in the short run, the war also presented him with what he soon saw as a rare opportunity to reshape the international order. As noted, he had been deeply shocked when the war started. Very much the product of the Victorian years of peace among major nations, he believed civilization had advanced to a point that ought to allow for the resolution of differences by nonviolent means. He also subscribed to the Progressive confidence in the power of reason to overcome all problems.[27] As the carnage in Europe worsened, Wilson became determined to prevent any recurrence. During the first thirty-plus months of the war, the president repeatedly sought to use his good offices to bring about a peace accord. He pursued this objective through his personal direction of American diplomacy, sending his advisor Colonel Edward M. House to Europe on several occasions and remaining in close contact with him.[28] After defusing the immediate crisis with Germany over the *Lusitania*,

Wilson resumed his search for a negotiated peace, a quest that would continue until American entry into the war. By 1916 his vision broadened to include the creation of a system of collective security that would offer an alternative to war. Such a mechanism would involve the United States, thereby marking an end to the nation's historic isolation from global affairs, though he tried to downplay the departure from tradition.[29]

The president made public his vision of a new international system in a speech on May 27, 1916, a speech that also pledged support for the ideals of government by some form of popular consent and freedom from aggression.[30] Thus, well before American policy makers seriously entertained the idea of direct participation in the war, Wilson contemplated how he might play a role in ending it in a way that would prevent future large-scale conflict. He issued a stirring call for "peace without victory" in January 1917 that included a pledge that the United States would join other nations to guarantee that peace would be maintained.[31]

For all of Wilson's sincere efforts to bring an end to the war, his initiatives would stimulate nothing more than an elaborate diplomatic charade by the other players. None of the belligerents had a serious interest in following up on his overtures. As the cost of the war increased and casualties reached incomprehensible totals, the warring governments concluded that their people would accept nothing less than victory for the sacrifices they had made.[32] Great Britain and France negotiated secret agreements about how to divide the spoils they would wring from their beaten enemies to compensate their own citizens for the deprivations they were enduring.[33] They also made promises about territorial gains to other nations, such as Italy, to induce them to enter the war on the side of the Entente.[34] As they cut deals among themselves, leaders of the combatants paid lip service to American efforts to broker peace. They hoped that the onus for failure would fall on their adversaries, who would state terms so extreme that Wilson himself would be forced to admit they could not be accepted. After winning reelection in 1916 as the peace candidate, he renewed his call for negotiations and asked the two sides to state their minimum conditions for peace. Berlin, while evading the president's request to state peace terms, announced a readiness to negotiate, putting the Allies on the spot.[35]

At this point, though, Wilson's diplomacy was subverted by members of his own administration. Both Lansing and House had become actively pro-British. Lansing went so far as to announce to the press that Wilson's December 1916 message was not a call for peace but rather an effort to clarify the belligerents' positions because the United States was moving closer to war. Although an angry president made the secretary of state issue a clarifying statement, Lansing was not forced to resign. Instead he continued to reassure the Allies privately (and unbeknownst to the president) that America would never enter the war on the side of Germany. House expressed the same message to his confidants in the British government. The Allies were encouraged, then, to state their most extreme peace terms, knowing these would not push the United States into the German camp. Lansing and House pursued a different foreign policy from that of their president.[36]

The fruitless quest for a negotiated settlement taught the president how little leverage he could actually exercise. The Allies in particular depended on the United States for war supplies and food. Any threat to shut off the flow across the Atlantic, though, would also alarm American businesses and farmers prospering from the markets created by the war. As far as the Central Powers were concerned, the British blockade had worked so well in choking off shipping from the United States that an embargo on their part would have little effect. Germany would only take account of a potential foe with significant military capacity. But although the U.S. Navy represented an important military chip, the main conflict in Europe had assumed the form of a clash of vast conscript armies. With an army at his disposal that barely sufficed to contain trouble along the Mexican border, Wilson could hardly threaten to intervene against Germany in a way that really counted. The German government and high command understood that it would take considerable time after an American declaration of war before American manpower began to matter on the battlefield.

Several factors contributed to the failure of the United States to create an army that might have sustained Wilson's diplomacy. Not the least of these was the president's own conviction that American influence did not rest on the threat of force. He had firmly maintained since the outbreak of war that the United States did not need a large army to promote his goal of a lasting peace.[37] For that matter, he remained certain until the end of 1916 that the country would not enter the conflict, notwithstanding the ongoing threat that Germany might resume submarine attacks. According to one oft-repeated (though likely apocryphal) story, when Wilson learned through a newspaper account that the U.S. Army general staff had developed a plan for war with Germany, he flew into a rage and threatened to dismiss any officers involved. In fact, the army's planning had been entirely defensive in character—the War College Division had devised a response to a hypothetical German attack on New York City.[38] With no indication that the president contemplated intervention in Europe, army thinking simply continued along its well-worn if archaic path.[39]

But not all the fault for the lack of military preparedness rested with the president. War in Europe had provoked a debate that was remarkably detached from the reality of the war itself. Arguments about modernizing the army had become entangled with the strident nationalism of certain influential Republicans, such as former President Theodore Roosevelt and General Leonard Wood. They saw preparedness as a vehicle for promoting patriotism and an ethic of service.[40] They also conjured up fanciful scenarios that envisioned the victor in the European war deciding that a weak United States was ripe for picking.[41] As one historian of the movement puts it, "Preparedness was almost purely defensive. Its thrust was isolationist, not interventionist."[42]

On the other side, Wilson's fellow Democrats in Congress, especially its powerful southern wing, had no enthusiasm for increasing the military power at the disposal of the federal government. War Department schemes to establish a trained reserve that might be ready in the event of war, moreover, collided with the lobbying influence of the state militia (recently renamed the National Guard).[43] The president, reluctant to alienate anyone in an election year, left it to Congress to fashion a compromise in the form of the 1916 National Defense Act. It served Wilson's immediate political needs—preparedness faded as an issue—but the result was useless for either diplomacy or war. The measure established a program to expand the regular army modestly over five years, established stronger federal oversight for the National Guard, and allowed the Guard to be used outside the continental United States. As critics observed, this was entirely inadequate for an actual war and larger than necessary for peace.[44]

In contrast with the president's lack of interest in building a major modern army, the administration did take certain steps to enlarge the U.S. Navy and to prepare for the mobilization of economic resources in the event of war. The president threw his political weight behind a bill to accelerate the construction of capital ships (battleships and battle cruisers) and expand the number of smaller vessels.[45] Again the initial benefit was political, because it would be several years before the ships would be ready. Just as bad, they would be the wrong kinds of vessels: the measure, drafted by battleship admirals, took little account of the growing submarine menace.[46] American leaders also realized that war would increase the demand for strategic resources and require government direction of economic activities to an unprecedented degree. With this in mind, the National Defense Act included a provision to establish a cabinet-level Council of National Defense to prepare for economic mobilization should war erupt.[47]

Wilson secured his reelection by a narrow margin, aided by his deft response to the preparedness movement, but found himself at a diplomatic dead end and subject to the policy choices of other nations. Despite his effort to use his good offices to broker an acceptable peace agreement, the warring alliances had staked out positions that could not be bridged. Neither would concede that victory was impossible or not worth the cost. At the same time, each experienced a rising sense of desperation, as nations reached the limits of their available manpower, foodstuffs began to run short, and political discontent percolated just below the surface. Finally, in Germany, a government reluctant to antagonize the United States gave way to one that heeded military demands to halt shipping to Great Britain. The German naval command expressed confidence that its U-boats could force the British people into starvation before the United States could put sufficient forces into the field to make a difference. When the Allies responded to Wilson's December 1916 call with extreme peace terms that would have amounted to a German surrender, Berlin decided the following month to initiate unrestricted submarine warfare, announcing the decision on February 1, 1917.

Wilson had left himself with no choice but to break diplomatic relations with Germany.[48] Soon thereafter the British intercepted and published a telegram from the German foreign minister to the Mexican government that offered it help if it decided to go to war with the United States. It was a foolish and clumsy move that angered the American public, but few took seriously the threat.[49] The submarine attacks were a different matter, however, and Berlin's refusal to revoke the order finally drove Wilson to ask Congress for a declaration of war in April 1917.

Taken as a whole, Wilson's efforts in the thirty-plus months of American neutrality demonstrated a mixture of political savvy, moral rigidity, and diplomatic naiveté that brought the United States into a global conflict. A skillful politician in the domestic arena, he understood American public opinion and what it would tolerate. Had he pushed harder for a military buildup after the start of the war in Europe, he might well have split his political coalition and found himself too far ahead of a reluctant public. Further, he came to grasp that German militarism threatened a global economic order in which the United States had assumed the leading role. Were Germany to prevail on the battlefield, it would coexist uneasily at best with the economic leviathan that had emerged in the Western Hemisphere. (Preparedness advocates and army planners who conjured up future German invasions overstated the underlying conflict of interests but did not misconstrue it.)

On the other side, Wilson was slow to appreciate that American economic leverage was a two-edged diplomatic sword: it could only be used in ways that would do grave harm to the power that wielded it. He could have avoided confrontations with belligerents had he accepted Bryan's recommendations that they ship American goods in their own hulls. Adamant on matters of principle, however, he insisted on neutral shipping rights of little practical significance. I have observed how this left the choice between war and peace in German hands. In his high-minded attempts to mediate an end to the conflict, Wilson also failed to recognize what the conflict had done to the psyche of the warring nations and their governments. They used his idealism—his vision of a settlement with no winners leading to a world without war—to manipulate him. As events would show, Wilson and his new British and French partners would continue to have very different conceptions about the goals for which they would now be fighting together.

War without Victory

Wilson told the U.S. Congress in a special session on April 2, 1917, that the country had no alternative but to recognize that a state of war existed with Imperial Germany. His speech presented an opportunity to frame for the American people the purposes for which he would ask them to fight. As the first expression of war aims, the address also let the president exercise most freely his agency as the political leader of a nation at war. That is, he could choose how to portray the struggle (including the character of the enemy), what level of destruction the nation would seek to inflict, and what kind of peace he would aim to build. Certainly he had offered hints earlier, but none of his previous expressions of his goals, such as a negotiated compromise acceptable to both sides, bound him now. By contrast, with America now about to go to war, his framing of what was at stake and what the United States would aim to achieve stood as firm commitments. Barring some dramatic change in circumstances (such as when Lincoln had realized that victory required the destruction of slavery), the initial presidential assertion of war aims would drive everything that followed. At no other point, then, would the president have such wide scope for exercising discretion.

Wilson's address began with a narrow, almost legalistic case for war that hinted at quite limited goals. Reminding his audience of the threat to peaceful trade posed by unrestricted submarine attacks, he reaffirmed the principle that wartime commerce should be governed by traditional rules. To this Wilson added a bill of lesser charges that included German espionage, efforts to disrupt American industry, and the recent bid to incite a Mexican attack on the United States. He blamed the autocratic character of the German regime for these actions, specifically noting that the German people ought not to be held responsible for what their leaders had done. Peace would require, then, the assurance of freedom to trade and an end to the threat of aggression by Germany. (Wilson refrained from asking Congress to declare war on the other Central Powers.) Although in theory it might be possible to achieve these objectives through a negotiated peace with the Imperial German government, he made plain that he believed future security depended upon, to use a phrase that gained currency in a later generation, regime change in Berlin. "We know that in such a government, following such methods, we can never have a friend; and that in the presence of its organized power, always lying in wait to accomplish we know not what purpose, there can be no assured security for the democratic governments of the world." Nonetheless, Wilson still called not for victory but a negotiated settlement, pointedly rejecting any goals grounded in the raw emotions that conflicts stimulate: "Our motive will not be revenge or the victorious assertion of the physical might of the nation." It made for a pretty tepid brew, hardly the stuff to stimulate the pulse of a people who would be asked to make great sacrifices.[50]

And so the president raised the stakes, by an order of magnitude. The United States would fight for something far more important, more worthy of great sacrifice. In going to war, Wilson continued, the nation would expend its blood and treasure

> for the ultimate peace of the world and for the liberation of its peoples, . . . for the rights of nations great and small and the privilege of men everywhere to choose their way of life and of obedience. The world must be made safe for democracy. . . . We have no selfish ends to serve. We desire no conquest, no dominion. . . . We are but one of the champions of the rights of mankind. We shall be satisfied when those rights have been made as secure as the faith and the freedom of nations can make them.[51]

Thus, beyond its own commercial and security interests, the United States would fight in pursuit of a transformative agenda, one that would radically alter the political status of subordinated peoples across the world. We shall fight, as he so grandly pronounced, "for the right of those who submit to authority to have a voice in their own governments." And to sustain that right, the United States would also commit itself to some kind of organization of free peoples "to bring peace and safety to all nations and make the world itself at last free."[52]

At this pivotal juncture, when Wilson needed to make clear why Americans had to join a war they had avoided for nearly three years, he conveyed mixed signals about what was at stake. He confused real but not very inspiring interests with an idealistic, indeed, nearly utopian vision of a world in which all peoples would enjoy self-government, justice, and peace. Wilson had broken relations with Germany and decided on war due to the submarine attacks, a narrow rationale the public grasped and evidently accepted. But he would not make great sacrifices in the name of balance-of-power politics, forestalling German hegemony, or preserving commercial opportunities. He could hardly ask his fellow Americans to do so, either. Something more seemed necessary, the kind of postwar settlement that had been taking shape in the president's mind over the many months of fruitless diplomatic overtures to the warring sides.

Yet in promising so much as the reward for war, Wilson vastly overreached, sowing the seeds for discontent with his postwar leadership and friction with the other powers at war with Germany. He had not yet secured the broad mandate from the American people that his expansive peace-building goals would require. In effect, the president had adopted a new foreign policy stance, one that implied, as one historian observes, "extensive and sustained intervention supported by the requisite military force."[53] Such a radical departure from American tradition called for a careful preparing of the political ground, something that a handful of speeches over the previous year could not accomplish.

Some months later, in January 1918, Wilson sought to clarify American war aims and articulate his conception of a new kind of postwar order. He laid out in a speech to Congress the Fourteen Points that he saw as a basis for bringing the war to an end.[54] Some of the terms represented hard-headed conditions that would reduce the probability of war (arms reductions), while others (eliminating economic barriers) would redound to America's advantage as the world's leading economy. He made clear, too, that the Central Powers could expect to retain no territorial gains they had made through wartime conquest. But Wilson also envisioned peace-building that encompassed justice for peoples who had been denied a voice in their own government, to be guaranteed through an instrument of collective security. He insisted upon the "free, open-minded, and absolutely impartial adjustment of all colonial claims," a process in which "the interests of the populations concerned must have equal weight with the equitable claims of the government whose title is to be determined." All of this would require, as the final point recognized, the creation of an international association with the power and responsibility to preserve the independence and territorial integrity of large and small states alike. Implicitly, the United States would be a member of this association.

Wilson's program put him on a collision course with the very nations beside which the United States would fight. Rather than join the Entente, the United States chose to wage war as a co-belligerent Associated Power, sharing a common enemy but not necessarily common war goals. Wilson understood that the Allied leaders would want to make Germany pay heavily for the human and material damage caused by the war. The United States, he made clear, would have no part in such a peace.[55] Indeed, where the Allies would want to make certain Germany could not again threaten them, the president stressed his continuing faith in "German greatness" and sought to reassure the German people that his program would allow for it.

Moreover, Wilson pledged himself broadly to a principle of self-determination and anticolonialism—even as the United States had yoked itself to the world's two leading colonial powers, Great Britain and France.[56] He might have anticipated that they would have reservations about his program, which could complicate peace-building. Although he would later claim that he knew nothing of the secret treaties among the Allies that promised postwar territorial gains, his assertion was not credible. Not only did the Bolsheviks publish the agreements to embarrass the Allies, but British Foreign Secretary Arthur Balfour reported that he had shown the treaties to the president in 1917. The territorial questions addressed in the Fourteen Points were themselves shaped by the secret treaties.[57]

Despite the gap between his program and the Allies' commitments, Wilson did not seek discussion with the Entente powers of the Fourteen Points or the proposed international association. One reason for his failure to do so was that he did not construe his commitment to self-determination as a broad-based attack on colonial empires so much as an approach to redrawing boundaries in Central and Eastern Europe.

Very much wedded to the prevailing racial assumptions of his age, he did not believe non-white colonial subjects were yet ready to fully manage their own affairs. He also saw that his ideas about a new kind of international order enjoyed growing popular support in the Allied nations, especially in Great Britain.[58] Possibly the president concluded that it would suffice to let those ideas percolate, generating a ground-swell of support that would compel Allied leaders to yield at the eventual peace conference.

Wilson's decision not to initiate conversations with the Allies about peace terms in early 1918 carried a risk: he left unresolved important differences about territorial settlements, responsibilities for war damages, and other issues. Only when an armistice was under consideration in October 1918 would it become clear that the British and French had only seemed to bless the Fourteen Points and Wilson's subsequent elaborations. How they might be induced to accept his transformative vision of a postwar settlement remained uncertain.[59]

Mobilizing a Nation for Modern War

The United States went to war in 1917 with a tiny regular army inca-pable of making even the slightest mark on the European battlefield. Designed as a glorified constabulary to maintain security on the nation's borders and in its recently acquired overseas possessions, the U.S. Army struggled to meet even those tasks. A punitive expedition against the Mexican rebel leader Pancho Villa, with fewer than 5,000 men, had taxed the army's capacity, forcing Wilson to call up National Guard units in 1916 to watch the southern border. This action revealed in turn the wretched state of the American militia force.

About the best that could be said of the entire preparedness debate was that it had accustomed American citizens to the idea of a mass army and compulsory military service.[60] The administration's quick decision to embrace conscription met with no serious political oppo-sition, an interesting contrast to the Union experience in the Civil War, and by mid-May 1917, Congress had approved enabling legislation. In terms of equipment, the army found itself with no tanks or gas masks, few aircraft, little artillery or ammunition for it, and obsolete machine guns.[61] American officers also lacked firsthand knowledge of battlefield developments: Congress had denied funding to send observers to Europe (the administration could have worked around this but decided not to) and army attachés in foreign embassies sent reports that were filed unread by civilian clerks.[62] Further, because some in Congress had suspected that senior army officers wanted to draw the country into the war, the 1916 National Defense Act had also reduced the size of the General Staff.

That no substantial U.S. Army existed posed a challenge to the president as he sought to achieve the objectives he had established in going to war. Initially, the Allies wanted American money, supplies, and shipping (especially to combat the submarine menace), rather than American troops. American financial might would power the Allies to victory, with American factories churning out weapons to be placed in the hands of British Tommies and French *poilus* fighting in the trenches. The formidable U.S. Navy would also sail for British waters, its battleships joining those of the Royal Navy to make certain the German High Seas Fleet did not again venture from port.[63] Toward that end, Wilson had sent Rear Admiral William S. Sims to arrange cooperation with the British in March 1917, before war had been declared.[64] Sims, learning from his hosts the true scale of sinkings to U-boat attacks, persuaded the reluctant British to adopt the convoy system that quickly reduced shipping losses.[65] So far as the Allies were concerned, the United States might assemble a token ground force as a gesture of solidarity, but anything more would be a misuse of scarce shipping capacity. Wilson, however, recognized that unless the United States made its weight felt on the great battlefields of Europe he could not expect to command the stage at a postwar peace conference. Immediately upon the declaration of war, he had asked Congress to establish an army of 1.7 million men that would constitute the American Expeditionary Force (AEF).[66]

Circumstances soon compelled the Allies to recognize the urgent need for American manpower. Visiting delegations of senior officers from Great Britain and France disclosed the sorry state of their respective armies after three years of unrelenting combat. The latest major French offensive failed miserably in spring 1917, precipitating near mutiny in the ranks; most British units had fallen far below their paper establishment. From the Allies' perspective, it would be best if

American troops were sent over quickly and incorporated into British and French units. British Major General George T. M. Bridges went so far as to propose that a half million American men be inducted, sent directly to England for training, and then sent as individual replacements to British units.[67] No American president would accept such a subordinate role, especially not Wilson, who saw at once the need for an American expeditionary force to make a clear, indisputable mark that would give him the political capital he would need in the subsequent peace negotiations. Grudgingly, the Allied military missions conceded the point, though this would hardly end debate over how American troops should be used.[68]

Having settled the matter of whether to send an army, the Wilson administration next faced the same task that had confronted the Lincoln administration in 1861—to put the requisite force in the field as quickly as possible. Although some of the framework had been established by the earlier preparedness summer camps and the 1916 legislation, the task would take time. Apart from the initial detachment designed to show the flag, an actual field army would not be available before mid-1918, and army planners anticipated that American numbers would not be decisive until 1919.[69]

As Lincoln had, Wilson faced a key decision: whom to place in command of this nascent expeditionary corps. Wilson believed that once chosen, this officer should be given great latitude in how he directed his troops. From the president's reading of history, Lincoln had interfered far too much in how his generals conducted their business. Wilson intended a much more "hands off" approach.[70] But that meant that the commander he selected would have to understand the administration's political objectives and be prepared to operate in manner designed to accomplish them. He needed, in short, to be a reliable agent. That ruled out someone such as the controversial former Army Chief of Staff Leonard Wood, who had been a strident proponent of American preparedness against the wishes of his commander in chief. Wood, a Republican closely associated with former President Theodore Roosevelt, also harbored known presidential aspirations, and Wilson was no more eager to enhance the prospects of a potential competitor than Lincoln had been. Instead, the president selected Major General John J. "Black Jack" Pershing, who had recently commanded the Villa punitive expedition.[71] There he had avoided antagonizing the Mexican government despite roaming freely over the border. Although Pershing, too, was a Republican, he had shown that he could pursue the administration's political objectives even without close oversight from Washington.[72]

Whether Pershing was the right general to command an army of a million or more men in battle remained a great unknown. We should recall again Eliot Cohen's observation that at the start of a war a political leader has no choice but to select from among unproven senior officers.[73] That was every bit as true for Wilson as it had been for Lincoln. In 1917 the U.S. Army had no officers who had commanded large bodies of troops in combat. Although Pershing's Mexican expedition had reached a maximum of 15,000 men, most of the time it had been a brigade-size force of about one-third that number.[74] He had handled it credibly, but Wilson quickly decided that the force to be assembled under the general's direction would be vastly larger, with correspondingly greater organizational, logistical, training, and planning challenges.

Pershing also had strong beliefs about how the AEF ought to fight: he was persuaded that the Allied armies had become too cautious, and he intended to imbue his troops with a strong offensive spirit. Here he revealed the risks that the army had incurred by the failure to send observers to study trench warfare firsthand over the previous three years. American officers had yet to comprehend the killing power of modern weapons and the advantage these gave to troops defending positions over those on the attack. Given the general's lack of experience in handling a mass army and the gap in his knowledge about the war in Europe, Wilson's decision to entrust him with broad discretion represented a major gamble.

It is striking, moreover, how little communication Wilson had with his key military subordinate before he sailed in May 1917. The president held only one face-to-face meeting with Pershing, and it was essentially a social visit. At that session, to the general's evident surprise, Wilson declined to discuss the pending campaign or ask for an explanation of military options.[75] Still, the two were on the same page. Secretary of War Newton Baker communicated to Pershing that his core mission was to make certain that American forces would operate independently and have a sufficient impact in battle to assure that the president could set the agenda at any postwar peace conference.[76] Confident that the general understood this, Wilson found no reason to inquire into just how Pershing would accomplish the task.

With Pershing dispatched to France, the administration set about raising, training, and equipping the AEF that would follow. Securing manpower was the easy part: hundreds of thousands of young men were inducted beginning in early summer 1917 to begin their basic training. Producing soldiers was one thing; creating an army in the age of industrial warfare quite another. As warfare became more complex, the need for specialized troops also increased, and they required longer training than did the soldier with a rifle. Much of the equipment needed for the AEF could not be produced quickly in the United States and would have to be acquired from the Allies.[77] Even to supply American troops with uniforms, vehicles, ammunition, fuel, and the vast range of goods the force would need required what was for the United States an unprecedented level of economic coordination.

The initial economic mobilization efforts went poorly, with Wilson exercising ineffective control. In August 1916, Congress had formed an advisory Council of National Defense (CND), staffed on a volunteer basis by prominent citizens. Following the declaration of war in April 1917, CND members established committees to supervise various aspects of mobilization, and these in turn spawned more committees until the total approached 150 separate bodies.[78] Wilson could only intervene selectively in the mobilization effort, and where he did so the results were unimpressive. At times he let political considerations override military needs. Thus, despite an urgent need for gun powder, the administration (with his active involvement) canceled a large contract to Du Pont for fear of how the public would react to rewarding a major corporation that had already earned huge profits from producing powder for the Allies.[79] Critics initially focused their ire on the War Department, which struggled to rouse itself from its peacetime slumbers.[80] But in early 1918, a coal shortage, brought on by Wilson's decision to set prices too low to assure steady production, forced factories to close and provoked broad attacks on the administration's mismanagement and calls for a bipartisan coalition war cabinet.[81] Rather than seize on this as an opportunity to broaden his administration (and preempt the critics by sharing ownership of the problems with them), Wilson saw only a challenge to his leadership that had to be thwarted.

To the president's credit, he responded decisively to the mobilization failures. A forceful advocate of presidential power who had demonstrated how it could be used to secure a domestic reform program before the war, Wilson did not hesitate to assert the authority of his office when circumstances seemed to require it. The voluntary Railroads War Board had failed to keep trains running smoothly, contributing to the loss of industrial output. Accordingly, the president drew upon his war powers and authorization language in the Army Appropriation Act of August 1916 to issue an executive order that placed the railroad industry under government control. Congress then passed the Federal Control Act of 1918 to assure railroads of compensation while under government management and promise the return of control to private ownership within twenty-one months following the end of the war.[82] Wilson also drafted new legislation, which became the Overman Act, to give the president sweeping emergency economic powers. (As these examples suggest, Wilson, like Lincoln, received congressional support for most of his actions.) Then he selected the noted financier Bernard M. Baruch to lead the War Industries Board (WIB), which became the linchpin of the mobilization effort. Production of war materials increased swiftly.[83]

The Wilson administration also mastered the financing of military expansion and operations, an important challenge that had bedeviled American leaders in several previous wars. Both James Madison and Lincoln had struggled to raise sufficient revenues to sustain their respective military efforts. Thanks to the constitutional amendment that legalized the income tax and to the creation of the Federal Reserve System under his auspices, Wilson had financing tools at his disposal that had been unavailable to his predecessors. Initially the president and Treasury Secretary George McAdoo hoped to pay for the war with an even mix of taxation and borrowing, and Wilson favored an equitable tax plan with progressive rates.[84] However, Congress refused to approve tax increases until after the 1918 elections, while expenditures escalated rapidly. The administration concluded it had no alternative but to borrow money, the old standby means for financing wars. To induce people to buy war bonds, the administration exempted the interest from taxation. People borrowed so they could buy the bonds, money flooded into circulation, and, with only ineffective price controls in place, inflationary pressures multiplied.[85]

Overall, the Wilson administration met the challenge of mobilization—creating a large army and providing it with the vital sinews of modern warfare—about as well as could be expected. Nothing like it had ever been attempted before in the United States. When the process began in spring 1917, it became evident that some of the wrong people had been placed in positions of authority, and a few were left too long in these assignments. But the president and his key subordinates such as Newton Baker were not afraid to make changes. For example, the latter brought back from France General Peyton March, Pershing's chief of artillery, in March 1918 to serve as army chief of staff when it became evident that greater urgency was needed.[86] Certainly the missteps at the outset were no worse than those that had plagued the Allies in the first year of the war (when the British Army nearly ran out of artillery shells and had to carefully husband the supply, much to the detriment of the troops in the front line).[87]

In judging the administration's mobilization record, we need to keep in mind that the United States planned to wage its victorious campaign in spring–summer 1919. Had the war proceeded on the anticipated timetable, the early stumbles in gearing up for war would have been passed off as inevitable hiccups in the shift from a peacetime economy. On the other hand, the Wilson administration's approach to mobilization, which relied heavily on voluntary cooperation, proved to be very expensive. The United States spent more per day than any other belligerent because the administration purchased cooperation through high profits and rising wages.[88]

Over There

General "Black Jack" Pershing arrived in France expecting to have ample time to prepare the AEF for the bitter combat he anticipated in 1918–1919. Although one division of American troops had been cobbled together with some difficulty and shipped with him, Pershing's initial tasks were preparatory. He and his modest staff (only about thirty officers)[89] had to identify a sector of the front where the U.S. Army would eventually fight, set up the logistical arrangements to supply this force, complete the training of units as they arrived, and finally plan his campaign. Already the French had started to build barracks for the Americans and identified a sector in Lorraine on the southern (or right) end of the Allied front that they would turn over to the AEF, a choice Pershing endorsed.[90] Troops from the United States arrived slowly due to the shipping logjam, with just 175,000 reaching France by the end of 1917, further confirming the expectation that the AEF would not be ready to conduct major operations until 1919.[91]

By late 1917, however, the Americans' neat plans had started to unravel in the face of setbacks in the Allied war effort. The Russian Revolution, which Wilson had praised in his war message to Congress as a hopeful stirring of democratic aspirations, took a more extreme turn with the seizure of power by the Bolsheviks. They signaled their readiness to conclude a separate peace agreement with Germany. This would allow the enemy to concentrate forces on the Western Front for a massive offensive in 1918, well before the AEF would be ready to take the field as an independent force.[92] With a new sense of urgency, the British offered to make available more shipping to transport American soldiers to France immediately. But the offer came with a catch: the British wanted only American fighting soldiers, not the full complement of support troops that an army needed to conduct its own operations. On top of this, Allied commanders, especially the British, used the newly formed civil-military Supreme War Council to renew their appeals for the "amalgamation" of American troops within the Allied armies.[93] Conceding that eventually Pershing would lead an independent army, British and French military and political leaders urged that as American combat elements arrived they be incorporated within Allied divisions already at the front.

Pershing would have none of it. Understanding his brief from the president—the AEF must achieve independent success for political reasons—the American commander rejected amalgamation. He would agree to no more than allowing some American units to be positioned behind the British sector for training purposes.[94] Wilson ratified his general's decision but granted him discretion to adopt amalgamation as an expedient if circumstances demanded it.[95] Although Pershing prevailed (the Allies had no leverage, given their dire need for man-power), the debate would continue and become more rancorous over the following six months.

The great German offensives that began in March 1918 routed several British and French armies, threatened to push the British out of France, and placed Paris in danger of capture. Both sides realized they had reached the ultimate crisis of the war. The German high command cal-culated that its forces could overwhelm the Allies before American numbers tipped the odds irretrievably against Berlin.[96] Using new assault tactics that emphasized bypassing enemy centers of resistance, German troops achieved breakthroughs that seemed impossible in the face of years of trench warfare stalemate, where gains of hundreds of yards had cost tens of thousands of casualties. For the Allies, defeat suddenly seemed possible. When the first attack against the British finally ran out of steam, the Germans launched another, then another, each yielding sizable gains.

Yet the German General Staff under Quartermaster General Erich von Ludendorff made fatal planning errors, failing to prepare the logis-tical support needed to consolidate gains so attacks could continue and neglecting to focus on a single strategic objective. Successive attacks through June bled white the German assault forces while achieving smaller and smaller advances. Still, the offensives provoked deep con-sternation, even gloom at times, among senior Allied political and mil-itary leaders. They finally agreed to a step they had resisted for almost four years, appointing a single supreme military commander, French General Ferdinand Foch. Pershing, who supported the move, pledged American cooperation, nominally placing the AEF under Foch's authority.[97]

Once more the Allies beseeched Pershing to release his troops, and once more he demurred. By spring 1918 several American divisions had entered the line, but they were in quiet sectors away from the German attacks. The Supreme War Council, including its American military representative, Major General Tasker Bliss, backed temporary amal-gamation. But Pershing believed that subordinating American units to Allied commands would interrupt the training of AEF senior staff and thereby delay the moment when an independent American force would enter combat. On this basis, he still rejected amalgamation.[98]

Enraged by his obtuseness amid disaster, the British again appealed over the general's head to his political masters in Washington. Initially Secretary of War Baker wanted to overrule his commander on the scene, but Pershing's objections led the secretary to reverse himself.[99] Pershing would contribute to the Allied cause, but strictly on his terms: in exchange for the temporary use of American troops, he secured a promise that excess shipping could be used to transport specialists he needed to fill out AEF higher formations (divisions and larger) plus a firm commitment that an independent AEF would become operational on a sector of the front by a specified date, with all American units returning to his command.[100] French Premier Clemenceau, who judged Pershing to be a mediocre officer, could not understand why Wilson had delegated so much authority to his field commander.[101] Pershing's insistence on an American sector, however, was fully in keeping with the president's definition of American national objectives.

Under the terms that Pershing extracted, American troops began to enter combat in late May 1918, with significant numbers engaged by July. Most fought in American divisional formations, some still suffering from lingering shortages in certain categories such as field artillery that had to be made up by the Allies. American units held relatively quiet positions, freeing up more experienced British and French troops to meet the later German attacks. Ludendorff realized by July that the arrival of American soldiers in significant numbers had turned the tide: they could be used to release enough veteran British or French units to hold any German attack.[102] In turn Foch promptly assumed the offensive. The Allied attacks included significant American contributions—some 270,000 American troops in two corps fought under French command in the July offensive on the Aisne Marne.[103] At this point Foch did not expect a breakthrough but instead sought to inflict "irreversible attrition" on the Germans.[104] On August 10, 1918, Pershing finally secured his long-sought goal, the activation of the First United States Army under his command near Saint-Mihiel.[105]

The first major American offensives, especially in the Meuse-Argonne sector, made clear how much the inexperienced AEF yet needed to learn about twentieth-century trench warfare. American soldiers would pay dearly for their commanders' lessons. Pershing's determination to instill an offensive spirit in his troops resulted in devastating losses among the units committed to the first attacks. Operations bogged down, too, because officers bungled the coordination of artillery support and failed to make adequate provisions to resupply men who had moved into enemy territory. Against an enemy with four years of combat experience (and sometimes as much time to prepare defensive works), the halting American performance should have surprised no one. Fortunately for the AEF, the Germans had weakened some of their positions, either to reinforce other sectors threatened by simultaneous British and French attacks or in preparation for withdrawal to a shorter and more defensible main line.[106] Pershing would never admit it, but the Americans fought mostly second- or third-rate German divisions already seriously depleted by earlier losses. Even with this, casualties swiftly mounted, and American battle deaths would exceed 116,000 in a bit more than four months of heavy combat, with an additional 200,000 wounded. (We should keep these losses in perspective: the British Army suffered nearly 60,000 casualties on the first *day* of its 1916 Somme offensive, while France absorbed more than six million casualties over the course of the war.)[107]

By August 1918 the German army had reached the limits of its endurance. The Allies launched one attack after another to drive the Germans back to their March starting positions, then continued with additional assaults that forced further withdrawals. Ludendorff, architect of the spring offensives, now concluded that the war was lost. On August 18, he advised his government to find a way to end the war by diplomatic means, but he withheld full information about how grave the situation had become. In the vain hope that some battlefield success might yet allow it to secure more favorable terms, Berlin chose to play for time rather than seek an immediate cessation of hostilities.[108]

One month later, after the British had broken through the main German defensive position on the Western Front (the Hindenburg line) and precipitated a full-scale retreat, Ludendorff lost his nerve and insisted the government seek an immediate armistice.[109] He subsequently disavowed his own recommendation, claiming that the army could continue to offer effective resistance behind the German border. (This reversal helped give rise after the war to the "stab in the back" myth—the inflammatory claim that the government decided to quit the war even though the German Army could continue to prevail on the battlefield—that helped spur German resentment of the peace treaty.) Despite the mixed and fluctuating signals from the German military high command, the German government concluded the time had come to seek peace.[110]

If the actual military results achieved by the AEF were modest, it accomplished what Wilson, Baker, and Pershing had intended. The U.S. Army shored up Allied lines at a critical moment during the German spring offensives, held quiet sectors to free up experienced French troops for operations in other sectors, and then added to the pressure that helped trigger German withdrawals in late summer–early fall. Thus the AEF provided the critical edge necessary for Allied success, even if the Americans scored no great victories. In all the AEF field operations in summer 1918, the hand of the American commander in chief never appeared.[111] True to his initial decision to run the war as the anti-Lincoln, Wilson disdained "active direction" and left Pershing to his own devices, demonstrating that a political leader could secure wartime national objectives on the battlefield without close supervision of military operations. American troops made a contribution that friend and foe alike would have to acknowledge, letting the president negotiate from a position of strength when the Central Powers sued for peace.

This moment came sooner than most on the Allied side had expected. Seeing Wilson as the best hope for reasonable terms, the Germans reached out to him in early October 1918 about the possibility of an armistice on the basis of the Fourteen Points, while pledging to replace the government's military leaders with civilians. Wilson replied with a note on October 8 to confirm that the German Army would withdraw from all occupied territory. He did so without first informing the Allies, who, afraid that the American president would pursue a separate peace on terms they could not support, then tried to add conditions (e.g., reparations for shipping losses). Wilson himself insisted the German government would have to be democratized—fulfilling his initial April 1917 demand for regime change—and made clear that the armistice terms would have to make it impossible for the Germans to recant later and resume fighting. In effect, the president tried to thread his way between American wishes for peace and excessive Allied demands.[112] When the Germans accepted the stiffer revised terms,

Wilson and the Allied leaders agreed on an armistice, to go into effect on November 11.

As the end game proceeded, Wilson encountered surprising difficulties from two of his key subordinates. General Pershing, heretofore so reliable an instrument of the president's will as to need almost no direction, suddenly objected that an armistice would be premature and that the war should continue until unconditional German surrender. Although the cause of his abrupt deviation from administration policy remains unclear, it seems reasonable to suppose that one source lay in his frustration at the AEF's failure to achieve a decisive battlefield victory.[113] The AEF had started to demonstrate improved prowess in its final combat operations,[114] but by that point the Germans had commenced their withdrawal all along the front. Under pressure from Washington, which deemed his stance inconsistent with the president's avowed desire not to humiliate Germany, Pershing backed down and accepted the armistice terms.[115]

Meanwhile, when the first German peace feelers arrived, Wilson again sent Colonel House to Europe to act as a go-between with the Allied governments. By this point the two men were no longer so close, and House appears to have been uncertain about exactly what Wilson wanted, beyond the Fourteen Points and a democratic regime in Berlin. House was surprised to discover that the British and French did not embrace his superior's peace conditions or an international league to sustain them. Hard negotiations were needed to gain their acceptance of the Fourteen Points, and that came only with important reservations attached. Of particular concern to the president, House agreed to let the Allied military commanders set the military terms of any armistice, failing to appreciate how these would have lasting political ramifications and an impact on peace talks. An angry Wilson turned on his emissary, convinced he had given away far too much and determined that he should not be permitted to negotiate the final peace treaty.[116]

For all the last-minute disputes, though, Wilson secured what he needed. Both sides had agreed that the peace conference would proceed according to his agenda. The German government had toppled, replaced by a new civilian-dominated provisional regime that claimed to speak for the German people. Berlin had accepted terms that would make it impossible for Germany to resume fighting, so all the leverage in shaping a postwar settlement rested with Wilson and the Entente leaders. As for the latter, they appeared to have endorsed Wilson's core principles, as embodied in his Fourteen Points, albeit with reservations that might yet prove disruptive. The AEF had provided the margin of victory. The Allies knew it, too: when they balked at accepting the Fourteen Points, House hinted the Americans might withdraw their army, and that sufficed to bring them into line behind the president.[117]

Making America Safe for Democracy

All wartime presidents dislike criticism of their policies and leadership, but none was more defensive than Woodrow Wilson. Presidents have a natural tendency when the country is at war to view themselves as the embodiments of the national interest. From that perspective, it is but a short step to the position that criticism of the administration expresses disloyalty and dissent reflects treason. Wilson crossed that small distance when the United States entered the war. In other nations, political leaders reached across party lines to form governments of national unity; Lincoln had bent over backward to woo Democrats to support his war. Wilson would have none of that. He rebuffed Republican calls to broaden his administration and turned the 1918 election into a partisan referendum on his war policy. As for domestic opposition to the war, his administration pursued the most repressive approach of any wartime president in American history.

The Wilson administration understood the importance of sustaining popular support for the war effort. Some of its measures reflected a shrewd appreciation of the challenges a government faces when it asks for broad sacrifices from its citizens. Conscription stands as an excellent illustration. American experience (the Civil War, to be specific) suggested that a draft would be very unpopular and might provoke active resistance. Although the preparedness movement, with its celebration of universal service, had laid the groundwork for conscription, popular acceptance was no certainty in 1917. Especially in the South, where the tradition of the citizen-soldier as willing volunteer remained the ideal, many preferred to see the government first try to fill the ranks of the planned army through conventional recruitment efforts. To help neutralize potential opposition, the administration decided to entrust the new selective service system to local boards rather than implement it through a national agency. Men would be chosen, exempted, or rejected, then, by distinguished members of their own community.[118]

In broad terms, the administration hoped to generate enthusiasm for society-wide war mobilization by building on the reform energy that Progressivism had stimulated over the previous fifteen-odd years. Progressivism encompassed a wide range of reformist ideas and initiatives. Varied though these were, they were linked by some shared threads, and these could be tapped to sustain mobilization. Progressive ideals, expressed by influential writers such as Herbert Croly, included a commitment to a new nationalism, a belief that individualism should be devoted to the service of a higher calling or purpose, and an abiding faith in the power of reason and science to solve social problems.[119]

Wilson had amassed solid Progressive credentials, too, by the time America entered the war. He had pushed through important measures to expand government regulation of corporations, offer better protection for the rights of working people to organize, and more. Various Progressive activists saw the war as an opportunity to extend their projects across the whole of American society, and took that to be their patriotic duty.[120] More than that, through its involvement in the war, the United States could extend Progressive principles beyond its own borders. The president had signaled as much in his initial war address to Congress when he hailed the recent revolution in Russia as a sign of the democratic aspirations the United States would advance.[121]

To promote popular support for the war and channel the Progressive spirit, the administration established the Committee on Public Information (CPI) under journalist George Creel in April 1917 and staffed it with dedicated reformers who believed the war could tap the Progressive spirit of service and self-sacrifice. The committee represented the first official American attempt at propaganda. Rather than censor negative reports from the front that might depress public morale, CPI stressed positive news and magnified the merits of the Allied cause. Progressives welcomed the Creel Committee effort to promote American values among immigrant groups, as well as its efforts to check prostitution and alcohol consumption.[122] The latter dovetailed with attempts to promote "social hygiene" around the burgeoning training camps where young men might otherwise be tempted by, well, all the things that tempt young men.[123] In support of these efforts, Congress approved a temporary ban on liquor sales in summer 1917, and the drive toward prohibition culminated in passage of the Eighteenth Amendment in 1919.[124] Whether the Creel Committee's broader propaganda efforts had a significant impact on public support for the war is difficult to determine. By exaggerating what the United States could achieve, moreover, the committee ran the risk of inviting broad disenchantment if the results fell short of the promise.[125]

Not even the most vigorous propaganda campaign could forestall criticism of the administration, to which the president was acutely sensitive. His response to some political opponents, however understandable, was small-minded. Former President Roosevelt had been a thorn in Wilson's side throughout the preparedness debate and the run-up to American intervention, accusing him of timidity. When the United States declared war and Wilson indicated plans to send troops to Europe, Roosevelt offered his services, hoping to raise a volunteer division akin to his Rough Riders of 1898.[126] The administration turned him down on the pretext that it had decided against the volunteer approach, but the action was clearly payback. (Roosevelt would get even, savaging the administration in the following months for its stumbles during the mobilization process.)[127]

Although Wilson paid lip service to the idea that in war the nation should rise above ordinary politics, he did not always practice what he preached. Recall his rejection of the suggestion by Republicans and some Democrats in the wake of the early mobilization failures to establish a bipartisan war cabinet. Wilson followed by embracing a partisan approach during the 1918 campaign, in which he suggested that patriotic citizens should choose Democratic candidates.[128] This backfired. Democratic losses were about average for the party in the White House during a mid-term election. But these were enough to cost the party its majority in both chambers of Congress. Republicans claimed the electorate had repudiated Wilson's leadership. Because the winners typically shape how an election will be interpreted, the Republican gloss on the outcome would influence the kind of reception Wilson could expect to receive on measures that required congressional approval. He would face troubles especially in the Senate, where Henry Cabot Lodge, a frequent critic, was the incoming majority leader.[129]

The Wilson administration's response to mainstream pro-war critics was tame in comparison to how it dealt with those who opposed American participation in the war. By stressing Americanism, the Creel Committee fostered suspicion of all things foreign, including political radicals born abroad or those who espoused "unAmerican" ideas. A series of laws targeted war foes and the means they used to express their dissent: the 1917 Espionage Act allowed fines and prison for interfering with recruitment and authorized the postmaster general to block the mailing of literature he found seditious; under the October 1917 Trading with the Enemy Act, all foreign language publications had to clear certain pieces with the post office before publication; the Alien Act of 1918 let the government deport or incarcerate foreign residents suspected of disloyalty or merely accused of belonging to organizations that advocated violent overthrow of the government; and the May 1918 Sedition Act permitted jailing anyone who said anything disloyal or abusive about the government or the army.[130] Some of these measures, of course, had historical precedents in earlier national security crises. But taken together the Wilson administration's laws against antiwar opposition represented a new order of censorship of dissent.

The administration followed with vigorous enforcement of the new statutes. Postmaster General Albert S. Burleson went after any publication he deemed disloyal, including socialist materials, effectively excluded from the mail by the end of summer 1917. In a striking demonstration of poor executive coordination, Burleson even banned publications that the Creel Committee urged Americans to read so they could better understand Germany.[131] Meanwhile, Attorney General Thomas W. Gregory sought to prosecute those he deemed radicals and subversives. Lacking adequate manpower to police the many threats he identified, Gregory turned to a private vigilante force, the ultra-nationalist American Protective League (APL). The APL, which grew to 250,000 members by November 1918, sought to destroy radical organizations, especially the Industrial Workers of the World (IWW), or "Wobblies."

If Wilson personally did not direct the repression of dissidents, he also never lifted a finger to stop it. Some historians contend that Wilson tried to check the more extreme expressions of anti-German chauvinism and urged restraint on the more zealous members of his administration, such as Burleson. And it is true that the president blocked a move by ultra-nationalists to make the United States a war zone, place it under martial law, try anyone who published anything that endangered the success of the military effort in a military court, and permit execution by firing squad of those convicted.[132] Apart from these isolated examples, however, the evidence suggests that Wilson supported the persecution of those opposing his war. He clucked his tongue over wartime limits on free expression even as he insisted they were necessary. Wilson ignored most complaints about Burleson's broad interpretation of his power to restrict access to the mails.[133] Although the president occasionally asked his postmaster general to reconsider an exclusion, Wilson never imposed his will on his subordinate and certainly never asked him to resign.[134] Further, the president never instructed his administration to cease cooperating with the ultra-nationalists. As a president who insisted on control over all aspects of his administration's war-related policies, Wilson plainly "owns" its record on civil liberties.

By extension, to him falls the blame for its political consequences. The mobilization of conservative forces in defense of wartime nationalism effectively destroyed the reform movement. War inherently is a force for social disruption and dislocation—exposing fissures, thrusting people into new roles, uprooting millions through military service or occupational demands—and World War I was no exception. One vivid example: as mobilization led women into new responsibilities, momentum built for women's suffrage, culminating in the Nineteenth Amendment in 1920. The result of war will be a new configuration of issues; American wars always have given rise to new political agendas.[135]

What direction the postwar agenda will take, however, is not preordained. The Civil War fostered the Republican program for promoting industrial development through government support. As I observed, Progressives anticipated that America's entry into the First World War would have a similar effect, spurring government activism in new areas. But that expectation presupposed the continued political effectiveness of various groups and movements that had boosted Progressive initiatives, especially forces on the political left—socialists who backed Eugene Victor Debs, the IWW, and various agrarian populists clamoring for action to shield small farmers against railroads and other elites. Many on the left, though, also opposed the war and became the targets of political repression by the Wilson administration, various state and local prosecutors, and deputized vigilantes. Meanwhile, conservatives used the left's opposition to the war to discredit not just radicalism but the very idea of reform.[136] By the time they had completed their work, which took a more frenzied form as fears of Bolshevism spread after the war, they had shattered Progressivism and its more radical manifestations beyond repair.

Nor was political repression the only factor that curtailed the possibilities for continuing the reform wave that Wilson had ridden into office. The administration's preferred approach to mobilization empowered conservative elements across the board. In part to satisfy the dominant southern wing of the Democratic Party, which distrusted a vigorous central state, the administration opted at first to encourage the voluntary cooperation of the private sector. Business leaders thus became key insiders in the mobilization efforts. When mobilization faltered and Wilson sought stronger executive authority, Congress cooperated but also made certain that enhanced presidential power would expire and the private sector would be fully restored. Thus, in the case of the railroads, I noted earlier that the 1918 Federal Control Act not only gave railroad owners a fair return as the price of national control but also guaranteed that nationalization would be strictly temporary. Mobilization might also be threatened by labor disruptions. Accordingly, even as radical elements of the labor movement faced persecution, the administration reached out to the labor mainstream, the American Federation of Labor (AFL) under Samuel Gompers. In exchange for a no-strike pledge for the duration of the war, the AFL received government backing in its efforts to organize workers. Membership rose sharply during the brief period of cooperation, but the gains were quickly reversed in the reactionary postwar climate.[137]

The brief time of American involvement in the First World War—by far the shortest of any of the conflicts examined in this book—makes it difficult to assess the effectiveness of the Wilson administration's efforts to sustain popular support for the war. American doughboys were in combat in France for only about six months before the armistice. Despite heavy losses in that short time, public support was not tested as it was during the Civil War or would be later in long conflicts in

Vietnam and Iraq. Certainly, the Wilson administration had grounds for concern, given the evidence of war weariness on the home front in other countries that had been beset by war for several years. Notwithstanding Wilson's paeans to the democratic aspirations of the Russian people, he knew full well that the revolution against the old regime in February 1917 expressed widespread discontent with the war.

Proactive measures to encourage popular enthusiasm and engage citizens in war-related voluntary activities, then, made a good deal of sense. (Or, to put it another way, no responsible government will trust to chance the willingness of its citizenry to make sacrifices for abstractions such as national honor or making the world safe for democracy.) The administration also demonstrated a capacity for innovation in its use of emerging advertising techniques as propaganda tools. On the other hand, administration propaganda inflated expectations about what the war would accomplish, making subsequent disillusionment more likely and undercutting support for Wilson's postwar peace-building project. Worse still, the Creel Committee contributed greatly to an atmosphere of heightened nationalism and chauvinism that even the most pro-Wilson historians describe as "a mob spirit."[138] Wilson paid lip service to the right to dissent, but he presided over a broad-scale assault on civil liberties without equal in the generally abysmal record of American leaders faced with significant domestic opposition to their wars.

Wilson Tries to Build His Peace

On one point about Woodrow Wilson as a war leader historians agree: he did not achieve the kind of peace he had promised when asking Congress to declare war on Germany. They differ, though, on two counts. To begin with, whether Wilson was right to aim as high as he did has long divided those who have examined his leadership. Some dismiss his vision as hopelessly and dangerously utopian, while others counter that he understood the vital importance of collective security arrangements for preserving peace but was too far ahead of his more narrow-minded contemporaries.

Moreover, there has long been debate about how much of the responsibility for Wilson's failure rests on his shoulders. One camp believes he spoke for the people of the United States and more broadly for the entire world, only to be undone by politicians at home and abroad who sought instead their own narrow interests. On the other side are those who insist the president might have achieved most of what he sought, but his self-defeating personality attributes, specifically a stiff-necked refusal (magnified by his ill health) to compromise with those who opposed him, led him to throw away a rare opportunity to transform America's international role.

I suggest that he gravely underestimated the difficulty of the peace-building tasks he set for himself—vision without awareness of obstacles does a leader no credit. At the same time, his rigid approach exacerbated a problem all wartime presidents face when fighting ends: Congress moves quickly to restore the institutional balance with the White House that war has tipped in favor of the Oval Office.

Peace-building preoccupied Wilson from before the United States entered the war through the November 1918 armistice. In comparison with Lincoln, who deferred postwar planning to the end of the Civil War, with unfortunate consequences, Wilson appreciated that American involvement would be justified by the kind of peace he could fashion. Not only did he articulate a transformative agenda for postwar order but his administration also promoted it both at home and abroad. The Creel Committee, for example, engaged in vigorous international propaganda activity, making certain that Wilson's speeches about the postwar international order and self-determination received wide notice.[139]

In addition, the president and his aides did not take it for granted that things would fall neatly into place once the shooting stopped. They understood the unsettled conditions and social turmoil that the war had provoked across Europe and beyond. Under Colonel House's oversight, American experts from various fields had started as early as September 1917 to prepare reports (called the American Inquiry) about the many territorial and governance issues that would have to be confronted at the end of the war.[140] Wilson stood confident as he prepared to attend the peace conference in Paris in December 1918 that the combination of American military and financial power, global public opinion, and the moral force of his vision would assure a successful outcome.

But the president's position began to erode as soon as the armistice went into effect. He thought that with the Allies so dependent on American loans and American troops, they would not dare refuse American demands. The tough armistice terms that the Allies had required, however, stripped Germany of the capacity to resume fighting. Thus American military power largely ceased to matter. Moreover, although the Allies owed vast sums to the United States, debt was a weapon that cut both ways. Unless France collected significant reparations from its defeated foes, it would be in no position to repay its American creditors. Wilson further weakened himself with self-inflicted political wounds. As many historians have commented, he erred by excluding Republicans from the American delegation to the conference. Partisanship had availed him little in the 1918 congressional elections, which as I noted cost the Democrats control of both houses of Congress. Now, despite the obvious need for opposition support for any peace treaty, Wilson let his personal distaste for Republican Senator Henry Cabot Lodge override the compelling argument for a bipartisan delegation.[141]

Rather than recount the negotiating process that took up most of the first half of 1919,[142] I focus here on Wilson's core goals, his successes and failures, and the elements that thwarted him from achieving a number of his key objectives.

His goals were ambitious, to say the least. First and foremost, the president insisted that the peace treaty include, among its opening provisions, a League of Nations that would address international tensions and protect small nations against aggression. Confident that various forms of arbitration or mediation would resolve most disputes, he understood that the organization still would need recourse to sanctions, including the possible use of force, to be effective.[143] Second, he expressed support for political self-determination, especially for people who had been subjects in multinational, multiethnic empires. The principle of self-determination also extended to colonized peoples, though Wilson considered them not yet ready for full self-rule and preferred mandate arrangements under League auspices as an interim measure of indefinite duration. Third, Wilson believed in what might be termed quick German redemption. Assigning much of the blame for the war to the Kaiser and his military, the president hoped for relatively mild peace terms, including very limited reparations and immediate German membership in the League of Nations. Germany would be most likely to behave as a responsible member of the international community if treated as such rather than as a pariah.[144]

Of the three goals, the president achieved in Paris something closely approximating what he wanted on the League plan but fell far short on the others. Despite Clemenceau's deep skepticism that an international organization could offer a meaningful security guarantee, the four leading powers (the United States, Great Britain, France, and Italy) agreed that the peace treaty would begin with provisions establishing a League of Nations. Included was wording to permit the enforcement of sanctions against aggressors violating the sovereignty of member states (Article X, of which more will be said later). The League design, however, was flawed, requiring unanimity on many matters that would stall action in a crisis.[145]

Self-determination proved a much more vexing concept than Wilson had appreciated, despite warnings from others in the American delegation. New nations were carved out of old empires in Central and Eastern Europe, but often at a steep price in the form of ethnic minorities being included within national boundaries, an outcome that pointed toward future political instability.[146] Moreover, nothing was done to make good on the notion of consent of the governed where colonial powers on the winning side were concerned. Quite the opposite happened: they also gained new imperial possessions (often under the fig leaf of League of Nations' mandates) through the dismemberment of the Ottoman Empire or stripping Germany of its colonial holdings in Africa, Asia, and the Pacific islands.[147]

The peace terms imposed on Germany scarcely resembled the ones Wilson had suggested in his various wartime speeches and that the Germans expected when they accepted his armistice terms. Among the articles sparking German objections were those that placed millions of ethnic Germans within the borders of Poland and Czechoslovakia, denied the possibility of a German union with the new rump state of Austria, placed the Rhineland under temporary Allied occupation, required that most German naval vessels be turned over to the Allies (their crews scuttled them before this could be done),[148] and severely limited the size and equipment of the German military.

Most offensive to German sensibilities, the Treaty of Versailles fixed on Germany the full responsibility for the war and made clear Berlin would be required to pay reparations for war damages, the amount to be determined later.[149] German disillusionment was deepened by the sense that Wilson had promised that German delegates would participate in the conference as equals, when instead they were invited only at the end to accept terms dictated by their enemies.[150] Notwithstanding contemporary depictions of the treaty as punitive, Margaret MacMillan observes that the "war guilt" language that so rankled Germans was no different from that contained in other treaties with defeated Central Powers, such as the Austro-Hungarian Empire, that provoked no similar reaction. Moreover, the reparations terms were not ruinous (and payments were first delayed and later repudiated when Hitler came to power).[151] But in politics, perceptions can be everything. German nationalists used the treaty as fodder for their extremist appeals while no German leaders would defend its terms.[152]

A number of factors contributed to Wilson's inability to achieve in Paris much of what he had promised. As MacMillan points out, wartime coalitions tend to split once peace arrives; national rivalries over competing interests reassert themselves.[153] This certainly held true in 1919, with participants pursuing their own interests as they saw them, frequently at odds with the president's agenda. During the war the Allies had agreed among themselves to various territorial settlements, as I earlier remarked, and they refused to drop many of their claims at the peace conference. Often these claims collided with the Wilsonian commitment to self-determination, as when the Italians wanted significant parts of emerging Yugoslavia, the Greeks and Italians laid claims to parts of Turkey, or the Japanese wanted the former German holdings in China. The American leader discovered quickly that he had much less leverage over the Allied powers than he had anticipated.

Allied territorial claims were only one of several reasons Wilson could not deliver on the promise of "self-determination." The concept itself was deeply ambiguous and effectively unbounded, and every minority took it as a pledge of political autonomy.[154] Even if limited to East Central Europe, as the president perhaps intended, his promise of self-rule failed to take into account the complex intermingling of different ethno-national groupings that centuries of warfare and migrations had produced. Within every proposed national territory could be found regions in which minorities formed majorities and now demanded their right to self-determination, and within these smaller regions were still other minorities asserting their own rights. Simply put, once self-determination became the defining principle for drawing boundaries, the process pointed ultimately toward anarchy.[155]

That outcome, of course, was unacceptable to the conferees in Paris, so they tried to impose limits. Here the Allies encountered another problem: their writ did not extend very far on the ground, especially as the rapid demobilization of Allied troops (and the declining willingness of the rest to risk their lives) meant that actual borders would be settled by the most powerful local forces.[156] Thus the eastern border of Poland would be determined through combat between the new Polish Army and Russian Bolshevik formations, with Ukrainian separatists adding to the confusion.[157]

Harsher terms for Germany reflected a combination of French intransigence and Anglo-American moralizing. Clemenceau had a very different view of how to assure French security than did Wilson. The French premier placed little faith in the League; he subscribed instead to traditional notions of alliances and a balance of power, expecting Germany to revive and again become a threat too great for France alone to contain.[158] Accordingly, he sought a defense treaty with Great Britain and the United States, control over parts of western Germany, tight restrictions on German military power, and other punitive terms at odds with Wilson's intention to normalize German status. France also faced enormous war debts and rebuilding expenses, which it hoped to cover through German reparations. In this vein, note that although Wilson asked for no direct German reparations to his own country, he expected the French to repay what they owed the United States and thereby increased Clemenceau's determination to pass on the burden to his vanquished foe across the Rhine.[159] Wilson himself was of two minds about Germany. He wanted it to rejoin the international community in good standing, yes, but he, like British prime minister David Lloyd George, believed the Germans should be chastised for their aggression. In this regard, they shared common ground with the French.[160]

Finally, beyond Wilson's difficulties with the other conferees, he miscalculated the role of public opinion on the peace conference. When he traveled in Europe before the conference began, he received the adulation of enormous crowds, very much the hero of the moment, the most famous and celebrated man in the world.[161] Doubtless he expected the Allied publics to continue to support him and his quest for a new kind of international order. Some have suggested that he committed a major blunder when he agreed to exclude the press from much of the conference, thereby denying himself the means to communicate over the heads of recalcitrant Allied leaders when necessary.[162]

But there is more to it than that. Wilson in December 1918 was very much like a president-elect before his inauguration, when every aspiration is projected onto him and he has done nothing to disappoint expectations or alienate his believers. That situation was bound to change as the leaders at the conference made hard choices certain to anger many. No amount of press access could have prevented disenchantment. In one country after another, as word arrived about decisions in Paris that betrayed what people had taken Wilson to mean, the local press turned on the American president.[163]

Notably absent from this list of factors that led to Wilson's disappointing results in Paris is one that has been popular since the ink dried on the Treaty of Versailles: the claim that he allowed himself to be outnegotiated by his more savvy European counterparts.[164] Wilson certainly did not grasp the complexity of the ethno-national mixtures in the European empires. Moreover, though he expected Allied leaders to pursue their parochial concerns, he still underestimated the domestic political pressures they faced.[165] Unlike Wilson, they arrived at the conference having promised their own citizens specific gains as their just reward for wartime sacrifices. These leaders were effectively trapped, for their governments would fall if they returned home empty-handed.[166] Wilson fundamentally overrated the means at his disposal for overcoming opposition.[167]

It is hard to square the picture of Wilson as gullible with the image of him as too stubborn to ever change his mind once he had reached a decision. Neither seems to reflect the president who participated in months of hard bargaining in Paris. On some matters he dug in his heels, even hinting he might leave the conference to force the French to back off their territorial demands on Germany,[168] while on others that he regarded as less central (Japan's claims in China, all matters of British or French colonial policy) he ceded ground. We might note that Lloyd George, caught between the demands of British public opinion and his own sense of sound policy, also vacillated on key issues such as German reparations.[169]

More than anything else, the view that Wilson was bamboozled by Clemenceau and company reflects the mistaken conclusion that other Allied leaders achieved more of their objectives at the conference than did the president. With the possible exception of Japan,[170] they all came off badly, failing to secure much of what they had promised their citizens. Consider, for example, Italy, which expected substantial territorial acquisitions, received less, and even then could not hold much of the additional land—a performance that set the stage for the fascist triumph several years later. The major Allied powers, Great Britain and France, suffered critical setbacks, both at the conference and as a consequence of what was or was not done there. Great Britain expanded its colonial holdings, but its refusal to make good on the Wilsonian promise of self-determination compromised its hold over India and provoked restiveness in Egypt. In addition, Lloyd George did not forge the strong Anglo-American partnership he sought; quite the contrary, he did not even secure language to forestall a naval arms race with the United States that his country could not afford.[171]

France came away as the ultimate loser, notwithstanding Clemenceau's hard-edged realism. Limited by his traditional outlook, domestic constraints, and General Foch's fierce determination to reduce Germany to third-rate military status, Clemenceau could not envision a different kind of relationship with France's old nemesis. What he most desired—a permanent alliance among the leading democracies to withstand a rearmed Germany—he did not achieve. Although Wilson signed a treaty with the French that promised American help in the event of an attack on France, he knew the U.S. Senate would never approve it. (He was confident, too, that the League of Nations would make such agreements unnecessary.)[172] Clemenceau also did not acquire for France the German territory west of the Rhine, settling instead for temporary occupation. Finally, reparations fell far below what he demanded, with no effective means to compel payments should the Germans renege.[173]

Negotiating a peace treaty, of course, represented but the first step in the peace-building process. Wilson also needed to secure the approval of the treaty by the U.S. Senate to assure American leadership in the new postwar international order he hoped to establish. Even before the negotiations were completed in Paris, signs indicated trouble. Historians contend that Wilson and the Creel Committee had done their work well enough to win over the American public to the idea of a League of Nations.[174] But there is good reason to doubt the level of popular support. In the first place, the polls conducted by magazines that showed a majority in favor of the League were notoriously unreliable.[175] Moreover, conservative forces had been mobilized during the war in the campaign against dissidents on the political left and continued active efforts to persecute those who seemed sympathetic to Bolshevism. The public as a whole already seemed to be turning inward, increasingly preoccupied with domestic issues ranging from inflation to racial strife.

Meanwhile, Senate Republicans, led by Lodge, indicated their skepticism about the League when Wilson returned to the United States in March 1919.[176] With too few Democrats to approve the Treaty, he needed significant Republican backing. Recall that he had antagonized Republicans during the 1918 elections and by excluding them from the peace delegation. To this we should add the eagerness of Congress, forced by wartime need to subordinate itself to the chief executive, to assert its institutional prerogatives as soon as the fighting ended. Due to the combination of his own political miscalculations and the institutional pendulum effect triggered by the return of peace, Wilson faced an uphill struggle to secure the Senate votes he needed.

How events played out over the months following the debate has been recounted in a number of excellent studies, so I will offer only a brief review here.[177] Wilson presented the treaty to the Senate in July 1919, urging acceptance of a new international leadership role for the United States. The Senate was divided into three groups: supporters of the treaty, who formed the largest bloc and counted most Democrats and several Republicans; those who might accept the treaty if certain reservations were attached; and a small bloc of opponents, the Irreconcilables, who rejected the treaty in any form.[178] Lodge, as majority leader and chair of the Foreign Relations Committee, led the opposition and sought to propose amendments or reservations to the treaty to induce enough senators to vote against it. Wilson tried first to persuade senators not yet publicly committed. However, because he would accept only explanatory reservations (which would not require actual changes in treaty wording and thus might have no legal force), he could not convince enough of the moderate foes to vote yes. By September it became evident that Lodge could either force major changes or defeat the treaty outright. Wilson, despite clear signs of failing health, decided on a speaking tour across the country, convinced he could mobilize public opinion to pressure the Senate to endorse the treaty as it stood. He collapsed after a speech in Colorado on September 25, 1919, returned to Washington, and suffered a major stroke that left him largely incapacitated for several months.

Lodge capitalized on Wilson's refusal to compromise by striking a deal with the mild reservationists: the anti-Wilson coalition would support approval with fourteen reservations, the most important of which declared that the United States would not support League sanctions against an aggressor (Article X) unless Congress approved. In November, Lodge and his allies defeated the treaty in its original form, while Wilson directed his Senate backers to reject it with the reservations attached. With the president still refusing to compromise, the Senate again voted down the treaty in March 1920, effectively ending any chance that the nation would join the League.

Wilson plainly missed opportunities for compromise that would have led to approval of the Treaty of Versailles with reservations and to American membership in the new League of Nations. By some estimates, as many as four out of five senators were prepared to back the Treaty in some form. Lodge did not reject outright the idea of American participation, though he preferred more traditional alliances grounded in the threat of force.[179] (Note the similarity between his position and Clemenceau's.) To be sure, reservations would have complicated American diplomacy, forcing additional negotiations with the Allies. But treaty approval in any form would have established the foundation for ongoing American engagement in the international organization Wilson saw as the cornerstone of a new framework of international relations. The president miscalculated his prospects for forcing the Senate to bend to his will, overestimating his ability to move the American people to take his side and perhaps the influence of public opinion on the Senate.[180] Just as important, he failed to take into account that Congress would reassert its prerogatives in peacetime, refusing to delegate its authority over the decision to go to war to an international body. Others shared responsibility for the treaty defeat—at some point Lodge became more interested in scoring a political victory over the president than in finding a constructive solution, while Senate Democrats should have followed their instincts to compromise.[181] But the lion's share of the blame rested on Wilson.

The defeat of the peace treaty accelerated the inward turn in American politics. Wilson's effort to alter the popular mind-set to embrace an expanded global role was curtailed by the short period of American participation in the war, by his extended absence while negotiating the treaty (a hidden price of his hands-on role), and by the collapse of his health. In truth, his rhetoric during the League fight had veered toward panic mongering about the Bolshevik menace and attacks on the patriotism of his opponents.[182] None of this did much to promote a new public commitment to sustain international order. After the Republican triumph in 1920, Lodge and President Warren G. Harding depicted the results as a popular repudiation of the League.[183] The voters probably intended no clear signal (voters often do not), but winners frame the interpretation of an election outcome, so the message stuck. Americans would return to "normalcy," as Harding put it, and that included a refusal to be much troubled by what happened on the other side of vast oceans.

Wilson as Prism: Revisiting Some Puzzles of Wartime Presidential Leadership

Wilson's actions before the United States entered the First World War cast a different light on one of the puzzles posed by wartime presidential leadership. In a political system designed to check executive power, how is it that presidents have been so easily able to lead the nation into war? Earlier I pointed to the key role of presidential initiative in deploying military forces in a manner likely to bring on a clash of arms. For instance, once Lincoln decided there was no alternative to war against the secessionist South, he sent supplies to Fort

Sumter, knowing that the rebels would be likely to fire upon the relief ships.

By contrast, Wilson hoped to avoid American entry into the war, and he managed to do so for more than two years. But his early steps, specifically his decision to confront Germany over its use of submarine warfare, made war much more likely. The president's stance on U-boat attacks left it up to Berlin to choose whether and when the United States would enter the war. By boxing himself in with his 1915 warning, Wilson also removed from Congress effective control over the decision to enter the war. He understood clearly the absence of real choice when he called upon Congress in April 1917 to "accept the status of belligerent which has thus been thrust upon it."[184] To the list of means by which presidents on their own can propel the United States into war, then, we should add the broad diplomatic powers invested by the Constitution in the presidency.

As a wartime commander in chief, Wilson accomplished several key leadership tasks. He determined that the United States must play a pivotal role at a postwar peace conference, so he would be in a strong position to shape what happened after the conflict ended. In Pershing, the president found a commander who could achieve the necessary results, despite the general's limitations. Pershing's success calls into doubt the claim that a political leader needs to exercise hands-on direction of military strategy and closely monitor the actions of military subordinates. Wilson purposefully chose not to supervise the commander of AEF, a reflection of the president's conviction that Lincoln had meddled too closely in military matters. (However, it might be recalled that over the course of the Civil War, Lincoln intervened less often in military decisions. Wilson's approach was not as different as he supposed.) That Wilson, as unmilitary a president as any who have led the United States during war, could succeed through his detached approach suggests that Eliot Cohen and others may be looking in the wrong place for the answers to what makes for effective wartime political leadership. Back home, despite initial stumbles, the Wilson administration managed to mobilize the American people and economy in time for the AEF to make a key contribution on the battlefield in 1918. An innovative propaganda campaign, both at home and abroad, helped boost support for Wilson's bold war goals.

On the other hand, the Wilson administration's approach to mobilization and to sustaining popular support for the war effort incurred a political price. Many Progressives had signed on in support of the war because they saw it as a vehicle to promote social justice at home and abroad. They could not have been more mistaken. The administration enlisted business and conservative labor leaders to manage economic mobilization and deputized nationalist vigilante groups to suppress antiwar dissent and hound radicals into silence. By the time the war ended, key constituencies backing social reform had been delegitimized, even as strong ties formed between government and business.

The Wilson administration thus offers an answer to another wartime leadership puzzle—the question of why wars undermine presidential domestic agendas and hopes for significant social reforms. In this case, the decisions by Wilson and key political appointees to empower conservative forces as key actors in the mobilization project and in the attacks on critics of the war (and radicals more generally) placed those forces in a far more influential position than they would have enjoyed had America not entered the war.

Wilson's inability to secure the kind of peace treaty that would justify American intervention points up how problematic presidents find peace-building. Much more than Lincoln, Wilson considered what the postwar order should be. But there was an enormous mismatch between his expansive vision for the future and his capacity to realize it. His experience suggests two observations. First, presidents face a dilemma when they seek to define war goals. If they aim for modest stakes, it becomes more difficult to justify the sacrifices that war entails. Wilson would have found it hard to summon Americans to the colors merely to make it safe for a handful of travelers to sail safely into a war zone. On the other hand, by promising that war would yield transformative results, such as the broad spread of democracy or an international order that will check aggression, presidents risk leaving people disillusioned, with potentially far-reaching repercussions.

Second, bolder goals require more resources, resources that presidents are unlikely to retain at the end of a war. To secure his main peace-building ends—the creation of an effective League of Nations, a generous peace with Germany, and self-determination for former imperial subjects—Wilson needed to dominate the peace conference in

Paris and the treaty debate in the Senate. Yet, as we've seen, a president's leverage over other political actors seems likely to decline quickly when the fighting ends. Abroad, Wilson found that his recent allies pursued their particular narrow interests; troops who might have helped impose order in the vacuum left by collapsing regimes instead were swiftly demobilized, while the few who were not became demoralized; and new political forces (armed groups, discharged soldiers, radical movements) seized the openings created when authority disintegrated. At home, Congress reasserted itself, as it did at the end of the Civil War, while the American people turned back to domestic concerns. Wilson might have secured some of his peace-building program were it not for his illness-driven rigidity, but he could never have accomplished most of it.

Had Wilson appreciated in 1918 or 1919 that his initial objectives were overly ambitious, however, he still would have found it impossible to back down. Like Lincoln before him, Wilson demonstrates how presidents lose flexibility over the course of a war, as their early choices increasingly constrain their options. Wilson started to frame his vision of a new postwar order in 1916 and early 1917, but he did not commit himself irrevocably to an epic peace-building agenda until he asked Congress to declare war. In view of his professed convictions—Americans must only be asked to make great sacrifices in exchange for commensurate gains in the broad betterment of the human condition and the promise of a global order that would prevent another such catastrophic conflict—he could neither accept himself nor justify to his domestic audience a peace that resembled a return to balance-of-power politics. His inspiring vision and soaring rhetoric created insurmountable obstacles to reaching common ground with realists such as Clemenceau and Lodge. When he arrived in Paris in December 1918, pledged to transform the world, he was a captive to that vision.

3

Freedom of Action
Franklin Roosevelt

ON DECEMBER 7, 1941, FRANKLIN D. Roosevelt suddenly found himself the leader of a nation at war—the wrong war. Japanese strikes on Pearl Harbor and the Philippines plunged the United States into conflict in the Pacific. But the president had regarded Germany under Adolf Hitler as posing the fundamental threat to American security. With that in mind, he had looked for ways to provoke a German attack that would justify American entry into the war on the side of Great Britain and the Soviet Union. Although Roosevelt also expected to fight Japan at some point, he intended to put off this conflict until American forces were better prepared, at least until spring 1942. Now he would have to ask Congress to declare war on the less dangerous enemy, and it seemed American military resources would have to be directed away from the principal menace. As Wilson had learned when he ceded to Berlin discretion over American entry into the First World War, Roosevelt discovered he exercised less control over events than he believed.

However, just days later, on December 11, 1941, Hitler unexpectedly declared war on the United States, resolving FDR's dilemma. This chain of events points to a critical element in war: a great deal depends on what historian Stephen Ambrose calls "dumb luck."[1] Roosevelt got the war he wanted, but not because of clever diplomacy or planning on his part.

More than any other American wartime president, Roosevelt consciously tried to retain his freedom of action. Preserving his options had been a hallmark of his domestic leadership style. He much preferred to test the waters before making a commitment. Notwithstanding his reputation as a public communicator, he was careful not to get too far in front of public opinion; when he erred in his reading of the public mood—such as during the scheme to pack the Supreme Court—he swiftly backpedaled. Both before and during American involvement in the Second World War, Roosevelt adroitly avoided and delayed making choices that would commit him to a course of action from which he could not retreat. Thus he serves as the ideal test case for the proposition that presidents lose the capacity to shape events over the course of a conflict. We saw this pattern first with Lincoln, then it recurred with Wilson. So, too, with Roosevelt: his decisions, the irresistible momentum they created, and the actions of others combined to narrow his range of choices.

That Roosevelt would be thwarted in his drive to dictate the course of the war became evident even in the several years before the Japanese attack on Pearl Harbor. The first task for a president facing the prospect of war is to determine whether the national interest of the United States requires that it resort to and prepare for the use of force. Roosevelt had grasped the threat posed by Germany under Hitler and concluded the United States must help stop him. Rather than act on that conviction, however, he worried more about holding open his options. But his efforts failed, in part because of events beyond his control and in part because the very steps he took to avoid being forced to choose backfired. As for preparing for war, Roosevelt acted even before Germany struck Poland in September 1939 to redress glaring weaknesses in American military readiness. Yet his hesitation about full preparedness, driven mainly by politics, delayed the military buildup and left Americans unconvinced about the wisdom of entering the war until the attack on Pearl Harbor settled the matter.

Roosevelt rebounded from his prewar equivocation to become a highly effective wartime chief executive. He approached the conflict with a clear (though often unstated) sense of national objectives, both for the war and its aftermath, which included a vision of the postwar world order more ambitious even than Wilson's. In the space of several years, American mobilization produced both an unequaled military force for waging global war and sufficient additional output to meet a significant part of the needs of the nation's allies. Massive military spending also revived American prosperity, but the president still paid a political price as mobilization and war-generated social tensions empowered his conservative opponents. American strategy on the battlefield reflected both immediate military considerations and the president's larger political purposes. Much like Lincoln, Roosevelt played an active part in shaping military decisions during the early part of the war, intervening less often as it became clear that the Allies were heading toward victory over both Germany and Japan. Roosevelt also showed himself to be the most astute strategic thinker among the leaders of the major belligerent nations. At home, the president preserved broad popular support for the war, thanks to an approach that limited battlefield casualties and because of his attention to the timing of military operations.

For all this, Roosevelt could not escape the loss of agency. Decisions had to be made; important campaigns took on a life of their own; and other Allied powers had their own agendas. Time ran out for Roosevelt, just as it had with his predecessors.

Stumbling into Infamy

Although hindsight makes World War II appear inevitable, it did not seem so to most contemporary eyes even in the late 1930s. The rise of Hitler in Germany in 1933 increased tensions in Europe, but many thought his ambitions might be curbed through alliances and diplomacy. Munich in September 1938 represented the culmination of the diplomatic approach: British Prime Minister Neville Chamberlain ceded the Sudetanland portion of Czechoslovakia to Hitler and in so doing believed he had assured "peace for our time." Even a civil war that erupted in Spain in 1936 and attracted external support from both fascists and communists did not spread beyond the Pyrenees and finally ended with the rout of the Republicans in 1939.

On the other side of the globe, Japan had occupied Manchuria in 1931, which whetted the appetite of Tokyo's militarists for greater conquests. Japanese army units staged an incident in Beijing in July

1937 that became the pretext for invading China. Despite its swift defeat of the Nationalist armies under Chiang Kai-shek and the capture of several major cities, Japan soon bogged down in a frustrating and costly low-intensity struggle with no apparent end. The Sino-Japanese conflict, though disturbing to other major powers, also appeared unlikely to spill beyond the immediate region.

Roosevelt, preoccupied with economic calamity at home, did not focus closely on foreign policy until 1937. Coping with the Great Depression claimed most of his attention, and he was immersed in the New Deal and the political conflicts that swirled around it. In the aftermath of his reelection landslide in 1936, he moved boldly to remake the Supreme Court, which had obstructed his economic reforms by voiding key New Deal measures. But his attempt to pack the Court with additional justices who would back his programs alienated conservative southern Democrats and drove them into a working alliance with Republicans that would discourage further large-scale reform. Meanwhile, economic recovery stalled and reversed, due in part to the president's ongoing fixation on balanced budgets. Unemployment increased again in 1937, and with it came a surge in labor unrest and workplace violence in places such as Flint, Michigan, where workers and union organizers clashed with strikebreakers and police. Frustration at home contributed to Roosevelt's newfound interest in foreign affairs.[2]

Domestic and foreign policies were connected, moreover, by the evolving economic agenda of his administration, which began to emphasize the revival of international trade as the key to domestic recovery. The president and several key advisors, including Secretary of State Cordell Hull and Treasury Secretary Henry Morgenthau Jr., worried that nations such as Germany, Japan, and England aimed to carve up the world into exclusive trading blocs. If they succeeded, American businesses would be barred from vital markets. Administration concern over international markets had a political dimension, too: businesses that advocated free trade (including banks, oil, and tobacco) had become an important component of the Democratic Party coalition by the late 1930s, among the few friends the president could claim in business circles.[3]

When Roosevelt turned his attention to developments in Europe in 1937–1938, he first aimed to prevent the outbreak of war. He believed

Wilson had erred in 1914 by not intervening early to head off violent confrontation.[4] Initially, Roosevelt tried to play the role of neutral broker. He pushed for the Munich conference, only to be dissatisfied with the outcome. Chamberlain and France's Edouard Daladier had failed to show sufficient firmness against Hitler's bluster, the president complained, though he was no more willing than they to stand up to the German führer. It quickly became evident that appeasement had failed to quench Hitler's thirst for a larger empire. In March 1939, only a few months after Munich, he resumed his expansionist approach with the bloodless occupation of the remainder of Czechoslovakia.[5] Tensions escalated in the wake of this move, as European nations accelerated their preparations for a clash that daily seemed less and less avoidable. Up to the very eve of war Roosevelt continued to issue appeals for peace and offered to mediate, but he did so mostly to make clear to the American people that the onus for war lay with Germany.[6]

Two factors persuaded Hitler that he could ignore the United States as he contemplated his next aggressive moves. First, Roosevelt did not possess the one thing that counted in the führer's eyes—a significant military force.[7] To reassure the British against the possibility of a simultaneous Japanese move against the key Royal Navy base at Singapore, the president in 1939 transferred much of the U.S. Navy to the Pacific. But this strategic relocation meant the American fleet did not matter to Germany. Nor did the president have any troops to send to Europe, because the Army had shriveled again after the First World War to fewer than 200,000 active duty personnel. In the wake of Munich, Roosevelt asked Congress to appropriate $500 million for defense. Where defense spending made up less than 7 percent of the federal budget in 1934, the share of defense outlays would roughly double by 1939. Most of the money, though, would go to building a large air force that might deter an aggressor from striking the United States, and none of those planes would be ready for several years.[8] Just as important, to impress Hitler Roosevelt needed to make a clear commitment that the United States would support Great Britain, France, and Poland. He had signaled through back channels to the British and French governments that the United States would put its enormous industrial resources at their disposal. But he refused the public declaration of American support that might have made Hitler flinch.[9]

Public timidity was something European dictators had come to expect from the political heads of the major democracies. Hitler dismissed Roosevelt as, in the words of historian Donald Cameron Watt, "simply another democratic halfling, half-dolt, half-dupe."[10] Toward such leaders, the führer felt only contempt, and his scorn had increased with their craven efforts to appease him at Munich. His disdain was shared by Joseph Stalin, who concluded that the Soviet Union also could not rely on feckless allies in the West and decided instead to cut a deal with Germany, the Non-Aggression Pact signed on August 23, 1939. For Stalin, the agreement at least bought time to put his country's defenses in better order.[11] Hitler, knowing the Soviet Union would not take the side of Great Britain and France, readied his final plans for Poland, whose only friends were too far away.

Germany's attack on Poland on September 1, 1939, left the Roosevelt administration groping for a new policy toward Europe. The president saw at once that a German victory would pose a grave threat to American national security. He now understood that Hitler's ambitions were insatiable. Better to oppose him in alliance with other significant powers than face him alone, much less confront him while also coping with the Japanese menace in the Far East. At the same time, however, Roosevelt refused to go beyond the offer to help meet the Allies' needs for armaments. He intended to assist them to prevent a German triumph (Benito Mussolini and Italy did not join the war on Berlin's side until June 1940), and thereby contain the war within Europe. But he expected the British and French to resist successfully without direct American military intervention—anticipating at worst a reprise of the Western Front stalemate of 1914–1917.

Above all, the president sought to retain his cherished freedom of action, to hold open all possible options. He approached the situation as a shrewd politician. Roosevelt's stance reflected his strong personal style: he preferred to let others advocate particular positions, to commit themselves, so he could gauge the reactions of various key players before reaching his own decision. The method had suited him well in domestic politics, where he would sometimes delay before attaching himself to a policy initiative until the political benefits were fully clear, yet still in time to secure much of the political credit. (The plan to pack the Supreme Court stood out as a rare misstep for so consummate a politician, the result of hubris born of the electoral landslide of the previous year, and he would exercise extra caution to avoid a repeat.) Always Roosevelt believed himself to be the master of circumstances, confident that he could steer events, if not right away then over time, in the direction he chose. A political consideration also figured in his refusal to make a commitment. Presidential positions can become public, either accidentally or because someone leaks them, at which point they become embarrassing to disavow, especially once enemies seize upon them as political fodder.[12]

Despite Roosevelt's caution, several factors intruded to undercut the president's capacity to manipulate American security policy. The first constraint was domestic public opinion. Isolationism had revived in the wake of the disappointing results Wilson had secured in the First World War. Many Americans felt they had been misled into a conflict that did little more than enrich certain sectors of American business, an impression fortified by congressional hearings that highlighted the huge profits that munitions manufacturers had earned during the war.[13] In the wake of the hearings and reflecting the public disillusionment, Congress had passed several neutrality measures between 1935 and 1937. These included the 1937 Neutrality Act, which precluded arms sales to belligerents when the United States remained neutral and aimed to inhibit American firms from doing business with nations at war. The Great Depression left hard-pressed citizens preoccupied with their immediate economic needs, too. With events in Europe or the Far East posing no direct danger, Americans showed scant interest in distant war clouds.[14]

It would be a mistake, though, to overstate the degree to which American public opinion tied Roosevelt's hands. Even before Germany struck Poland, Gallup opinion polls showed more than 80 percent of Americans believed the United States ought to back Great Britain and France against Hitler and Mussolini. Just as striking, by a two-to-one margin they favored sending material aid to the Allies.[15] Roosevelt also possessed extraordinary rhetorical gifts; his occasional radio "fireside chats" did much to boost spirits amid the Depression (and to make the presidency itself a more popular office). Yet he declined to push the limits of popular support on matters of foreign policy that were removed from his listeners' everyday concerns.[16] To the contrary, the vox populi served as an excuse when he preferred inaction. A case in point: when the British pressed him to join in an official protest against Japanese actions in China, he demurred, insisting the American people would not stand for it.[17]

Congress stood as a more significant obstacle to the president. He found it hard to persuade lawmakers to give him the latitude he wanted to steer the national course through treacherous times. In broad terms, he had been weakened by the defeat of his court-packing measure and his subsequent failure in the 1938 congressional primaries to oust anti–New Deal Democrats. Lawmakers came away confident they could oppose the president with impunity on both domestic affairs and matters of foreign and military policy. To take one pivotal example, the administration could not rely on unified Democratic support to revise the Neutrality Act to permit arms sales to Great Britain and France. The administration tried to work around the law, but its efforts sometimes resulted in public embarrassment and provoked congressional anger.[18] When administration allies in Congress adopted a more direct approach to repeal the arms embargo in spring 1939, the move proved deeply divisive and stalled.[19] Only after war started in Europe did Congress agree to revise the neutrality legislation, and even then important restrictions (such as a requirement that all purchases be paid for in cash and carried by the belligerents' own ships) remained.[20]

Easy as it seems in retrospect to condemn Roosevelt for his timidity in dealing with Congress, he and his advisors appreciated that they could ill afford to lose key votes on foreign and military policy. Legislative results were observed closely at home and especially abroad. Hostile powers delighted in evidence of American division, while allies found it disheartening. Cordell Hull, often involved in tense negotiations with Japan, worried that the defeat of interventionist measures would subvert his diplomatic position. Understandably, then, the president timed his overtures to Congress to maximize the prospects for success. He would await some international crisis, then call for legislative action he deemed urgent to meet the emergency. Thus the fall of France in June 1940 opened an opportunity for a major increase in defense appropriations, with a focus on expansion of the (suddenly frontline) U.S. fleet.[21]

Within the ranks of the administration itself lay a third impediment to the president's freedom of action. The federal government expanded dramatically during the New Deal, with new agencies springing up constantly and old ones adopting new responsibilities. To direct this enlarged administrative apparatus, Roosevelt had added White House staff, often borrowing personnel from other departments. Still, he exercised only loose control over his subordinates and the federal bureaucracy. He also preferred a management style aptly described as competitive: his aides vied for his attention and favor, but none enjoyed his full confidence. It was not uncommon for a senior official to leave a meeting with FDR believing the president had been persuaded to take action, only to learn later that he had backed away from a decision. For Roosevelt, this seemed to preserve the latitude he so prized. However, in the void left by presidential inaction and non-decisions, factions within the administration often chose to pursue the course they believed the president ought to have taken. "Rather than a smoothly functioning, harmonious machine," observes historian Jonathan G. Utley, "the foreign policy establishment in the Roosevelt administration was a snake pit of influential leaders and faceless bureaucrats working at cross-purposes, striking deals, and not infrequently employing sleight of hand in order to move the nation in the direction each thought most appropriate."[22]

The multiple agendas below the president tugged American policy in directions Roosevelt was not yet prepared to go and set different policies at cross-purposes. Japanese aggression, first against China and later aimed at points farther south, exposed the deep rifts within the State Department and elsewhere in the federal bureaucracy. On one side were hard-liners determined to punish Japan and force it to quit China entirely; on the other stood cooler heads, such as Secretary Hull, who realized that European colonial powers in Asia lacked the military means to face down Japan and Germany at the same time.[23]

The bureaucratic factions clashed repeatedly and pursued their respective notion of proper American policy in a no-holds-barred contest of wills. In 1940 the president decided to prevent Japan from purchasing aviation gasoline needed by the U.S. armed forces, so he ordered it placed under an embargo. Treasury Secretary Morgenthau, a strong proponent of using economic coercion to influence Japanese behavior, altered the language to broaden the embargo to cover *all* petroleum products, added scrap iron and steel to the list, and sent the revised order to the president without alerting him of the change. Roosevelt signed the Morgenthau version, but the State Department struck back and replaced the initial directive with one more narrowly drawn. Even that did not end the matter, for lower-level bureaucrats managed to establish a tighter oil embargo on Japan (though not on the fuel Japanese planes used).[24]

To this odd policy stew we can add the military, which had its own agenda. Because the president declined to set clear security goals, military planners adopted a very conservative course that emphasized defense of the Western Hemisphere.[25] This reflected the low level of military readiness—only the U.S. Navy could be deemed combat-capable before 1941. When diplomats urged that the United States take over from the Royal Navy the responsibility for blocking Japanese expansion in the Western Pacific, senior naval officers balked and insisted that the fleet not go beyond Hawaii. Roosevelt declined to resolve the conflicting policy views between civilians and the military, while letting each believe he shared its perspective.[26]

The political calendar, specifically the pending 1940 presidential election, imposed yet another constraint on what Roosevelt believed he could do. All wondered whether he would seek an unprecedented third term. To his critics, who worried that he had already amassed more power than any other peacetime president, another reelection bid would mark a move toward an elected dictatorship. Others wondered about the wisdom of breaching a political norm set by George Washington himself. Ever the attentive politician, Franklin Roosevelt understood the reservations and appreciated that he would have to tread softly when it came to expanding presidential powers. He declined to override restrictions set by the Neutrality Act, even though some key figures within his administration advised him in 1939 that he might do so under his constitutional authority over foreign policy.[27] When he did pursue a third term, he promised American mothers that their sons were not going to be sent off to war.[28]

Last and most important, unanticipated events in the war itself deprived Roosevelt of alternatives he had taken for granted. The swift collapse of France under the German blitzkrieg stunned the president and his military advisors, who had regarded the French army as the finest in the world. More than that, French defeat and British evacuation at Dunkirk swept away the foundation of Roosevelt's initial wartime grand strategy: no longer could the United States assume that its role would be limited to supplying the Allied armies as they checked Hitler on the European continent. During summer and fall 1940, as the fate of England hung in the balance, the administration debated whether it made sense to ship additional scarce American war supplies to the British. The president's military advisors warned that American forces were dangerously short of weapons and equipment for a last-ditch defense of the Western Hemisphere in the event of a Nazi attack.[29]

Fortunately, the British under Winston Churchill's determined leadership stoutly resisted German air attacks over the second half of 1940, while British and Commonwealth forces won victories over the Italians in the Middle East. Reassured that the British Empire would continue to fight, then, Roosevelt resolved to support it at all costs. But this decision necessarily implied others that would push the president down a path from which there could be no turning back.[30] By late 1940, Churchill informed the president that Great Britain was running out of the money needed to pay for war orders. Just as important, the Royal Navy faced a rising menace from U-boat attacks, much like 1917, and it would do little good if American supplies could not be delivered to the war zone.[31]

The crisis provoked by the German triumph in Western Europe in spring 1940 spilled over to the Far East. Western defenses against Japanese southward expansion had always been fragile, more bluff than substance. Still, the combined Asian forces of Great Britain (positioned in India, Burma, Malaya, and, above all, Singapore), France (in Indochina), the Netherlands (in the East Indies), and the United States (in the Philippines) should have sufficed to deter Japanese aggression. Japan also had to anticipate that its potential regional adversaries would receive major reinforcements from their homelands. With the defeat of France and the Netherlands, though, their colonial outposts could expect no help. Japanese expansionists recognized the vulnerability and, with no objection from the new Vichy regime, sent troops into northern Indochina to close off one supply route to the Chinese Nationalists.[32] Great Britain meanwhile needed all its military resources to forestall

Germany and Italy. Accordingly, the British drew major formations from Australia, New Zealand, and India for service in the Middle East, replacing them with untrained troops, and sent obsolete equipment to defend its key Far Eastern outposts.[33]

These developments again compromised American options. Where previously the Roosevelt administration had relied on other nations to take the lead in blocking the Japanese, it now found itself assuming that role. This posed hard choices for Washington. Should America stand by as the Japanese upped their demands on the orphaned colonial governments as, for instance, when Tokyo insisted on increasing oil purchases from the Netherlands East Indies?[34] Or should the United States demand firmness and take steps more likely to provoke war? From a pure military standpoint, the answer seemed plain enough—draw in American forces to the Western Hemisphere until they were sufficient to meet wider threats. In that spirit, the commander of the U.S. Navy's Pacific Fleet, Admiral James O. Richardson, recommended recalling it from Hawaii to San Diego.[35] Such a move, however, would remove the fleet as a chip in the effort to deter Japan, and the president rejected it and found himself a new admiral, Husband E. Kimmel, who served until the Pearl Harbor disaster.[36]

One other pivotal event transformed the set of choices open to the president: on June 22, 1941, Germany attacked the Soviet Union. The immediate effects were far-reaching. With Germany committing the bulk of its army to the east, any threat of invasion of Great Britain vanished. But initial Russian defeats and rapid German advances raised the grim possibility that the Nazi war machine would gain control over all the resources—particularly the oil fields in the Caucasus—it needed to become self-sufficient.[37] As Soviet armies surrendered or retreated, Moscow's requests for aid became more urgent, another major call on American military production. But with output of war items still very limited, help meant the diversion of equipment that would further slow the buildup of American forces.[38] Here, repeating his approach when Great Britain seemed on the verge of defeat the year before, the president overruled his military chiefs and insisted that help be sent to the Russians. No significant aid could reach them in time to stem the German tide in 1941, but Roosevelt understood the value of making a good-faith gesture in their moment of peril.[39]

The war between Germany and the Soviet Union also had important repercussions for the Far East. Japan had been weighing two options for aggressive military action, a move into Siberia to force the Soviets into a two-front war versus one southward to obtain control over strategic resources. Although Tokyo had a neutrality accord with Moscow, key Japanese officials, including the foreign minister, favored an attack on the Soviet Union to destroy a powerful enemy once and for all. Other Japanese military leaders countered that the real menace came from the West, which controlled access to oil and other vital resources, while the Japanese army in Manchuria preferred not to attack the Soviets without first securing a large numerical edge.[40]

In early July 1941, a Japanese imperial conference chose to risk confrontation with Great Britain and the United States. Both the Russians and the Americans, through their intelligence sources, soon learned of the decision. It led Stalin to transfer forces from Siberia to defend Moscow in late 1941, where the Soviets finally threw back the Nazi onslaught. But the Japanese response to the German invasion of the Soviet Union also meant time was running out for Japan and the United States to find diplomatic solutions to their differences.[41]

Notwithstanding the march of events that pushed America closer to war, Roosevelt still resisted making key strategic decisions. He refused to define defense priorities for senior military planners, leaving them to guess at his intentions. Even after he reviewed their plans, such as a recommendation by his military chiefs in November 1940 to concentrate the U.S. fleet in the Atlantic, he declined to endorse or reject them.[42] When he did make a choice, he favored the option that seemed most likely to buy him more time. His fascination with air power reflected his determination to thwart Germany and Japan without actually going to war or risking the lives of American soldiers. Beginning with the president's post-Munich embrace of aircraft production, his fixation on the deterrent value of bombers persisted until late 1941. Because the United States could strike potential enemies at long range, he remained confident they (either the Germans or Japanese) would not risk aggression that might provoke American retaliation.[43] As a practical defense policy the president's stand was absurd (and he soon modified it), but it tells us everything about his wishful outlook.

Yet much as the president wished to hold open all possibilities, each step, even some designed to avoid definitive choices, drew the United States closer to war. Roosevelt's election to a third term in November 1940 relieved him of immediate electoral considerations. He soon announced to the American people that the United States would function as the "arsenal of democracy." In March 1941, responding to Churchill's plea, the administration secured congressional approval of the Lend Lease Act to increase the volume of war supplies.[44] Billed as a way to avoid direct American involvement in the war, Lend-Lease also increased the American investment in British survival. For example, unless the additional armaments and goods reached England, the program would be useless, and the Royal Navy could not adequately protect shipping from America while also meeting its other vital obligations. The U.S. Navy therefore took on greater responsibility for the transit of ships from American ports across the Atlantic, including so-called neutrality patrols to warn merchant vessels of nearby U-boats. Meanwhile, the president, skirting the neutrality legislation by creatively redefining "Western Hemisphere," extended the U.S. security zone as far as Greenland.

Events in the Atlantic in 1941 demonstrated again that an American president exercises initiative over foreign and military policy that can dramatically increase the likelihood of war without congressional approval. Roosevelt, still worried over public reaction, denied that U.S. Navy ships were serving as escorts for convoys to and from Great Britain. Instead he called operations within the expanded American security zone "reconnaissance."[45] As his critics pointed out, this was a distinction without a difference. Neutrality patrols invited confrontations with German U-boats that would surely result in both American and German losses. Nor was Roosevelt done. Convinced by September that the time had come to provoke Germany into submarine attacks that would justify going to war, the president ordered the U.S. Navy to shoot on sight at any U-boats. The action seemed designed to goad Hitler into war, but the führer side-stepped confrontation by directing his submarines to avoid engagements with U.S. Navy vessels.[46] He was not quite ready to add another enemy.

Meanwhile, the mounting prospect of war in early 1941 prompted high-level military consultations between Great Britain and the United

States. In late 1940, Admiral Harold Stark, Chief of Naval Operations, proposed and endorsed Plan Dog, a strategic overview that called for concentrating on the defeat of Germany, avoiding war with Japan or remaining on the defensive in the Pacific, and sending major ground and air forces to the European theater for an offensive against Germany. Roosevelt again declined to commit himself to a grand strategy for war, but he did approve staff talks with the British.[47] For two months, beginning at the end of January 1941, senior American and British military commanders held the American-British Conversations Number 1 (ABC-1) to begin planning for the day the United States finally entered the war. Absent clear policy guidance from their political leader, the American officers could make few concrete suggestions. Even so, both sides quickly confirmed that Germany represented a much greater threat than Japan, defeating the Nazi war machine would be the first priority, and American and British resources would be concentrated in the Atlantic.

Differences arose over the Far East, where the British expected war and wanted an increased American presence, while the Americans hoped Japan would remain neutral and refused to promise additional forces. Nonetheless, here, too, the two countries' military representatives found common ground in the position that every effort should be made to delay war with Japan as long as possible. In keeping with his conduct throughout this period, Roosevelt did not endorse the resulting report. American commanders, with no other instructions, used it anyway as the basis for planning.[48]

If American grand strategy in the latter half of 1941 intended to postpone a clash with Japan, though, Roosevelt neglected to coordinate the pieces of American policy toward that objective.[49] Denying Japan access to oil made sense in military terms—Japan would be unable to wage a long war without a secure supply—but asking the Dutch to resist Japanese demands for increased oil shipments from the Netherlands East Indies in mid-1941 merely confirmed for Tokyo its strategic vulnerability and gave it added incentive to seize what it could not purchase. In this instance appeasement would have better served the immediate security interests of the United States and its allies.[50]

The president's minimal control over junior-rank officials within his administration again made matters worse. In response to the Japanese occupation of southern Indochina in July 1941, Roosevelt ordered a freeze on all Japanese assets in the United States, with a committee to decide selectively to release assets to pay for exports. He intended the move to increase pressure incrementally on Tokyo. But hard-liners at the lower levels of the federal bureaucracy again pushed economic pressure beyond the president's design. When these aggressive officials refused to release any Japanese assets to permit purchases, the provisional freeze on Japanese assets in the United States became a total embargo.[51]

Nor were American military preparations in the Pacific or Far East properly calculated to delay a Japanese attack. Roosevelt still believed that the Pacific Fleet at Pearl Harbor would inhibit any Japanese naval move against the Philippines and other targets in the Far East. But he ignored the military corollary: were they to strike the British in Malaya/ Singapore and the Dutch in Netherlands East Indies, the Japanese could not afford to ignore a major hostile fleet in the Central Pacific.[52] Much the same could be said for belated American efforts to bolster the defenses of the Philippines. At the urging of General Douglas MacArthur, who had come out of retirement to command there, Roosevelt agreed in mid-1941 to send major reinforcements.[53] These included most of the new B-17 long-range bombers in the inventory of the U.S. Army Air Force, on the assumption that Japan would be terrified by what bombing might do to its fire-prone cities. The president overlooked the possibility that the B-17 threat would force Japan to strike preemptively at the bomber bases before their defenses were ready. His decision to recall MacArthur and rush him troops and equipment went against the recommendation of senior American military leaders.[54]

The day of reckoning arrived a good six months sooner than Roosevelt intended. Despite his determination to dictate whether, where, and when the United States would enter the war, it found America at a time and place not of his choosing.

Some of his decisions did buy him time and protected American strategic interests. Operating within what he took to be narrow political constraints, he stood with Great Britain in its hour of need and with the Soviet Union as it bent under the Nazi onslaught. The president and his key civilian and military aides also identified Germany as the principal threat to American national security.

For the most part, though, events framed and limited Roosevelt's options, narrowing his freedom of action even before the United States became a belligerent. So far as he did establish a clear grand strategy, moreover, he did not follow through ruthlessly on its logic. "Germany First" implied greater efforts to placate Japan, by assuring it of access to resources and curtailing aid for China. Instead, heavy-handed economic pressure magnified Tokyo's sense of vulnerability, while the feverish American military buildup led Japan to attack before the odds tilted against it. Had Hitler not played into the president's hands by declaring war on the United States in December 1941, the entire Anglo-American grand strategy might have unraveled.

OHIO

When Germany struck Poland on September 1, 1939, the United States Army ranked as the seventeenth largest in the world, sandwiched between Portugal and Bulgaria. With 174,000 officers and men, the Army stood well below its authorized strength of 250,000.[55] Only a nation confident it faced no significant threat would maintain such an insignificant military establishment. The puny size of the army testified to the failure of the Wilsonian attempt to have the United States accept broad responsibilities for preserving peace. By comparison, as we've seen, the U.S. Navy was a force that might give a potential adversary pause. Yet rather than capitalize on American industrial might after World War I by building the world's largest fleet, American policy makers chose to negotiate naval arms limitation treaties (beginning with the 1922 Washington Naval Treaty) that restricted the number and size of American vessels. The American fleet still matched the Royal Navy as the world's largest, but unlike Japan, which could concentrate in the Far East, the United States faced hostile powers on two oceans. Moreover, by the mid-1930s Japan and Germany each renounced treaty restrictions and started major naval rearmament programs before the United States, so they enjoyed a head start.[56]

When a president recognizes American vulnerability, as Roosevelt did by late 1938, or concludes war is likely, as he did by early 1941, his next task is to prepare for war. This task has military, socioeconomic, and political dimensions. He must make certain the armed forces under his command are sufficient and ready to wage war successfully. For a major military conflict on a global scale, with key allies also depending on American war production, the president also has to mobilize and coordinate enormous economic resources. Last, as a political leader, the president must make certain the citizenry is ready for the sacrifice that war will entail. The people have to accept the necessity for war, understand what it will cost, and consent, at least passively, to become participants.

The Roosevelt administration began economic and military mobilization as the war clouds gathered over Europe in late 1938, and preparations accelerated in the next three years. As noted earlier, after Munich the president secured a large appropriation to build aircraft, announcing a goal of building 15,000 planes per year. After the fall of France in 1940 the administration also embraced a major shipbuilding program.

But these important first measures were already late. Modern military hardware had become so complex that the lead time between when weapons were ordered and their actual availability was several years. (Compare this to the Civil War, fought largely with weapons already in production that needed only to be manufactured on a larger scale.) The aircraft carriers put in production in 1940, then, would not begin to appear in the battle zone until early 1943.

Another flaw in the initial mobilization lay in its purpose. Everything the president wanted—from long-range bombers to capital ships (aircraft carriers and battleships)—was designed to deter an aggressor, not to fight him. One historian goes so far as to conclude, "From the beginning of rearmament, Roosevelt sought, not rearmament, but the appearance of rearmament."[57] Had the president had been left to his own devices, the United States would have entered the war with a hopelessly unbalanced force structure, lots of planes and ships but virtually no ground troops. For that matter, much of the new equipment would have been shipped to allies already at war.

Fortunately, Roosevelt did not surround himself with sycophants, and he solicited views that differed from his own. Several of his key aides objected to his approach to military mobilization. In particular, he was challenged at a November 1938 meeting on his plans to focus so heavily on aircraft production by then Brigadier General George C. Marshall Jr., recently promoted to Army Deputy Chief of Staff.

Roosevelt respected the willingness of a relatively junior staff officer to speak freely, and thus began a relationship that would prove to be of enormous value. Marshall's star rose: he assumed the chief of staff post on the day Germany invaded Poland.[58]

To Marshall would fall the herculean task of turning the neglected U.S. Army into a military machine capable of defeating adversaries on either side of the globe. In this he would be supported by other capable military leaders, but Marshall took the lead in persuading the president to build up a military organization in which he had taken little interest. Key civilian figures in the administration, such as Morgenthau, presidential aide Harry Hopkins, and (after June 1940) Secretary of War Henry Stimson, made certain Marshall had direct access to the White House.[59] The president also took an important step to establish a direct line of communication with his military chiefs by issuing a rare presidential Military Order in July 1939 that placed them under his supervision.[60]

Their efforts were hampered, though, by the political cautiousness of the man they served. For just as Roosevelt avoided making hard choices about foreign policy and defense strategy, so, too, did he evade decisions that might result in a battle in Congress or stir public opposition. Conscription serves as a good illustration. Marshall pointed out in May 1940 just how unready the army was—it could put no more than 15,000 poorly organized and equipped soldiers into combat at a time when Germany already had 2 million troops under arms.[61] The United States would need to expand the Army to several million men. As the First World War had demonstrated, no method other than conscription would suffice. Yet when he and others pointed out to Roosevelt the need for a draft, the president demurred. He consented reluctantly to a peacetime conscription measure only after the French surrender, which lessened public and congressional opposition, and he let Marshall serve as the administration's point man in Congress to make the case for the bill. (As a measure of the president's timidity, consider that in the summer of 1940 nearly 70 percent of Americans favored a draft.)[62] Even then, the draft bill called for only one year of active duty (due to end in October 1941) and restricted the use of conscripts to the Western Hemisphere. Much like the 1916 National Defense Act, then, the 1940 draft law represented a halfway defensive measure, far too little if the country found itself at war.[63]

If political considerations hindered military readiness, they had the opposite effect on the production of armaments. Unemployment had remained stubbornly high throughout the 1930s, despite many New Deal initiatives.[64] Increased government spending on relief and public works had not sufficed to offset the loss of aggregate spending power. But with the beginning of large orders for military hardware, first from abroad[65] and then from the American armed services, defense contractors started hiring in large numbers. The demand was so large that new factories had to be established.[66] Every new job and new defense plant, of course, was located in some senator's state and congressman's district, so there was ample political credit to be shared. The Roosevelt administration thus discovered that Congress was eager to appropriate funds for the military buildup. By fall 1940, total military appropriations exceeded $17 billion, more than nine times the 1939 total.[67]

Problems arose in the administration's attempts to impose some kind of rational order on the procurement and production processes. Much as in 1917–1918, no organizational structure existed to establish priorities or identify bottlenecks. Bernard Baruch, who had directed the War Industries Board effectively under Wilson, advised Roosevelt to vest overarching mobilization authority in a similar business-guided structure. But the president, still smarting from his antagonistic relations with much of corporate leadership, did not want to turn over control of economic mobilization to the private sector. He also refused to cede so much authority to a single economic czar of the kind that Baruch himself had been. Instead, Roosevelt approached the challenge with a succession of improvised agencies, frequently reshuffling and renaming them.[68] The administrative confusion resulted in competition for scarce resources and slow production of war materials. By summer 1941, they amounted to a mere 10 percent of total industrial output,[69] and the latter still reflected sluggish private demand.

As a result, the American armed forces approached the war lacking modern weapons and equipment. Every battleship at Pearl Harbor on December 7, 1941, was more than twenty years old, a holdover from the First World War. When conscription finally yielded a substantial influx of new men, the U.S. Army had little to put in their hands that might defeat an enemy. The shortage was exacerbated by the president's decision to ship the most modern equipment to Great Britain. Photographs of army maneuvers in the prewar period depict the embarrassing state of readiness. At a time when German panzers had conquered much of Europe, American armored troops drove trucks with the sign "tank" affixed to their sides. But they were in no danger. The anti-tank "guns" aimed by their war-game opponents were wooden poles resting on stakes.[70]

Roosevelt invested the least effort on the third dimension of mobilization, readying the American people for war. Prior to the 1940 presidential election, where he expected a tough battle, electoral calculation may have played a role. Copying a page from Wilson in 1916, Roosevelt chose to downplay the likelihood that the nation would become a belligerent. Less comprehensible was his refusal after winning a third term to mount an effort to influence American opinion in favor of entering the war. He limited himself to speeches, often highly effective, explaining the importance to the United States of British success and defending aid to Great Britain. Especially compelling was his March 11, 1941, justification for Lend-Lease:

> Suppose my neighbor's home catches fire, and I have a length of garden hose four or five hundred feet away. If he can take my garden hose and connect it up with his hydrant, I may help him to put out his fire. . . . I don't say to him before that operation, "Neighbor, my garden hose cost me $15; you have to pay me $15 for it." . . . I don't want $15—I want my garden hose back after the fire is over.[71]

The president still declined to make a public case for American belligerency, even when he recognized by mid-1941 that war could not be avoided much longer. He feared that an official propaganda effort would spark a political backlash. As Americans had soured on the results of the First World War, critics had looked back at the Creel Committee and condemned it for promoting chauvinism, intolerance, and hysteria.[72] Roosevelt, pressed by interventionists to make a case for war, finally established a war information committee in summer 1941 under New York Mayor Fiorello La Guardia, but its tepid efforts did nothing to sway the public.[73]

Just how little had been done to mobilize public support for war became evident in the six months before Pearl Harbor. Draftees spoke eagerly about returning to civilian life as soon as their year of training was complete. Their attitude was captured by the slang term "OHIO"— over the hill in October, the month the conscription law would expire. Barely more than half the public backed extending the draft law, and a clear majority wished to continue the restriction that conscripts could serve only in the Western Hemisphere. Again General Marshall put his influence on the line to sway lawmakers to continue the draft.[74] After a fierce battle in the House of Representatives, the bill to reauthorize conscription and extend the term of service passed by a single vote, with the geographic restriction still in force.[75] This despite a declaration by the president of an unlimited state of national emergency amid rising tensions with both Germany and Japan. Polls taken in November 1941 made evident just how little progress the president and his administration had made in their effort to sway the public toward American intervention. Although most Americans favored aid to the Allies, only one in three would vote for war.[76] Indeed, the American people were no more willing to enter the war at the beginning of December 1941 than they had been after the French surrender in June 1940.

Did the slow American mobilization for war matter? A harsh critic of Roosevelt's direction of prewar policy, Stephen Ambrose poses the most provocative "what if." Had the United States mobilized early for war, he avers, "the Axis almost surely would have been deterred."[77] Possibly so, though that would have been the case only if the country were fully armed by 1939, which in turn would have required remarkable prescience on Roosevelt's part—the buildup would have had to commence several years before Munich.

It seems more reasonable to suggest that serious American preparations should have started when Germany attacked Poland. Even that would have done little to alter the disastrous results in the months immediately following Pearl Harbor. At root, early American defeats stemmed from the mental habits of peace: on December 7, 1941, modern battleships would have been just as unready to defend themselves against the surprise Japanese attack, while more B-17s in the Philippines simply would have meant more of them caught on the ground. On the other hand, belated mobilization slowed the American counter-offensive in all theaters. An invasion of Northwest Europe in 1943 might have ended the war a year sooner—saving millions of lives, including countless civilians who perished in 1944–1945 in battles, bombing raids, and gas chambers.[78]

Unconditional Surrender and Beyond

From the moment the first Japanese bombs fell on Pearl Harbor, it was clear that the United States would settle for nothing less than the complete defeat of its enemies and the utter destruction of their capacity to ever threaten peace again. Roosevelt would offer no Fourteen Points with a promise of generous terms; there would be no armistice while either Germany or Japan still had strong armies in the field that might give rise to another "stab in the back" myth. He spoke to his advisors early in the war of how the German people had been "Prussianized," drawn into a militarized culture that would need to be uprooted thoroughly.[79] At this point, when Nazi plans for extermination camps were just beginning to move from drawing board to reality, he still had only a limited grasp of the nature of the Hitler's regime. But he understood that Germany would need to be beaten in a way that would open the door for a thorough remaking of German popular attitudes. Similarly, the political influence of the military in Japan would have to be eliminated once and for all, while Japan would have to be evicted from all its holdings in Asia, especially China.

For some fifteen months after Pearl Harbor, though, America's basic war aims remained implicit. Not until the president met Churchill in Casablanca in February 1943 did Roosevelt declare publicly that the Allies would insist upon the unconditional surrender of Germany and Japan. (The prime minister later claimed that he was surprised by the announcement, which may have been true, but he and the president had discussed the policy in advance and agreed upon it.) Stalin agreed with the call for the total defeat of Germany; the Soviet Union would not enter the war against Japan until its final days.

"Unconditional surrender" stirred controversy during the war and later. German Propaganda Minister Joseph Goebbels exploited the Allies' goal to stimulate German determination. After the war, some German generals claimed it left them no alternative but to stand behind Hitler to the end. Even among American military commanders, there were a number who worried that the demand for the enemy to lay down his arms unconditionally would prompt him to resist more fiercely. The result might be heavier Allied casualties than would be incurred with the offer of more lenient terms.[80]

But the arguments against the unconditional surrender policy do not stand up under inspection. In the case of the Pacific theater, Japanese soldiers had already demonstrated that they would almost never surrender, no matter how hopeless their military position. They had been thoroughly indoctrinated in the view that capitulation was worse than death. Their conduct on the battlefield did not change in the aftermath of the Casablanca announcement. Nor did that of the Germans. Notably, the most serious attempt on Hitler's life, the July 1944 bomb plot, occurred when the officers involved knew full well of the Allied demand. It did not stop a number of the most senior German officers, including two field marshals (Erwin Rommel and Günther von Kluge), from giving at least tacit endorsement to the effort to kill the führer and overthrow the regime. The plotters expected a temporary military government to open surrender negotiations with the Allies immediately. Further, large numbers of German troops, even entire armies (as in Tunisia in May 1943), capitulated when they recognized their positions to be hopeless. If anything encouraged fanatical German resistance to the end of the war, it likely was the fear of Soviet revenge for German atrocities and the order by Heinrich Himmler in 1944 that the families of deserters would be executed.[81]

The policy decision to pursue unconditional surrender brought clarity to the Allied cause, perhaps a mixed blessing. On one side, both those on the front lines and those at home could have no doubts about whether their leaders intended to carry the fight to final victory. The dirty business of war would be pressed to the end. On the other, in making the commitment to the total defeat of the regimes in Berlin and Tokyo, Roosevelt did something he had always taken pains to avoid— he constrained his own discretion. Unless the military situation became deadlocked, the goal could not be revised downward. Much like Lincoln after emancipation, Roosevelt left no room for peace overtures to either government.[82]

For the president, the commitment to the total defeat of Germany and Japan represented only the proximate Allied war goal, the essential first step. After a second cataclysmic war in a generation, Roosevelt was determined to succeed where Wilson had failed and create a stable, peaceful international order. Here Roosevelt avoided definitive statements and firm commitments. He moved cautiously toward his objectives, retreating or hedging his bets at times.[83] Still, a vision of the postwar world that Roosevelt sought emerges from his diplomacy, comments to the press, speeches, and actions. He looked forward to a system of collective security in which four great powers—the United States, Great Britain, the Soviet Union, and China—would assure peace and resolve disputes, within the framework of an inclusive international organization (which in 1945 took the specific form of the United Nations). This arrangement would replace the older system of spheres of influence that the president believed to be a source of international friction.[84]

Roosevelt was also convinced that colonialism must end, for it, too, represented a source of competition among major nations, while colonial peoples would not accept permanent subordinate status. They might not be ready for self-government—Roosevelt reflected the casual racial prejudices of Western elites that non-white peoples would need a period of careful supervision before they could fully manage their societies—but they could be set on a path toward independence. (The same off-hand racism led the president to bow to pressure in early 1942 to intern Japanese Americans.)[85] To avoid the stifling economic effects of exclusive trading blocs, moreover, the postwar order would rest upon a liberalized set of economic arrangements, with few obstacles to free trade.[86]

Several elements in this Roosevelt vision deserve scrutiny. To begin with, although the president and his advisors saw the arrangements he favored as universally beneficial, they were plainly American-centric. The four great powers included a Great Britain that would be deeply in debt to the United States and hobbled by its crippling wartime expenditures. Thus the British lion could be expected to dance to Washington's tune. Likewise, China would be recovering from a long war, protracted Japanese occupation of key cities, and internal political turmoil. The United States would need to guide China as it gradually assumed a leading role in Asia.[87] In economic terms, free trade would play to the strengths of the United States as the dominant industrial power and the only one not directly ravaged by the war. That the arrangements Roosevelt proposed favored his own national interests would not go unnoticed by other Allied leaders. They in turn would pursue their national goals, and it was to be expected that a divergence of purpose would emerge over the course of the war and especially at its conclusion, when victory would snap the bond forged by opposition to a common adversary.

Differences over war objectives, moreover, became clear from the outset, especially with Great Britain. The Atlantic Charter, a pre–Pearl Harbor Anglo-American declaration of principles, promised self-determination as an Allied war goal. In Roosevelt's view, the statement put the British on record as pledging an end to colonialism.[88] Churchill saw things otherwise: he had not become the king's first minister, he declared in 1942, "to preside over the liquidation of the British Empire."[89] The anticolonial implications of the Atlantic Charter in his mind thus excluded British possessions, and he intended that Great Britain not only retain its current imperial holdings, such as India, over American objections but reclaim those lost to Japan, including Burma, Malaya, and especially Singapore.

Here, clearly, the prime minister was in denial. Not only would the creation of a huge Indian Army to fight the Axis powers make a return to colonial subordination on the subcontinent impossible, but Asian peoples who had seen fellow Asians (the Japanese) defeat Western armies would never again recognize claims by colonial powers as legitimate. The prime minister also did not subscribe to the president's view that spheres of influence were dangerous and destabilizing. At least insofar as they were accepted among the great powers, they might in fact remove a source of tension.

Finally, Roosevelt's conception of postwar order rested on very optimistic expectations about the other two members of the Big Four: China and the Soviet Union. He treated Chiang Kai-shek as the leader of a major power, despite indications that the Nationalists were doing little for the Allied cause. Instead they husbanded resources for the expected postwar showdown with Chinese communists.[90] But Roosevelt needed a major Asian power other than the Soviet Union to replace Japan, and China would have to be made to fit the part. As for Moscow, the president correctly foresaw as early as 1941 that the Soviet Union would take its place among the great nations after the war. Questions arose, however, about what kind of role the Russians would assume. They might take a narrow view of Soviet interests and seek domination over bordering states. Roosevelt hoped instead that if real Soviet security anxieties could be addressed, Stalin might gradually become a responsible partner in the collective security arrangements that would follow the war, while Russian participation in a liberal economic order might eventually open the Soviet economy. His positive view of future Soviet behavior set him apart from many within his own administration, not to mention Congress and the broader American public.[91] But even the president's sanguine expectations for Stalin had its limits: the United States would not share the secrets of the atomic bomb project with the Soviet dictator. When Stalin learned of the bomb anyway through his espionage network, it merely served to confirm his suspicions about the Anglo-Americans.[92]

Under Roosevelt's leadership, the United States fought the Second World War in pursuit of both military and other long-term politico-economic national objectives. Defeat of Germany and Japan came first, to be sure, but that goal did not crowd out all others. As a clear indication, the United States sent significant military resources to China under Lend-Lease and recommended to the British that they pursue major military operations in Burma to reopen the land route to the Nationalists, the Burma Road. American aid to China continued even after it became evident that Chiang Kai-shek would not pursue offensive operations against the Japanese. The British viewed Burma differently, as a stepping-stone in the reconquest of other Japanese-occupied British possessions to the southeast (Malaya and Singapore).[93] In a like spirit, the United States refused to back Churchill's scheme to attack in the Greek Dodecanese in 1944. "God forbid if I should try to dictate," General Marshall told the prime minister bluntly, "but not one American soldier is going to die on that goddamned island."[94] As the Americans saw it, the British pushed the idea not as the best way to defeat Germany but as a step designed to restore a British presence in the Balkans and Mediterranean after the war, a design at odds with Roosevelt's opposition to spheres of influence. Roosevelt, then, fully appreciated that the war was an appropriate instrument to pursue a range of national war goals.

"Doctor Win-the-War"

Total war entails a broad redirection of economic activity, with far-reaching social consequences. Even with expanded wartime powers, government in a market-oriented society such as the United States must still induce the voluntary cooperation of major private actors. To meet the challenge of mobilization for global war, Roosevelt found it necessary to reach out to some of his most bitter political adversaries, but the political cost was high. They already had checked the momentum of his New Deal. They used their enhanced wartime leverage to gnaw at its political underpinnings and make certain its advocates would not frame the terms for postwar politics. Meanwhile, as a consequence of social forces set in motion by mobilization—demands by African Americans for equal treatment in factories and in the military—the president's political coalition threatened to fracture on racial lines. Racial polarization struck another blow against the fading prospects for further social reform.

American mobilization for total war began months before Pearl Harbor but would still require several years to bear fruit. After Roosevelt finally accepted the need to commence planning for war in mid-1941, military and civilian planners quickly generated a document referred to as the Victory Program. This anticipated that American forces would be ready for full-scale offensive operations by summer 1943. Although based on key assumptions that proved incorrect (such as the possibility that both the Soviet Union and Great Britain might be defeated), the program's estimate of 8.8 million Army and Air Force personnel was very close to the actual mid-1945 figures.[95] Adding estimates for the navy and for Lend-Lease, the Victory Program arrived at total economic requirements for the 1943 target date much higher than the initial mobilization program had anticipated. Skeptics questioned whether such production goals could be achieved, but the president announced them as targets in his State of the Union message to Congress one month after Pearl Harbor. Remarkably, the American economy would achieve the production miracles the Victory Program promised: besides meeting nearly all of its own military needs, the United States supplied an additional $40 billion in defense output for its allies.[96]

Through the massive program of war production, Roosevelt took the first step toward rapprochement with his erstwhile antagonists in corporate America. The War Production Board (WPB), directed by Donald M. Nelson, a former retail business executive, sought to steer economic mobilization through a system of committees. Much as the Wilson administration had drawn upon the expertise of corporate leaders in the First World War, the WPB tapped businessmen to staff its functional divisions and industrial advisory boards. Business leaders also were invited to comment on all plans, and large firms did especially well because Nelson, other WPB officials, and the military believed only major corporations could fill big orders quickly.

As a further sweetener, procurement contracts were on a cost-plus basis that provided, in the words of historian David M. Kennedy, "ironclad guarantees of profits beyond the most avaricious monopolist's dreams."[97] These inducements to business helped to address one of the president's long-standing political problems—the alienation of American capital from his administration. Alas, the committees and contracts did little to clear up production logjams stemming from a decentralized procurement process under which the military services placed their own orders and made demands for scarce resources. Various administrative expedients were tried in 1942–1943 that eventually led to a more efficient allocation of resources.[98]

Political and military leaders also quarreled about what to build. For instance, in the first months after the United States entered the war, the president and his advisors debated whether it made more sense to meet the U-boat threat by building anti-submarine warfare ships or more merchant vessels. Sometimes, too, the allure of glamour weapons like battleships eclipsed the appeal of the humble equipment that meant at least as much to the war effort. Allied operations were compromised until well into 1944 by the lack of landing craft with which to move troops onto enemy beaches. (To appreciate how important these little vessels were, note that every significant American campaign of the war began with an amphibious operation.) Eventually American factories turned out more than 40,000 landing craft of all types, but that impressive total masks the inattention to the need that characterized early war mobilization and the resultant shortages that forced Allied planners to choose between or delay operations.[99]

Roosevelt believed that setting ambitious targets would goad industry to produce more than most believed possible, but his approach also had a downside. The focus on quantity above all else, for example, led to an emphasis on older and cheaper aircraft models rather than modern types the Army Air Force needed for its strategic bomber offensives.[100]

Although hardly brilliant, the Roosevelt administration's economic mobilization efforts stand up well in a comparative light. Interestingly, the time needed to rationalize war production after Pearl Harbor was about the same as the Wilson administration required to sort out its economic efforts following American entry into World War I. It helped that the lingering effects of the Depression left the United States in early 1942 with considerable slack industrial capacity and unused manpower that could be converted quickly to military production.[101] Compared to the military output of the other belligerents, the American mobilization record shines. American industry in 1944 produced 40 percent of total world military output. Great Britain, which began full rearmament in 1938, could not come close to meeting its needs in either quantity or quality, and relied heavily on Lend-Lease to equip its forces. This dependence gave the United States economic leverage, too, that the administration used to secure open access to the British Empire.[102]

By contrast, the Soviet Union outproduced the United States in tanks, with a basic design in the T-34 that surpassed the American M-4 medium tank in many respects. But with little need for a navy, Soviet industry was free to concentrate on a narrower range of armaments, while the Red Army relied heavily on some 350,000 trucks supplied under Lend-Lease to keep moving in its great offensives in the last two years of the war. American equipment for the British and Soviet militaries traveled across the oceans in the 2,700 Liberty ships built between late 1941 and 1945, a remarkable total that still represented less than half of the ships built in American yards during the war.[103] As for the Axis powers, Germany suffered from divided and wasteful industrial production until Albert Speer became armaments minister in 1942, Italy never came close to equipping a modern army before its 1943 surrender, and American industry outproduced its Japanese counterpart in every category, including at least eighty more aircraft carriers during the war.[104]

The president and his advisors weighed how best to pay the enormous cost of mobilization but often were compelled to sacrifice their preferred solutions to political necessity. As with other wartime administrations, Roosevelt's settled on a mix of new taxes and borrowing. Even before the United States entered the war, policy makers lowered exemptions, imposed a surtax on higher incomes, and increased corporate taxes. The 1942 Revenue Act sharply lowered the personal exemption that had spared most Americans the need to file a tax return and added 13 million new taxpayers to the system.[105] Revenues continued to lag behind administration goals, though, leading the Treasury Department to propose a radical policy departure in 1943: rather than pay taxes on income in the previous year, payroll deductions on current income would be combined with the previous year's obligations to generate a one-time revenue surge.

But the measure, however sound as a device to boost revenues in a time of national need, proved too unpopular in its original form. Over administration objections, Congress approved taxing current 1943 income through withholding, but also forgave 75 percent of 1942 tax liabilities. This pattern continued the following year as a rising federal deficit prompted the president to request new taxes and Congress responded with a bill (passed over a presidential veto) that offset some of the increase with a freeze on or rollback of other taxes. For lawmakers, 1944 was an election year, and they had something besides a war to win.[106]

Despite the tax increases, expenditures still outpaced revenues, forcing the Treasury Department to borrow heavily. Bond drives yielded more than $150 billion, while also serving as an activity to engage the broad public in supporting the war effort. As a measure of administration success, the United States never faced the possibility of running out of money to pay for the war, and inflation, though worrisome at times and a political flashpoint, never spiraled out of control.[107]

Mobilization for total war also generated political effects that forced Roosevelt to choose between political constituencies whose support he needed. On one side stood the core of his New Deal coalition, organized labor and reformers deeply invested in the future of social reform. On the other were aligned many of his political enemies, now indispensable to war production and legislation required for the war effort.

The president did his best to appease both factions, an impossible challenge. Much as they had done under Wilson, conservative forces became bolder, picking off parts of the New Deal that lacked broad popular backing. Bowing to the new political reality, the president professed his enduring commitment to reform even as he eschewed confrontation with the political right.

Wartime labor demands initially empowered the union movement. As conscription absorbed working men, labor shortages drove up wages and encouraged union militancy, evident as early as 1941 in a wave of strikes that affected defense industries. Roosevelt responded by establishing a National War Labor Board (NWLB), with government, business, and labor representation, to avert strikes or lockouts for the duration. Through a "maintenance of membership" policy established in May 1942 that required newly hired workers in unionized workplaces to join the union, the NWLB offered organized labor a sturdy shield— so long as union leaders kept their members in line. Union membership soared to nearly 15 million workers during the war years.[108]

For many workers, however, the government seemed to take away more than it gave. As part of the effort to restrain inflation, the NWLB imposed limits on wage increases that did not quite match rising prices. This set the stage for confrontations between business management and rank-and-file workers. Strikes without the backing of American Federation of Labor or Congress of Industrial Organizations leaders became more frequent in 1943. Not all work stoppages took place against the wishes of top figures in the labor movement, however. John L. Lewis, the independent and cantankerous head of the United Mine Workers, led his members on a strike in 1943 when the NWLB rejected his demand for significant wage increases. For Roosevelt, the miners' strike was a political nightmare—it pitted national security, strongly backed by conservatives, against a key constituency within his political coalition. The president seized the mines and ordered the union members back to work, but Lewis also achieved a favorable wage settlement that provoked sharp criticism of the administration.[109] In the wake of perceived administration leniency toward illegal strikes, conservative attacks on the New Deal political order gathered steam.

Roosevelt's political foes soon got their chance. With few battlefield successes in the first eleven months after Pearl Harbor to offset the annoyances of increased wartime bureaucracy and rising prices, voters vented their frustrations on the party in power in the 1942 elections. Democrats took it on the chin—a loss of forty-seven seats in the House of Representatives and seven in the Senate, along with several governorships that included the president's home state of New York (to Thomas E. Dewey, the Republican candidate for president in 1944 and 1948). The incoming Congress had a pronounced rightward tilt, with a majority consisting of anti-Roosevelt, anti–New Deal members, including southern Democrats and conservative Republicans.[110] As conservative business leaders became central players in wartime economic mobilization, so, too, did conservative political leaders now assume a dominant role in the legislative process. They used their position to begin undoing the reform structure the president and his political allies had put in place over the previous decade.

The New Dealers, though, refused to admit that their day had passed. In their view, the war confirmed that government spending could achieve full employment, but they worried that the end of massive defense outlays when peace returned would plunge the economy into a new depression. Social spending, they suggested, might serve as a substitute, providing the necessary economic stimulus.[111] Their analysis missed the transformative economic effects of the war—how the explosive economic resurgence laid a foundation for sustained postwar consumer demand and how the dominant international economic position of the United States would give it a trade advantage that would last for decades. Instead, the New Dealers looked back to the severe downturn that had followed the hasty demobilization after World War I. (Evidently generals are not alone in fighting the last war.) The reform impulse found its fullest expression in the National Resources Planning Board (NRPB), which issued reports that urged comprehensive postwar planning to secure full employment. Still wedded to a Depression-era sensibility, the NRPB assumed a permanent need for government stimulus.[112]

Conservatives, including southerners in the president's own party, saw the domestic political future very differently. With the New Deal effectively blocked even before the war—no major domestic legislation passed after 1938—conservatives set out, in David Kennedy's apt phrase, "to drive a stake through its heart." The 73rd Congress by the end of

1943 had eliminated such New Deal mainstays as the Civilian Conservation Corps and the Works Progress Administration. Rejecting the New Dealers' approach to planned demobilization, Congress also voted to terminate the NRPB. At the same time, however, Roosevelt's foes declined to test their strength against popular New Deal programs such as Social Security and minimum wage laws, while southern Democrats remained attached to agricultural programs that favored their constituents.[113]

The unpopularity of wartime strikes, especially the disruptive mineworkers' stoppage, also created an opening for conservatives to legislate against organized labor. Congress overrode a Roosevelt veto to pass the Smith-Connally Act, which permitted the president to seize companies or industries in response to a strike and imposed criminal penalties on a union that promoted a strike after such a seizure. In a direct slap at the pivotal role organized labor played in the Democratic Party, the measure also prohibited union campaign contributions.[114]

Social dislocations generated by the war brought the president's political coalition under acute pressure from yet another direction, too. During Roosevelt's first two terms, he had drawn together an uneasy alliance of white southern Democrats, working-class white ethnics in northern cities, liberals who favored racial moderation, and a modest but growing number of northern African Americans. This was an inherently unstable mix that could endure only so long as he and his party could keep racial issues off the agenda or address them with symbolic gestures.[115]

The war made that impossible. In search of jobs in the expanding war industries, blacks migrated from the rural South to cities there and elsewhere, only to find themselves barred from most openings. African Americans demanded that the United States practice at home the values the president claimed Americans were fighting for abroad. When A. Phillip Randolph threatened a march on Washington on July 1, 1941, to protest the exclusion of blacks from defense plants, Roosevelt agreed to issue an executive order to assure that hiring in defense industries would be done without regard to race and establish a Fair Employment Practices Commission (FEPC) to investigate and act on complaints.[116] In his 1942 State of the Union Address he also declared that racial discrimination in hiring impeded war mobilization. But even the smallest steps to assure fair treatment aroused the ire of southern politicians in his own party, who condemned all federal intervention in race relations in their home region and hinted at grave electoral consequences for the Democratic Party.[117]

Meanwhile, as the military continued to segregate black troops and assign them to menial duties, racial incidents, including violence, increased on military bases. Unions also resisted pressures to accept non-white members, despite federal government prohibitions on discrimination. As black workers began to secure factory jobs that previously had been open only to whites, resentful whites interrupted production with "hate strikes" to protest such things as having to share restrooms with their black co-workers. The friction spilled over outside the plants, too, and led to episodes of broad-scale violence in a number of cities, including Mobile and Detroit in 1943.[118]

Roosevelt sought to remain above racial controversy, preferring to allow various agencies to address the conflicts. Race relations represented his worst political nightmare: any stance he took would have carried a political price that might cost him reelection or split his party. Consider the FEPC: after Roosevelt bowed to southern white demands in 1942 to curb the commission by subordinating it to the War Manpower Commission, he faced so much liberal criticism that he felt compelled to backtrack the following year, restoring its independence and increasing its budget and staff.[119] Not surprisingly, most of the heavy lifting against racial discrimination was done below the presidential level—the War Labor Board banned racial differentials in wages in 1943, the U.S. Employment Service prohibited race-specific job listings, and the National Labor Relations Board ruled it would not certify unions that barred minority members.[120] The armed forces also responded to the racial challenge by desegregating bases, beginning an educational campaign against racial prejudice, and taking the first tentative steps to integrate units, mostly on an ad hoc basis and in response to manpower shortages.[121] Apart from an occasional speech, however, Roosevelt avoided action on matters of race. He feared, with cause, sparking a revolt by his party's powerful southern wing. The Democratic vote in the South declined in 1944, an omen of the fate of the party in the postwar era.[122]

At a press conference in late 1943, Roosevelt seemed to recognize that the Great Depression and the reformist political momentum that it had inspired were gone for good. The crisis had necessitated bold steps for recovery, he said, but these had succeeded and "Doctor New Deal" was no longer needed. Now the time had come for "Doctor Win-the-War" to organize the great effort to defeat the menace posed by German Nazism and Japanese militarism. Yet just a few weeks later, in his 1944 State of the Union Address, the president issued a stirring call for an economic bill of rights to guarantee every citizen a job, a living wage, adequate housing and medical care, education, and protection from a range of circumstances that would leave people insecure. It may have been his most radical speech in terms of advocacy of public social provision, and liberals reacted enthusiastically to his call. But the speech could amount to little more than campaign posturing for the 1944 race, something with which to inspire the political legions of the left. Major legislative proposals did not follow, for the sensible reason that they would have gone nowhere in the conservative Congress and done no more than highlight the president's political weakness.[123]

Strategies for Global War

Franklin Roosevelt picked outstanding men to help him plan and direct American military operations in the Second World War. It helped, as historians have noted, that the president already knew how to build an effective political coalition because that exercise resembled assembling a powerful military force.[124] Typical of Roosevelt, he rejected recommendations to appoint an overall military commander (whose power might have offset his own) and let the membership of the new Joint Chiefs of Staff (JCS) evolve in the early war period, without ever giving the body formal authority.[125]

In George C. Marshall, the army chief of staff, the president found a truly extraordinary military leader to guide the formation of the largest field army in American history, select many of its key leaders, and keep Allied strategy properly focused.[126] Ernest J. King, installed as commander in chief of the United States Navy just after Pearl Harbor and soon thereafter also as chief of naval operations, demonstrated a keen grasp of global strategic tensions. Although seen by many, especially the

British, as fixated on the Pacific, King understood the need to balance the demands of what were effectively two simultaneous wars.[127] General Henry "Hap" Arnold, brought into the JCS structure at Marshall's behest, oversaw the air campaigns against both adversaries. Strategic bombing was a particular concern of a president who regarded air power first as a key deterrent and then as an essential instrument of victory.

Beneath this senior troika, the leadership team included a striking array of military and political talent. The war brought to the fore a number of excellent commanders, particularly General Dwight Eisenhower and Admiral Chester Nimitz. Eisenhower held the most sensitive commands in the European theater, for which political and diplomatic skills mattered at least as much as military talent. Nimitz assumed control of the Pacific Fleet after the Pearl Harbor disaster, guided it through the crucial first year when the Japanese enjoyed naval superiority, and then directed the counteroffensive across the Central Pacific toward Japan. Other key advisors included Admiral William D. Leahy, who headed the JCS and served as the president's go-between with the three service chiefs. On the civilian side, no man was of greater value to Roosevelt than the versatile Harry Hopkins, who functioned as an intermediary between Marshall and the president and acted as the president's personal emissary with key Allied leaders such as Churchill and Stalin.[128]

Among the senior American commanders, the president found General Douglas MacArthur to be the most problematic, at once politically valuable and politically difficult. MacArthur started the war badly, overestimating the capacity of air power in the Philippines to deter the Japanese and then seeing his bombers caught on the ground hours after receiving word of the Pearl Harbor attack. Compounding his initial mistakes, he then ignored the established plan for an early, prepared retreat into Bataan in the event of a Japanese invasion in favor of a futile attempt to throw back the attackers on the beaches. Still, when American and Philippine soldiers quickly fell back to Bataan anyway, they waged a valiant defense, which endured until Corregidor was overwhelmed at the beginning of May 1942.[129] The president by then had ordered MacArthur to leave for Australia, from which he famously pledged to return.

Here the politics began. MacArthur had many friends among American conservatives, and if he voiced complaint about the abandonment of his Philippine forces (an outcome long expected in American war planning), the administration could face a firestorm of criticism at a time when American military fortunes were at low ebb. Better, then, to secure the general's silence by portraying him as a hero (hence his Congressional Medal of Honor) and giving him a command far from the center of press attention (hence he would operate from Australia). Historian Eric Larrabee succinctly captures the president's problem with his most egomaniacal general: having built up the MacArthur legend, Roosevelt could not thereafter undo it. He would have to live with MacArthur, headaches and all, and manage him.[130]

The military situation the president and his advisors faced in the first months of the war was bleak. The Japanese followed up their successful opening air attacks with a bold offensive that brought them control not only over the Philippines but also Malaya, Singapore, Burma, the Netherlands East Indies, and a number of Pacific Islands such as New Britain (with its important harbor at Rabaul) and Papua New Guinea. Convinced that the United States lacked the stomach for a long war, the Japanese strategists sought to establish a thick defensive shell, its outer perimeter far from their homeland. This would force the U.S. military to exhaust itself in costly battles until the American government agreed to sue for peace on terms that would leave Japan in possession of the strategic resources it needed. Japan's capture of Burma also isolated China by land, so that supplies to Chiang Kai-shek's forces could only be delivered via a difficult air route. By spring 1942, the Japanese had advanced far enough to threaten vital lines of communications between the United States and Australia.

On the other side of the world, the Germans had been thrown back in their attempt to capture Moscow in late 1941, but American and British leaders still doubted whether the Soviet Union could survive. England, having been spared from a possible invasion when Hitler turned east, continued to face heavy bombing raids. In the Middle East German and Italian forces battled British Empire troops in Libya, while the two sides fought for control of the Mediterranean shipping lanes. Wide-ranging U-boat attacks that extended as far as the American East Coast and Caribbean inflicted mounting losses on Allied shipping.[131] In the face of these multiple threats, the United States as yet had few combat-ready units.

Confirming the understanding arrived at before the United States became a belligerent, Anglo-American grand strategy treated Germany as the main enemy.[132] Roosevelt, Churchill, and their military advisors agreed that only the Nazi regime could potentially defeat the Allies, particularly if the Russians were beaten on the European mainland and German U-boats severed the sea lifeline from the United States to Great Britain. Already Stalin clamored for the Anglo-Americans to open a second front to draw off German forces. Increasing losses to German submarine attacks meanwhile raised doubts about whether the United States could meet British supply needs and build up a field army for an eventual attack on the European mainland.

"Germany First" did not mean, however, that the war in the Pacific could be ignored. As King understood, a strictly defensive posture in what was primarily a naval war made no sense—the ocean itself cannot be held. He insisted that protecting the sea route to Australia and New Zealand required at least opportunistic attacks, a position the president shared.[133] Further, the president remained determined to keep China in the war, believing at this early stage that Chiang's Nationalist armies could make a substantial contribution to Allied victory. For political reasons, too, the Pacific theater demanded attention. The Japanese had struck Pearl Harbor and inflicted humiliating defeats on U.S. forces in the Philippines, on Wake Island, and elsewhere. Americans felt a much deeper hatred for their Japanese enemies—a passion heightened by racial animosity—than for the Germans.

For Anglo-American political leaders and senior military commanders, the great strategic debate about the war against Germany involved how best to engage the enemy on terms likely to bring Allied victory. This debate, which started in early 1942, continued to the very last months of the war in Europe and has been the focus of extensive historical commentary.[134] I will concentrate here on the central themes and the factors that shaped the final resolution. At the heart of the dispute lay the question of when to launch an invasion of France across the English Channel. Narrow though the issue may appear, it embodied a range of others, primarily political in nature—how best to maintain the cooperation of the Soviet Union during and after the war, the political fate of postwar Europe, the relative influence of the United States and Great Britain in wartime policy and the postwar order, and more.

The American view, expressed forcefully from the outset by Marshall, held that the cross-Channel assault should be made as early as possible because the Germans could only be defeated by a direct clash on the main battlefront. Sometimes mischaracterized as an unimaginative attrition strategy (which is how the British chose to see it),[135] this approach did not preclude operational creativity and flexibility. But the American perspective also recognized that the Allies did not have unlimited time with which to work. The longer the delay before an invasion, the stronger the Germans could make their defenses. There was an "opportunity cost" to be paid in the Pacific, too, where time would allow the Japanese to better fortify their positions.[136] Moreover, the relationship between the Anglo-American allies and the Soviet Union remained fragile. Too long a delay before the cross-Channel invasion, American planners worried, might result in Soviet defeat (a concern until the German surrender at Stalingrad in early 1943), provoke Stalin to seek a separate peace with Hitler (a persistent fear), or let the Red Army advance all the way across Europe (a prospect that loomed larger as Soviet forces drove the Germans back from the second half of 1943 onward).

Although the British agreed that an invasion would be necessary at some point, they countered that a premature attack could result in catastrophe. Having fought the Germans in Norway, France, Greece, Crete, and North Africa and come off second best each time, the British had a healthy respect for German military prowess. They wanted to meet the Germans on favorable terms.[137] To Churchill and his senior military aides, such as General Alan Brooke, Chief of the Imperial General Staff, this meant using their forces and American troops in campaigns that would wear down the Axis and draw off enough German resources from France to give an invasion a fair chance of success.[138] The British preferred to continue and extend the war in the Middle East, including assaults on North Africa and later Sicily, Italy, and perhaps Greece and the Balkans. Churchill spoke of the approach as striking the "soft underbelly of Europe," an evocative phrase but one that rang hollow to the Allied troops sent there who found it anything but yielding. Still, fighting in the Mediterranean did hold the prospect of driving Italy out of the war and would force Hitler to defend not just Italy but other points where Allied forces might land. At the same time, the Red Army would engage the main mass of the *Wehrmacht* on the Eastern Front, inflicting heavy losses though at the price of enormous Soviet casualties. (The British were willing to fight to the last Russian,[139] but Stalin would have done the reverse without remorse.) British caution reflected another legitimate fear as well: the cross-Channel invasion would be a colossal gamble, because if it failed it could never be repeated.

Upon the two political principals, Roosevelt and Churchill, fell the unenviable task of adjudicating between the competing approaches. Each man shared the outlook of his military subordinates. Churchill worked relentlessly to postpone the cross-Channel invasion virtually to the moment it was launched in June 1944. However, to mollify the Americans—and prevent them from shifting their main war effort to the Pacific—he reaffirmed the British commitment to a campaign in northwest Europe at a date unspecified.[140] He never did fix the date.

Roosevelt thus became the pivotal figure in determining whether and when the invasion would proceed. Over the objections of his own military advisors, he recognized compelling reasons in 1942 to delay the attack at least until 1943, and then did so again early the following year when he agreed to postpone it until 1944. But when he concluded in late summer 1943 that the necessary conditions for a successful assault were present, he insisted the invasion be scheduled for spring 1944 and never wavered in his commitment, notwithstanding repeated pleas by Churchill and Brooke.[141]

Several considerations entered into Roosevelt's initial decision to take sides against Marshall and the American military in 1942 and order the invasion of Vichy-controlled North Africa. The Victory Program did not anticipate the availability of major American ground forces before mid-1943, so any early invasion would be a largely British affair. Delayed American mobilization thus had an obvious consequence: lacking troops to put into battle, the United States was in no position to insist on a campaign in which American troops would not bear the brunt of the fight. Vital equipment needed for an invasion—especially, for reasons I examined, landing craft—was in short supply and would remain so for many months. More important, British planners pointed out that the Germans could reinforce any invasion site in France much faster than the Allies could build up a beachhead.[142]

To postpone all U.S. military operations against German forces until sometime in 1943, however, would have political repercussions. The president hoped American troops would enter combat in the European theater before the 1942 elections. More important, with American eyes riveted on the Pacific, where U.S. troops from August 1942 onward were already fighting the Japanese in savage battles on Guadalcanal and New Guinea, popular pressure would mount to send greater resources there, potentially undercutting the "Germany First" commitment.[143] By accepting the British position, Roosevelt also gained a political advantage in Allied war councils. He showed that he could rise above national parochialism. This would enhance the legitimacy of his decision when the time arrived to press for the land campaign in Northwest Europe. There were the Russians to consider, too. If the Anglo-Americans could not open a true second front to satisfy Stalin, they needed to demonstrate a commitment to broaden their operations against Germany as the Soviets faced another major offensive in summer 1942.[144] Last, where a cross-Channel attack represented an irrevocable toss of the dice, North Africa, though risky, meant an encounter with French forces, which might not resist.

Instead of invading France, then, American and British troops landed in Morocco and Algeria in November 1942 (Operation TORCH), a campaign that drew American forces deeper into the Mediterranean theater. (To the president's credit, he did not insist the operation be mounted before Election Day and raised no complaint when TORCH came a week later.)[145] The notion that TORCH would not compel a particular subsequent path of operations proved, as Marshall had feared, illusory.[146] In early 1943, a combination of circumstances—the need to continue active operations somewhere in the European theater after the defeat of German-Italian forces in Tunisia, the impossibility of transporting many Allied soldiers back to England, and the desire to force Italian capitulation—led to the decision to invade Sicily (Operation HUSKY).[147] The American leadership again capitulated to the British agenda: grand strategy at times, as one historian puts it, "has to be a question of taking the least bad compromise alternative."[148]

HUSKY resulted in Mussolini being deposed and arrested. The inevitable next step saw Allied forces land in Italy. As hoped, Italy surrendered (and promptly switched sides), and the Allies secured useful air bases around Foggia from which to mount strategic bombing assaults on parts of the Third Reich out of range of aircraft based in England.[149] But the Germans swiftly moved additional units into Italy, and the Allied campaign stalled in late 1943 well south of Rome.[150]

Meanwhile, the British-American debate over the best course to pursue in Europe continued. Invading Italy made a cross-Channel invasion impossible in 1943, but it left open the next step. Churchill and the British preferred to continue the main effort in the Mediterranean, with attacks in the Dodecanese that would tie down German divisions away from France or from use against the Red Army on the Eastern Front and might induce Turkey to enter the war on the Allied side.[151] Further, Churchill and some of his officers (Brooke and Harold Alexander, commanding in Italy) maintained that the best route into central Europe lay through Italy, despite overwhelming evidence that the mountainous terrain there favored the defense.[152] American military leaders, on the other hand, dismissed further investments in the Mediterranean as a wasteful diversion from the main event. They also suspected that the British were motivated by a desire to restore their political influence in the Balkans and Turkey.[153] Hovering in the background were increasingly tense relations with Stalin, who by mid-1943 had lost patience with the Anglo-Americans and their repeated promises to open the Second Front in France.[154]

This time, at the Anglo-American Quebec conference in August 1943, Roosevelt came down firmly on the side of Marshall. He rejected the British alternatives in Italy and the Mediterranean in favor of the invasion of Normandy, Operation OVERLORD, on or about May 1, 1944. (Weather led to a one-month postponement, so D-Day came on June 6, 1944.) By this point, the American buildup in England was well under way and the Allied navies had defeated the U-boat threat in the Atlantic. With American forces in the European theater finally surpassing those of Great Britain, the president no longer felt he needed to defer to the British.[155] He also concluded that the invasion must have an American commander (Eisenhower rather than Marshall, for a number of reasons),[156] though the key deputies would be British. The American percentage would increase until by the end of the war the United States contributed approximately two-thirds of the Anglo-American troops fighting in Germany. As for the British role in northwest Europe, it would be limited as its manpower began to decline during the Normandy campaign—the price paid for pursuing campaigns designed to wear down German strength around the periphery of Europe. The president also stood behind Marshall's demand to make available seven American divisions that had been fighting in Italy for use in France.[157] By stripping troops from Italy and rejecting further ventures in the Mediterranean, he also denied the British, especially Churchill, the prestige they desperately wanted of leading a major campaign at the close of the war. Henceforth Italy would be a backwater, where Allied advances (and heavy casualties) after mid-1944 did little to bring on German defeat.[158]

Having made the pivotal decision of the war in the European theater, Roosevelt receded into the background.[159] He did not intervene directly in the conduct of the invasion or the subsequent campaign across France to the German border in summer and fall 1944. To Marshall and Eisenhower he left the operational choices (whether to advance on a broad front or, as the British preferred, in a single thrust), but the defeat of Germany became a matter of time once the Allies gained a foothold in Normandy. Nor did he interfere in the relentless strategic bombing campaign that laid waste German industries and cities. Only on rare occasions, such as the ill-fated raid on the Ploesti, Rumania, oil facilities in 1943, did he involve himself directly.[160] In the last year of his life, Roosevelt focused his attention in Europe not on military matters but on the postwar settlement, an appropriate concern for a political leader.

By contrast with the deliberate approach Allied strategists adopted in the war against the Third Reich, the struggle with Japan forced the American military to respond to events and seize opportunities as they appeared. Here, too, Roosevelt initially played an active role. He supported the morale-lifting Doolittle Raid in April 1942. When the Japanese responded with a strike aimed at Midway, the stage was set for Nimitz to direct the pivotal American naval victory. King saw this as the moment to begin his own limited counteroffensive by U.S. Marines in the Solomon Islands, again with the president's backing.

The result was an epic campaign on an island virtually no American before the war could have found on a map—Guadalcanal. In the seesaw struggle that followed, American military leaders several times considered withdrawal, especially when the Japanese landed massive reinforcements in October. Roosevelt insisted that all possible help be sent to Guadalcanal, and the U.S. troops held.[161] Although both sides lost heavily, especially in ships, the American losses would soon be made good while the Japanese would never recover. The president also looked ahead to the day when the Japanese homeland could be subjected to more than a nuisance bombing raid. He supported the enormous investment in a new, very heavy bomber project that became the B-29 bomber—and the Manhattan Project to create the atomic weapon that the B-29 would deliver.

The arrival of more American troops, more and better aircraft, and new ships made possible a general counteroffensive across the Pacific.[162] So much arrived by mid-1943, in fact, that U.S. commanders could advance along two axes.[163] In the southwest Pacific, U.S. and Australian forces under MacArthur moved in jumps along the northern coast of Papua New Guinea, bypassing and cutting off Japanese garrisons. By summer 1944, the Allied advance had neutralized the key base at Rabaul and MacArthur contemplated his return to the Philippines.[164] The second line of approach, directed by Nimitz, carried American forces across the Central Pacific, with costly invasions in the Marshall, Caroline, and Mariana Islands. In June 1944, at the Battle of the Philippine Sea, American naval aviators effectively destroyed their Japanese opposites, which meant that the U.S. fleet no longer needed to fear carrier attacks.[165] The capture of Saipan and Tinian in the Marianas also meant that Japan itself could be reached by the new B-29 bombers. In all these campaigns, the president played little direct role, with the decisions about where and when to attack left largely in the hands of the military professionals.

An important exception occurred in mid-1944, when the president traveled to Hawaii to meet with MacArthur, King, and Nimitz. MacArthur's and Nimitz's successes raised the question of where to attack next. MacArthur adamantly urged the liberation of the Philippines. Navy opinion was split: King preferred a jump to Formosa (Taiwan); Nimitz saw value in seizing airfields and sea bases in the Philippines;

other senior officers preferred seizure of Iwo Jima and Okinawa. The matter might have been resolved within the military through compromises, especially since the loss of American airfields in eastern China in the previous months meant the Formosa option would yield fewer military returns and little was expected by this point of Chiang Kai-shek's forces.[166] But 1944 was an election year, and the president faced another campaign. Indeed, the Hawaii conference functioned in part as an opportunity for the president to be photographed with his victorious commanders, much to the chagrin of MacArthur and King, who disliked being turned into campaign props.

But MacArthur knew how to play the political card, too. The general told his commander in chief that the American people would never stand for abandoning the Philippines after its people had fought so hard for the United States at the start of the war. Perhaps "blackmail" is too strong, but the implied threat—in Max Hastings's words, "the general's political friends would raise a storm among American voters"—was not lost on the president. Given the lack of a clear military rationale for an alternative, the political calculations likely tipped the balance.[167] MacArthur got his invasion, with full support from the navy.

As often happens in war, the decision had unforeseen consequences, some salutary but others not. The invasion of Leyte in September 1944 drew out most of the remaining Japanese fleet for an epic clash in Leyte Gulf. The U.S. Navy destroyed what remained of Japanese sea power. But once started on his campaign to reclaim the archipelago, MacArthur would not stop. His liberation continued with a series of landings and engagements that led to heavy American casualties and far greater losses among the civilian population, while doing nothing to speed the end of the war.[168] The violence was pointless—the Philippines would be fully liberated when the Japanese surrendered, without MacArthur's ongoing ego offensive. Still, Roosevelt and the Joint Chiefs declined to incur the political price of arousing the general's friends to stop him.

While American forces advanced across the Pacific toward Japan, a separate war was waged by the Allies in the Far East in what they designated the China-Burma-India (CBI) theater. Militarily, it meant little to the outcome of the war against Japan, which is why the theater command received the fewest resources of any Allied front. On the other hand, in political terms, the region mattered greatly to leaders in Great Britain and the United States. Both Roosevelt and Churchill saw the CBI theater as vital to the postwar order within the region and beyond, though their visions for the future were very different.

Roosevelt, as we've seen, intended that China play the part of a great power, one of the Big Four, in his postwar order. He first sought to supply the Nationalist armies so they could tie down major Japanese forces. But Chiang Kai-shek had his own agenda, one that did not include risking his troops against a Japanese enemy they had failed time and again to defeat in battle. No amount of aid or cajoling by American emissaries could make him fight.[169] The sober realization that China could contribute little to Allied victory prompted Roosevelt to cancel a planned amphibious operation across the Bay of Bengal in 1943 to recapture Rangoon and reopen the Burma Road—one of the rare times he overruled his own military chiefs.[170] The president also believed long-range bombers in eastern China might strike directly at Japan. At enormous expense, airfields were constructed, only to be captured easily in 1944 by Japanese troops.[171] Still, it served the president's long-term political purposes to prop up Chiang, so both leaders continued the pretense that China was contributing to the Allied cause.[172]

Roosevelt also aimed to prevent the reestablishment of colonial control in Southeast Asia, putting him directly at odds with Churchill. Versions of international trusteeships for erstwhile colonial holdings had been under discussion among leaders of the Big Four since 1943 but faced British and French objections.[173] The president refused to approve the addition of French officers to the Allied command in Southeast Asia because he feared it would signal a commitment to restore French control over postwar Indochina. He hoped to see Chiang's government assume some kind of temporary stewardship over the former French colony, in keeping with China's anticipated role as a major power. (For his part, the generalissimo preferred immediate independence for Indochina, expecting it would fall permanently under Chinese dominance.)[174]

In stark contrast, Churchill maintained that the old colonial order could be reestablished and preserved. The British leader refused to concede Indian independence, despite evident popular support for the Congress Party and its program.[175] Churchill also intended to use India as the gateway back to Burma, Malaya, and Singapore. Accordingly, after defeating a last-throw-of-the dice Japanese attack against Imphal and Kohima near the Burma-India border in the first half of 1944, British and Indian troops under General William Slim launched an offensive that utterly destroyed the Japanese army in Burma in 1945. Like MacArthur's later assaults in the Philippines, Slim's campaign did nothing to hasten the defeat of Japan—its forces in Burma were already cut off and could contribute nothing to the defense of the homeland. But as part of Churchill's postwar program, the venture acquired a political logic.[176] In the same spirit, invasions of Malaya and then Singapore were in the planning stage when the war ended.

Roosevelt's hands-off posture in the latter stages of both the European and Pacific wars raises the question of how much direction he really exercised over the course of events. That he continued to seek freedom of action remains clear from his determination to avoid on-the-record decisions as much as possible. Testimony by Marshall and other senior military commanders confirms that they often discussed with the president the political implications of military options, but Roosevelt insisted that no notes or minutes be taken. (For example, we do not have a record of the 1944 Hawaii conference on the Philippines invasion; the putative exchanges were reported subsequently by the participants and are open to question.)

Just the same, much as the president wished to hold open his options, the decisions he made compelled or invited others, choices that could not be reversed except at a high political price. When he approved the invasion of North Africa in 1942, American forces entered a path that led deeper into the Mediterranean than his military commanders deemed wise or necessary. The soldiers fought in Sicily and then Italy, a campaign that went on too long and cost too many lives because halting it outright would further antagonize the British.[177] Much the same could be said for the Philippines and the bloody invasions that marked the closing months of the Pacific war. For all the self-sacrificing courage demonstrated by U.S. Marines on Iwo Jima, capture of the island was unnecessary either for the blockade of Japan or to secure a route for a possible invasion of the Japanese mainland. Enemy civilians also suffered, too, from the irresistible momentum of strategic bombing campaigns. Roosevelt (and then Truman) let the raids continue past the point where the destruction contributed to the reduction of the war-fighting capacity of either enemy.[178]

Prisoner of Events

Roosevelt initiated planning for peace almost as soon as the United States entered the Second World War. With a peace-building agenda at least as ambitious as Wilson's had been, Roosevelt enjoyed important advantages over his predecessor. By preference and circumstance, Wilson had tried to build a postwar order largely by his own hand. He insisted on tight control over diplomatic initiatives; he also had a very modest government organization on which to draw. Roosevelt recognized that the tasks of reconstructing the world after the most destructive war humanity had ever suffered would far exceed what he alone could manage. Fortunately, the state apparatus at his disposal had grown enormously during his time in the White House, first as an outgrowth of the New Deal and then as a result of sustained wartime mobilization. The military general staff organization, for example, had matured into a complex, specialized structure capable of managing extraordinary planning challenges.

But that enlarged government structure also introduced a political complication. Planning for the postwar order provoked a fundamental division, with the military and conservatives on one side and New Dealers on the other. Looking to the end of the war, the former group favored a military occupation of Germany and Japan for a relatively short period, which implied a less thorough effort to remake social institutions.[179] The New Dealers, by contrast, called for more far-reaching social engineering to uproot institutions and traditions that seemed the underlying source of militarism. (Although the respective positions paralleled domestic debates over the limits of government, some participants broke form—Cordell Hull, for example, was a domestic conservative who wanted extensive remaking of Germany and Japan.)

Interestingly, the arguments about how to treat the vanquished enemies echoed those at the end of the Civil War. Then, Radical Republicans favored broad efforts to uproot the old slaveholding order and promote black political inclusion, while Republican moderates and war

Democrats anticipated a brief occupation of the defeated Confederate states followed by a return to self-government under white control. Lincoln evaded the tension by postponing consideration of Reconstruction until the end of hostilities. Roosevelt would also delay decisions as he sought to hold open options, only to discover that events circumscribed the possible choices as the war drew to a close.[180]

The president faced an additional obstacle that besets all bold peace-building projects. As the agenda becomes more ambitious, the number of conditions involved increases, too, as do the number of things that can go awry. It is hard enough for a president to control his own military and administration. Earlier presidents had learned that they could not count on the continuing cooperation of Congress or the ongoing support of the American public for peace-building initiatives. Even less could Roosevelt depend on the willingness of key foreign leaders to stick to his script. For, as Wilson had learned, victory immediately frays the association of the victors, with each nation instead pursuing its own interests as it sees them. That this pattern of difficulties would repeat itself after the Second World War became clear well before the conflict ended.

The fate of Germany ultimately rested upon the willingness of the United States to absorb the costs of remaking German society. At Teheran in 1943, the president, Churchill, and Stalin endorsed in principle the idea of dismembering Germany to prevent it from ever again posing a threat to peace.[181] Their accord fit with the 1944 Morgenthau Plan, developed by the treasury secretary, to divide Germany and reduce it to an agrarian society. Roosevelt initially endorsed the plan.[182] But Hull, Stimson, and other key advisors repudiated the "dismember Germany" approach. As American military commanders pointed out, any scheme to fragment Germany likely would face resistance from the German people, a situation that would strain military resources while the war against Japan continued. Even proponents of thorough efforts to root out Nazism and militarism from German society acknowledged the process could require a military occupation lasting at least a generation. The president and his advisors doubted the American public's willingness to sustain a large-scale military commitment for so long a period. Debate continued into 1945, as here, too, Roosevelt declined to force closure.[183]

Rather than the outcome of a clear political decision, Germany's postwar future reflected military expedients and the erosion of cooperation between the Soviet Union and the West. At Yalta in March 1945, Roosevelt again put off a decision on splitting Germany, though Stalin still seemed to prefer dismemberment. (He also wanted to impose severe reparations on the Germans to block any quick recovery, but neither Roosevelt nor Churchill was prepared to reenact what many viewed as the error of Versailles.) The immediate solution took the form of zones of occupation for each of the Allies, including France. Stalin chose to bide his time because Roosevelt hinted that he expected American occupation forces to remain for only two years. To the Soviet leader's surprise, however, as tensions between the Soviet Union and the West quickly worsened after the war and the exhaustion of British resources became more evident, the Americans stayed and thus assured a great power balance in Europe.[184] The boundary between the Soviet occupation zone in Germany and the others hardened into a permanent one that would endure for almost fifty years.

On Eastern Europe, though, Stalin would have his way. As the Red Army rolled back the Germans in 1944, it claimed control over countries that Hitler's troops had conquered early in the war (Poland) and those that had chosen to ally themselves with the führer (Bulgaria, Hungary, and Rumania). Only Yugoslavia, which was largely liberated by Tito's communist-led partisans, managed to escape the smothering embrace of Soviet liberation. Stalin made clear, too, that he intended to impose a Soviet-style system wherever his troops marched. In a cold demonstration of his intentions, he had ordered his forces to give no assistance to Polish underground forces that staged an uprising in Warsaw in August 1944, going so far as to refuse the British and Americans permission to drop supplies to the beleaguered resistance as it was systematically crushed by the Germans. The uprising had been orchestrated by leaders tied to the London Polish government-in-exile, while Stalin had formed his own acting government in a liberated town, Lublin. Stalin also insisted on redrawing Poland's borders, effectively moving the entire nation to the west to give the Soviet Union more territory and requiring the forced relocation of ethnic Poles unfortunate enough to live within the transferred land.

The Anglo-American Allies could do nothing to alter the situation. It became fashionable after the war, especially on the American right, to accuse Roosevelt of being naive about Stalin (whom the president referred to privately as "Uncle Joe") and claim the Soviet dictator duped the president about the future of Eastern Europe.[185] But this presumes the president, otherwise coldly calculating in his dealings with advisors and political enemies alike, somehow lost his political sense when dealing with Stalin. A more persuasive explanation exists: the president recognized how little leverage the Anglo-Americans exercised over the fate of Eastern Europe. They did not for a moment consider using force to expel the Red Army.[186] Roosevelt still believed he could draw the Soviet Union into his design for a postwar security order,[187] and the American military continued at the time of Yalta to believe Soviet participation in the war against Japan would be vital in holding down American casualties.

For these important objectives, acceptance of Soviet dominance in Eastern Europe was a necessary price. Churchill knew it, too, despite his later public statements and warnings about Soviet behavior. When he tried to negotiate Soviet and British shares of influence in the Balkans with Stalin in fall 1944, the prime minister recognized as a fait accompli Soviet control over Poland and much of the region. (He was much more concerned with the fate of the Mediterranean, and satisfied when Stalin agreed to let the British dictate what happened in Greece.)[188]

Explaining the price for Soviet cooperation to the American people was another matter, and here Roosevelt flinched. When the double-edged nature of liberation by the Red Army became visible in mid-1944, especially at the time of the Warsaw Uprising, he faced a closely contested reelection. The many Americans of Eastern European extraction, especially Polish Americans, watched with concern as the Soviets established communist-led governments.[189] To reassure them, the president insisted he had secured promises from Stalin that the future government of the liberated countries would be open to representatives of all factions (a formula that sounded democratic without actually being so). Reelection did not put a stop to the posturing for American public opinion. At Yalta, Roosevelt cynically admitted he wanted a fig-leaf promise of a democratic process for

Poland because he needed to mollify the large number of Polish Americans. The president risked provoking the same kind of disillusionment that had helped defeat Wilson's peace treaty and that later fed isolationism.

Unlike Europe, where the United States never dominated the war against Germany, the Pacific counteroffensive against Japan was overwhelmingly an American enterprise. American military leaders were divided over the benefits of retaining this near-monopoly. Late in the war, Churchill sought a larger British role, principally so Great Britain might earn through its sacrifices its title to its former colonial holdings. Admiral King opposed the prime minister's offer of a British fleet to support Pacific amphibious operations, raising weak logistical objections. At heart, King sought to minimize the role of any other power in shaping the postwar Asia-Pacific order. But the president overruled him—he could never have explained to the American public why, in the face of appalling losses in the late war Pacific battles, he had refused Allied help—and a large British fleet entered the war against Japan in the final months.[190]

How best to end the war in the Pacific quickly and with the least loss of American lives was the issue that vexed American political and military leaders in 1945. They hoped to avoid a direct invasion of the Japanese home islands and bring about surrender instead through blockade and strategic bombing. However, although the Japanese military already had been cut off from its sources of vital strategic materials and Tokyo and other cities were being reduced to ashes by B-29 firebombing, the Japanese leadership gave no sign it was ready to quit. The rigidity of the "unconditional surrender" formula sparked new debates among senior American officials. Military commanders feared it would prolong the war by encouraging Japanese resistance, and they worried that the heavy casualties suffered during an invasion would damage both military and civilian morale for little gain over what might be achieved with slightly more flexible terms. State Department officials countered that no other formula could give the Allies effective control over Japan, which was necessary to assure the demilitarization of Japanese society.[191] Amid this impasse, Roosevelt at Yalta secured a promise from Stalin to enter the war against Japan three months after Germany surrendered.[192] Meanwhile, secret development of the atomic bomb continued, with the goal of having one or more weapons ready during summer 1945.

The end of the war against Japan would rest in the hands of Roosevelt's successor, but the cumulative weight of decisions made since December 7, 1941, left Harry Truman with few real choices. In his first speech to Congress after taking office, he declared that unconditional surrender would remain the Allies' demand. For several months he adhered to this position, which was reflected in the Potsdam Proclamation issued in July 1945 by the United States, Great Britain, and the Soviet Union. The horrific casualties on Iwo Jima and Okinawa left American leaders determined to explore every alternative to invasion itself.

Once the first atomic bomb test succeeded, then, Truman moved ahead with the plan to drop the weapon on a major Japanese city. Notwithstanding pleas from some scientists involved in the Manhattan Project, senior American officials never seriously revisited the decision to use the bomb. The new president, still feeling his way in office, did not yet feel comfortable questioning his advisors on military matters, but no evidence suggests that Roosevelt would have acted differently. After the vast investment in the bomb project ($2 billion, larger than the entire 1941 defense budget), it was destined to be used unless a president forcefully interrupted the process. Truman did finally tweak the surrender terms slightly, to make it possible for the Japanese emperor to remain on the throne in some capacity.[193] By that point, the first atomic bomb had tumbled from the B-29 *Enola Gay* onto Hiroshima, and a second bomb would fall on Nagasaki before the Japanese finally capitulated. Soviet troops meanwhile invaded Manchuria on August 8, 1945, fulfilling Stalin's pledge and making plain to Tokyo that it invited national obliteration if it continued the war.

As the Pacific war approached its violent climax, events elsewhere in Asia showed starkly the limits of Roosevelt's capacity to shape the postwar order in the region. The United States had almost no ground troops in the China-Burma-India theater. When the war ended, British forces were mopping up the last disorganized remnants of the Japanese army in Burma. The British moved quickly to reoccupy Malaya and Singapore following the Japanese surrender. Roosevelt had hoped to prevent the French from reestablishing themselves in Indochina.

However, by early 1945 he was forced to acknowledge that he had no alternative but to agree to make France the sole trustee over its erstwhile colony.[194] Thus the stage was set for the first Indochina war. Meanwhile, Chiang Kai-shek bided his time and husbanded his forces for the inevitable showdown with the communists. Roosevelt had counted on the generalissimo to take a seat at the table as one of the postwar Big Four. But, as he had throughout the war, Chiang would continue to disappoint his American patrons. Incompetence, corruption, and indifference to the suffering of the Chinese people contributed to the collapse of the Nationalist regime and its ignominious retreat to Formosa (Taiwan) in December 1949.[195] Roosevelt proved no better able to shape political outcomes where there were no American troops than Wilson had been after the 1918 Armistice.

In one key respect, though, the lessons from the previous war had been well learned. After victory, Roosevelt believed, the United States could not retreat from its global responsibility to preserve peace. Central to his vision for postwar security was a new international organization that would not suffer from the liabilities that had crippled the League of Nations. The president insisted that the United States not merely belong to but also lead the organization. In October 1944, after several years of planning by the State Department, American, British, and Soviet diplomats agreed on the basic structure of a United Nations organization, called the Dumbarton Oaks Proposals. Roosevelt had observed Wilson's failure to secure ratification of the League of Nations and resolved to avoid his predecessor's errors, especially his assumption that the Senate must follow presidential direction in postwar foreign affairs.[196]

To secure American membership, then, the Roosevelt administration mounted an organized campaign designed to generate strong popular and U.S. Senate support for the United Nations. Isolationist ("unilateralist" might be more apt[197]) sentiment in the United States remained strong if subdued, and critics of the Proposals worried that participation would compromise American independence. Leaving nothing to chance, the State Department underwrote a concerted campaign through which a wide range of private organizations urged Congress to ratify the UN Charter. Roosevelt also studiously avoided Wilson's partisan approach by reaching out to isolationist Republican Senator

Arthur Vandenburg, appointing him to the U.S. delegation to the April 1945 San Francisco conference to finalize the organization's charter. This time around there would be no Henry Cabot Lodge.

The administration's timing, moreover, was exquisite: the campaign to win public support came at a time when Americans were tired of war and thus open to ways to prevent another, and before the squabbling that resumes among allies at the end of a conflict had left the public jaded about the possibilities for international cooperation. (Possibly this consideration also entered into Roosevelt's determination to minimize differences with Stalin over Eastern Europe.) By the time of the San Francisco conference, more than 80 percent of Americans who had heard of the United Nations supported American participation.[198] And the consequences went beyond mere membership in the new international body. As a recent study of the administration's campaign to win public support concludes, "In essence, Roosevelt made American entry into the United Nations a national referendum on the postwar posture of the United States and its willingness to prevent World War III."[199] This national commitment to backstop an international organization for collective security set apart Roosevelt's peace-building efforts from Wilson's.

The United Nations, moreover, was but one support beam in an extraordinary framework of international organizations designed to promote free trade and an international market economy. Before the war ended, the United States took the lead in establishing the International Monetary Fund and the World Bank. These were followed by the Marshall Plan, for which Congress appropriated $17 billion in 1948, and the North Atlantic Treaty Organization in the following year.[200] Clemenceau's and Lloyd George's old nightmare—of the European democracies abandoned by the United States while a powerful adversary lurked across the border—lay banished for good. Of course, the new structures did not reflect pure altruism on the part of Roosevelt or other American policy makers. The economic institutions established at war's end helped assure strong overseas markets for American goods at a time when no competitor could hope to compete with American industry. Once seen by American business as its archenemy, the Roosevelt administration laid the groundwork for an unprecedented era of global American economic hegemony.

The Prime Minister and the President

Judged against the performance of his adversaries, Roosevelt stands out as an exceptionally effective wartime leader. The Axis leaders waged brilliant opening campaigns followed by unimaginative defensive ones that often facilitated the great Allied counteroffensives. In the Pacific, no single Japanese political leader directed the far-flung campaigns of the Imperial forces. Rather, army and navy commanders negotiated with each other over strategic options, operational priorities, and the allocation of strategic resources. The lack of a single overarching authority did not inhibit Japanese advances into mid-1942, but the absence of a leader with sufficient authority to overcome inter-service rivalry and focus resources against the main threat meant the Japanese military reacted in an ad hoc, piecemeal manner once the American counteroffensive began. Weak political control over the military also contributed to fatal strategic failures, notably the refusal to recognize the threat American submarines posed to vulnerable shipping lanes.

In Europe, Hitler committed the war's single greatest mistake at the level of grand strategy when he opted to begin a war on a second front against the Soviet Union in 1941 before he had defeated Great Britain. He later made the Allied task immeasurably easier by his rigid refusal to withdraw from any piece of occupied territory. Allied commanders, especially General Brooke of the British Imperial General Staff, recognized the flaw in Hitler's approach and used it in their calculations— the führer would not make best use of interior lines to concentrate all of his forces against a major attack or invasion because that would necessitate a strategic retreat elsewhere.[201] Hitler's many other strategic and operational blunders have filled numerous books and need not be rehearsed here.

More interesting comparisons can be drawn between Roosevelt and the other two primary Allied leaders. Joseph Stalin fought a very different war from that waged by the Anglo-Americans—on a single front, against a direct invasion of his country, and almost entirely land-based. Just as the president and his senior commanders chose to wage a war that made maximum use of America's greatest strategic advantage (industrial resources), so, too, did Stalin capitalize upon the Soviet Union's key assets—space and manpower. Russian defenses were overwhelmed in the first weeks of the war, due in part to Stalin's rigidity, and suffered as many as 2 million casualties. But where the French never recovered from their shattering defeat in May 1940, the Red Army withdrew into the vast Soviet interior, while vital Soviet heavy industry was swiftly dismantled and relocated to new factories east of the Ural Mountains. Stalin was profligate in his use of human resources, too, and the final butcher's bill for Soviet victory was staggering. No alternative, though, presented itself. After all, the Red Army engaged the main mass of the German *Wehrmacht* for three years, from June 1941 until the Normandy invasion in June 1944, while the Anglo-Americans nibbled on the perimeter of German-occupied Europe as he cajoled them in vain to open a real Second Front. Although Soviet forces benefited most from Hitler's obsession with holding every foot of ground, winning major encirclement battles at Stalingrad and elsewhere, no other Allied army fought a longer, more brutal campaign, or paid so high a price.

Stalin pursued far more modest war objectives than those of either Roosevelt or Churchill. The Soviet dictator fought for security in a narrow and very concrete form: he intended to establish a much larger buffer zone between his country and a potentially resurgent Germany or any other threat from the West. He was willing to participate in a postwar international organization, yes, but he did not expect much from it and preferred to rely on an old-fashioned sphere-of-influence approach, consisting of satellite nations compelled to adopt the Soviet system (an innovation in power politics). His cold realism led him to dismiss the Chinese communists as weak challengers to the Nationalists, and so he initially backed Chiang Kai-shek after the war. Stalin also took an opportunistic approach to war gains. He expressed support for dismembering Germany, but the lack of separatist movements there helped convince him the cost would be too great and he wearied of Anglo-American equivocation on the matter. He also hoped to secure reparations to compensate for Soviet material losses. When the Anglo-Americans refused in the end to cooperate, Soviet troops instead stripped bare all territory they occupied, ranging from Germany to Manchuria.

Churchill, stalwart leader of Great Britain in its darkest hour, remains a captivating figure. Probably no other British political leader could have kept his nation afloat in summer 1940 after the defeat of France and the Dunkirk evacuation. Apart from his contribution to British morale over the following months, his single greatest contribution to ultimate British success may have been his ability to convince Roosevelt that Great Britain would not succumb to Hitler if the United States came to its aid. Churchill's engaged style of directing the British war effort also appeals to some astute students of wartime political leadership. Eliot Cohen, for one, regards the prime minister as an archetype of the hands-on leader who regards any and all aspects of his nation's war effort as his legitimate domain.[202]

And accounts of Churchill certainly bear out this image: the prime minister insisting that a reluctant General Archibald Wavell launch an early offensive to relieve Tobruk from a German siege in summer 1941, holding court with Brooke and others late into the night, scribbling "action this day" in the margins of yet another report, encouraging the development of specialized tanks to crack open German defenses during the cross-Channel invasion, urging British landings in the Aegean in 1944 to gain control of Greece and induce Turkey to enter the war on the Allied side, and on and on.[203] By contrast, Roosevelt plays a background role in many accounts of the American war effort, especially after 1942.

But high energy and enthusiasm do not themselves win wars. If we focus instead on Roosevelt's and Churchill's conception of their respective national war objectives and their ability to pursue a military strategy that would achieve those objectives, the president emerges clearly as the more effective leader. Both men had ambitious war aims beyond the defeat of Germany, Italy, and Japan, some of which exceeded their own or their nation's capabilities. I have touched upon Roosevelt's quixotic aspirations, including his belief that colonialism could be eliminated quickly after the war, his expectation that China might replace Japan as the major power to stabilize Asia, and his hope that the Soviet Union might be induced to act as a responsible member of the postwar Big Four if the Anglo-Americans acquiesced in Stalin's brutal solution to Soviet security concerns. To his credit, the president realized that the prewar international order with its white-dominated empires was gone for good, destined to be swept aside by surging demands for independence among colonial peoples. He was mistaken in his belief that he could dictate the pace of the transition, a reflection of his assumption that non-white populations were unready for self-government and required a period of tutelage under international auspices.

By contrast, Churchill clung to the past, refusing to recognize that the foundations of white rule had been swept aside by the war, especially in Asia, where the Japanese proved that the colonial intruders could be beaten. He also failed to appreciate the full magnitude of both American ascendance and the enfeebled economic condition of his own country. A virtually bankrupt Great Britain would be in no position to afford the costs of preserving its empire, the pieces of which rapidly began to fall away after the war, beginning with Indian independence in 1947.[204] Notwithstanding his own revisionist efforts to rewrite his record in dealing with Stalin, moreover, Churchill accepted as readily as Roosevelt did the reality of Soviet hegemony over Poland and the rest of Eastern Europe.[205] The prime minister's call for Anglo-American forces to advance as far across Germany as possible and capture Berlin was rightly rejected as pointless by Eisenhower, who understood that the troops would need to withdraw immediately following a German surrender to the prearranged occupation zones.[206]

As military strategists, both men had their limitations, but Roosevelt demonstrated a greater ability to focus on the central military tasks.[207] He made his worst mistakes before the United States entered the war, as he tried to balance the competing threats posed by Germany and Japan. Once war came, he remained steadfast in his commitment to the Germany First strategy and shrewdly appreciated the need to get American forces into combat against the Germans before American public opinion might compel a shift against the more hated Japanese enemy. But he also did not follow the advice of his own senior commanders, especially General Marshall, to push for an early cross-Channel invasion. Instead the president waited until Americans constituted the majority of Allied formations in the European theater and then held firm on the spring 1944 invasion timetable. Not only would this be the fastest way to defeat Germany, but it also countered the possibility that the Red Army would liberate all of Western Europe and establish permanent Soviet control over the region. In the Pacific the president backed selective moves to check the Japanese advance and initiate limited offensives, such as at Guadalcanal. His leadership faltered only when American victory became certain: he let MacArthur's Philippine gambit go too far and, arguably, waited too long to seek alternatives to the absolute unconditional surrender formulation.

Churchill showed a willingness to make tough decisions and showed broad strategic imagination. Notwithstanding the distasteful aspect of waging war upon a former ally, he ordered attacks on the French fleet in summer 1940 to keep its ships out of German hands and against Vichy forces in Lebanon and Syria in 1941 that secured British control over the Middle East and its vital oil supplies. He risked leaving Great Britain itself vulnerable to invasion to reinforce Commonwealth armies in the Middle East. Although his decision to aid Greece in early 1941 led to a stinging military defeat there and on Crete, he acted according to a legitimate political concern—Great Britain had strong ties to Greece. The invasion of North Africa in late 1942, which the prime minister strongly urged, let the Americans gain experience fighting the Germans, promoted cooperation between U.S. and British commanders, and made possible a major victory over the Axis that finally cleared them from North Africa and the Middle East. Additional operations in the Mediterranean in 1943 brought significant gains, such as the surrender of Italy and relocation of more German formations into Italy and Greece.[208] Perhaps most important, Churchill showed an early appreciation for the critical Atlantic supply line, which, if severed, would doom any prospect of bringing American military might to bear upon Germany.

But there are marks to enter on the negative side of the ledger, too, including excessive haste, a preoccupation with "prestige" objectives, and a fascination with operational sideshows and glamorous special operations bereft of strategic return. Churchill's incessant hectoring of Wavell to strike the Germans at Tobruk resulted in a premature offensive and defeat, for which only the general was held accountable.[209] The prestige of the British Empire and how it was perceived by its colonized non-white subjects also weighed too heavily in the prime minister's decision making. When British defenses collapsed in Malaya in December 1941–January 1942 and it became evident that Singapore was doomed to fall, he still permitted another 25,000 men to be shipped in for the final defense. Somehow he persuaded himself that this gesture would make a positive impression upon Asian and Commonwealth audiences. All the reinforcements were killed or captured within a few days.[210] (Contrast this with Roosevelt's cold-blooded acceptance of his military chiefs' assessment that the Philippines could not be held in 1942, leading to the decision not to attempt major reinforcement.)

Once the Anglo-American Allies were prepared to go on the offensive, Churchill liked to conjure up operations that would have diverted their effort to the periphery of occupied Europe. For example, he repeatedly urged an attack across northern Norway (Operation JUPITER) to link up with the Russians, an enterprise that would have neither aided the Red Army significantly nor engaged a substantial part of the *Wehrmacht*.[211] His enthusiasms extended to colorful leaders like Ord Wingate and their ideas about unconventional operations. With the prime minister's staunch backing, Wingate mounted a large behind-the-lines operation in Burma in 1944 that failed to preempt the massive Japanese offensive at Imphal and Kohima.[212]

Churchill's most glaring failure is the mirror image of Roosevelt's wisest decision: the timing of the cross-Channel invasion and the attendant shift in Anglo-American effort from the Mediterranean to northwest Europe. As I earlier noted, the prime minister paid lip service to the idea of invasion but never committed to a particular date, a hesitation that reflected early British defeats at the hands of the Germans. Circumstances had changed by mid-1943—the Allies had won against the U-boats, their equipment had improved, they had achieved victories on the ground in North Africa and Sicily, and American troops were arriving in England in vast numbers—but he ignored the implications of the changes.[213] His outlook also reflected a British preoccupation with the importance of the Mediterranean and secure sea lanes and his desire to see the main campaign led by a British commander and fought primarily by Commonwealth troops.[214] Even after Roosevelt decided the Normandy invasion must proceed, Churchill refused to give up his obsession with Italy, Greece, and the Balkans.[215] He wrongly persisted in arguing that the best route into Central Europe led through Italy into Austria (where again his fixation on prestige led him to proclaim the quaint notion that the power that controlled Vienna controlled Europe.)[216] In pressing for campaigns in Greece and Yugoslavia, he also wanted to deny them to the Red Army. Certainly the Anglo-Americans could have liberated the region first, but at the price of the Red Army advancing at least to the Rhine and quite possibly to the Channel coast. Postwar geopolitics would have looked very different, and not to the advantage of the West.[217]

Comparisons between Roosevelt and Churchill tend to exaggerate the differences in their approach to wartime leadership. Roosevelt prudently relied upon the massive military organization the United States created to wage a global war and intervened selectively. He gave, as we've seen, strong support to the B-29 bomber program, which at $3 billion represented an extraordinary investment in a weapons system for the time and so needed extra political muscle behind it.[218] On certain matters of military technology, such as carrier aviation, he learned a great deal and asked sharp questions, just as the prime minister did.[219] But the president was also the kind of hands-on leader who often preferred *not* to leave his fingerprints on a decision.[220] Recall his insistence that no minutes or notes be taken in most of his meetings with senior advisors. Such an arrangement suited a man who might want to hold open his options or change his mind. Roosevelt's informal organizational structure funneled power to him and let him make the final decisions on many matters, even if his role was not visible.[221] He rarely overrode his military chiefs because they understood his political objectives and strategic priorities.

Wartime presidents inevitably lose their capacity to alter direction over the course of a war. Roosevelt did everything he could to preserve his freedom of action. He placed himself at the center of the decision-making apparatus and kept his subordinates focused on his broad objectives. He put off choices and binding commitments as long as possible, weighed carefully different means to achieve his goals, adjusted his tactics to changing circumstances. Yet in the end, his path was tightly circumscribed—he could not halt the unnecessary ongoing campaign in the Philippines or the strategic bombing that pounded ruined German cities, prevent the imposition of Stalinist government across Eastern Europe, or halt the restoration of colonial regimes in Asia.

The Good War

As Roosevelt faced the prospect of war, he hoped to have a unified public behind him. Pearl Harbor gave him what he wanted. No organized effort was needed to suppress dissent of the sort the Wilson administration had backed in the First World War. Opposition to the war scarcely existed after Pearl Harbor, sparing him one challenge that had beset all of his wartime predecessors. Isolationists were immediately silenced, sometimes vilified. Readers of the anti-interventionist *Chicago Tribune*, which had published key details of the Victory Program just days before the Japanese struck, canceled their subscriptions by the thousands.[222] Most foes of American intervention fell into line behind the war effort. A mere handful of dissidents faced government repression.[223]

"Remember Pearl Harbor!" might do for a start, but vengeance alone would not suffice to sustain popular support for a war effort that promised to be long and costly. Early on, the president voiced certain core principles as the moral basis for the Allied war effort. The 1941 Atlantic Charter expressed an American commitment to a peaceful world order based upon a commitment to self-determination, very much in the Wilsonian spirit. Shortly after the United States entered the war, Roosevelt improved upon that initial statement of purposes by celebrating what he denoted as the "Four Freedoms"—freedom of speech, freedom to worship, freedom from want, and freedom from fear. The list was part reiteration of basic civil liberties, part extension of the New Deal principle of economic security, and part promise of protection against aggression. Opinion polls suggested that Americans drew a broader sense of purpose from the president's words, though they more often saw the war not as a noble struggle but as a dirty job that had to be done.

Popular support for the war reflected the unique manner in which Americans experienced their participation in the global struggle. Not only was it a good war in moral terms, but it was a good one in its economic benefits. Alone among the citizens of the belligerent nations, Americans enjoyed a rising standard of living, notwithstanding wartime shortages. Further, building upon the president's prewar "arsenal of democracy" approach, political and military leaders continued to stress the material contribution the United States would make to the Allied war effort. This helped to limit American casualties, which Roosevelt believed important in sustaining morale among a population that he suspected still had strong isolationist impulses.[224] Indeed, the approach worked almost too well before 1944: Americans felt detached from the war and fixated on the inconveniences caused by the lack of certain goods and by wartime regulations. After shielding the public from visual images of American casualties, the administration finally approved the publication of photographs of dead GIs in *Life* magazine in late 1943.[225] Those sobering reminders of the cost of victory reinforced public resolve and steeled Americans for the heavier casualties of the later battles in both Europe and the Pacific.

With Americans at home spared serious deprivations and actually living better than they had during the Depression, the burden of the war fell almost entirely upon those called to serve in uniform. Their sacrifice in turn led to the one significant piece of social legislation enacted during the war period. In June 1944 the president signed into law the GI Bill of Rights, which offered veterans generous benefits for vocational training and higher education, plus low-interest housing loans.[226] Social provision was earned through military service, a well-established American principle, rather than by citizenship alone. And the gains would take the form of individual social mobility, rather than, as with earlier New Deal legislation to promote unions or establish a federal minimum wage, assuring the advance of an entire economic class. In Great Britain, by comparison, the war led to much broader social legislation, including comprehensive national health insurance— but, then, the British people as a whole had suffered far more during six years of war, with thousands of civilians killed by German bombs, many more left homeless, and all suffering privations from severe wartime rationing.[227]

One other key element helped in the effort to keep up home front morale in the United States—the timing of military operations. Roosevelt understood the domestic impact of battlefield success. Thus the Doolittle Raid in April 1942 was staged when the Americans had suffered a string of defeats in the Pacific and was intended to demonstrate that the United States would soon begin to strike back. Operation TORCH in North Africa aimed to get U.S. forces into combat against a German enemy toward whom most Americans harbored less animosity than they did toward the Japanese, thereby forestalling pressure to shift the balance of effort to the Pacific. Especially in the first year of the war, the president took military risks for morale-building reasons, a necessary part of wartime political leadership in a democratic society.

The post-TORCH operations in the Mediterranean into mid-1944, moreover, followed a political as well as military rationale. They reflected Roosevelt's judgment that the American people would not tolerate a long period of inactivity in the European theater while the press pointed out the insufficiency of resources devoted to beating the Japanese and some on the political left called for a Second Front (now!) to help the gallant Red Army. Against these political considerations, Roosevelt had to weigh the lives of the troops sent into battles that might not be justified in strictly military terms. But for a wartime democratic leader, no decision can ever be purely military—if the people cease to believe in the conflict, it is lost.

Time Runs Out

Like Lincoln, Roosevelt died before the end of the war through which he had led his fellow citizens. And, like Lincoln, Roosevelt's passing has prompted much speculation about how the future would have differed had he survived. But by the time of his death each president had lost most of his capacity to shape the world after the war. Their successors inherited situations over which no president could have exercised significant control. Roosevelt had believed he could influence Stalin's behavior by drawing him into a fabric of postwar international institutions and economic arrangements. Truman quickly adopted a more confrontational style to what he regarded as Soviet violations of commitments. Those commitments, of course, had never been anything more than window-dressing, designed for consumption by Roosevelt's and Churchill's domestic constituencies, and both men knew it. Stalin did not respond positively to Truman's abrasive tone, but there is no reason to think the Soviet leader would have given in any more readily to Roosevelt. Stalin had his own postwar agenda, and it came to the fore when the glue of a common enemy dissolved. Poised with their own plans, too, were key domestic actors: the conservative members of Congress and business leaders eager to get back to civilian production and to curb union militancy. No president would determine the postwar agenda for American politics.

In one important respect, Lincoln was more successful than Roosevelt as a wartime leader. Lincoln demonstrated a deeper trust in the

American people and their capacity to endure the terrible price of civil war. He explained his policies directly and with striking respect for the intelligence of the citizenry. In sharp contrast, Roosevelt often feared public opinion; he shied away from efforts to persuade and opted for dissembling rather than candor, especially in election years. His failure to move Americans toward interventionism represented a singular shortcoming of his prewar leadership. Toward the end of the war, he refrained from speaking plainly about the parts of the nascent postwar order that did not fit the vision he had touted. He denied the implications of Soviet control over Poland even after his 1944 reelection. Similarly, because he needed Chiang Kai-shek to be something he wasn't, Roosevelt chose to remain silent about the weaknesses of the generalissimo and his Nationalist regime. Into the void stepped that regime's American enablers, conservatives who would later deny Chiang's obvious limitations and seek scapegoats among American diplomats for the "loss" of China to the communists.

The curious aspect of the president's reluctance to share his own realism with the American people is that his administration demonstrated, in the case of the United Nations, a striking capacity to shape public attitudes on international affairs. Nonetheless, by declining to address the limits of American power, he purchased short-term acceptance of the Yalta agreements and other end-of-war accommodations at the price of future popular disillusionment. Although the public would not retreat into an isolationist shell again, international engagement would be driven by unreasoning fear of the Red Menace, an attitude no more conducive to the sober consideration of foreign affairs than the cynicism that had followed Wilson's war.

Roosevelt's capacity to shape outcomes over the 1938–1945 period followed an arc. Before the United States entered the war, the president maneuvered, at times desperately, to retain his freedom of action so he might decide whether, where, and when the country would become a belligerent. He juggled multiple goals—to defeat Hitler without actually fighting him, to force the Japanese to withdraw from China without provoking them to launch a wider war in Asia and the Pacific, to help Great Britain without arousing isolationist ire, to deter enemies with American might without building the kind of military needed to fight a global war. By late 1941, events left him waiting for an expected

Japanese strike with no way to get into the European war he thought the United States needed to wage and a military far from ready.

Pearl Harbor and Hitler's reckless decision to declare war on the United States gave Roosevelt broad initiative. The American people stood behind the war effort and Congress was prepared to cooperate fully. Roosevelt could articulate expansive war goals, and he enjoyed nearly complete strategic discretion about where to concentrate the American military effort. This was also the period in which the president intervened most directly in decisions, down to the operational level, because assuming military risks had profound political repercussions. In late summer 1942, Marshall proposed a small, cross-Channel invasion as a gesture to the Soviets, then desperately clinging to Stalingrad. But failure, almost certain, would have shattered fragile domestic morale. The choice hinged on competing political considerations, and Roosevelt rightly turned down Marshall's scheme.

As the war continued, the president's flexibility eroded, with each major decision driving a host of lesser ones, the cumulative weight of the sequence of choices leaving progressively fewer important decisions for him to make. At the peak of U.S. military power in 1944–1945, when Roosevelt commanded the world's dominant armed force, his actual capacity to shape results had been dramatically circumscribed. He read lines off a script he had written before America could flex its muscles.

For as long as he could shape events, Roosevelt handled the tasks of wartime leadership with much distinction. He stands with Lincoln as our most accomplished wartime chief executives. Both achieved their primary military and political objectives, despite significant domestic opposition (Roosevelt's came before the war, Lincoln in its darkest days). Their natural political talents helped them enormously, setting them apart from the unyielding Wilson. Yet despite records that command respect, Roosevelt and Lincoln's made their fair share of miscalculations and missteps, and the peace that followed fell short of what they sought. That neither man mastered all of the challenges he faced speaks to the impossible demands of wartime leadership.

The Second World War was the last total war of the industrial age. With the advent of nuclear weapons, major powers could not risk open conflict. Divided into two main power blocs, their competition thereafter shifted to peripheral regions around the globe, ones just emerging from colonialism. The United States henceforth would find itself engaged in limited wars, conflicts that did not threaten its survival or even disrupt most of the routines of everyday life. For the presidents who led the nation in these wars, leadership would present new complications, ones for which the lessons of Lincoln, Wilson, and Roosevelt might not apply.

4

Staying the Course
Johnson and Nixon

THE VIETNAM WAR CLAIMS TWO dubious distinctions: it was the only American conflict to end in unequivocal defeat and, in the process, it dragged down two presidencies. In part, this outcome reflected the nature of the war itself, which American leaders, from Eisenhower onward, misunderstood. They insisted on treating a minor regional struggle as a major Cold War test of wills, even though that meant staking everything on a weak client government in Saigon. They did not help themselves, either, by the manner in which they directed the conflict. Under Lyndon B. Johnson, the United States pursued military strategies and fought under self-imposed constraints that assured a military stalemate; Richard M. Nixon then sought to extricate the United States from the war in a way that guaranteed the ultimate collapse of its ally.

No leader could emerge unscathed from such a debacle. Johnson found himself deserted on both political flanks, first by liberals who saw the war as unnecessary and wanted American troops brought home, and then by conservatives who believed he had thrown away all chance for victory. Nixon, by insisting on violent measures that yielded transient military gains, sacrificed any possibility of building a domestic consensus in favor of long-term support for the Saigon government.

His paranoia about antiwar critics, moreover, backfired in the political scandal that eventually doomed him, and with that removed the slim chance that the United States might intervene again to punish enemy violations of the peace agreement by which American forces left the conflict. Vietnam represented the nadir of wartime presidential leadership.

From the moment Johnson assumed office, Vietnam hovered over him. He reaffirmed the commitment made by his two predecessors to sustain the noncommunist regime in South Vietnam against a growing insurgency backed by communist North Vietnam. Sharing the conventional wisdom that no communist threat could be ignored, he opted to escalate the scale of American intervention. At the same time he failed to clarify American national interests in going to war, refused to choose between costly domestic and military commitments, did not explain American objectives clearly to the public, and never defined a coherent military strategy that would force the communist adversary to accept a political solution on his terms.

In short, Johnson quickly surrendered his freedom of action. By 1967, senior administration officials concluded that the war had become a stalemate, a treacherous political situation for a wartime leader. Elite and public opinion at home began to turn against Johnson. The president and his key military commanders compounded their difficulties by claiming by late 1967 that American troops had turned the tide. When Hanoi launched its Tet Offensive in early 1968, the attacks, though a military debacle for the communists, undercut the Johnson administration's assertion of progress and ultimately ended his fading quest for reelection. Negotiations to find a political solution finally began in his last months in office.

Richard Nixon inherited the military stalemate and fitful peace talks, but as a new president he regained a measure of latitude. When campaigning for the White House in 1968, he had pledged to pursue "peace with honor" in Vietnam, a vague stance that ruled out only immediate withdrawal or all-out war. Over the next several years, his administration shifted the burden of fighting to the South Vietnamese and reduced American troop levels. But Nixon found it hard to give up the ghost of victory. Several times he ordered the use of increased force in a futile effort to bully the communist leadership in Hanoi to bow to

American terms. On the home front, Nixon failed to see that the gradual withdrawal of American forces triggered the political dynamic we have seen as characteristic of postwar politics—other political institutions push back against presidential power, while the public loses interest in what happens abroad. A president finds himself with declining leverage to shape a postwar settlement. Nixon and his key aide, Henry Kissinger, tried to parlay a weakening hand into an acceptable peace agreement. South Vietnamese president Nguyen Van Thieu harbored no such illusions. He recognized the terms being negotiated by his American benefactors as meaning ultimate defeat. Nixon pledged privately to punish treaty violations by the North Vietnamese, but his words proved hollow: neither the American people nor Congress stood behind them, while Watergate left him too weak and distracted to act. It remained only for the final humiliating act to be played out in Saigon in 1975 as the last Americans fled on their helicopters.

Beginnings

The Vietnam conflict traced its origins to the close of the Second World War, when Roosevelt had sought to prevent the French from reasserting their control over Indochina but lacked the means to do so. Following negotiations with the occupying British and Nationalist Chinese, French officials and troops reentered the region in early 1946. In the brief interlude before their return, a communist-dominated nationalist coalition led by Ho Chi Minh declared Vietnam independent. The French refused to recognize the new Democratic Republic of Vietnam (DRV) government and in late 1946 drove it from Hanoi. This precipitated a war that continued until Ho's forces, known as the Vietminh and commanded by General Vo Nguyen Giap, triumphed over their adversaries in the epic siege of Dien Bien Phu in May 1954.[1]

That same month, a peace conference convened in Geneva to resolve the political future of Indochina. Notwithstanding their military success, the Vietnamese communists were pressured by the major communist powers, the Soviet Union and the People's Republic of China, to accept a temporary partition of the country, with the Vietminh in control of the DRV north of the 17th parallel.[2] The Geneva accords called for an election within two years to unify the country, and the communists were confident that as the only legitimate anticolonial independence movement they would easily triumph. (American intelligence estimates suggested that Ho might win 80 percent of the vote in a free election.) Many communist troops in the southern part of Vietnam, following orders from the party leadership, regrouped to the DRV in anticipation of a quick return, while party political cadres remained behind to organize for the election.[3]

The expected vote to reunite Vietnam, however, never occurred. President Dwight Eisenhower decided not to recognize the Geneva accords or treat them as binding on the United States. Instead he backed the newly formed government of South Vietnam (GVN), under its leader Ngo Dinh Diem, as a noncommunist state. Stepping gingerly around the Geneva terms (which barred either of the temporary governments from entering a military alliance), the Eisenhower administration formed a regional security pact, the Southeast Asia Treaty Organization (SEATO), and placed South Vietnam under its protection.[4] On this basis, the United States supplanted France as the principal benefactor of Diem's regime, training his army from 1956 onward and providing it with weapons and equipment.[5] Diem declined to hold the reunification election stipulated by the peace agreement and set out to consolidate his political grip. Over the next several years, his army and police rounded up political opponents and began to destroy the stay-behind communist political apparatus.[6] The communists reciprocated by engaging in a campaign of violence against the government, especially assassination of local officials, while communist troops sent north began to return to South Vietnam to conduct larger military operations. Hanoi also established the National Liberation Front (NLF) in December 1960 to give local direction to the rebellion in the South.[7] By the time John F. Kennedy entered the White House in January 1961, the Diem government faced a mounting insurgency.

Where Eisenhower had enjoyed a free hand after Geneva, Kennedy did not have the same luxury. In his presidential campaign, he called for a restoration of American firmness; he followed in his inaugural address by affirming his determination to oppose communist expansion at any point, calling explicitly for Americans to be prepared to make sacrifices in the name of freedom. This stance did not accommodate sober reflection on whether specific communist challenges endangered American security or that of its key allies. Accordingly, as the communists in South Vietnam, referred to as the Vietcong or VC (for Vietnamese Communists), upped their pressure on Diem's regime, the Kennedy administration reacted. The president and his key advisors, notably Secretary of Defense Robert S. McNamara, did not lack for confidence that they knew how best to meet the threat. The administration included proponents of counterinsurgency warfare, a politico-military approach designed to bolster popular support for an established government—winning hearts and minds, as it was called—while denying guerilla forces the grassroots backing they needed to sustain a protracted campaign of subversion. Kennedy increased the number of American advisors in South Vietnam as well as the level of military assistance to the Diem government. In early 1962, the first U.S. Special Forces (the Green Berets) arrived to help train and advise the regime's forces.[8]

Yet reports from the field suggested that the growing American involvement was not stemming the erosion of the South Vietnamese government's position. In combat with the Vietcong, troops of Diem's Army of the Republic of Vietnam (ARVN) usually came off worst, displaying a reluctance to fight despite American coaching and superior equipment.[9] Given that Diem picked commanders for their political loyalty rather than their military competence, the poor ARVN performance was predictable.[10] The Americans could do little to alter the situation, though, because Diem demonstrated a strong streak of independence and rejected their efforts to influence his choices of senior officers. He also ignored pleas from American diplomats to broaden the base of his regime. By mid-1963, political opposition to Diem, especially from Buddhist monks, erupted in street demonstrations that included spectacular acts of self-immolation captured on camera and published in American newspapers.[11]

Kennedy began to doubt whether South Vietnam could be held and contemplated drawing down the American commitment. But facing what seemed like a difficult reelection bid in 1964, he also appreciated his need to forestall anything that looked like a communist victory.[12] Meanwhile, South Vietnamese military leaders initiated plans to overthrow Diem, and their scheme received at least implicit blessing from some U.S. officials. A coup on November 1, 1963, toppled the regime and resulted in the murder of both Diem and his brother.[13]

Kennedy's assassination just days later placed Lyndon Johnson at the helm of U.S. policy in Vietnam. Coping with the worsening situation in South Vietnam became one of Johnson's first priorities. The coup against Diem brought to power General Duong Van "Big" Minh, who disappointed American hopes by voicing interest in a political settlement that might include the communists in a power-sharing arrangement. To Washington's relief, another military revolt in January 1964 displaced Minh with the more staunchly anticommunist General Nguyen Khanh.[14] Political stability in South Vietnam proved elusive, one junta quickly following another, sometimes with intervals of government by civilian figureheads. Making matters worse, communist gains on the battlefield continued, aided by increasing infiltration through Laos on what was known as the Ho Chi Minh Trail. That route brought supplies to support the Viet Cong and may have also seen the passage of the first regular units of the North Vietnamese Army (NVA).[15]

In the Americans' view, the war had entered a new and more dangerous phase marked by what they regarded as overt North Vietnamese aggression. (The Vietnamese communists always rejected such claims on the grounds that, as the Geneva accords acknowledged, Vietnam remained a single country, and troops from the North merely fought to restore national unity.) Senior Americans, including the incoming head of the U.S. Military Assistance Command Vietnam (MACV), General William Westmoreland, warned in early 1964 that the enemy might achieve decisive victory on the battlefield. The new American president, then, would not be given the luxury of addressing Vietnam on his own timetable.[16]

Meeting the Test

Even as Vietnam demanded Johnson's immediate attention, the conflict left the president with very limited options. He took it as a given that the United States must resist communist-inspired aggression wherever it arose. At the same time, though, the danger of nuclear confrontation with major communist powers and the possibility that China might enter the conflict dictated that the response be limited. The political consequences of his choices also weighed heavily on the mind of a president who had not yet secured the backing of the American people in his own right. Johnson knew that to withdraw from Vietnam could undermine his electoral prospects in 1964. Further, he intended to pursue a dramatic, in many ways radical, approach to domestic problems, an agenda that would collide with mobilization for a major military conflict.

Upon taking office, Johnson decided to retain his predecessor's entire cabinet and foreign policy team. This alone did much to push his Vietnam policy further along the same path that Kennedy had followed. Kennedy had embraced a muscular liberalism that demanded resistance to communist expansionism.[17] His defense and foreign policy advisors reflected this eager determination to meet any and all threats—as the nation had seen in the Cuban Missile Crisis in 1962. Key holdovers included, besides Defense Secretary McNamara, Secretary of State Dean Rusk, Attorney General Robert F. Kennedy, and national security assistant McGeorge Bundy. They outnumbered and outranked the few skeptical voices, most notably Rusk's deputy, Undersecretary of State George Ball. The new president was also a relative novice on matters of foreign policy. Supremely confident in his abilities as a legislative leader, Johnson lacked the same self-assurance in the international arena, leading him to rely heavily on the expertise of his advisors.[18] He consulted, too, with a number of long-standing political friends and lawmakers he knew well, such as Clark Clifford. Most of them shared the same worldview as Kennedy's inner circle and tended to echo the dominant recommendations rather than examine them critically.

American leaders, including Johnson, viewed the Vietnam conflict through the prism of recent Cold War confrontations and their memory of the world's failure to block dictators before the Second World War. To American policy makers, the communists since the end of World War II had seized upon every opportunity to expand their areas of control—Eastern Europe under Stalin, China, Korea, Cuba, and Vietnam. They could be checked only by resolute action, including, as Korea had demonstrated, the use of military force. At the moment, Soviet and Chinese leaders identified the Third World as the new site of struggle against Western powers, championing the cause of national liberation movements that opposed colonial or American-leaning governments. Of course, the split between Moscow and Beijing had not escaped notice. But the fracturing of the erstwhile communist monolith and the friction between the two communist giants merely aggravated the danger. Now the Soviet Union and China competed to demonstrate greater support for radical insurgencies.[19] Whether Moscow or Beijing directed them remained a matter of dispute in Washington policy circles, but either way the United States could not permit communist powers to capitalize on revolutionary fervor and upheaval. Failure to respond, moreover, would merely embolden them. Johnson took to heart the "lesson" of Munich in 1938: dictators must be confronted early, lest they gather strength. That meant Washington, which alone had the military and economic wherewithal to stem the communist advance, needed to backstop government resistance to insurgencies wherever these erupted.

To make transparent the connection between communism, liberation movements, and American interests, American leaders beginning with Eisenhower used the metaphor of falling dominos.[20] A particular country might be of little or no strategic importance in itself, but its collapse and absorption into the communist orbit would undermine its neighbors, and their defeat would in turn trigger a sequence of failures. Thus communist victory in South Vietnam would precipitate the surrender of neutral Cambodia and Laos, eventually lead Thailand and Malaysia to submit to communist dominance (whether Hanoi's, Beijing's, or Moscow's was never entirely clear), dishearten South Korea and Taiwan, embolden communist insurgents in the Philippines, and drive Indonesia into communist arms. Policy makers were not so simple-minded as to believe communist-dominated liberation movements could easily jump borders, much less oceans. Rather, it was held that defeat of an American-backed government at any point would destroy the faith of neighboring states in U.S. security guarantees and lead them to seek accommodation with the communists.[21] And from the experience of Eastern Europe after World War II, Washington policy makers drew the conclusion that any government that included communists would soon be controlled by them. The causal logic behind the domino theory could be questioned and the historical analogies were suspect, but still it exercised a powerful grip on both the elite and popular imagination. In February 1965, an opinion poll found that four out of five Americans believed that a withdrawal from Vietnam would result in a communist takeover of all of Southeast Asia.[22]

Important though Vietnam might be, from this perspective, the war there also had to be kept within bounds. Neither the United States nor the major communist powers wanted direct conflict, which could quickly spin out of control. Both sides had been sobered by the Cuban Missile Crisis, which had pushed the world perilously close to the brink of nuclear Armageddon. China would enter the nuclear club in 1964. From that point forward, American leaders had to reckon with the likelihood that a confrontation might escalate to the nuclear level.[23]

Moreover, if the war in Vietnam came too close to China, Beijing might intervene with conventional forces. Still fresh in the memory of American policy makers was the Korean War. When UN forces approached the Yalu River that separated China from North Korea in October 1950, General Douglas MacArthur had dismissed indications that the Chinese would send troops to assure the survival of their North Korean ally. Massive Chinese attacks then inflicted a stunning operational defeat on MacArthur and extended the war for several years. To preserve its credibility among national liberation movements, China could not allow the collapse of North Vietnam. Although it was not possible to know just what might provoke the Chinese to enter the Vietnam War, prudence dictated that the United States avoid certain military actions likely to compel Beijing to respond.[24] For example, the Korean precedent suggested the Chinese would defend a communist buffer state on their border. Accordingly, the Johnson administration ruled out any attempt at regime change in Hanoi.[25]

Balancing the risks, the president saw that only a narrow course remained open to the United States in Vietnam. Johnson, encouraged by most of his civilian and military advisors, concluded that the United States needed to meet the communist challenge at its most threatening point, in the jungles of Southeast Asia, but in a way that would contain the conflict. The underlying rot of the Saigon government made it a poor bet, one that would need much help before it could stand on its own. Nevertheless, withdrawal would be worse, for it would undermine American prestige and initiate the terminal retreat of the West before the communist menace. Equally important, Vietnam must not be allowed to increase the risk of nuclear confrontation with a major communist power or expand into a wider war against China. Circumstances thus dictated a war limited in both goal and method: American objectives would not include military victory in the classic sense of forcing an enemy surrender or occupying the adversary's territory, and military measures would exclude actions deemed likely to provoke either communist superpower to enter the conflict directly.

Not everyone was persuaded of the need for the United States to stand behind the Saigon government. A number of Western leaders believed Saigon a hopeless case due to the endemic weakness of the regime, its lack of popular support, and the powerful claim of the Vietnamese communists to nationalist legitimacy. Charles de Gaulle proposed the neutralization of Vietnam, but Johnson dismissed the idea as too vague.[26] At home, many Americans, including some in the military, remembered bitterly the stalemate in Korea and insisted that never again should the United States permit itself to be caught up in a land war in Asia. Skeptics included Ball, Senator Mike Mansfield, the majority leader, and, at times, Johnson's confidant Clark Clifford and Vice President Hubert Humphrey. Ball repeatedly argued against direct American military intervention. South Vietnam, he insisted, did not represent a vital American interest, American prestige and influence would be compromised by backing an unpopular military government, escalation would beget the same by the other side, and the prospects for success were poor.[27] But although Johnson heard out Ball, the assistant secretary's voice was drowned out by the larger chorus of interventionists around the president.

The president's conviction that the only choice in Vietnam lay along a narrow path between ignominious retreat and reckless escalation was reinforced by political considerations. Even had Johnson wanted to walk away from the conflict, the likely political fallout would have prevented him from doing so. To abandon Saigon or accept neutralization would have left him vulnerable to charges of weakness. He had witnessed the damage done to the Democrats by the virulent "Who lost China?" debate and feared a repeat.[28] (Eisenhower had survived Castro's communist triumph in Cuba, but he enjoyed credibility on national security that Johnson could not claim.) Indeed, the consequences might be worse, with a tragic revival of American isolationism that the world could not afford.

Johnson was nonetheless determined that Vietnam not define his presidency. The president intended to make his greatest mark on domestic policy. He envisioned a broad legislative program to provide health care for the elderly, secure voting rights for African Americans, alleviate poverty, and rebuild cities—in short, to outdo even the New Deal by erecting what he would call the Great Society. It was an ambitious agenda, one made possible only by the remarkable prosperity of the United States since the Second World War. But even American affluence had its limits. If he sought to mobilize the nation for full-scale war, moderate conservatives in Congress, already opposed to the Great Society, would use the cost of the war to insist he curtail his domestic program. Vital though Vietnam might be, Johnson did not intend to let it interfere with the completion of the domestic political project that would be his enduring legacy.

Sliding into Intervention

Lyndon Johnson led the United States into war in Vietnam through a series of small decisions and policy shifts between early 1964 and summer 1965. Ready to move ahead with his domestic agenda at the beginning of 1965, the president continued to find himself beset by the dire predicament of the Saigon government. He escalated American military intervention in Vietnam, first through a sustained bombing campaign against North Vietnam and then with the introduction of ground forces in South Vietnam. Although his decisions, especially the authorization of major troop reinforcements, occasioned extensive discussion within the administration, the outcome was foreordained. The president's actions expressed the assumptions that drove American foreign policy at the time. But Johnson had full discretion over whether to take Congress and the American people into his confidence. Political calculations led him to minimize the Americanization of the war.

In a brief exchange of fire between North Vietnamese torpedo boats and a U.S. Navy destroyer in international waters in the Tonkin Gulf on August 2, 1964, the Johnson administration saw an opportunity to demonstrate American firmness to audiences both at home and abroad. The initial incident was followed by a report, later retracted, of a second encounter.[29] With little regard for the accuracy of the information, the administration hurriedly prepared a resolution for Congress that would authorize a limited military response and shared it with legislative leaders. Enraged at the attacks, the lawmakers encouraged the administration to broaden the wording to permit wider use of force. The revised Tonkin Gulf Resolution passed both houses of Congress with minimal opposition (two senators voted nay; there were no negative votes in the House of Representatives).[30] Within days American aircraft struck the torpedo boat bases and a fuel storage facility.

The Tonkin Gulf incident and its aftermath played directly into the president's hands during the 1964 campaign. Public support was strong for both the resolution and the administration's measured military response. Through his restrained initial use of the mandate Congress had given him, Johnson met his immediate political needs. He demonstrated responsible firmness against communist provocations. American voters could see the striking contrast between the president's approach and the reckless bellicosity advocated by his 1964 Republican presidential opponent, Senator Barry Goldwater.[31]

At the same time, Johnson refrained from making any specific commitments about future American actions in Vietnam, including pledges not to send American troops to fight in foreign wars of the sort that had haunted Roosevelt after his 1940 reelection campaign. In a speech in late September 1964, Johnson chose his words very carefully: "I have not thought we were ready for American boys to do the fighting for Asian boys. What I have been trying to do was to get the boys in Vietnam to do their own fighting—we are not going north and drop bombs at this stage of the game."[32] A careful listener would have noted that Johnson kept open every military option. The president's deft campaign and his foe's extreme positions resulted in a landslide Democratic victory, including huge congressional majorities. Johnson emerged well positioned for sweeping legislative success the following year. If Vietnam could be contained, the Great Society appeared within his reach.

But the war would not stay in its place. The downward trajectory of the Saigon government continued through 1964 and into the following year, marked by a series of negative indicators—ongoing political turmoil among South Vietnamese leaders, loss of government control over the rural population, increasing VC guerilla attacks, and worsening ARVN combat performance. Further, the Vietcong began to strike American installations more frequently, inflicting significant casualties and prompting further retaliatory U.S. air strikes against the North.[33] The president approved a sustained bombing campaign, Operation Rolling Thunder, against targets in North Vietnam, and raids commenced on March 2, 1965. It marked another turning point in the war, but still the administration made no public announcement.[34]

That month General Westmoreland requested deployment of two battalions of U.S. Marines to protect the major American base at Danang. Soon thereafter, he asked for substantial ground troop reinforcements, two full divisions, to make possible offensive operations in South Vietnam, warning that otherwise the government faced probable military defeat. His bleak assessment of the situation was confirmed by the Joint Chiefs of Staff (JCS) in June 1965: the Chiefs recommended even larger reinforcements and concluded the United States would need to assume the primary combat role while the ARVN was rebuilt and retrained. Westmoreland outlined his requirements to McNamara when he visited the following month—some 175,000 men by the end of the year and another 100,000 in 1966—and the defense secretary forwarded the request to the president on July 20, 1965.

A week of intensive discussions within the administration and between the president and leading politicians followed, but the die had already been cast. Johnson would Americanize the war. With each new proposal to take the next step deeper into the war—to move from specific retaliation for VC attacks on American installations to a sustained air offensive, to use American troops not just to defend the bases but take the war to the enemy—presidential advisors reenacted their now-familiar roles. George Ball, seeing Saigon as hopeless, urged the president to cut his losses by seeking a political settlement that would put the best face on defeat.[35] In July he found more support within the administration: Clark Clifford darkly predicted the war would generate heavy losses to no gain, and both he and Vice President Humphrey warned the American public would never support the kind of war Johnson proposed to fight.[36] The president would listen attentively and appear almost swayed by their warnings. Then McNamara or Bundy would crisply discount their arguments, warn against the extremes of either withdrawal or all-out escalation, and leave, as the only responsible choice, the latest version of the superficially reasonable middle course that most of the president's civilian, military, and political advisors had long favored.[37]

In March 1965 this middle course meant a shift from retaliatory air attacks to an ongoing bombing campaign against North Vietnam; in July, it meant the introduction of enough American troops to stabilize the situation and then turn the tables on the VC and NVA. Most of the politicians with whom the president conferred likewise counseled him to meet mounting communist violence in kind, though they voiced serious misgivings about the prospects for success. A few, especially Senator Mansfield, continued to dissent and urged the president to eschew intervention. Each time, Johnson, after admitting his own doubts (partly, one suspects, for the historical record), would agree with the mainstream recommendation, which after all fit his own guiding assumption that Vietnam must be held.[38]

His approach and his decisions cast the idea of presidential freedom of action in a new light. Given the assumptions that guided American foreign policy and prevailing popular attitudes, any American president of the era would likely have adopted a similar course in Southeast Asia in 1964–1965. Defeat in South Vietnam would compromise the American international position. Of note, the few advisors who dissented from the dominant interventionist view still subscribed to the larger Cold War perspective. They tried to argue that even the mighty United States needed to choose its battlegrounds, and Vietnam was simply the wrong place to fight. But to most of those around the president, history suggested that as the guarantor of international stability the nation must take up the communist challenge wherever it presented itself. Put another way, within the conventional foreign policy outlook of American leaders in 1964–1965, a president facing the situation that confronted Lyndon Johnson exercised no real agency or choice on the decision to go to war.[39] As with the wartime presidents before him, circumstances drove Johnson in only one possible direction. All that differed was the nature of the circumstances, here more ideological than practical but no less binding.

Johnson did exercise full control, by contrast, over the politics of going to war in Vietnam—whether to seek a declaration of war or explicit congressional approval for a major commitment of American forces. Although the Tonkin Gulf Resolution's broad wording met the formal test of legislative approval, to rest escalation entirely on that foundation represented a gamble. Harry Truman had based his authority to intervene in Korea on the United Nations Charter, even though congressional leaders unanimously endorsed his decision and he easily could have secured legislative support in June 1950. When the war stalled and popular disillusionment followed, he could not fall back on the approval of Congress.

Johnson had seen this and understood the risks: a president becomes politically vulnerable if a war becomes unpopular. A close student of Roosevelt, he had also learned that sacrifice abroad requires consensus at home.[40] Yet he chose not to seek additional congressional authorization when he resolved to Americanize the war because he rejected the derailing of his domestic agenda. On the same basis he decided not to support intervention by calling up the military reserves, contrary to a JCS recommendation. To activate reserve forces for more than a year required an act of Congress, and the price might be suspension or reduction of domestic programs.[41] American forces would be stretched thin around the world, though the troop requirements estimated by McNamara and Westmoreland in 1965 suggested it would be possible to fight the war *and* pursue the Great Society simultaneously.

Besides declining to ask Congress to endorse large-scale military intervention, Johnson preferred not to test public support for his decision. No public announcement accompanied the beginning of Rolling Thunder, so it appeared at first to be no more than an extension of the earlier pattern of retaliatory raids.[42] As early as April 1965 the president approved the wider use of Westmoreland's Marines in offensive operations. Again he issued no statement. After the change became public in a low-key press release two months later and attracted some worried editorial comment, administration dissembling continued. The White House claimed that there had been no change in the mission of U.S. ground forces. More remarkably, when Johnson in late July 1965 approved the large-scale commitment of ground forces in Vietnam, he announced his action at a midday press conference at which he denied that the additional troops represented a change in American policy.[43]

Johnson's refusal to bring the American people into his confidence troubled both his military and civilian advisors. The Joint Chiefs had favored a reserve call-up in part to remind the American people that the nation was going to war. All the more troubling, Johnson had been warned that defeating the communists would require a long struggle, one certain to test the patience of the citizenry. Nevertheless, he took no steps to rally the public behind his decisions to escalate American involvement, even though polls showed the war to be popular.[44]

Johnson's refusal to explain his decision to the American people posed a risk for his wartime leadership. A president has to prepare the citizenry. Roosevelt had also done little to move public opinion in favor of American involvement, even when he saw war approaching in 1940–1941, but Pearl Harbor proved a godsend, uniting Americans at one stroke behind a full-scale war effort. The Tonkin Gulf incident did not rise to the same level. Nonetheless, popular support for retaliation indicated that Johnson would find it much easier to sway the public on the need for military intervention. Americans were already primed to meet any communist threat their leaders identified—"to pay any price, bear any burden," as Kennedy had put it in his inaugural address. But that support, as Humphrey and Clifford realized, was shallow. It would not sustain a prolonged conflict or heavy losses unless the president secured an informed popular commitment upfront, likely at the price of the Great Society. Johnson led the nation into the Vietnam conflict on a very fragile political foundation.[45]

Peace without Victory

Johnson first laid out American goals in Vietnam in a speech at Johns Hopkins University on April 7, 1965, before he had decided whether to commit American ground forces.[46] As the first goal, the United States sought to secure the independence of South Vietnam as a nation free to determine its own future. A clear parallel could be drawn in recent American experience to South Korea. There the United States had intervened in June 1950 to preserve a noncommunist state that faced a direct invasion and had succeeded after a protracted conflict. The president stated the situation in terms that echoed the Korean precedent: "The first reality is that North Viet-Nam has attacked the independent nation of South Viet-Nam. Its object is total conquest." The United States would assist South Vietnam in meeting this aggression. "Our objective is the independence of South Viet-Nam, and its freedom from attack." The young nation must be guaranteed the opportunity to shape its own future and its relations with the rest of the world. Without specifying what an independent South Vietnamese state would look like, the president made clear that the United States would not withdraw "under the cloak of a meaningless agreement."[47] Political expedients such as neutralization did not meet the test of independence.

Of course, the situation in South Vietnam was by no means as straightforward as the South Korea parallel implied. Johnson acknowledged that a substantial domestic insurgency threatened the collapse of the Saigon government. Yet that should not be permitted to deflect attention from the real struggle: the war continued because of a steady stream of men and supplies from North Vietnam. More critically, the aggression drew upon a larger and far more dangerous wellspring. "The confused nature of this conflict," Johnson continued, "cannot mask the fact that it is the new face of an old enemy." Communist China, the source of much of the violence across the globe, lurked behind the aggression in Vietnam, urging on the leaders in Hanoi.[48] This external pressure invested the conflict with more than local significance. At stake in Vietnam was international stability writ large, and the United States remained determined to preserve world order.

Beyond guaranteeing the independence of South Vietnam, Johnson identified a second fundamental national objective. Every president since 1954 had pledged to maintain the integrity of South Vietnam. American credibility was therefore at stake. By halting aggression at this point, the United States would reassure other nations that relied upon American security guarantees, and thereby check the possibility that disorder and violence would spread across Southeast Asia and beyond.[49] The sanctity of our word, Johnson insisted, meant that the United States did not have the luxury of choosing when it might be too difficult or costly to uphold it. We would demonstrate that we had the means and will to meet aggression in any place in the world, even one as admittedly unpromising as South Vietnam.

Unlike Wilson and Roosevelt, Johnson did not seek to transform the international system. He had inherited a world divided into two power blocs, Western and communist, and would honor the American commitment to prevent the latter from gaining ground. The American role, then, was at its core a conservative one: to preserve the local status quo as an expression of the larger balance of power. Johnson's war goals were conservative in a second critical sense, too. In sustaining the independence of South Vietnam, his primary objective, he would take no risk of provoking either Soviet or Chinese intervention and thus widening the war. And so he added that American intervention sought to do only what was "absolutely necessary" to secure South Vietnamese independence and security.[50] The United States would fight a war for a limited, specific goal in a manner intended to avoid any danger of a general war.

The president's expression of war goals masked several potential problems. Johnson stated American objectives in stark, even rigid terms. In doing so, he painted himself into a corner, a curious move for a politician renowned for his shrewdness. By insisting absolutely on South Vietnamese independence and ruling out withdrawal under a political agreement, he left little space for political compromise. He also declined to define any expectations for the South Vietnamese government, despite the fact that American policy makers blamed much of the deterioration in the regime's military fortunes on its political failings. Thus he could not use a corrupt and inept Saigon to justify disengagement; indeed, he gave South Vietnamese political leaders great leverage over any possible political settlement. Political initiative was placed largely in communist hands, too, for Johnson said the other side would determine when peace would come.[51]

Basing American credibility on South Vietnam represented a broader risk, too. Success in international power politics requires strategic flexibility—sometimes retreat is the wiser course. Strong as America was in the 1960s, its power was not unlimited, and its leaders understood this.[52] They worried that if the United States became too deeply enmeshed in Southeast Asia, American resources would be insufficient to meet crises elsewhere. This consideration weighed on the Joint Chiefs, who advised the president to mobilize the country fully for war, and on key foreign leaders. All feared the United States would be less able to meet its broad-ranging security obligations, in Western Europe,

Asia, and the Pacific, if it became bogged down in Vietnam. Thus, by upholding promises to Saigon, other American guarantees became *less* credible. Johnson compounded the danger that American military means would not suffice to meet multiple security challenges, moreover, by his determination to press ahead with the Great Society program. In effect, he gambled that Southeast Asia would be the only place where the steadfastness of the United States and its allies would be tested.

Finally, the war goals that Johnson established presumed that the American people would share his willingness for a protracted conflict in which the full military power of the nation could not be deployed. Reminding his fellow countrymen that the conflict required "the will to endure," he asserted that success would come when the communist adversary realized that "our patience and our determination are unending."[53] He asked, in short, that the American people bear the sacrifices of war indefinitely. There was an obvious tension between his efforts to downplay the war by refusing to make it the centerpiece of administration policy and the potential cost Americans would be called upon to pay. Further, as Korea had demonstrated, public patience would be severely tested by a limited war and the accompanying political restrictions on how the American military could apply force. American ideas of victory had been shaped by the experience of the Second World War, in which the destruction and occupation of the enemy's homeland had served as clear markers of success. General Douglas MacArthur had tapped this memory when he had challenged the Truman policy in Korea by proclaiming that "there is no substitute for victory." If the enemy proved resilient and the conflict dragged on, the president would face mounting public pressure to make full use of American military power and expand the scope of the conflict. Popular frustration might outweigh the abstract concern about provoking intervention by the major communist powers.

No Meeting of the Minds

Johnson enjoyed an advantage over every one of his wartime predecessors in that he would not have to wait for the creation of a substantial military establishment. How suitable that force was for the Vietnam conflict was another matter. Military leadership would vex Johnson throughout the war. Problems started at the top, where the president inherited a climate of mutual mistrust between his senior civilian advisors and his military chiefs. He believed he had found an effective, aggressive field commander in General Westmoreland. But where Westmoreland stood out as a fine conventional officer, he was asked to take charge of a war that was anything but conventional.

After the Second World War, with the burden of frontline defense of anticommunist interests around the world thrust on the United States, peacetime disarmament was no longer possible. The U.S. military again had lapsed into a low state of readiness by the start of the Korean War, but major reinforcements were available to MacArthur within a couple of months to permit him to undertake his bold amphibious riposte at Inchon. At the end of the conflict, the United States had retained a vast military establishment, sustained by peacetime conscription and a robust defense sector that churned out the most advanced weaponry in the world. As the United States entered the Vietnam conflict, the American military establishment claimed more than 2 million active-duty personnel. A rapid military buildup in Southeast Asia was possible even without mobilization of reserve forces; political calculations and logistics[54] would determine the pace of deployment, not troop availability.

On the other hand, neither advanced equipment nor large troop numbers guaranteed that American soldiers were prepared for the kind of combat they would meet. The United States military had been configured first and foremost to deter a massive Soviet attack in Europe and a Soviet nuclear strike. However, as the Kennedy administration recognized, many weapons intended for possible use in such a potential war—ranging from tanks to interceptors designed to shoot down approaching Soviet bombers to intercontinental ballistic missiles—would be of little or no use in the brushfire wars ignited by national liberation struggles. To deal with the mismatch between a military establishment designed for one kind of war but facing another, Kennedy and a number of his key aides had to step on toes at the Pentagon. Counterinsurgency advocates pushed creation of the Green Berets, an elite unit that would train and advise the armed forces of threatened friendly governments.[55] But the Special Forces could not cope with the expansion of the Vietnamese communist war effort in 1964–1965 beyond the guerrilla phase. The task now fell to arriving American conventional troops.

They would find themselves up against a complex political-military challenge. American troops faced an enemy who was more familiar with the terrain and adept at camouflage, and who could seek sanctuary in places ruled off-limits to American forces. They would need to take care, too, not to alienate the population from the Saigon government. Similarly, American aircraft would be expected to disrupt heavily defended enemy supply efforts while operating within tight constraints laid down for political reasons. Johnson's decisions not to mobilize reserves and to limit the tour of duty in Vietnam to one year posed further challenges. American units would be forced to cope with inexperience and high turnover, both damaging to unit cohesion, throughout the conflict.[56]

That lack of cohesion spread to the highest ranks. Lincoln had struggled to put together a military team to realize his purposes; identifying commanders in tune with their objectives quickly was the good fortune of both Wilson and Roosevelt. Johnson stepped into a situation of poor civil-military relations at the Pentagon that fed ongoing tensions between top civilian advisors and their counterparts in uniform. He found himself sharply at odds with his military chiefs, quickly creating a poisonous climate that destroyed mutual confidence.

Friction at the Pentagon dated back to Kennedy's selection of Robert McNamara as secretary of defense. With a reputation for both brilliance and arrogance, McNamara arrived to find a Defense Department mired in outdated management practices and stale strategic thinking. He promptly introduced new management systems, including rigorous reviews of new and proposed weapons systems for cost effectiveness, which antagonized old Pentagon hands. He and his civilian assistants showed no greater sympathy for how uniformed commanders approached military problems. Evidently persuaded of the old adage that generals prepare for the last war, McNamara and company turned instead to academic strategists for guidance in how to meet current military threats. The Kennedy administration had to prod the military to take seriously the challenge of low-level national liberation struggles. (Army Chief of Staff General George H. Decker was ousted quickly after he expressed a dismissive view of guerilla warfare, and Kennedy hinted that future promotions would be based on experience in counterinsurgency operations.)[57] None of this boded well for mutual understanding when the United States found itself engaged in a major war quite unlike recent conflicts and posing daunting, interwoven political and military problems.

At the most fundamental level, McNamara and other civilian advisors had a different conception of the nature of war, especially limited conflicts such as the one in Vietnam, from that of the military leadership. To the civilians, war represented an extension of politics as a rational form of human activity. An adversary could be deterred or discouraged if the price imposed on him outweighed the potential gain from fighting. Actual war required inflicting sufficient pain to make the enemy accept a political settlement—in this instance, compelling Hanoi to respect the independence of South Vietnam. The point at which the other side would be prepared to accept terms might not be known in advance, but it could be identified through a gradual increase in violence, each additional increment of which would also communicate American seriousness of purpose and the intention to continue raising the level of destruction.

For the military, by contrast, war was a messy, imprecise business that unleashed powerful emotions, undermining any effort to calibrate the level of violence or connect it to a predictable political response. Military commanders, such as General Earle "Bus" Wheeler, JCS chairman during the escalation phase of the Vietnam War, believed that past conflicts, especially the Second World War, demonstrated the need to cripple completely an enemy's capacity to continue to fight. Victory, however defined, required inflicting maximum punishment on the enemy, and doing so as quickly as possible to break his will and minimize losses on both sides—what a later generation would refer to as "shock and awe." The JCS pressed the president to fully exploit American military assets and complained about civilian Pentagon leaders who refused to do so.[58]

Johnson found himself caught between these incompatible views of warfare. He sympathized with the uniformed commanders' view that military resources should be used to overwhelm an adversary. Still, he subscribed to the belief that the war must be contained and all measures that might widen it avoided.[59] The military conception of how to fight fit poorly with a war waged under such tight political constraints. In addition, the JCS chafed under the decision not to mobilize for war and repeatedly recommended that the president call up reserves, an option Johnson had rejected at the outset and would continue to shun. He dealt with his commanders through a version of what has been called the "Johnson treatment": a mixture of bullying and flattery, his well-honed technique for dominating interpersonal relations. When the chiefs responded to the lack of progress by urging a turn to their kind of warfare, the president lashed out at them, excoriating them for their utter lack of imagination, their inability to come up with any better idea than more or heavier bombing.[60] At the same time, he suggested that he saw merit in their arguments and never ruled out their requests once and for all. He also knew when to throw them a bone. After their frustrations with McNamara became public in summer 1967, the president decided the secretary of defense should be eased out. The president also started to include General Wheeler or another JCS member in his small Tuesday meetings on the war. These occasional sops sufficed to deter his military commanders from resigning as a group to protest the restraints under which the military fought.[61]

Both the president and the nation might have been better served had they done so. Johnson should have found commanders more in tune with his policies or revisited his assumptions. And the chiefs, who believed the war unwinnable under the terms the administration had established, should have accepted Wheeler's suggestion amid the 1967 dust-up with McNamara that they resign. An open rupture over the political limitations imposed on military operations might have promoted better public understanding of and support for the administration policy, or at least led to an earlier reassessment of its viability. Instead, an unworkable situation was allowed to continue, with president and military commanders at loggerheads, an institutional stalemate that mirrored the one that took shape on the battlefield.[62]

In General Westmoreland, Johnson had a more complaisant commander with whom to work in the battle zone itself. Based on Westmoreland's military assessment, the administration decided that the South Vietnamese military was on the brink of defeat in 1965. The general also recommended that American troops be used in offensive operations, and he requested sufficient manpower to permit U.S. forces to assume

Abraham Lincoln led the nation through its greatest existential crisis, the Civil War. Over the course of the conflict, he showed himself to be an exceptional wartime leader. Yet even Lincoln fell into a trap that has often ensnared his wartime successors—waiting too long to begin planning for peace.

Secretary of War Edwin M. Stanton served as Lincoln's key civilian advisor.

In General Ulysses S. Grant, President Lincoln found a commander who understood how the Civil War had evolved into a total war and was prepared to prosecute it ruthlessly.

Wartime presidents should be judged in comparison to their opposite numbers. Abraham Lincoln proved a far more gifted leader than Confederate President Jefferson Davis, whose pedestrian strategic vision and misguided decisions about field commanders contributed significantly to the Confederate defeat.

Woodrow Wilson with Entente leaders (from left, Lloyd George of Great Britain, Orlando of Italy, and Clemenceau of France) in Paris in May 1919. The conference revealed how little leverage a president has over allies after the fighting ends.

General John J. Pershing commanded the American Expeditionary Force in France in World War I. Given a free hand by President Wilson, Pershing frustrated the British and French by insisting that American troops fight independently. His forces scored only modest military successes but contributed to the exhaustion of the German Army in summer 1918.

To promote popular support for the war, the Wilson administration established the Committee on Public Information (CPI) under journalist George Creel in April 1917. The committee represented the first official American attempt at propaganda.

Republican Henry Cabot Lodge, as Senate Majority Leader and Chairman of the Foreign Relations Committee, led the opposition to the Versailles peace treaty and American membership in the new League of Nations.

Franklin Roosevelt actively encouraged the military to launch the Doolittle Raid against Japan on April 18, 1942. Later in the war, the president left most key military decisions to his senior commanders.

Army Chief of Staff General George C. Marshall was Franklin Roosevelt's indispensable military aide. Assuming his position at the time of the German invasion of Poland in 1939, Marshall pressed for balanced American rearmament and helped sell peacetime conscription to Congress. Once the United States entered the war, he pushed for a second front in northwest Europe before Allied forces were ready, but also appreciated the need to resist misguided British pressure to extend campaigns in the Mediterranean.

General Dwight Eisenhower served as the supreme Allied commander in Europe, a role that was as much diplomatic as it was military.

Franklin Roosevelt meets in Hawaii in 1944 with his top commanders in the Pacific, General Douglas MacArthur (left) and Admiral Chester Nimitz (holding pointer) to discuss the possible invasion of the Philippines. Managing MacArthur, who had strong ties to American conservatives, was a recurring political challenge for the president. Admiral William Leahy is also present.

The Yalta meeting of the Big Three—Churchill, Roosevelt, and Stalin—highlighted the fragile basis on which the wartime alliance rested. Stalin intended to establish a Soviet sphere of influence in Eastern Europe and the Western powers had no means to reverse his determination. Roosevelt's ailing health is evident.

Lyndon Johnson and his field commander, General William Westmoreland. Johnson's failure to oversee Westmoreland's conduct of the war represented a critical failure of presidential leadership.

Lyndon Johnson with two key advisors, Secretary of State Dean Rusk (left) and Secretary of Defense Robert McNamara (right). An early advocate of escalation, McNamara soon began to question whether the United States military could achieve the political goals the president sought and urged limiting the American commitment while seeking a negotiated solution.

The Tet Offensive in 1968, though a military debacle for the communists, demolished the Johnson administration's claims of progress in the war. Here the president and Vice President Hubert Humphrey, meet with General Creighton Abrams, who would soon succeed Westmoreland in command.

By 1968, the war in Vietnam and domestic strife had exhausted Lyndon Johnson.

Richard Nixon, Henry Kissinger, and General Alexander Haig discuss Vietnam at Camp David in November 1972, seeking to resolve the negotiating stalemate created by South Vietnamese President Thieu's refusal to accept the preliminary Paris peace agreement.

Secretary of Defense Melvin Laird (left) was the lead architect of Richard Nixon's policy to turn over the fighting in South Vietnam to President Thieu's army. But Laird was marginalized within the administration because he dissented from the president's impulse to flex his muscles against North Vietnam.

Transfer of command: in early 2007, General George Casey, who finally lost the confidence of President Bush in the wake of the ongoing insurgency in Iraq, gave way to General David Petraeus, a strong proponent of the troop surge and counterinsurgency methods. Petraeus would later command in Afghanistan under Bush's successor, Barack Obama.

Army Chief of Staff General Eric Shinseki warned before the invasion of Iraq in 2003 that the United States might need 400,000 troops in the event of an insurgency. Though his estimate was dismissed by the Bush administration at the time, this was roughly the number of U.S. and Iraqi troops that finally stemmed the tide of violence in Iraq beginning in 2007.

President Bush retained Secretary of Defense Donald Rumsfeld long after it became clear that U.S. policy in Iraq was failing. Rumsfeld disdained "nation building," but he could offer no better alternative than to let the Iraqis fail on their own. Finally, after the Republican defeat in the 2006 mid-term elections, the president accepted Rumsfeld's resignation.

President George W. Bush in 2002 flanked by National Security Advisor Condoleeza Rice (far left), Secretary of State Colin Powell, and Secretary of Defense Donald Rumsfeld. Powell was the most skeptical of the wisdom of invading Iraq, but played a significant role in promoting the case against Saddam Hussein before the United Nations.

the burden of fighting VC/NVA regular formations. His suggestions received a favorable response from the president; indeed, Johnson at the very least signaled to his general that he would be receptive to a call to commit American ground forces. Westmoreland certainly did not welcome the restrictions that civilian leadership imposed,[63] but he accepted them and never voiced public criticism of the kind that had led to MacArthur's firing in Korea. He asked repeatedly for more troops than either the president or McNamara was prepared to approve. Every time, he accepted without open protest the smaller increases he was given, merely pointing out that the result would be to extend the conflict.[64]

Westmoreland became the target of criticism during and after the war, much of it justified.[65] Given the military constraints Washington imposed, his military options were severely limited. That said, his operational approach to fighting the war through search-and-destroy operations was unimaginative and led to heavy American casualties. He dismissed arguments that the emphasis should be shifted to providing better security to the population and extending government control over rural areas.[66] He also was slow to appreciate the need to prepare the South Vietnamese military to resume the lead in combat. In the period before the Tet Offensive in January 1968, moreover, he misinterpreted the main focus of enemy plans, with the result that many U.S. and ARVN units were poorly positioned, though in the end the troops under his command repelled the enemy attacks. Sometimes, most notably in the months before Tet, he declared that his forces had turned the corner in the war and had defeated the enemy on the battlefield.[67] But he also faced enormous political pressures from Washington to claim success, leading him to interpret ambiguous evidence in a way that suggested dramatic gains. One lesson seems clear: in a situation like the one confronting Westmoreland, no military commander could have emerged untarnished.

Johnson might have replaced Westmoreland as signs of a military stalemate became unmistakable, but the very criticism directed at the MACV commander paradoxically made his position more secure. The situation recalls the Lincoln-McClellan relationship: both the president and his senior civilian aide (then Stanton, now McNamara) were frustrated with the lack of results achieved by the key military commander.

In a summer 1967 trip to Vietnam, McNamara blurted out to reporters that he thought Westmoreland had enough men and simply needed to make better use of them. Rather than bite the bullet as Lincoln had, however, Johnson stood by his ineffective general. The president did so not because he still had confidence in Westmoreland but because removing him would amount to an admission that his initial selection had been a mistake.[68] Refusing to admit error is a luxury no wartime president can afford. Lincoln seems to have been the rare president to appreciate this.

Choosing the Least Bad Strategy

Johnson declined either to put his stamp on the conduct of the war or shape military operations to meet his goals. Beyond translating the underlying assumptions about how to keep China out of the war into a set of restrictions on American military operations, he and his senior civilian advisors provided little guidance for the military. This was unfortunate, because in Vietnam the U.S. military confronted an unfamiliar kind of conflict, waged on several levels by a sophisticated enemy. Given the complexity of the challenges, field commanders needed effective direction and oversight. Instead, the military chafed under the limits that Washington imposed, while those in uniform and civilians pointed fingers at each other for the lack of progress.

The Vietnamese communists conducted multiple, interlocking political and military campaigns. Adapting the approach of Mao Zedong—as tested in their earlier war against the French—they pursued a strategy that evolved through three stages. Phase one took the form of a low-level insurgency designed to erode government authority and win allegiance of the people. This had commenced in South Vietnam in the late 1950s and continued throughout the Diem period. His ouster and murder had coincided with the beginning of the second phase of the struggle, in which guerilla forces launched more ambitious attacks on government troops, undermining their morale and further eroding the regime's authority. Vietcong (and possibly NVA) troops engaged in successful assaults on ever-larger ARVN units, backed by the increasing flow of men, equipment, and supplies down the Ho Chi Minh Trail. By mid-1965 communist forces seemed on the verge of

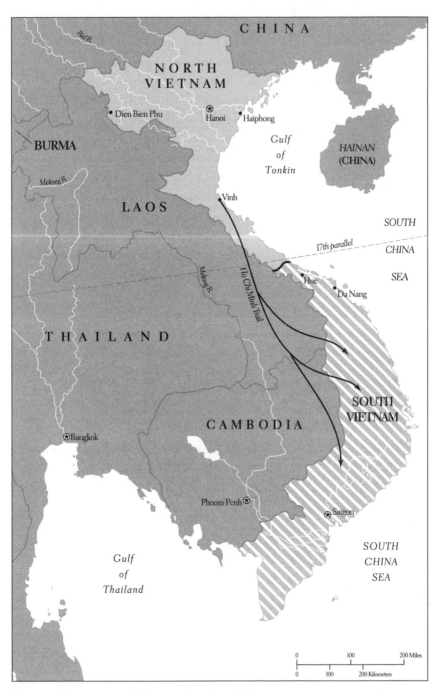

Map 4.1 Communist Infiltration into South Vietnam

moving to the third phase, a general offensive to topple the Saigon government, which they were eager to accomplish before American troops might arrive in significant numbers. (See map 4.1)

The United States escalated its military effort in time to forestall what seemed an imminent communist triumph, but American forces arrived to find themselves engaged in a multitiered struggle. In villages and hamlets, U.S. troops would need to mount a counterinsurgency campaign against communist guerillas and their political infrastructure, competing for the support of the population, "winning hearts and minds." Simultaneously, American troops would attempt to reverse enemy gains in conventional warfare. Since the communist forces in South Vietnam relied heavily on reinforcement and resupply from the North, moreover, the United States needed to interdict the communist lines of communication, disrupt enemy sanctuaries, and raise the cost of supporting the war so that Hanoi would cease the effort and negotiate. Breaking the North-South communist link, American commanders believed, depended on an effective bombing campaign.

Presidents typically exercise their greatest discretion early in a military conflict. Over time, as the cumulative weight of their decisions makes it harder to shift direction, they lose the capacity to shape the course of events. Lincoln represented a partial exception because he redefined war goals when he embraced emancipation. Roosevelt, on the other hand, made his most important decisions—ranging from ratifying the Germany First grand strategy to his insistence on operations in North Africa and his support for the Marines on Guadalcanal—during the first year after Pearl Harbor. Where Lincoln, Wilson, and Roosevelt all took care to preserve their freedom of action upon going to war, Johnson surrendered his, evidently with little reflection. Instead he simply took in stride the limits on American operational flexibility that derived from assumptions about Chinese behavior and how much guns and butter Congress would buy at the same time. He further tied his hands when, for the sake of the Great Society, he decided not to put the nation on a war footing.

Thus, although on paper a conflict between the United States and the Vietnamese communists appeared a mismatch, politics helped even the odds. Overruling the military, the president and key civilian advisors rejected a number of military actions deemed too inflammatory to the

Soviet Union or China.[69] The administration barred the mining of Haiphong harbor, the key port for the delivery of Soviet munitions, for fear that the sinking of a Soviet vessel with significant casualties might force Moscow to respond in Vietnam or elsewhere. American aircraft would also stay well clear of the China–North Vietnam border. Further bombing limitations reflected a concern for public relations: American officials believed air raids on major population centers on the scale of the World War II strategic bombing of German and Japanese cities would alienate public opinion at home or abroad. The administration also worried that extending the war into Laos to block the Ho Chi Minh Trail or into Cambodia to disrupt communist sanctuaries would be overly provocative, especially since the United States had recently agreed to assure Laos its neutrality.[70]

Military manpower ceilings represented the other key limitation on the American war effort. Because the president decided against the mobilization of reserves, the war would be fought within tight personnel constraints. The initial 1965 approval for a major increase in U.S. forces in South Vietnam meant Westmoreland would receive the troops he needed to halt communist advances plus enough to take the offensive in 1966. But as he asked (with JCS endorsement) for more men, his new requests ran up against competing American military obligations elsewhere around the world, especially to NATO in Europe and in South Korea. The military leadership soon expressed alarm that U.S. forces were stretched too thin.[71] Other nations, including South Korea, Taiwan, and Australia, sent troops to South Vietnam to augment the American commitment, but the administration could ask only so much of these allies; other Western powers refused to support the war effort.[72] As an added complication, maintaining a large military force on the far side of the globe required a major logistical establishment, so a high percentage of American forces in Southeast Asia consisted of support personnel who did no fighting. American and ARVN combat troops accordingly enjoyed at best a modest numerical advantage over their adversaries, though they also had much greater firepower and mobility.

From the outset of the Rolling Thunder bombing campaign against the DRV, the president's military and civilian advisors split over policy. Civilian officials regarded bombing both as a military tool to hamper

North Vietnamese support for communist forces attacking South Vietnam and as a means to pressure Hanoi to negotiate. Under close civilian oversight, the attacks increased in scale and frequency over a number of months. Ratcheting up the pressure, it was felt, sent a signal to the enemy that worse would come if he refused to discuss ending his effort to destroy South Vietnamese independence. Military leaders rejected this logic and called for an all-out campaign to block supply efforts, including attacks that would impede the flow of materials into the DRV from China and the Soviet Union. Gradual escalation, moreover, let the enemy adjust to each increment of violence, neutralizing its psychological impact. The North Vietnamese also gained ample time to strengthen their air defenses around likely targets, with a resulting increase in U.S. aircraft and pilot losses.

McNamara and other civilian advisors quickly concluded that bombing would never accomplish more than to limit enemy infiltration.[73] As the civilian side saw it, evidence failed to substantiate military assertions that lifting most target restrictions would severely impair the communist resupply effort. Civilian officials also worried over the negative publicity the bombing attracted. Despite restrictions to avoid hitting densely populated areas, air raids killed and maimed noncombatants and destroyed nonmilitary targets, and the North Vietnamese made sure these mistakes were publicized. Popular sensibilities had changed in the generation since Dresden and Hiroshima, too, and world opinion recoiled from the destruction. Last, as in the Second World War, bombing seemed to harden the resolve of enemy civilians and bolster their support for the Hanoi leadership.[74]

Civilian-military discord also erupted over the frequent bombing pauses the administration imposed as part of its diplomatic efforts. Sometimes the pauses would be accompanied by very public diplomatic overtures designed to show American willingness to seek a peace agreement. Each pause angered American military commanders, who pointed out that the communists used the opportunity to increase their rate of reinforcement and resupply to the South. The JCS also maintained that the enemy would interpret these halts as evidence that the United States lacked the will to win. Rather than make gestures to induce the North Vietnamese to meet at the conference table, General Wheeler argued, the tempo of air operations should be increased.[75] And each time, following some delay while the arguments were rehashed, Johnson would agree to resume the air raids.

On the ground within South Vietnam, meanwhile, the United States would fight what amounted to two separate wars. In response to the threat posed by the Vietcong and its NLF political wing, American and South Vietnamese forces continued the counterinsurgency effort. They aimed to win over the rural population through a combination of security measures and economic development. The task was daunting, however. Most peasants likely did not care who won and thought instead in more immediate terms about their security; they might go either way, depending upon which side could better protect them. The communists had built up a strong political infrastructure and intelligence network that would take time to dismantle. For its part, the Saigon government had demonstrated little capacity for pacification, and its troops often alienated the population they were supposed to safeguard by indiscriminate harsh treatment of anyone suspected of sympathizing with the communists.[76] Despite the obvious importance of counterinsurgency, pacification proceeded haphazardly during the first several years of the Americanized war. General Westmoreland reported at the beginning of 1968 that the South Vietnamese government seemed to have made very little progress, suffering from widespread corruption and inefficiency, while the VC infrastructure remained intact.[77]

There was ample blame to go around. Part of the problem was institutional: no U.S. agency owned the responsibility for making a real nation out of South Vietnam. By default, then, the task fell to the American military, which lacked either the experience or the capacity for pacification. Westmoreland showed far more interest in tackling regular communist forces, which he deemed the greater threat, than in the slow work of bringing security to the countryside. His own intelligence chief said pacification bored the MACV commander. When an army study found that pacification depended on successful small-unit operations that improved security at the local level, Westmoreland rejected the report, which implied that his approach was misguided.[78] He treated local security and his military operations as unrelated. (Regular communist units understood the importance of political support among the rural population because they depended upon local

VC cadres for intelligence and supplies.)[79] In 1967, with pacification stalled, Robert Komer, a senior civilian official, was placed in charge of the effort. But his abrasive personal style put off Americans and South Vietnamese alike and he accomplished little.[80]

To defeat regular VC/NVA forces, Westmoreland pursued a strategy of attrition. Attrition presumes greater military resources than the adversary possesses, so combat erodes his fighting power and eventually forces him to recognize that he cannot prevail by military means. Westmoreland believed U.S. troops, backed by massive air support and enjoying far superior firepower, could destroy the combat effectiveness of VC and NVA regular (or "mainforce") units whenever these were brought to battle. Because the elusive enemy avoided fighting on terms the Americans preferred, it would be necessary for American troops to engage in "search-and-destroy" operations to find and eliminate him. The savage encounter in the Ia Drang Valley in November 1965 pointed to what Westmoreland intended: some 300 Americans were killed but inflicted roughly five times as many communist deaths.

The search-and-destroy approach promised to be both costly and time-consuming. American troops would have to operate on terrain chosen by communist troops to help nullify American technological advantages. The enemy could often avoid contact when tactical circumstances placed him at a disadvantage. Still, U.S. military commanders believed that, with determination and sufficient patience, the mathematics of attrition would work in favor of the U.S., South Vietnamese, and allied forces. In his initial assessment of his force needs in summer 1965, General Westmoreland estimated that if given the manpower he requested, he could blunt the tide of communist success by the end of the year, move to the offensive during the next eighteen months, and clean out remaining enemy sanctuaries over the following year—a timetable that placed success in the summer of 1968.[81]

An insoluble tension existed, however, between the geographic constraints imposed on American military operations and Westmoreland's attrition strategy. Attrition fails when the enemy can replenish his losses. Since Washington had decided against ground operations in Laos and Cambodia, these served as sanctuaries into which the enemy could retreat under pressure, safe from pursuit. Communist forces decided when to enter combat and when to exit the battlefield, a fact that soon became apparent back in Washington if not to MACV.[82] Cutting off resupply of the enemy rested entirely on air interdiction. Yet air attacks could do no more than hamper infiltration down the Ho Chi Minh Trail. And if the Americans and South Vietnamese could not isolate the battlefield, the communists could maintain their force-in-being, possibly even expand it.[83] The result would be a military stalemate in the conventional war, neither side able to defeat the other. Ultimately, the outcome would be determined by whichever side had greater staying power, and, loath though Johnson was to admit it, that equation in turn would disadvantage the United States as the external combatant.[84]

Again and again, American military commanders pressed to remove the restrictions on U.S. military operations, but the president and his civilian advisors resisted. Through 1966 and 1967, the administration reluctantly added new bombing targets to the list, until nearly all the worthwhile military ones were struck. It was still not enough to satisfy the JCS: the Chiefs wanted to mine Haiphong harbor, the principal DRV port through which many supplies arrived, and extend bombing to near the Chinese border to block rail deliveries, too. McNamara and other civilian leaders continued to insist that the risk of widening the war was too great and cautioned that world opinion would turn even more sharply against the United States, already seen to be bullying a small nation. Johnson sided with his civilian advisors and became frustrated when, amid mounting evidence of a stalemate on the ground, the JCS seemed unable to recommend anything better than more bombing. Similarly, military suggestions to allow American ground forces to attack communist sanctuaries in Cambodia and block enemy supply lines through Laos by assaulting westward from the northern neck of South Vietnam met the same political objections as earlier—such actions, Washington repeated, posed too much danger of expanding the war.[85] (Later events would demonstrate that both sides were mistaken about the effects of removing the limits on military operations.)

The attrition strategy also fell afoul of political constraints. Early estimates minimized the number of NVA troops available for service in South Vietnam, so it seemed possible—if just barely—that communist soldiers might be killed off faster than they could be replaced.[86] It soon became painfully clear, however, that American intelligence had greatly underestimated Hanoi's will and capacity to reinforce its army in the

South. Westmoreland asked for additional troops to match the North Vietnamese effort and sustain the logic of attrition. But as McNamara warned in 1966, mutual reinforcement pointed to a new stalemate at a higher and more costly level, with victory denied to either side. He spoke of limiting the American commitment to a level that could command durable domestic political support while denying North Vietnam success. Eventually, seeing it could not prevail through trial by arms, Hanoi would negotiate a political solution that would assure some semblance of South Vietnamese independence.

By November 1967, the increasingly disillusioned McNamara went further, recommending a complete halt to the bombing of the North and a study of how best to shift the burden of fighting from American troops to the South Vietnamese.[87] The military pressed for a more robust American commitment that would allow troop increases the communists eventually could not match. Then attritional math would work its ruthless logic against Hanoi. The argument brought the debate back to the sticking point for the president: to achieve the troop levels the JCS sought would require broad national mobilization, a price he believed the American people would not pay.

Although Johnson voiced displeasure that the military leadership seemed unable to think of anything beyond more men and more bombing,[88] much of the fault for the failure to rethink policy rested with him. The president overlooked opportunities to reclaim flexibility and steer military strategy in a new direction. Having bought into the need to halt communist expansionism while keeping the Chinese and Soviets out of the Vietnam War, he never revisited the bases behind these working assumptions. Yet the world did not stand still, and the likelihood that either communist superpower would either capitalize on a drawdown in the American commitment or intervene was not a constant. In 1966, the Cultural Revolution in China sowed disorder, distracted its political leadership, and drew its military deeply into domestic political turmoil. The communist tide in Asia, moreover, no longer seemed to be advancing, as evidenced by the brutal suppression of leftists in Indonesia.[89] One year later, Johnson met Soviet Premier Alexei Kosygin at Glassboro, New Jersey, in a precursor to detente. The altered positions of China and the Soviet Union might have opened either of two paths—toward a negotiated withdrawal (because the expansionist impetus of communism had stalled) or toward a more aggressive use of force (because the likelihood that it would induce a Chinese or Soviet military response had declined significantly).[90] Instead, old fears that the major communist powers would exploit or overreact to a new American policy remained the default setting that stymied fresh thinking.

In the final analysis, the internal stalemate in the administration's Vietnam debates reflects poorly on Johnson as a wartime leader. He involved himself closely in certain details of the war—picking out specific bombing targets or having a sand table set up in the White House in early 1968 to follow the siege of the Marine base at Khe Sanh. But his selective absorption in the minutiae of warfare masked just how little meaningful direction he exercised over any aspect of American military operations. He never questioned Westmoreland about his tactics, even though American ambassadors with close knowledge of the fighting (General Maxwell Taylor and Henry Cabot Lodge Jr.) doubted the efficacy of major search-and-destroy operations.

Moreover, the exercise of promoting a full airing of policy options became a substitute for actually resolving the differences between civilians and the military. Despite McGeorge Bundy's reminder that retaining the confidence of both the public and his own government required the visible assertion of presidential leadership, Johnson never seized control of the key policy discussions, never resolved the contradictions that bedeviled military policy, and never established a coherent strategy to achieve his war goals. The president, as one later critic puts it, "refused to abandon his no-win policy."[91] Nor did he grasp the openings that a shifting international setting offered him to regain freedom of action—which, as is worth stressing again and again, is the single most vital resource a wartime political leader can possess. Put bluntly, for nearly three years, from July 1965 until February 1968, Lyndon Johnson was a commander in chief in name only.

Eroding Political Support

Sustaining public support for the Vietnam War may well have been an impossible leadership challenge. Johnson needed to stir the right amount of popular enthusiasm: enough to back a limited war of indefinite duration, but not so much that political pressure would force an all-out military effort. He never struck the proper note. On one side, a growing number of leaders from his own party and ordinary citizens did not see the struggle as important enough to risk the nation's blood and treasure, and they looked for a way out, bestowing legitimacy on a burgeoning antiwar movement. On the other side, the president's fears of stirring too much bellicosity were realized: by 1967 the largest segment of the public favored an escalation of the American war effort.[92] Squeezed between the two extremes was the smallest group, the dwindling cohort that backed the administration's constrained war.

Contentious relations with the mass media did not help the administration's efforts to communicate its version of the war. Even during the Kennedy years, reporters in Saigon had become skeptical about official accounts, and matters worsened once the war was Americanized. Correspondents soon dismissed Westmoreland's official briefings as "Five O'Clock Follies" that bore little or no relationship to the war they observed when they went into the field with U.S. or ARVN troops.[93] In part the discrepancy reflected the nature of the war itself, with its lack of visible benchmarks of progress; military operations appeared repetitious, even pointless. Government-media relations had also changed fundamentally since World War II: reporters no longer saw themselves as part of the war effort and refused to boost public morale. Doubts about the veracity of administration claims spread to Washington, so that by late 1966 the press spoke openly of a credibility gap between what administration spokesmen claimed and what was happening on the ground. The president, miffed when media interpretations of administration war policy deviated from the official line and chagrined by the attention given the growing opposition to the war, often lashed out at influential news outlets and at individual reporters.[94]

As an added obstacle to the administration's efforts to frame coverage of Vietnam, it became the first war to be witnessed in all its savagery by the American public. Television networks had expanded their news coverage, and video reports from the battlefield made for dramatic viewing.[95] Where censorship in the Second World War had insulated the home front from images of dead American soldiers, in Vietnam no such buffer existed. Scenes of mayhem and destruction became nightly newscast fare, with very little context. Haunting images of American dead and wounded seemed to negate administration claims of progress, while the occasional television report of an atrocity committed by American troops undercut the official rationale that they were there to help the South Vietnamese people. (For obvious reasons, the coverage frustrated the president because cameras did not record similar abuses by the enemy.)[96]

Elite support for the war, strong at the outset, eroded with the lack of progress on the battlefield. Where Wilson had been able to marginalize dissent during the First World War because intervention commanded broad support among mainstream leaders, Johnson faced a situation that more closely resembled Lincoln's in the Civil War—an initial surge of enthusiasm followed quickly by disappointment as casualties rose with no sign of victory. In Johnson's case, antiwar expression came not from the partisan opposition but from within the ranks of his own Democratic Party. The first critics of American involvement, leftist college students and a handful of liberals, could be ignored or dismissed. By 1966, however, the position that the United States should cease bombing North Vietnam and begin negotiations without preconditions found a growing number of mainstream advocates.[97] Foes of the war gained visibility early that year when Senator J. William Fulbright, an erstwhile Johnson backer who had turned against the war, used his position as chairman of the Senate Foreign Relations Committee to hold televised hearings on the conflict in which the critics received a full opportunity to voice their reservations.

With each passing month, additional liberal Democratic politicians broke with the president over the war. These included Robert F. Kennedy, who had strongly supported American assistance to South Vietnam while serving as attorney general under his late brother.[98] On November 30, 1967, Senator Eugene McCarthy of Minnesota, a staunch foe of the war, announced he would challenge Johnson for the Democratic presidential nomination in 1968.

Distressed though the president was about the opposition from the left, the attacks from the other end of the political spectrum caused him deeper alarm. Republicans and conservative Democrats picked up the theme that too many restrictions had been imposed on the use of American military power. In August 1967, Democratic Senator John Stennis of Mississippi, chairman of the Preparedness Investigating

Subcommittee of the Senate Armed Services Committee, held hearings on the bombing campaign that brought into public view the disagreements between the JCS and McNamara. Stennis made no bones about where his sympathies lay when he explained that the hearings were intended to examine whether the opinions of the military were being heeded so as to end the war quickly and save American lives. In its report issued at the end of the month, the subcommittee sided strongly with the military leadership. Bowing to this pressure from the right, Johnson overruled his defense secretary and authorized bombing several targets that had been placed off-limits earlier.[99] His action reflected his appreciation of the political danger conservatives represented to his agenda. Although the administration did not believe hawks might make common cause with the antiwar opposition, the possibility that they would prefer a hard-line Republican in 1968 weighed heavily on the president.

Further, conservative lawmakers held in their hands the fate of Johnson's domestic legacy, the Great Society. The president had sought from the beginning of the Americanization of the war to minimize its fiscal price tag. He went so far as to keep his budget planners out of meetings with defense officials to discuss expenditures for the war and to insist that war appropriations be approved by Congress outside of the regular budget process.[100] By the beginning of 1967, though, rising military expenditures coupled with the Great Society–induced surge in domestic outlays led to a widening federal deficit and worsening inflation. The president called for a 6 percent tax surcharge to slow the inflation rate, even as he held fast to his commitments abroad and at home. Hawks were prepared to support tax increases to pay for the war. But they made it clear that in exchange they would expect full-scale mobilization or the scaling back of Johnson's domestic agenda. Representative Wilbur Mills, chairman of the powerful House Ways and Means Committee and a Democrat from Ohio, rejected any tax bill that did not include domestic spending cuts on the same order.[101] To sustain the scale of the American commitment in Vietnam, Johnson grudgingly conceded to their demands.

As more and more political leaders rejected administration war policy from either left or right, public opinion followed. The initial broad backing for the war gave way to a downward trend, as did approval for the president's overall job performance.[102] In summer 1967, as popular disenchantment with the war increased, 65 percent of Americans in a Gallup poll said the administration was not being truthful about the war, a vivid demonstration of the magnitude of the credibility problem. That August the president's approval rating bottomed out at 39 percent, with 54 percent disapproving of his conduct of the war; in October, a Harris poll showed that backing for the war itself declined to 58 percent, a new low and down from 72 percent in July.[103]

Hidden within the overall numbers was a sharp division within the public that mirrored the split within elite policy circles. On one wing were doves who believed the United States should either withdraw unilaterally from Vietnam (still few in number by late 1967) or halt the bombing of North Vietnam and negotiate a prompt exit from the conflict. At the other end of the spectrum stood a larger fraction of the public in favor of fighting the war more vigorously. A sizable percentage of the public endorsed hawkish positions that frightened administration decision makers: in April 1967 just over a quarter of those polled favored the use of nuclear weapons in Vietnam, while the following December nearly half endorsed a ground invasion of North Vietnam. Sandwiched between these two camps was the smallest group, Americans who backed the administration's war policy.[104]

The administration debated internally how best to present its case but could not settle on a single theme. Veering from a principled defense of freedom wherever threatened, to America's own self-defense, to the need to fight a small war to avert a much larger one, the inconsistent messages did not make things clearer to the American people.[105] Citizens puzzled, too, over why, if the war mattered so much, they were not being asked to make greater sacrifices. The president's conviction that support for the war would collapse if the price became too great clashed directly with popular expectations that any conflict worth the cost ought to impose a price on everyone.[106] The public also voiced confusion over the actual war policy, a predictable consequence of the administration's effort to strike a delicate balance between being firm without becoming too bellicose.

Meanwhile, Johnson found it impossible to discredit the antiwar movement. It continued to gather steam, staging larger demonstrations in 1967 that attracted considerable media attention. The president and his spokesmen often attacked the critics who urged an early withdrawal from South Vietnam as agents, perhaps unwitting, perhaps not, of Hanoi. Although this aggressive response scored well with a significant segment of the public, antiwar activists enjoyed too much support from major Democratic leaders to be neutralized. Unlike Lincoln, who used his public rejoinders to his critics so effectively to explain his actions, Johnson never made a persuasive public argument for his limited war approach.

Tet: The Mutual Disaster

A war of attrition between two adversaries who are relatively evenly matched threatens to become a drawn-out slogging match. Consider the bloodletting that continued for years on the Western Front in the First World War, ending only when the infusion of American man-power in 1918 gave the Entente a decisive advantage. Vietnam by 1967 appeared to be heading down a similar path. Understandably, the course of the war yielded frustration on both sides, and provoked the adversaries to desperate measures, though of a very different sort.[107] For the Johnson administration and its military commander in the field, there arose a strong desire to interpret any fragment of good news as a marker of real progress. The administration touted these gains to the American public, creating a fragile illusion that the end lay in sight. On the other side, Hanoi decided to gamble on a new strategy involving a general offensive and popular uprising to topple the Saigon regime and force an American withdrawal. The Tet Offensive in early 1968 shattered the hopes on both sides of bringing the war to a quick conclusion.

From the beginning of American ground intervention in 1965, the president and other American leaders searched for some indication that NVA and VC troops were being put out of action more quickly than they could be replaced. Westmoreland and his MACV subordinates, under heavy pressure from both the White House and military higher-ups, tried their best to demonstrate that attrition was showing results.[108] As they compiled figures on enemy losses, the U.S. military command looked for the magic "crossover point," the moment when enemy losses eclipsed reinforcements and initiated a downward spiral that would leave the communists unable to exercise strategic initiative. Then West-moreland's troops would dictate the pace of operations, driving the enemy away from population centers into isolated sanctuaries from which he could do no more than mount nuisance attacks. Several times in 1967, military commanders believed they had crossed this threshold, and they announced it with much fanfare.[109]

Their claims set off fierce debates within the administration, fed by doubts about the accuracy of the information on enemy losses and arguments over which communist forces ought to be counted in the enemy order of battle (OB).[110] Skeptics in American intelligence circles knew there were good reasons to question the reported number of enemy dead. To disguise their losses, the communists removed many from the battlefield. American officers in the field, often pressured by superiors to report higher totals of communist dead than they actually found, submitted inaccurate "body counts" of VC/NVA killed, and these figures were further inflated as they moved up the chain of command. In a war with many corrupting elements, one former officer writes, the "body count may have been the most corrupt—and corrupting—measure of progress in the whole mess."[111] Everyone involved (except perhaps the MACV commander) knew the system to be flawed, but in a war of attrition, success could not be measured in any other way. Meanwhile, Westmoreland insisted that as many as 200,000 VC irregulars and political cadres not be included in the enemy OB because they did little or no actual fighting. Without them, of course, the NVA/VC totals seemed much less imposing.

Finally, after extended wrangling within the administration, the president came down on the military's side and a special national intelligence estimate published in late 1967 adopted something close to MACV's preferred counting system.[112] The American military command thus inflicted far greater losses on the enemy by the stroke of a pen than it did that year in actual combat. The new way of calculating enemy strength naturally did not escape criticism from a skeptical press. Still, when coupled with evidence of tactical victories over NVA and VC mainforce units in the latter half of 1967, the new OB figures might be taken as evidence of a decline in regular communist forces in South Vietnam.[113]

Eager, even desperate, for positive news, the Johnson administration boasted of turning the corner. To sell the claim of significant progress, the administration decided to use its field commander as a political pawn. Westmoreland was brought home to speak to Congress and the press about the turnabout. He suggested that if the trends continued, American forces might begin to withdraw within two years, turning over the war to the South Vietnamese.[114] In a speech to the National Press Club on November 21, 1967, he went so far as to declare that the enemy was now losing the war.[115] Johnson repeated this optimistic refrain before friendly audiences, pleased at last to answer the naysayers on both flanks. Public opinion polls showed that the message had been received: approval of the war and the president's performance both rebounded (though the results were short-lived).[116] Westmoreland and other administration spokesmen warned that the communists might yet stage a major attack, but the cautionary words were lost amid the broader upbeat message.

The administration thus staked its credibility—already left in doubt by previous misstatements and exaggerations—on a very fragile foundation.[117] Should the enemy show greater resilience than official U.S. pronouncements implied, the blow to the president and to his field commander would be severe. And even the administration understood the possibility that the reported battlefield gains were but temporary. As Johnson himself had observed several times, nothing seemed to prevent Hanoi from increasing its infiltration rate to offset losses or match American troop increases.

The communists meanwhile had decided to pursue a radical strategic departure. Although Hanoi believed the Americans would eventually tire as had the French and seek a face-saving political accommodation that would pave the way for reunification of the nation, significant elements within the Politburo (the communist leadership body) pressed for a more rapid successful conclusion to the war. The heavy casualties inflicted by American firepower took their toll on morale among fighting troops—even highly dedicated soldiers get discouraged when they see no evident gains from their sacrifices. Some senior communists, including the military commander in the South, General Nguyen Thich Thanh, decided that it made more sense to focus on the Saigon government as the point of vulnerability. Attacks in the Central

Highlands of South Vietnam and along the Cambodian border would first draw away American troops from population centers. Then, through nationwide attacks on South Vietnamese cities, communist forces, led by indigenous VC mainforce and part-time troops, would spark a popular uprising that would topple the "puppet" regime. Without a Saigon government to defend, the Americans would have no choice but to depart quickly. Other communist leaders, among them the redoubtable General Giap, questioned the wisdom of a general offensive in the face of obvious American advantages in firepower. Despite these reservations and Thanh's death from wounds suffered during an American air attack in mid-1967, plans proceeded for the sequence of attacks that would culminate in the general offensive during the Tet holiday at the end of January 1968.[118]

Tet represented a bold military gamble, even a reckless one. The offensive violated the basic military principle of concentration of effort. Individual attacks, even if temporarily successful, could be defeated in detail (that is, one by one) by a foe, the U.S. military, which enjoyed superior mobility and could assemble more quickly. Unless the attacks sparked a massive popular uprising from a largely apathetic or cautious population and toppled the Saigon government in short order, the participating VC forces would be exposed, isolated, and vulnerable. If they were defeated, moreover, it would take years to rebuild them, while the Saigon government would have an opportunity to solidify its control over the population. Only with great reluctance (and possibly under enormous political pressure from others in the Politburo) did Giap accede to the scheme.[119]

A further danger lay in the possibility that detailed orders for the offensive would fall into American and South Vietnamese hands, giving them time to prepare. In fact, communist plans were captured, so American intelligence knew that a major attack was pending, which led to the public warnings by Westmoreland and others. What the Americans learned about the offensive, however, made it seem so misguided that they discounted the authenticity of the information.[120]

At a high price in casualties, the communists succeeded in setting the stage for the Tet Offensive. Attacks on isolated outposts near the demilitarized zone (DMZ) dividing North and South Vietnam and along the Laotian and Cambodian borders in fall 1967 drew the attention of

American commanders.[121] As a further distraction, NVA forces placed the U.S. Marine base at Khe Sanh, on a major infiltration route from Laos into the northern part of South Vietnam, under siege in January 1968. American military and political leaders suspected the communists were trying to replicate their success against the French at Dien Bien Phu and resolved to reinforce and hold the base.

Whether the NVA actually intended to assault Khe Sanh has never been certain, but as a diversion the siege worked: from Westmoreland to the White House, where Johnson began to wake up early to request updates on the battle, American eyes fixed on the obscure outpost.[122] Westmoreland became convinced that the main enemy effort would come in the north. By late January 1968 the MACV commander had concentrated more than half of his maneuver battalions in the I Corps area of operations below the DMZ (the region including Khe Sanh).[123] That month, American intelligence detected ominous signs of enemy buildups elsewhere across South Vietnam. Despite requests from American officials, however, South Vietnamese President Nguyen Van Thieu declined to cancel holiday leaves for his troops and only reversed himself at the last moment when premature enemy attacks confirmed the accuracy of the intelligence reports. Due to his hesitation, nearly half of the ARVN was absent at the beginning of the Tet celebration.[124]

Viet Cong and North Vietnamese forces launched well-coordinated assaults on January 31, 1968, that initially caught U.S. and ARVN forces off-guard. Communist troops struck thirty-nine of forty-four provincial capitals and numerous district capitals, as well as other prominent targets.[125] The most visible was the U.S. Embassy in Saigon: VC soldiers failed to penetrate the embassy itself, but a number were killed in and near the neighboring residence for embassy personnel. Although many of the communist attacks achieved temporary local success, the expected popular uprising did not materialize. Heavy American firepower soon wore down the enemy, though the urban battlegrounds also meant a terrible toll among civilians. Only in a few places did the communists make a protracted stand, though eventually U.S. forces recaptured all urban centers. The fighting in Hue, the ancient Vietnamese capital, was especially bloody. U.S. Marines fought to clear the city house by house, and before the communists finally quit they massacred thousands of civilians in an attempt at political intimidation that backfired. ARVN forces, with American air support, also fought stoutly.

As Giap and other doubters of the Tet strategy had feared, the offensive depended too heavily on optimistic assumptions and left communist forces fighting on exactly the terms the American military preferred. The entire plan was grounded more in the ideology of people's war than a sober assessment of political realities. Most South Vietnamese civilians were simply waiting to see which side would prevail. Contrary to expectations that the demoralized South Vietnamese military would welcome the opportunity to eject its American overlords, no ARVN units switched sides. Urban warfare also left communist forces far from their sanctuaries. All along, American tactics had sought to draw VC/NVA regulars out into the open, where massive U.S. firepower could inflict crippling losses. Viet Cong troops in the Tet attacks suffered especially heavy casualties—more than half of their committed forces—from which they would never recover.[126] After the offensive, North Vietnamese soldiers made up the bulk of nominal VC units for the remainder of the war.

For the Johnson administration, the Tet Offensive became a debacle of a different sort. The first video images and photographs of the attacks, especially the abortive assault on the American embassy, pointed up the continuing enemy capacity to strike anywhere in South Vietnam. A carefully crafted narrative of steady progress collapsed overnight, victim of its own overselling.[127] The indiscriminate use of air strikes in built-up areas also backfired in the public relations war. When bombing leveled Ben Tre to beat off a communist assault, an American officer told reporter Peter Arnett, "It became necessary to destroy the town in order to save it." The quote took on iconic status as an expression of the self-defeating character of the American war effort.[128]

Damaged beyond repair, too, was the reputation of General Westmoreland, who had been thrust (however reluctantly) into the role of administration propagandist. Even as he accurately announced that the communist attacks had been defeated, few were listening. Moreover, intelligence reports made clear that many of the Tet attackers had come from the very categories Westmoreland and his MACV staff had sought to exclude from the enemy order of battle. Success also came at a heavy cost: in one week in mid-February, American forces suffered more than

3,000 casualties, the highest one-week total of the war. Westmoreland was soon "kicked upstairs" to become Army Chief of Staff, a promotion that fooled no one, and replaced by his deputy, General Creighton Abrams.[129]

The political fallout was immediate. American public opinion, which had started to turn against Johnson and the war again after the fall 1967 uptick, continued on its downward course, with presidential approval falling to 41 percent in February.[130] By early March, a Gallup survey reported that only one in three Americans believed the United States was making progress in Vietnam. Two events confirmed the degree of media and public disillusionment with the war. On February 27, 1968, CBS anchor Walter Cronkite—the "most trusted man in America"— declared the war a stalemate, an announcement even the president knew marked a turning point from which there could be no recovery.[131] Two weeks later, on March 13, Senator Eugene McCarthy came within a handful of votes of defeating Johnson in the New Hampshire Democratic primary. McCarthy drew stronger support from hawks than those who favored a U.S. withdrawal—clear evidence that the administration position had been repudiated on both flanks.[132] His strong showing prompted another candidate with broad appeal, Robert F. Kennedy, to enter the race. Communist strategy had always treated public opinion as a vulnerable point in the American war effort. Although the Tet Offensive failed to bring down the Saigon regime, the aftershocks in the United States confirmed Hanoi's political insight.

The Tet Offensive had far-reaching repercussions for American war policy and the president who directed it. Once again, military commanders urged extensive reinforcements, initially because the situation was still dangerous and, later, to capitalize on the enemy's defeat. General Wheeler, who asked in late February to reinforce MACV with another 206,000 troops, hoped the request would finally compel the president to mobilize the reserves.[133] Before Johnson would decide, he asked Clark Clifford, who recently had replaced McNamara as defense secretary, to review U.S. policy options. Unlike his predecessor, Clifford enjoyed a strong position with the military: he was a longtime Johnson ally and, despite voicing early doubts about the wisdom of American intervention, had been a loyal, even hawkish backer of the president on the war. But his post-Tet assessment led him to recommend a sharp change of course. Rather than continued escalation, Clifford advised taking measures, particularly a bombing halt over most of North Vietnam, which he believed more likely to bring about negotiations with the communists.[134]

Following intensive debate within the administration, the president agreed to an unconditional bombing halt above the 20th parallel and a very modest increase in the American troop ceiling in Vietnam that signaled a definitive rejection of the JCS mobilization alternative.[135] Never again would all-out war be an option for the United States. Johnson explained his policy decision in a nationally televised address on March 31, 1968, and concluded with the surprise announcement that he was withdrawing from the presidential race. The war that he had been so determined to keep within bounds so as to preserve his legacy had instead consumed it.[136]

Diplomacy and the Elusive Quest for Peace

In framing American political objectives as securing the independence of South Vietnam from North Vietnamese aggression, the president established two diplomatic relationships as central to the outcome of the war. At some point the United States would have to negotiate a political solution with the DRV. The president vainly sought to bring Hanoi to the negotiating table for nearly three years after he Americanized the war. It proved no easier to secure the cooperation of his South Vietnamese allies, who stubbornly pursued their own agenda and feared any negotiations with the communists would doom them. The partial bombing halt that Johnson announced in his March 31, 1968, address finally broke the ice with Hanoi; significant progress on the shape of a settlement seemed in the offing seven months later, when he declared a complete end to the air attacks. With the prospect of a more friendly Nixon administration in Washington, however, the Saigon government balked at joining the talks.

Johnson hoped to induce the North Vietnamese leaders to negotiate via a carrot-and-stick approach. Through a sustained American military commitment, he would beat back the communist attempt to overwhelm South Vietnam. At the same time, he hoped to encourage the communists to adopt a more reasonable stance by offering them a strong economic incentive to cooperate. In the April 1965 Johns Hopkins University speech in which he laid out American war aims, the president also offered American funding for a massive regional Mekong River development project that he regarded as the foundation for prosperity across an impoverished Southeast Asia. The idea represented a twist on the New Deal Tennessee Valley Authority, which Johnson saw as the cornerstone of economic progress in the American South. From the perspective of a canny politician like the president, the offer would be too good for Ho Chi Minh and company to resist—give up the dream of conquest, fated now to be thwarted by American might and resolve, for the sure thing of economic development.[137]

Hanoi saw it otherwise. The communists would not be deflected from their central objective, reunification. On the day following Johnson's address, Pham Van Dong responded with the Politburo's terms: the United States must observe the Geneva accords, withdraw its forces, cease attacks on the DRV, and sever its ties to the Saigon government. The people of South Vietnam would settle their own future, and eventually all Vietnamese would decide on reunification of the nation. Effectively, then, the communists insisted on the terms earlier framed by the National Liberation Front, which Johnson had made clear he would not accept.[138]

For the better part of the next three years, the two sides tried to communicate through intermediaries and a process of signaling that led to ambiguity and confusion. Messages via third parties involved extended delay, caused misunderstanding or—worse—aroused suspicion of bad faith, or simply never elicited an answer. In response to an early bombing pause in May 1965, the North Vietnamese indicated to the French that they would not make American acceptance of their conditions a prior condition for talks; they wanted another Geneva-type conference, and they would not demand that American troops leave the South until negotiations were completed successfully. The French never received an American reply.[139] Once the bombing raids resumed, the North Vietnamese made clear they would not talk, even through intermediaries, unless the attacks ceased unconditionally.[140]

In summer 1967, the North Vietnamese indicated flexibility on a timetable for American withdrawal and a willingness to delay reunification. Rather than communicate directly, the communists passed along the message through a new back channel opened by Henry Kissinger, still a Harvard professor, who served as an informal conduit. The United States also gave ground: in a speech at San Antonio in late September 1967, Johnson offered to stop air attacks on the DRV as a step to initiate discussions, with the understanding that so long as talks were under way in good faith the communists would not take advantage of the cessation. Modifying its demand that Hanoi cease infiltration before a bombing halt, the administration instead said North Vietnam would have to agree merely not to increase its military effort. Again, however, an increase in the intensity of the bombing campaign suffocated the peace feelers.[141]

If anything, the South Vietnamese government (GVN) proved more frustrating to the Johnson administration than did Hanoi. Despite constant American urging to introduce reforms to improve political stability and win popular support, South Vietnamese military leaders, the power behind the regime, demonstrated greater concern for their own security than for creating a workable government. The arrival of American troops did not put an end to the turmoil; coup followed coup. Generals Nguyen Cao Ky and Nguyen Van Thieu finally emerged as the two officers with the strongest backing. At Johnson's behest, they agreed to draft a new constitution, with a number of American features, and then combined in a single ticket, with Thieu at its head, in a national election in September 1967. Despite winning just one-third of the votes, the Thieu-Ky ticket placed first.[142] American officials hailed the results as conferring legitimacy on the government, ignoring the fact that no candidate who advocated a coalition government with the NLF could run. When newly elected President Thieu proceeded to arrest various political opponents, the American embassy had to arrange to have them released.[143]

The episode was yet another symptom of the underlying problem: neither the United States nor the GVN trusted each other. South Vietnamese officials feared an American sellout in any political settlement. When in late 1967 Johnson raised the possibility of negotiations between Saigon and the NLF, Thieu rejected the idea out of hand. As if to hammer home the point, a senior GVN police official in October 1967 arrested two NLF representatives who were heading to a meeting with U.S. embassy officials to discuss a prisoner exchange.[144] To their frustration, American officials found that vast U.S. assistance yielded little leverage over the South Vietnamese government and military. On the other hand, had Americans managed to assert greater control, they would have confirmed communist propaganda that Saigon was nothing more than an American puppet—a crippling label in a country trying to shed its colonial past.

Johnson's March 31, 1968, decision to restrict bombing to the part of the DRV below the 20th parallel finally created the opening for negotiations. The two sides agreed to meet in Paris, with the American delegation headed by two experienced diplomats, Cyrus Vance and Averill Harriman. Le Duc Tho assumed leadership on the North Vietnamese side. He was uncompromising in public, but the American team believed private talks offered a more promising path. Battlefield setbacks had persuaded the Politburo to accept terms consistent with its minimalist position—reunification over time. At a private meeting on September 12, 1968, Tho said South Vietnam could remain independent and neutral, while Washington and Hanoi might establish diplomatic relations. But the United States must halt all bombing, and the war would continue, too, if the Americans tried to shift the fighting to its allies in the "neocolonial" South. Harriman answered that American forces would withdraw when the NVA did, and he restated the American commitment to provide reconstruction aid. In a subsequent meeting, Tho offered to let GVN representatives join the discussions in exchange for a complete cessation of air attacks, though he remained vague about when the talks might start.[145] Johnson agreed to the full bombing halt, though he held off a public announcement.

The South Vietnamese were another matter, however: as a lame duck, Johnson had even less leverage than before over Thieu and Ky. When Clifford made his first Saigon visit since replacing McNamara, the GVN leaders demanded enormous quantities of new equipment, hedging against an American pullout that might leave them to face the communists alone. Later, as the private talks in Paris made progress, Thieu grew increasingly anxious. He also became convinced (not without reason) that his government would do better under the following American administration, expecting Richard Nixon to be elected. Harriman and Vance still hoped to begin the next phase of negotiations before the election. Having earlier agreed to begin the talks on November 2, 1968, Thieu backed off his commitment. Johnson announced the unconditional bombing halt on the last day of October and said new negotiations would commence one week later, while Thieu, still determined to draw out the process, replied that his government would not participate. If he believed that the next American administration would be prepared to sustain Saigon with American blood indefinitely, he was soon disappointed. His representative in Paris informed him that Nixon would disengage from Vietnam, but do so more slowly than a Democrat would.[146]

Johnson's success with diplomacy was on a par with the other elements of his wartime leadership. The early Johns Hopkins University speech pointed to some of the difficulties that would dog him. In that address, Johnson left himself with precious little space for diplomatic maneuvering: almost any negotiated outcome, because it would have to allow for either power sharing, neutralization, or eventual reunification of the two Vietnams, would appear to be a defeat. He also established no standards for the GVN's performance, denying the United States any rationale for disengagement and the leverage over Saigon this might have provided. And in stating that it was up to Hanoi to decide when to cease its aggression, he let the communists determine when negotiations would begin. Further, the confidence that military force could be manipulated precisely to send clear signals to the other side proved misplaced. Time and again, attempts to communicate a message did not align with military action; witness the resumption of bombing before Hanoi could respond to diplomatic overtures. Washington also sent signals inadvertently that were quite at odds with what the Johnson administration intended. By announcing a firm ceiling on American troop levels in Vietnam, as Clark Clifford pointed out to the president in late 1967, the administration communicated very plainly that its commitment to the war was limited.[147] Hanoi understood that it need not fear American force increases it could not hope to match.

Above all, Johnson misunderstood his communist adversaries and underestimated their will. His Mekong River development proposal betrayed the president's profound parochialism. In making the offer, he revealed that he saw Ho Chi Minh and the other Vietnamese communist leaders as conventional politicians who would bargain away any goal for pork-barrel projects. This approach had served Johnson well in the U.S. Senate, but not with determined revolutionaries.[148] The only way to persuade such a foe to negotiate the kind of peace Johnson wanted would be to threaten to undo what the communists had already accomplished in their part of Vietnam. The president, though, had ruled out an invasion of the DRV and the threat of regime change and refused to revisit the option. In the end, he left himself no way to achieve his war goals unless Hanoi's determination faltered. The domestic response to the Tet Offensive revealed the exhaustion of Johnson's diplomatic quest. He would leave office seeking talks on terms closer to Hanoi's minimal conditions than on those he had first enunciated at Johns Hopkins.

"Peace with Honor": Nixon (Briefly) Reclaims Flexibility

A president elected during an ongoing war, at least one that appears stalled, stands to regain significant freedom of action. Assuming that he refrained from making firm commitments while seeking the White House, he can pursue options not available to his predecessor. He is also not weighed down with the psychological and political burden of past choices. Eisenhower broke the Korean stalemate in part by threatening publicly to unleash a massive bombing campaign. Vice president at the time, Richard Nixon had witnessed this, and he had absorbed the lesson. The window of opportunity for changing course, however, opens only briefly. Once the new president begins to make choices, the wartime pattern resumes—his decisions draw him down an ever-narrowing path.

Campaigning in 1968, Nixon made sure not to tie his hands on Vietnam. He understood that the next president would have to end the war, though he left open exactly how he might do so. As a candidate, he promised to secure "peace with honor." It was a clever political phrase that ruled out only three possibilities an incoming president might have considered. First, he could not continue Johnson's course, which had been an obvious failure. Second, he would not end the war immediately through a unilateral American withdrawal or anything that looked too much like defeat: "honor" was a code word for "no capitulation." Immediate unilateral withdrawal, in fact, was the one option removed from a list of possible policies drafted during the transition period.[149]

Finally, having promised "peace," Nixon would find it difficult to sell full-scale mobilization to a Congress controlled by the opposition party, especially with an overheated American economy showing serious inflationary strains.

The new president knew what he hoped to accomplish—withdrawal that was not surrender—but had no clear policy to achieve it.[150] Ideally, the United States still would secure an independent South Vietnam that could decide its own future. Nixon reaffirmed this objective in a speech on May 14, 1969, and soon thereafter in a private message to Ho Chi Minh.[151] But another goal was now at least as important—extricating the United States from the conflict. Working with his new national security advisor, Henry Kissinger, the president expected to pursue a diplomatic track, particularly through secret talks between Kissinger and DRV negotiators. If Nixon and Kissinger believed they would make quick progress toward a negotiated settlement, the first sessions with Tho and his colleagues in summer 1969 disabused them of their optimism. Hanoi would continue to be obstinate, even when Nixon threatened to use greater force.[152] Other measures would be needed to demonstrate progress toward ending the war to the American people.

Seeking a military policy the public would accept, Nixon embraced an idea proposed by his secretary of defense, Melvin Laird: a prompt shift of battlefield responsibility to the ARVN and a concomitant drawdown of U.S. forces. McNamara had first broached an approach along the same lines a couple of years earlier, but Westmoreland had remained so fixated on defeating the enemy with American troops that he took no steps to turn over the fighting to South Vietnamese forces. Likewise Clifford in 1968 anticipated that ARVN troops would assume more of the combat burden over time. Laird thus became the third successive defense secretary to identify the transfer of responsibility as the path forward (and, for the United States, toward the exit door).[153] Now, though, the policy gained a name, "Vietnamization," and became official, with a specified withdrawal timetable for American forces.

To make it appear as though Vietnamization would not be construed as a tacit admission the United States was abandoning its post–World War II role as guarantor of security for small nations facing communist aggression, the administration joined the policy to what the president proclaimed as the "Nixon Doctrine." This held that countries would be expected to provide the troops to defend themselves against insurgencies and local adversaries, while the United States would only intervene against attacks by major communist powers or to deter nuclear threats.[154] The doctrine provided a neat rationale for Vietnamization: Saigon would henceforth be given the same support any other nation would receive. Predictably, President Thieu did not see it that way, but after pressure from Washington he agreed in mid-1969 to the first American troop withdrawal.[155]

Although Vietnamization met a pressing political need, the policy also contained traps, some not fully appreciated at first by the president and his advisors. Americans might be pleased to see the boys coming home, but as the stakes for the United States in Vietnam declined, the public would also have less reason to care about the outcome of the war or the fate of the Saigon government. Put another way, Vietnamization set in motion the dynamics of postwar politics even as the conflict continued. Once started, moreover, the process would be irreversible, difficult even to slow down, no matter what happened on the battle-field. After all, Vietnamization represented an administration initiative that was not tied to reciprocal actions by the other side. So if the North Vietnamese chose to capitalize on the American withdrawal by stepping up their own infiltration and attacks, Washington could not claim bad faith or use it to justify a new American military escalation.[156] Nixon quickly saw his freedom of action reduced, his military options constrained.

By choosing unilateral (if gradual) withdrawal, moreover, the Nixon administration weakened Kissinger's negotiating position. The United States had been unable to compel the North Vietnamese to agree to mutual troop withdrawals even when it had more than a half-million soldiers in South Vietnam. As they started to depart, what incentive would Hanoi have to agree to American terms?[157]

Finally, Vietnamization did not take into account the capacity of the Saigon government to defend itself with less American help, indeed, possibly without any American support whatsoever. Unresolved at the outset was whether the United States would leave behind a residual force or, if not, continue to backstop the ARVN with air power based in the region.

Taking the Gloves Off

Between January 1969 and January 1973, when a peace agreement was finally signed in Paris, the United States fought in Vietnam under a peculiar dual-command system. On one side, a relatively straightforward relationship ran from defense secretary Laird through MACV commander Creighton Abrams to the troops in the field. This chain of command embodied the administration's commitment to Vietnamization. Over four years, as American troops withdrew, Abrams improved pacification efforts and turned over increased responsibility to the ARVN. The results made plain both the strengths of Vietnamization and its limits. On the other side, the White House intervened fitfully to direct military operations, usually to meet some domestic political need or influence the ongoing peace talks. These episodes saw Nixon flexing his muscles: he unleashed military power in ways his predecessor had not allowed, satisfying, if only briefly, the military's desire to be allowed to fight with the gloves off. Despite short-term military benefits, the results proved transient, and the spillover effects at home and in Indochina called into question the judgment behind the impulse.

Abrams reoriented American strategy, rejecting Westmoreland's methods and emphasis, and introducing a new approach that fit well with Laird's agenda. Where Westmoreland shunned pacification and minimized the role of the ARVN, Abrams saw the handwriting on the wall—after 1968, the United States was certain to disengage from the war, so the survival of South Vietnam depended upon achieving more effective governance and upgrading ARVN combat capability. Defeats inflicted on VC/NVA mainforce units in the Tet Offensive and in subsequent attacks over the following year sharply reduced the threat from regular enemy units. With VC troops decimated, moreover, the communist political infrastructure became vulnerable. Abrams altered the politico-military approach to that of fighting "one war" designed to improve population security: as pacification established the presence of the South Vietnamese government among the rural population, American and ARVN troops would provide local security, shunning search-and-destroy operations in favor of "clear-and-hold" tactics that saw smaller units remaining in place to demonstrate government control. Meanwhile, he stepped up training of South Vietnamese forces, especially the expanded paramilitary local units (Regional Forces/ Popular Forces), and the United States supplied modern weapons and equipment on a much vaster scale. From a force of 700,000 in 1968, the South Vietnamese military increased to 1.1 million in 1973. When Laird informed Abrams that the American troop levels would be reduced, then, he had already started a program designed to replace the soldiers who would be leaving. He continued to cooperate dutifully with the Pentagon even as it accelerated the withdrawal timetable or when the NVA recovered to present new threats.[158]

Abrams's efforts paid off in several ways. Better integration of military and pacification efforts brought more of the population under the effective control of the Saigon government, which also contributed to winning popular loyalty through a significant land-reform program. Under the Phoenix Program, the Vietcong infrastructure was targeted, with many operatives captured or killed. (Critics charged that many innocent civilians were caught up in the net, too, and prisoners were tortured or executed without trial.)[159] It became increasingly difficult for communist troops to operate near the larger population centers of South Vietnam because they lacked the local support on which they depended for supplies, concealment, and information.[160] ARVN troops demonstrated their combat prowess on several occasions, most notably in the face of massive conventional attacks by the NVA in its spring 1972 "Easter Offensive." As the ARVN took over for the departing Americans, moreover, the toll in American lives fell steadily.

Still, the military picture presented disquieting elements. Although ARVN leadership had improved, too many senior officers still owed their position to their political ties to President Thieu. Always wary of a possible coup, he retained in key senior commands generals he knew to be loyal. Critical military operations unraveled when these political generals were given too much responsibility, as happened during the incursion into Laos in early 1971 (operation Lam Son 719) and again in several critical sectors during the heavy fighting in 1972.[161]

Overall, ARVN combat performance remained uneven. Properly led, ARVN soldiers were the equal of their communist adversaries. But South Vietnamese units remained prone to panic, fleeing and abandoning their (American) equipment on the battlefield, and even surrendered en masse when their leaders lost their nerve. This lack of steadfastness extended all the way up the South Vietnamese chain of command to the president: in the face of mounting NVA pressure, Thieu called off Lam Son 719 when his forces reached Tchepone in Laos before they could destroy many enemy supplies, long before the scheduled end of the operation.[162] ARVN troops gave a good account of themselves so long as they had ample American air power behind them. Overwhelming air strikes shielded the Laotian operation and repelled NVA attacks in 1972.[163] Nothing in these episodes, however, suggested that South Vietnamese forces left on their own could withstand future NVA offensives. Yet as early as November 1969, Laird had informed Congress that the administration had initiated planning for a phase after July 1, 1973, when the United States would provide no continuing support against either external or internal threats.[164]

Complicating matters for Abrams, orders and instructions sometimes came directly from the president or others close to him. Nixon centralized sensitive military decisions in the White House and the National Security Council (NSC) under Kissinger rather than trust them to Laird. At times Kissinger and his NSC staff, including General Alexander Haig, went around the defense secretary to work instead with the JCS. Four pivotal operations—the secret bombing of Cambodia that began in early 1969; the ground incursion into Cambodia in spring 1970; Lam Son 719; and the Linebacker bombing campaign directed against North Vietnam in response to the 1972 NVA offensive—appear to have originated with the president and his immediate circle of advisors, though each one reflected long-standing military requests to widen the scope of the war. Much as military commanders welcomed the operations, they occurred under constraints that dramatically lessened any military benefits they might have produced. They also generated consequences that damaged the long-term prospects for the success of Vietnamization or American policy in Southeast Asia.

Nixon decided soon after taking office to reprise the Eisenhower move that helped break the Korean stalemate, but with a twist motivated by his desire to dampen political tensions at home. For years the military had wanted to strike communist sanctuaries in Cambodia by air and on the ground, a request reiterated by Abrams.[165] Just as Eisenhower had threatened wider strategic bombing, Nixon wanted to impress upon Hanoi that he would not be bound by the previous administration's self-imposed restrictions on air attacks. At the president's behest, the JCS developed plans for a much-expanded air campaign against the DRV and Cambodia. However, cautioned by Laird that the raids would trigger massive protests at home without preventing the North Vietnamese from continuing the war, Nixon temporized.[166] He settled for bombing areas in Cambodia adjacent to South Vietnam, which would serve the double purpose of disrupting enemy military preparations and letting Hanoi know that the rules had changed. But the president still worried that wider bombing might arouse the antiwar movement. So, unlike Eisenhower, who made his intentions quite public, Nixon and his White House aides decided to proceed in secret.[167] Laird objected to the secrecy but was overruled, the first step in marginalizing him on critical decisions.

The bombing began in March 1969 and continued intermittently for fourteen months, with the attacks concealed officially through an elaborate reporting subterfuge by which aircrews would record the Cambodia missions as raids within South Vietnam. Only once did the veil over the operation get pulled back, in a report in the *New York Times* on May 9, 1969, but it drew little notice.[168] Although the administration succeeded in keeping the American people in the dark, the raids failed to have any impact on the communist negotiators in Paris.

In a second attempt to destroy enemy sanctuaries, the administration decided to launch a ground offensive into Cambodia in spring 1970. An American-leaning regime had taken power in Phnom Penh in January when Prime Minister Lon Nol had seized power during a foreign trip by head of state Prince Norodom Sihanouk. The new government demanded the departure of NVA troops, which instead attacked the ill-prepared Cambodian forces, threatening to overrun the country.[169] Determined to prevent so serious a reversal, the White House dusted off old military designs for an assault to destroy communist base areas that had served as safe havens since American forces had arrived in 1965. Unlike bombing raids, a ground attack by U.S. and ARVN troops into Cambodia could not be kept secret. But the administration in early 1970 saw the antiwar movement as a spent force: protest demonstrations in October 1969 drew smaller crowds than organizers expected. Nixon had followed on November 3, 1969, with his effective speech on behalf of what he famously termed "the silent majority" of Americans who wanted to see the war concluded honorably. Polls showed that public approval for the president's war policy had soared from 58 percent to 77 percent.[170] It seemed an opportune moment, then, to act aggressively on the battlefield. Apart from the military argument for attacking the sanctuaries, Nixon seemed to personalize the challenge they presented—as though the communist troops, by hiding behind an international boundary they felt free to disregard, were thumbing their nose at him.[171] Thus he spoke of how failing to respond would make it appear that the United States had become "a pitiful, helpless giant." Again Laird found himself in opposition to a major policy decision on the war and again he was overruled.[172]

Politics would also shape what the cross-border assault sought to accomplish and determine when it ended. Abrams wanted to advance far into Cambodia and to remain there for several months to ensure that the enemy's logistical base was destroyed. This would delay any communist plans for another major offensive in South Vietnam, leaving a breathing space for progress on Vietnamization and further American troop withdrawals.[173] Instead the president stated the operation was designed to destroy the communist headquarters for the war, the Central Office for South Vietnam (COSVN). Abrams and MACV knew that this enemy organization was widely dispersed and mobile, which meant there was virtually no chance that it could be located and destroyed. Despite the field commander's cautions, pressure came from above (specifically, Al Haig) to destroy COSVN.[174]

The attack aroused fierce protests on college campuses across the country, including demonstrations that resulted in the shooting deaths of students at Kent State and Jackson State universities by the National Guard. With the nation again seeming on the verge of splitting apart at the seams, the White House flinched: Nixon limited the depth of the incursion to thirty kilometers and announced that all American and ARVN troops would leave Cambodia by the end of June.[175] This was far sooner than MACV had intended, and it assured that the incursion would have few long-term military benefits. Abrams ruefully conceded that the entire operation had done little more than cause the enemy "some temporary inconvenience." Worse yet, no longer confident that their border sanctuaries were secure, the communists moved much deeper into Cambodia.[176] This marked the first step into the heart of the nation for the Cambodian communist insurgents, the Khmer Rouge, a course that would ultimately spell tragedy.

Lam Son 719, the ambitious 1971 operation to sever communist supply lines through Laos, was a third White House–inspired initiative. Here, too, the idea had been around for years, because aerial interdiction, even with refined techniques, could at best slow the movement of men and materiel south from the DRV. By the time the NSC planners embraced the concept, however, the circumstances made it a much riskier proposition. In the aftermath of the 1970 Cambodian attack, Congress had passed legislation, the Cooper-Church Amendment, banning the use of funds for American military personnel in Laos or Cambodia. The White House insisted on going ahead with the Laotian attack anyway, but it directed the Pentagon to plan an ARVN-only affair. (Haig's opinions on how to conduct the war evidently counted for more with the president at this point than did those of either Abrams or the JCS.) U.S. forces would provide long-range artillery support from within South Vietnam and air support. Once South Vietnamese troops crossed into Laos, though, they would be on their own, not even accompanied by their American advisors. This was precisely the kind of operation for which the ARVN had not been prepared. Abrams faced the task of inducing President Thieu to cooperate, which he did with considerable reluctance and only for as long as absolutely necessary. When the operation ended, badly, Kissinger and Haig sought to pin the blame on Abrams and MACV.[177]

Fear that South Vietnam might collapse—and cost him reelection—provoked Nixon to order another military operation in late spring 1972. The American military command voiced alarm that ARVN forces might break under the severe pressure of the communist Easter Offensive. By this point, with American forces in South Vietnam reduced to fewer than 100,000 troops, the president's options were limited. Even though Hanoi had virtually denuded the DRV of troops to throw everything into the attack, an American countermove into North Vietnam above the 17th parallel was not possible. Setting aside the practicalities of quickly amassing the needed forces, such an action would reverse Vietnamization and amount to an admission that it had failed. Nixon instead ordered intensive bombing of North Vietnam, including military options Johnson had rejected—air raids on transportation lines up to the Chinese border and the mining of all North Vietnamese ports, including Haiphong. He calculated correctly that his recent overtures toward Beijing and Moscow would stop them from intervening directly. The NVA offensive was beaten back, after the communist forces lost more than 50 percent of the 200,000 troops committed, a staggering casualty rate. Although the heavy bombing of North Vietnam impeded Hanoi's resupply efforts, the decisive air strikes were tactical raids in the South in support of the ARVN defenses and counterattacks. However, notwithstanding the terrible cost the communists paid, NVA troops retained control of significant territory within South Vietnam near the DMZ, in the Central Highlands, and along the Cambodian border. This strategic gain would prove important in the ongoing peace talks and beyond.[178]

On the whole, Nixon's episodic efforts to direct military operations proved ineffective, sometimes even counterproductive. He showed no better appreciation of the enemy's determination than Johnson had. That the secret air raids in Cambodia yielded no progress in Paris should not have surprised the president and Kissinger: if bombing the DRV had not forced Hanoi to bow to American military might, there was no reason to expect better results from bombing the jungles of Cambodia. Whatever the temporary military gains from the spring 1970 Cambodia incursion, moreover, they did not nearly offset the political turmoil at home.

The administration also showed a poor grasp of the limits of Vietnamization. Despite ample warnings from Abrams and MACV that the ARVN on its own should not be expected to undertake a major offensive operation into heavily defended enemy territory, the administration pressed ahead with Lam Son 719. The results did little for the confidence of President Thieu and his army. Nixon showed a willingness to expand the scope of military operations in the war, including a resumption of bombing of the DRV in response to the 1972 NVA offensive that included the mining of the port of Haiphong. But for all his keenness to shed restraints, he had no more to show for it than Johnson did. The gains achieved by Laird and Abrams through Vietnamization were dissipated by ill-conceived, politically misguided White House interventions.

Peace Building amid an Unpopular War

To achieve the objective he established in Vietnam, Nixon needed to build political support at home for an American commitment to guarantee the independence of South Vietnam. Vietnamization could never make the South Vietnamese military self-sufficient (no underdeveloped country could sustain a million-man military purely on its own resources)[179] or give it the capability to defeat an all-out NVA attack. Through negotiations in Paris, of course, the administration hoped to defuse the immediate threat posed by communist forces. But long-term survival of South Vietnam required either a permanent residual American presence, as in South Korea, or massive and continuous military aid backed by a credible threat of American retaliation should Hanoi launch another invasion on the scale of the spring 1972 attack.[180] Both depended upon a political consensus at home, at a time when familiar postwar political dynamics began to express themselves: the American people were turning their attention to other concerns and Congress was starting to reassert its will. Faced with an increasingly inhospitable domestic climate, the Nixon administration never fashioned a political strategy that could secure the necessary consensus.

Any possibility that U.S. troops might remain indefinitely in South Vietnam vanished early in Nixon's tenure. Laird initially advised Abrams to pursue Vietnamization on the Korean model, that is, to plan around the presence of a small American force to guarantee any cease-fire arrangement. Within months, the instructions from Washington changed: Abrams was told to proceed on the assumption that no U.S. troops would remain. The president and Kissinger learned quickly that Hanoi would never accept a negotiated solution permitting an ongoing American military presence. Since ending the war via peace talks remained the top priority, the administration quietly shelved the notion of another Korean-style truce. Abrams focused instead on modernizing the ARVN and the various paramilitary organizations to fight on if necessary without American troops. Thieu and his senior officers pressed relentlessly for more American arms and equipment, but Abrams told them they needed to learn how to make better use of what they had already received.[181] He doubted whether they could ever withstand a major communist offensive absent substantial American air support. Even after the American withdrawal was complete, then, South Vietnam would need not just munitions on a vast scale but also, if attacked again by the North, a resumption of U.S. bombing.

Past conflicts pointed up the peace-building dilemma confronting the Nixon administration. Weary of the sacrifices of war, the public refocuses on domestic concerns when the fighting ends. Any significant ongoing postwar involvement requires careful political groundwork. Neither Lincoln nor Wilson had managed the challenge effectively, postponing peace-building efforts until it was too late. Roosevelt had done somewhat better at the end of the Second World War with the well-orchestrated campaign to establish the United Nations. When he entered the White House in 1969, Nixon had inherited a situation in which no real planning had been done for the postwar future of Southeast Asia, and conditions at home were not the least bit promising for securing a long-term commitment to Saigon. With the drawdown of American forces and the decline in American casualties, people back home turned their backs on Vietnam. Popular protests weakened after the spring 1970 domestic upheaval, aided by the end of the draft, yet the war still became less popular over time. By the end of 1971, polls showed that other issues had eclipsed Vietnam in the public mind; Americans were nearly three times as likely to identify the economy as their major source of concern.[182]

Congress had also rejected the war, though legislative expressions of disapproval initially took a merely symbolic form. For example, the Senate repealed the Tonkin Gulf Resolution during the 1970 Cambodia incursion, knowing full well that this would not influence the course of American policy.[183] The real power of the legislative branch lay in its control over appropriations. However, so long as American troops fought in Vietnam, Congress would not terminate funding for the war. The reason was political. Lawmakers would not wish to face accusations that they had abandoned U.S. troops, even in an unpopular war.[184] Nevertheless, Congress began to apply pressure. Lawmakers introduced measures to restrict American military operations, including the withdrawal of all American forces from South Vietnam by a specified date (the end of 1970). Unsuccessful in the initial legislative skirmishes, proponents like Senators Frank Church and George McGovern kept at it, capitalizing on the sizable Democratic majorities in both chambers.

They began to taste success on December 29, 1970, when they passed the aforementioned Cooper-Church ban on the introduction of American troops into Laos or Cambodia.[185]

Given the unpromising political circumstances, Nixon had little time. The opportunity to build a consensus in favor of post-withdrawal "offshore" military support for South Vietnam would be brief. The policy might have been sold as the essential foundation for Vietnamization (which is exactly what it was). To be persuasive, the president in 1969 needed to take congressional leaders into his confidence, agreeing on a timetable that would promise a definitive end to the American ground combat role. Nixon would have been negotiating with the Democratic leadership from a position of strength, especially after his "silent majority" address. With hundreds of thousands of American troops still fighting the war at that point, he also might have sold a postwar commitment to South Vietnam's security as the quickest exit from the conflict and the best way to save American lives.

But the president let slip the chance. Possibly he convinced himself that, through improved diplomatic relations with the Soviet Union and China, he could persuade them to limit their resupply of Hanoi. He and Kissinger believed in diplomatic "linkage," the notion that improved relations at the superpower level might have spillover benefits in other parts of the world.[186] It seems more likely, though, that like his wartime predecessors, Nixon did not appreciate that he would soon lose the capacity to shape the aftermath of the conflict. He and his advisors ignored the early warning signs of congressional restiveness. They may have been misled, too, by the fading antiwar movement, never to regain its May 1970 peak. Scarcely did Nixon realize that the biggest obstacle to a security commitment to Saigon was the growing apathy of the American people. Once the troops came home, nothing could make the public care again about the fate of South Vietnam. A Gallup poll conducted at the time of the January 1973 Paris peace agreement revealed starkly the degree to which Americans had washed their hands of Southeast Asia: though most expected North Vietnam to violate the agreement and seek to take over the South, more than 70 percent opposed responding with renewed bombing of the DRV and nearly four out of five rejected a return of American troops.[187]

Wasted Talk

Nixon's quest to end the war "with honor" led him on a diplomatic path that extended the war for little gain. As I discussed earlier, when talks began between American negotiators and North Vietnamese representatives in Paris in 1968, the outlines of a possible settlement were already in place. Le Duc Tho indicated that South Vietnam might remain neutral and independent for a time in exchange for an American withdrawal. The settlement reached by Tho and Henry Kissinger in October 1972, and ultimately signed in very similar form in January 1973, scarcely improved upon these terms. Indeed, the language for several planks in the final Paris Peace Accords repeated verbatim parts of the NLF's ten-point peace plan for 1969.[188] Although the communist side dropped its demand that President Thieu be forced to step down, the United States conceded far more by giving up its insistence on a mutual troop withdrawal. The Nixon administration stumbled over the same obstacle that had thwarted its predecessor: Washington exercised little diplomatic leverage over either its adversary in Hanoi or its client in Saigon.

Initially, Nixon and Kissinger believed they could browbeat Tho and his colleagues into accepting a better settlement for South Vietnam than the one Johnson might have secured. In exchange for a mutual withdrawal by American and North Vietnamese forces, the United States would be prepared to accept the freely expressed will of the South Vietnamese people, including the choice of reunification if they wished. The American proposal called for the military cease-fire to precede any political solution. As these proposals were being tabled (that is, submitted for discussion), the administration also warned that it was losing patience and would be prepared to use greater force if Hanoi did not show flexibility, establishing a pattern of ultimatums that would characterize the American negotiating stance in the years that followed.

In response, the communist delegates restated the NLF program, which called for a complete withdrawal of American forces, the release of all prisoners of war (POWs), and the creation of a coalition government in South Vietnam. For three years the DRV stance—that the United States must withdraw and Thieu step aside—remained firm.

Kissinger found Tho no more flexible when parallel private talks commenced in January 1970. Moreover, threats to increase the level of violence against the DRV or expand the war only served to make Tho more rigid.[189]

As the North Vietnamese had perceived, time worked against the United States. Hanoi shrewdly grasped that the American position was weakening in both political and military terms. The communist leadership closely monitored public opinion in the United States—and tried to influence it through propaganda and occasional gestures such as POW releases into the hands of visiting peace activists.[190] If that led Hanoi at times to overestimate the effectiveness of the antiwar movement, the signs of flagging public support for the war were readily visible, as was the evidence of a growing wish among Democrats in Congress to disengage from the conflict. Further, the unilateral withdrawal of American troops gave the North Vietnamese ever less reason to agree to a corresponding drawdown of their soldiers in the South. As Tho pointed out to Kissinger, if the United States could not win with more than a half million troops in Vietnam, it could not hope to prevail with fewer.[191]

The Nixon administration also erred when it made the return of American POWs a central U.S. negotiating demand. This was unnecessary, as prisoner return had always been a feature of postwar settlements. Worse yet, Nixon and Kissinger discovered that they had turned the POWs into bargaining chips that communist negotiators would use to extract better terms. The public focused increasingly on the return of POWs as a major condition for ending the conflict honorably, so much so that for many Americans the issue surpassed in importance the fate of South Vietnam.[192]

Patient to the point of ruthlessness, Tho and his Politburo colleagues let the Nixon administration's desire for a peace agreement mount until the Americans made decisive concessions while offering far less in exchange. Kissinger tried in March 1970 to establish mutual withdrawal as a nonnegotiable American demand, only to have Tho dismiss the possibility. Six months later the White House conceded: on October 7, 1970, the president stated in a national address that the United States would accept a cease-fire in place, which meant NVA soldiers would remain in South Vietnam as the American forces departed. Kissinger tried to put the best face possible on the shift, insisting no negotiations could remove the NVA troops if they could not be expelled by force and also claiming they did not represent a threat to the South's survival. Thieu, who understood both the determination of his enemy and his own army's limits, knew the truth.[193] Meanwhile, Tho refused to bend on the question of Thieu's departure and a coalition government.

Each side sought new leverage, the Americans through opening diplomatic relations with Beijing, the North Vietnamese by launching their 1972 Easter Offensive to win militarily or at least establish control over some South Vietnamese territory. Nixon's China card paid no dividends in the Vietnam negotiations, while Hanoi's offensive yielded limited battlefield gains but failed to dislodge the Saigon government. Finally, seeing that Nixon would be reelected, the North Vietnamese on October 1972 dropped their demand that Thieu be forced from office as an immediate condition of a settlement. They separated cease-fire terms from political questions, as the United States had insisted all along. But the concession meant little. The preliminary agreement called for a reconciliation commission that would become a coalition government. Of much greater importance, the deal left NVA forces in possession of the territory they had gained earlier in the year, and it was clear to both sides from the outcome of the Easter Offensive that the ARVN could prevail only when backstopped by substantial American air power.[194]

While Kissinger negotiated with Tho in Paris, the Nixon administration repeatedly misled President Thieu about its diplomatic efforts. When he reluctantly went along with Vietnamization in June 1969, he had also acquiesced in the idea of secret talks between the United States and Hanoi. American officials had agreed to keep him informed about the course of negotiations, but Kissinger failed to honor that commitment. Political scientist Larry Berman, who has provided the fullest account of the Nixon administration's negotiations with the DRV, finds that the reports to Thieu by U.S. Ambassador Ellsworth Bunker after the private Kissinger-Tho sessions "were invariably sanitized."[195] American officials sometimes chose not to inform Thieu of new proposals before sharing them with communist negotiators, and his approval was not sought. If anything, mistrust between Washington and Saigon worsened over the course of time. Thieu never accepted the idea of a coalition government or the presence of NVA troops within South Vietnam, two conditions the Americans came to recognize as essential components of any deal Hanoi would accept. His worst fears were confirmed, moreover, when a provisional commitment he made in 1971 to step down (part of an offer that Al Haig told him Hanoi would reject) became public.[196] Once out in the open, such a pledge could never be fully renounced, and Kissinger felt free to bargain away Thieu's status as part of a post-cease-fire political arrangement.

Thieu's suspicion that Nixon and Kissinger planned to betray him and his nation erupted into open refusal when he learned the terms of the proposed peace agreement in late October 1972. He had already made plain his opposition to any scheme for a three-sided (Saigon/NLF/neutralist) reconciliation or electoral commission that might be seen as the basis for a coalition government, as well as to any agreement that permitted NVA troops to remain in the South. By this point, the American position had diverged too sharply from that of the South Vietnamese government for the two to be reconciled. Thieu reasoned that his best chance lay in sabotaging the agreement, and he insisted on multiple changes in the text sure to be unacceptable to Hanoi. Even when promised additional rush deliveries of military equipment to beat a proposed cease-fire deadline, or when threatened by American officials that they would conclude a deal without him even as Congress cut off all aid to his government, he refused to sign, and he made his objections very public through a Saigon TV and radio broadcast.

He succeeded in temporarily derailing the deal. Although Kissinger announced on October 26, 1972, that "peace is at hand," his introduction of the many amendments Thieu wanted caused the North Vietnamese to suspect bad faith on the American side and in turn led them to withdraw some of their earlier concessions. The Paris talks collapsed in mid-December. Nixon ordered a resumption of B-52 raids against Hanoi in what became known as the Christmas bombing, the largest heavy-bomber attacks since the end of World War II.[197]

The bombing represented one final violent exercise in diplomatic signaling by the United States, and it was as misconceived as most of the earlier gestures. Nixon intended to send a message to the North Vietnamese that he would punish them for any renewal of aggression and to reassure Thieu that he could rely on the United States to enforce the peace agreement through firm military action. In several messages via intermediaries and in letters directly to Thieu in the preceding weeks, Nixon had vowed to continue backing South Vietnam when the communists violated the pending agreement. When Saigon emissaries asked for something in the agreement to establish a legal basis for American retaliatory action, however, he brushed aside such language as unnecessary. He knew full well that by that point Congress would never go along with an open-ended commitment to send bombers back to Vietnam.[198] Saigon would have to trust his word, and by unleashing air attacks of unprecedented ferocity he showed that he meant business. However, even as the bombs fell, American officials told Thieu that they expected the communists to return to the table soon and conclude an agreement much like the one the two sides had arrived at in October.

The South Vietnamese leader had played his last hand, and it was a weak one. He failed to force a North Vietnamese withdrawal, his essential objective. For minimal and meaningless changes in the terms of the deal, Nixon had inflicted significant civilian casualties (Hanoi claimed that over 1,600 civilians had been killed) and caused serious losses in American aircraft (15 B-52s were either shot down or crashed) and their crews. On January 23, 1973, Kissinger and Tho signed the peace agreement that brought to a close American involvement in the war.

Final Reckoning

To the surprise of no one, the Paris accords never brought a day of peace to Vietnam. Nixon and Kissinger had evinced little interest in the implementation and enforcement arrangements, a clear indication they expected fighting to continue. As the time for the cease-fire approached, both Thieu and the communist leadership ordered their respective forces to launch attacks to improve their positions. Thieu also ignored language in the agreement that called for the release of civilian detainees, choosing instead to follow Kissinger's advice that he use them as hostages to bargain for NVA troop withdrawals.[199] (Why either one might have expected Hanoi to give up a key military advantage in exchange for captive VC cadre remains a puzzle, given the communists' cold-blooded willingness to sacrifice lives for their cause.) For their part, the North Vietnamese moved immediately to reinforce their units in the South, also violating the agreement terms that permitted no more than replacement of troops and worn-out equipment. Thieu and his government accordingly felt no compunction about ignoring the provisions that called for elections and a political settlement. Only the provisions calling for a final American troop withdrawal and the return of American POWs were carried out completely. More people died in fighting in South Vietnam in 1973 than in any year of the war.[200]

Nixon refused to make good on his private assurances to Thieu to punish North Vietnamese violations through stern military action. Various excuses were offered by the White House and other American officials—the United States did not wish to jeopardize the return of the later batches of American POWs, the onset of the rainy season would lessen NVA infiltration, bombing attacks again would merely impede enemy reinforcement, and so on.[201] Over the course of the year, moreover, the Watergate investigations started to close in on the president. Kissinger and Nixon later claimed that Watergate made it impossible for the president to honor his private pledges to Thieu. But even without political scandal, public and congressional support for renewed intervention would have been absent. A definitive legislative ban on a resumption of military action was therefore inevitable, Watergate or no. In August 1973, Congress barred the use of force in Vietnam, nullifying any promise Nixon had made to Thieu.[202]

The final chapter came with the abrupt collapse of the Saigon government in spring 1975. By that point Nixon had been forced from office, Congress had reduced aid to the South Vietnamese military to levels below what it needed to maintain itself at full strength, and Hanoi had rebuilt its forces (though not quite to the level of the 1972 Easter Offensive). The North Vietnamese became confident they would win when Nixon resigned, seeing his successor, Gerald R. Ford, as a weak leader. When Ford did not respond to the NVA capture of Phuoc Long province in South Vietnam in early 1975, Hanoi realized it could launch a broad offensive without fear of American retaliation. Thieu had made the communists' military task easier through his stubborn refusal to surrender territory to concentrate his forces. Although the attacking units were weaker than in 1972, the ARVN command again faltered and South Vietnamese morale, no longer backed by American muscle, broke.[203] Congress refused a last-gasp request from the Ford administration for a supplemental appropriation to send additional military assistance to Saigon. City after city fell quickly to the advancing NVA legions until they arrived at the outskirts of Saigon itself. There, in a scene that summed up the futility of two decades of American intervention, the last Americans fled the U.S. embassy in helicopters. Victorious communist troops burst into the grounds of the presidential palace—Thieu had resigned days earlier, to no avail—and raised their banner in triumph.

Defeat in Vietnam closed a dismal chapter in wartime presidential leadership. Neither Lyndon Johnson nor Richard Nixon could fulfill the core tasks. The former compiled a weak record. He never established a coherent military strategy to meet his political goals, and he did not keep a firm grip on the conduct of the war or alter direction when battlefield success proved elusive. Reluctant to make hard choices about national priorities, Johnson could not bring himself to level with the American people about the true cost of the war. His diplomacy with either Vietnam proved halting and ineffective. By 1968, Johnson's domestic agenda, his cherished dream for a Great Society, had unraveled, a political casualty of the war.

Nixon fared even worse. He let the war drag on for four years at a cost of another 20,552 American lives in combat and countless thousands of Vietnamese deaths, military and civilian, for an agreement no better than what Johnson might have secured.[204] From 1969 to 1973, American policy in Vietnam veered unpredictably between gradual disengagement and quixotic drives for victory, reflecting the instability of the president's temperament. American and South Vietnamese security gains did not add up to a basis for the long-term survival of the Saigon regime. And like Johnson, Nixon gravely underestimated the will of the Vietnamese communists to reunify their country. Any prospect for an independent South Vietnam following the departure of U.S. forces required engaging in a deliberate, open approach to peace-building, generating domestic support for an ongoing American commitment. Instead Nixon preferred to offer expressions of toughness and private pledges to Thieu, neither an adequate substitute.[205]

The Vietnam War provoked deep angst about presidential war powers and a political push to check them. On the political left, the war prompted talk of an "imperial presidency," to use the phrase of liberal historian Arthur M. Schlesinger Jr.[206] Excesses there were, including domestic espionage against political foes, illegal surveillance, efforts to harass war opponents by misusing government agencies for political purposes, and the other abuses that culminated in Watergate. Ultimately, Congress tried to regain some control over the decision to go to war by passing the 1973 War Powers Resolution. It was designed to force a president to seek legislative approval when sending American troops into harm's way. Few advocates of the resolution acknowledged that intervention in Vietnam had occurred with the full consent of Congress in 1964 and enjoyed broad public backing at the outset.

Despite the focus on presidential overreach, the Vietnam conflict really highlighted how little presidents can do to shape what happens in a war. Critics scarcely noticed that both presidents quickly dissipated their power. Johnson never asserted control over the war, even in the initial phase when presidents historically have exercised the greatest direction over military matters. Nixon on taking office did recover a degree of latitude. However, obsessed with showing how tough he was, he missed the brief opportunity he had to build a durable American security commitment to South Vietnam. For peace-building, he offered a mixture of secrecy (his private word to Thieu to meet communist transgressions with force) and cynicism (did he really believe Congress would support recurrent bombing?). It was an exit strategy that reflected the exhaustion of presidential war power, not its imperial apogee.

5

The Perils of Optimism
George W. Bush

PRESIDENTS SOMETIMES FIND WARS FORCED upon them, whether by circumstances or their own commitments. Lincoln inherited a secession crisis that left him no alternative to war besides disunion; Wilson allowed the decisions about whether and when the United States would enter the First World War to be made in Berlin; Franklin Roosevelt responded to threats from Germany and Japan in ways that made war inevitable; and Cold War logic drove Johnson to resist communist aggression in Vietnam.

For George W. Bush, by contrast, Iraq represented a war of choice.[1] In the wake of the September 11, 2001, terrorist attacks, nothing dictated that the United States must overthrow Saddam Hussein. Presidential discretion extended to how the United States might conduct a military operation in Iraq. Bush had at his disposal a large, technologically advanced military with no immediate competing demands on American troops.

This striking degree of latitude did not last. The president let much of it slip from his grasp by delegating responsibility for preparing for war, particularly to his secretary of defense, Donald Rumsfeld, and by not exercising close oversight over the planning process. Because Pentagon civilian planners paid too little attention to the difficulties implicit in Bush's goal of establishing a liberal, democratic Iraq, the military requirements for a successful invasion were not reconciled with his ambitious peace-building agenda. The military force used to topple Saddam Hussein proved insufficient for postwar security and reconstruction. When U.S. troops faced a widening insurgency in the months after they ousted Saddam, the initial decisions could not be undone. The war drifted, directionless, while Bush contented himself with exhortations to his subordinates to remain firm and warnings to the American public that defeat would open the door to terrorism here. Three years into the war—as casualties mounted, sectarian violence worsened in Iraq, and support at home eroded—even the president could no longer deny that his approach was failing. By that point, though, few options remained on the table, and all came with a high political price.

Faced with the prospect of defeat, Bush finally asserted some active control over the Iraq War, and in so doing managed to stave off disaster. He listened, as it were, to his "inner Lincoln." Against the view of his own top military people, many key advisors, and a broad range of political figures, the president decided to send to Iraq the few additional troops who could be made available and appoint a new commander who would pursue a different operational approach. New tactics and unexpected developments in Iraq, notably the willingness of many insurgents to cooperate with U.S. forces against their extremist enemies, yielded a significant lessening of violence. Iraq seemed to have stepped away from the edge of an abyss. Gone, though, was the hope of establishing there the kind of government that might spark the political transformation of the Middle East. And by then the American people had turned their backs on the war.

Unfinished Business, Unexpected Opportunity

When George H. W. Bush decided to respond forcefully to Iraq's invasion of Kuwait in 1990, he hoped not only to expel Saddam Hussein from the territory his troops had conquered but to see the dictator toppled from power.[2] The United States deployed a massive military force to the Persian Gulf under General Norman Schwarzkopf, commander of U.S. Central Command (CENTCOM). Through patient and extensive diplomacy, the Bush administration also assembled a broad multinational coalition and secured the approval of the United Nations for military action if Saddam refused to withdraw from Kuwait. After negotiation and sanctions failed to bring about an Iraqi pullback, the administration decided it had no alternative but to use force to liberate Kuwait, a course narrowly approved by Congress. Bush made clear that the United States hoped to go beyond restoring Kuwait's independence to eliminate Iraq as a threat to peace in the Gulf region and the Middle East—a signal that the administration would welcome "regime change" in Baghdad.

For diplomatic reasons, however, the United States could not explicitly pursue this broader objective. Just as importantly, American leaders had no wish to become responsible for governing a postwar Iraq that might prove highly unstable.[3] Washington hoped instead that once Saddam Hussein's army was crushed on the battlefield (especially the dictator's most loyal force, the Republican Guard), his military might turn against him or the Iraqi people rise up and overthrow him.[4]

To the disappointment of the Bush administration, the rout of Saddam's army in Kuwait in Operation Desert Storm did not precipitate his ouster. Coalition forces scored an overwhelming triumph in a mere four days after their ground offensive commenced on February 22, 1991. Most of the Republican Guard troops, though, escaped back to Iraq.[5] Further, Washington allowed the commander on the scene, Schwarzkopf, to negotiate cease-fire terms, and he permitted the Iraqi military to continue to fly helicopter missions. When the anticipated popular uprisings against Saddam erupted, the dictator used his helicopters and loyal troops to crush them. The United States intervened quickly in northern Iraq to protect the Kurds from reprisal attacks, establishing an autonomous zone under American protection. Elsewhere, however, coalition forces stood by as Iraqi troops suppressed rebellious elements and killed all those suspected of supporting or sympathizing with the opposition. The violence took on a sectarian cast: Saddam's regime drew its support from Iraq's Sunni minority, while the resistance was based primarily in the majority Shiite community, mainly around Basra in the South. Saddam Hussein concluded from the decision of American leaders not to pursue his forces all the way to

Baghdad that the United States had little taste for casualties and was unprepared to pay the price for toppling his government.[6]

For the next decade, the United States and its allies settled on a policy of containing the Iraqi regime while trying to weaken it. Under pressure from the United Nations, Saddam agreed to dismantle his nuclear, chemical, and biological weapons development programs and submit to UN-directed inspections. Few believed that he had complied fully with the mandate to eliminate the programs, referred to collectively as weapons of mass destruction (WMD).[7] Saddam saw the ambiguity as a means for protecting his regime: he believed that both internal enemies and external foes, specifically Iran, would be less likely to move against him if they thought he still possessed unconventional weapons. How the United States might view his possession of WMD capability evidently did not enter into his calculations.[8] In addition, the United Nations supported ongoing sanctions against the Iraqi regime designed to prevent him from rebuilding his battered military. However, to ease the pain that sanctions inflicted on ordinary Iraqis, a program was established that permitted Baghdad to sell oil for food, which in turn led to Western suspicions that Saddam had found ways to exploit the loopholes to acquire more lethal goods.[9] The United States and Great Britain also continued to enforce a no-fly zone over both northern and southern Iraq with regular aerial patrols. On several occasions the Iraqis challenged the restriction by firing on Allied aircraft, provoking retaliatory strikes. Saddam decided to test containment in another way: in 1998 he ordered out the UN weapons inspectors. That prompted President Bill Clinton to launch Operation Desert Fox, which not only damaged Iraqi air defense capabilities but briefly caused Iraq's Arab neighbors to fear Saddam's regime might collapse.[10]

That the Iraqi leader survived and occasionally stuck his finger in the American eye frustrated Washington and led some to conclude that it had been a grave mistake to allow him to remain in power after the 1991 Gulf War. The cost of enforcing a no-fly zone was not trivial (about \$1 billion per year), and no end was in sight.[11] Worse, Saddam Hussein remained an irritant in the region, a potentially destabilizing element in a strategically vital part of the world. Neoconservatives, an ideological faction deeply hostile to the Clinton administration's preferred multilateral approach to foreign policy, regarded Saddam as a menace to the region, especially to Israel, and as a criminal who had used WMD on his own people. Influential "neocons" such as Paul Wolfowitz urged a shift in American policy to support efforts to bring about regime change in Iraq.[12] In 1998, Congress passed the Iraq Liberation Act (ILA) that declared the United States should back efforts to remove Saddam's regime and promote a democratic government in its place. Because the legislation did not commit the United States to a specific course of action, President Clinton signed the bill, thereby avoiding the political attacks he might have incurred through a veto.[13] The Clinton administration, though it knew that Saddam was sidestepping UN sanctions, did not see Iraq as a major source of terrorism and chose not to engage in more aggressive action against Baghdad.[14] Other threats were more alarming, notably Osama bin Laden's al-Qaeda network.[15]

With the election of President George W. Bush in 2000, advocates of regime change moved closer to the seat of power, but American policy toward Iraq did not immediately change. Several leading neoconservatives assumed important second-tier positions within the administration; Wolfowitz, for example, became deputy secretary of defense for policy. He and a few others proposed that the United States back regime change "at a distance," that is, by supporting Iraqi insurgents and exile groups that might weaken Saddam Hussein, possibly even letting the Shiite south break away from Baghdad's control. Neither the new president nor his senior officials endorsed more direct measures against Saddam.[16] Secretary of State Colin Powell, Vice President Dick Cheney, and others had backed the 1991 decision not to press the coalition offensive to the point of overthrowing the dictator, lest the United States become too deeply enmeshed in the political fate of a post-Saddam Iraq. Although Cheney later concluded it had been an error to let Saddam remain in power, he still did not endorse military action to remove him.[17] Despite impatience with containment, then, the Bush administration initially continued the policy.

The terrorist attacks on September 11, 2001, abruptly transformed the policy calculus. Bush resolved at once to remove the threat of future attacks. Over the following days, Wolfowitz urged the president to send a strong signal of his commitment to stop terrorism by pursuing regime change in Baghdad.[18] However, all signs suggested that 9/11 had been the handiwork of bin Laden and al-Qaeda, and they were being sheltered not by Saddam Hussein but by the Islamic fundamentalist Taliban regime in Afghanistan. The president saw value in a final reckoning with Saddam—Iraq occupied a far more important geo-strategic position than did Afghanistan—but he recognized that domestic opinion would demand prompt retaliation against the 9/11 perpetrators. Accordingly, the Iraq option was shelved in favor of a military campaign to topple the Taliban, destroy al-Qaeda's Afghan sanctuary, and eliminate bin Laden.[19] Rumsfeld oversaw the planning of a military campaign, which would be launched under the auspices of CENTCOM commander General Tommy Franks. The operation, which relied on a combination of air power, light Special Operations forces, and anti-Taliban Afghan troops, drove the Taliban from power in a few short weeks.[20] Although bin Laden eluded capture, it seemed but a matter of time before he would be brought to heel.

With things proceeding well in Afghanistan, the president began to weigh his next move. The administration found itself in extraordinarily permissive circumstances. In part, these reflected the aftermath of the collapse of the Soviet Union and the end of the Cold War a decade earlier: the United States enjoyed a position of hegemony or primacy in international affairs without any recent historical parallel. Still, American leaders had reacted tentatively to their newfound strength in the 1990s, hesitating to use force other than under the auspices of international organizations and multilateral frameworks.[21] The 9/11 attacks swept aside all hesitation about using American power.

Equally important, the attacks revived American anxiety about threats looming in distant places that might endanger the homeland. Such anxiety has often primed the citizenry for military action abroad, even absent an immediate risk to American national security. Post-9/11 popular fear manifested itself in a willingness to tolerate significant curbs on civil liberties, as evidenced in October 2001 by passage of the USA PATRIOT Act. Gideon Rose captures the situation facing the president and his advisors: "Primacy removed constraints coming from the world at large, and the 9/11 attacks swept away constraints coming from the domestic political system. The administration's leading figures found themselves with extraordinary freedom of action, greater in some ways than that any of their predecessors had ever had, and the only question was how they would use it."[22]

It took little time for the administration to identify another target. Eyes turned again to Iraq. In late November 2001, the president directed Rumsfeld to order General Franks to begin planning for a possible invasion.[23]

The (Non) Decision to Invade

George W. Bush never made a clear decision to invade Iraq. That is, it is not possible to point to a particular meeting or a specific moment when he chose to go to war. Instead, the planning for a major military operation against Saddam Hussein took on a life of its own, generating an irresistible momentum within the administration.[24] It became evident to key advisors in summer 2002 that, barring a profound change in Iraqi behavior, the president had settled upon war.[25] By not insisting upon an open discussion of the risks of military action, Bush neglected the first important task of wartime leadership. The administration focused instead on justifying its preferred course of action to the American people and the international community.[26] With Americans already fearful of a terrorist follow-up to 9/11, making the case to the domestic audience proved simple enough. Not so foreign leaders and their publics, and the effort to induce their support by renewing UN inspections slowed the march to war.

From the standpoint of actual threats to American security, Iraq ranked low, even after 9/11. Saddam's military, badly damaged in the 1991 war, no longer represented a significant danger to its neighbors, let alone to the United States. American attention focused instead on the possibility that the Iraqi dictator might join forces with al-Qaeda or other terrorist organizations and make available to them his presumed stock of WMD. He had kicked out UN weapons inspectors in 1998, and the common assumption in the United States and elsewhere was that he had restarted his efforts to acquire nuclear weapons and revived his capability to produce chemical and biological weapons. (Indeed, his own military commanders shared the same belief and expected their leader to use WMD when American forces approached Baghdad.) On the other hand, his relationship with Islamic terrorist groups seemed tenuous. Saddam's Baath Party embraced a secular pan-Arab ideology that bin Laden condemned. Among "rogue" states, Iran in particular had closer ties to known terrorist networks than did Iraq. Even allowing for the heightened sensitivity to catastrophic terrorist attacks expressed by Vice President Cheney and others, Iraq represented a curious choice as the next administration target.[27]

But dealing a fatal blow to Saddam Hussein held other appeal. Iraq lay at the heart of the strategic Middle East, and the possibility of transforming the country into a free society with democratic and market institutions captured the imagination of the president and those around him. If Iraq could be remade, the effects might be felt across the region. For the first time, the Arab world would see a successful liberal alternative to either the stagnant authoritarian regimes that predominated or the backward-looking fundamentalist orders that Islamic extremists sought to promote.[28] Realist caution had guided past American policy to a dead-end: the United States had propped up dictatorships in the name of stability. Now, with American power at its peak and the world recoiling from the terrorist agenda after 9/11, the opportunity beckoned to set in motion a different dynamic that might usher in a new era of liberation.[29] As one critic later said of the administration's view, "Iraq was a blank slate on which the United States could impose its vision of a pluralistic society."[30] Other rogue states would get the message, too.[31] Last, taking down Saddam's regime would resonate with an American people still reeling from 9/11— better by far to strike a blow against an avowed enemy of the United States than to sit back and await the next act of terrorist violence.

It was all heady stuff, and certainly plausible on the surface. Bush saw himself standing at a crossroads, a rare moment when a political leader seems to have within his grasp the opportunity to alter the course of history. The circumstances created by 9/11, he believed, might allow for more than a conventional defensive response to extremists. But the very boldness of the emerging administration agenda also demanded close critical scrutiny. Questions needed to be asked about every assumption undergirding the transformative aspiration—about the real nature of Iraqi society that was deemed ripe for a liberal remaking, about whether democracy could be implanted quickly, about the agendas of different Iraqi actors both within Iraq and in exile, about how other regional actors might exploit a power vacuum created by a weakened Iraq, and more. In short, the situation begged for a rigorous, structured decision process, one designed to compensate for the president's own professed shoot-from-the-hip, instinctive leadership style.[32] But the following months would show that no such decision process existed within the Bush administration.

Although blame for the process deficiencies has been placed on various officials, ultimate responsibility rested with the president himself. It is certainly true that Condoleezza Rice, Bush's national security advisor, failed to play the role of an "honest broker" who would make certain that her boss heard conflicting viewpoints and understood the risks of war and its aftermath. Instead, she tended to tell the president what he wanted to hear.[33] Vice President Cheney enjoyed an outsized role in the administration that he used to promote his conviction—despite the lack of evidence, then and now—that Saddam Hussein had an active connection to al-Qaeda.[34] But these and other key subordinates had been chosen because they embraced Bush's view of the world, and he did not invite those around him to question his commitment.

The outliers in the administration who worried over the unexamined drift toward war with Iraq, such as Secretary of State Colin Powell, found themselves marginalized in the process.[35] They would make themselves heard, as George Ball had voiced his reservations about Vietnam escalation to Lyndon Johnson. Powell pressed his concerns forcefully enough to slow the timetable for military action. However, when a president signals that he has resolved on a course of action and asks his key subordinates to support him, few will risk their positions to stand in opposition. In the end, Powell and nearly all the other doubters swallowed their reservations.[36]

The Bush administration invested its energy, then, in building a case against Saddam Hussein that would justify regime change. Since the president and his team believed the Iraqi dictator posed a danger because he might share WMD with terrorist groups, much of the effort went into demonstrating that he possessed unconventional weapons and that his regime had strong ties to Islamic extremists. Neither claim would be easy to substantiate. Not only had UN weapons inspections ceased in 1998, but American intelligence services lacked credible sources within Iraq.[37] This left the intelligence community dependent upon Iraqi exiles, who naturally wanted to encourage the United States to overthrow Saddam.[38] The Central Intelligence Agency also found reason to doubt reports of contact between Saddam's government and al-Qaeda operatives or other known terrorist groups.

Frustrated by the failure of the established intelligence apparatus to connect the dots, senior administration officials decided to sift through the raw intelligence data themselves to ferret out the incriminating evidence they believed had been overlooked. A working group was established in the Defense Department under Wolfowitz's subordinate Douglas Feith to conduct an independent review. Grabbing hold of fragments of information and unconfirmed reports, Feith and company began to amass a picture of Iraqi activities that bore a much closer relationship to the administration's convictions.[39] This ad hoc intelligence shop passed along its discoveries to senior administration officials, who saw the new findings as confirmation of their suspicions. Further, many intelligence analysts reported intense pressure from above to report conclusions about Iraqi–al-Qaeda ties that supported administration contentions.[40]

The president and top officials next set out to prepare the American people for military action against the Iraqi regime. In his 2002 State of the Union Address, Bush identified Iraq, Iran, and North Korea as an "axis of evil," an obvious throwback reference to the enemies of the United States in the Second World War.[41] He took care not to suggest an explicit alliance among the three states (unlike the formal one that Germany, Italy, and Japan had established). Rather, he intended the association to suggest that Iraq and the others stood apart in their determination to undermine the global order for which the United States served as steward. Several months later, in a speech delivered on June 1, 2002, to the graduating class at the United States Military Academy at West Point, the president presented what became known as the Bush Doctrine:

> Deterrence, the promise of massive retaliation against nations, means nothing against shadowy terrorist networks with no nation or citizens to defend. Containment is not possible when unbalanced dictators with weapons of mass destruction can deliver those weapons on missiles or secretly provide them to terrorist allies. . . . [O]ur security will require all Americans to be forward looking and resolute, to be ready for preemptive action when necessary to defend our liberty and to defend our lives.[42]

He and other officials made clear over the following weeks that Iraq fit the criteria, with the vice president going so far as to claim on August 26, 2002, that the United States had firm proof that Saddam had WMD. (Cheney's assertion evidently caught the president, Rice, and others off guard, but they picked up the alarmist refrain.) Lest Americans underestimate the potential danger of letting Saddam Hussein remain in power, senior administration officials warned that conclusive evidence of his nefarious designs might come in the form of a "mushroom cloud." Bush declared in early October that the containment policy had failed and that Saddam already possessed chemical and biological weapons.[43]

The drumbeat of warnings achieved the desired effect. With 9/11 still a fresh memory, it was easy to stoke popular fears, which is exactly what the administration's propaganda campaign intended. The administration chose its words with great care, too, to avoid saying explicitly anything that it knew to be untrue or unsubstantiated, such as that Saddam Hussein had been involved in the 9/11 attacks. Few in the media questioned the assertions, while administration officials were quoted far more often than the skeptics.[44] As is always the case when media coverage slants overwhelmingly in favor of the official side of an issue, the public bought the administration position and its insinuations. An overwhelming majority of Americans believed Saddam Hussein still possessed WMD, while a lesser majority drew the conclusion that he had connections to al-Qaeda and even that he had participated in the planning for 9/11.[45]

Beneath the broad trends in public opinion, partisan differences still appeared—Republicans were more likely to accept the administration's line. Best, then, to get Democratic leaders to sign off on military action. In mid-October, the administration capitalized on the upcoming midterm elections to secure congressional approval for the use of force to compel Iraq to give up its WMD programs. To address lawmakers' concerns about the quality of evidence on Saddam's WMD program before they voted on the resolution, the administration prepared a Special National Intelligence Estimate, with the summary sanitized of all earlier caveats and official dissents about the WMD intelligence.[46] Many Democrats, concerned about appearing soft, voted in favor, and the measure passed by wide margins in both chambers.[47]

International audiences, as suggested, proved much less receptive to Bush administration arguments. Apart from a few of Saddam Hussein's neighbors, foreign leaders did not regard him as an immediate threat. Some nations, such as France, benefited from trade with Iraq under the oil-for-food program, as well as more illicit dealings. Moreover, if al-Qaeda terrorism prompted concern, so did unchecked American bellicosity, and the Bush Doctrine justifying preventive war stirred fears of the destabilizing effects when one nation acquires disproportionate power in the international system.

The administration struggled to reassemble the kind of broad multinational coalition that stood against Saddam Hussein when he had invaded Kuwait a decade before. Erstwhile American allies such as France declined to participate; Turkey held back, complicating any invasion plan that would have involved entering Iraq from the north.[48] Colin Powell urged Bush to build international support for military action by seeking a UN resolution to demand that Iraq submit to inspections of its suspected WMD programs.[49] Although this would mean putting the invasion plans on hold, the president agreed, and Powell led a diplomatic effort that secured unanimous support for Security Council Resolution 1441 on November 8, 2002.[50] Later, the secretary of state would put his prestige on the line when he returned to the United Nations in early 2003 to present the administration's evidence that Saddam had continued his WMD programs in violation of UN resolutions. But the intelligence that seemed to the Bush administration to confirm its worst assumptions about the Iraqi dictator failed to sway other nations.[51] (In time, the shoddy basis for Powell's assertions became public and badly tarnished his reputation.)[52] If the president decided to move against Iraq, he would do so with many fewer allies than his father's administration had recruited in 1990–1991.

McNamara Redux

The invasion of Iraq occurred against a backdrop of civil-military tensions strikingly similar to those that marked the Vietnam era. As we saw in the previous chapter, Robert McNamara took up his position as secretary of defense determined to reform the Pentagon from top to bottom, and he clashed fiercely with the military leadership throughout his tenure. Much the same pattern characterized Donald Rumsfeld's management of the Defense Department. He arrived with a mandate from the president to pursue a thoroughgoing transformation of how the American military fought wars. In the process, he would reestablish firm civilian control of the military, a principle that neoconservatives felt had eroded under recent administrations. Rumsfeld intended to solidify these twin themes—military transformation and civilian authority—in the preparation for war against Iraq.

From the perspective of neoconservative defense intellectuals, American military leadership had been permitted too much of a policy voice during and after the Gulf War and remained wedded to outmoded ideas about how best to wage war. Neoconservatives, as noted earlier, believed the unsatisfactory outcome of the 1991 Gulf War resulted from the willingness of political leaders to cede too much control over when and how the fighting ended to General Schwarzkopf. Military assertiveness continued through the Clinton administration, when uniformed commanders pushed back hard against proposed military interventions in Rwanda and the Balkans. To discourage intervention, for example, the military tended to overstate force requirements.[53] Hence neoconservatives welcomed Eliot Cohen's defense of hands-on political control of wartime military matters and made certain it came to the attention of Clinton's successor in the White House.

Meanwhile, both reform-minded officers and many defense experts argued that the American military had adapted grudgingly and incompletely to the revolutionary potential of new weapons and communications technologies. Senior commanders still planned for conflicts fought with massive armies that differed only in degree from those Eisenhower had commanded a half-century earlier. Advocates of military transformation insisted that the United States could use its vast technological edge over potential adversaries to wage lighter, faster campaigns that would yield victory at a much lower human and financial cost.[54] When Rumsfeld interviewed for the position of secretary of defense, he persuaded Bush that the emerging revolution in military affairs needed a revolutionary leader—a strong civilian head at the Pentagon who could overcome the military's entrenched habits.

Rumsfeld and his top civilian aides set about to remake the military virtually overnight, taking no prisoners along the way. The secretary of defense deluged the Pentagon with his "snowflakes," memos demanding explanations or justification for anything that struck him as symptomatic of the old way of conducting business.[55] Some senior officers wilted under his incessant pressure. Others expected to outlast him, however, knowing that few cabinet secretaries stay in office more than a couple of years.[56] So Rumsfeld leveraged his control over senior personnel decisions to induce cooperation. As under McNamara a generation before, Rumsfeld tied career advancement to support for his program of military transformation.[57]

The first key test of the new approach to warfare came with the campaign against the Taliban in Afghanistan. Rumsfeld wanted to mount an operation within days or weeks, only to find that General Franks and CENTCOM envisioned a lengthy buildup of conventional forces that would require months. By contrast, the CIA was able to place its operatives in the field with the anti-Taliban Northern Alliance virtually overnight. Rumsfeld harangued Franks to accelerate the deployment timetable and rely on Special Operations military personnel. It took just a few weeks for the CIA/Northern Alliance/special ops/air power combination to disrupt the Taliban regime and compel it to quit Kabul.[58] The operation demonstrated the new mode of warfare that Rumsfeld took to be the wave of the future. A number of high-ranking officers were not so sure. They worried that the military leaders charged with overall direction of the campaign had focused on short-run objectives that led them to mistake capturing the capital city (Kabul) for winning the campaign.[59] No matter—the defense secretary trumpeted his kind of victory.

When attention turned to a possible invasion of Iraq, however, Rumsfeld was dismayed to find that the military expected to reprise its 1991 Gulf War campaign. Franks started with a plan developed by his CENTCOM predecessor, Marine General Anthony Zinni, that called for some 350,000 troops.[60] It would take many months to position such a force, during which time it would be vulnerable to an Iraqi counter-strike and might stir unrest in the Arab world. In the defense secretary's view, this represented the kind of stale thinking he had come to the Pentagon to sweep aside. He demanded that Franks redo the plan to take better advantage of the capabilities that had been demonstrated in Afghanistan, making full use of Special Operations forces and carefully targeted air power.[61] Rumsfeld went so far as to entertain the possibility of mounting the invasion with less than a single division of American troops, fewer than 17,000 all told.[62] Whether he actually believed the scheme possible or merely used it to whittle down the troop commitment in Franks's plan is open to question, but it had the desired effect. CENTCOM produced successive iterations of an invasion plan that would be executed by about 100,000 American and allied (primarily British) troops.[63]

In asserting firm political oversight in the planning process, Rumsfeld exercised the kind of active direction that Cohen recommends, with a twist. Cohen advocates hands-on control by the political leader. Bush, though, introduced his own management style, one based on his business background: he believed a leader ought to set the general direction and tone for his organization and let trusted subordinates execute his vision within their particular domains. Thus he delegated full responsibility for planning the Iraq invasion to others, particularly his defense secretary. Rumsfeld and General Franks presented the successive versions of the plan to the president and his principals (the heads of major agencies and the national security advisor). At no time did Bush engage in a searching critique of the plan or explore the assumptions behind it. From the beginning of the planning process to the outset of the invasion, the entire enterprise was Rumsfeld's show. He intended it as definitive proof of his ideas about military transformation.[64]

Certainly there was unease in military circles about the invasion plan that emerged.[65] It presumed a swift advance to Baghdad, so rapid that the Iraqis would be unable to organize a coherent defense. But the attacking forces would depend upon a long, vulnerable supply line that would stretch some 300 miles. With so few troops on the ground, the enemy might easily ambush lightly guarded supply columns. Better to have a larger margin of safety, many military planners believed, by increasing the size of the invasion force.[66] There was also the matter of securing all the suspected WMD sites—an unreliable list of more than 900 had been developed by American intelligence agencies. To permit unguarded WMD to fall into the hands of extremists would defeat a main purpose of the war, yet there simply were too few troops for both the thrust to the Iraqi capital and protection of WMD sites.[67]

The defense secretary conceded on some points, and the officers most directly involved in commanding the operation seemed satisfied. Through the back-and-forth between the Pentagon and CENTCOM, the invasion plan had been refined, and Franks assured the president that the military had what it needed. Rumsfeld intended to monitor closely the flow of troops into Kuwait to make sure no extra unnecessary units would be deployed.[68] He later insisted that senior commanders never voiced their reservations to him.[69] Possibly this is so; possibly he chose to disregard the murmurings. Either way, one thing is clear: concerns raised lower down the military chain of command about the sufficiency of the invasion force never rose to the level of the president.

Regime Change . . . and Then What?

The most serious defects in the invasion plan arose from its relationship to the larger war goal that George W. Bush had established—to transform Iraq into a liberal society that would be a beacon to the oppressed masses of the Middle East. Neither the president nor his defense secretary was comfortable with the concept of "nation building." Yet unless post-invasion Iraq followed a best-case scenario, the United States would face a daunting challenge of remaking a deeply divided nation. Rumsfeld, however, minimized the complications and insisted that the United States would quickly hand off responsibility for the future of Iraq. At the same time, he was a skilled and ferocious bureaucratic infighter who insisted on control over all aspects of postwar planning. Preparation for postwar peace-building started late, ignored identified risks, rested on sunny assumptions, and left key questions unresolved.

Nation building enjoyed little favor in the early days of the Bush administration. As a presidential candidate, Bush had explicitly dismissed the idea, asserting that it had been an error to let the U.S. military dissipate its energies on peacekeeping missions. American armed forces should be reserved for what they did best, engaging in and winning violent conflicts.[70] Nation building, if necessary, ought to be left to other nations and their less capable militaries. The secretary of defense similarly viewed the extended American commitment to peacekeeping in Bosnia and Kosovo as a mistake. Apart from misusing U.S. military resources, Rumsfeld maintained, these operations encouraged dependency on outside intervention rather than forcing people in war-torn societies to solve their own problems. He was adamant that the United States must foster a more rapid return to self-sufficiency. The aftermath of the operation against the Taliban in Afghanistan represented the model he believed the United States ought to follow: a minimal commitment of military force to police postwar rebuilding, allies stepping in to assume much of the burden, and a quick return to self-government under a friendly leader.[71] Within the military establishment, the administration's distaste for nation building met a positive reception.[72]

Early Pentagon planning for post-Saddam Iraq reflected the defense secretary's premises and the Afghanistan experience. Rumsfeld and Franks focused almost exclusively on the invasion itself.[73] Other military planners likewise gave little thought to the postwar stability phase (referred to as "Phase IV" in current military jargon), having been assured initially that it would be the responsibility of other government agencies.[74] Civilian leaders at the Defense Department made a number of assumptions about what would happen after the regime was overthrown that were based on an optimistic view of underlying conditions in Iraq. The Iraqi state would continue largely intact, "under new management," while the Iraqi economy would quickly recover and the society would progress smoothly to a tolerant, multisectarian order. In political terms, regime change meant a neat decapitation procedure: the removal of the dictator and his inner circle of family members and henchmen, followed by their replacement by democratic leaders. Any costs incurred to rebuild the economy would be self-financed as Iraq quickly resumed pumping oil in large quantities to an eager world energy market.[75] As for ongoing security issues, these would be minor, easily handed over to some combination of multinational troops and police and reconstituted Iraqi security forces.[76]

Within the military and other parts of the Bush administration, many were not so sanguine. Some military planners feared that the power vacuum created by Saddam's ouster would encourage disorder. Experience from previous postwar stability operations suggested that security was best assured by maintaining an adequate force-to-population ratio.

Extrapolating from the Balkans examples, some 300,000 to 400,000 troops would be needed in Iraq, a number far larger than the invasion force Rumsfeld envisioned. Meanwhile, the State Department prepared a massive, multivolume study of Iraqi postwar challenges and potential problems, "The Future of Iraq." Although too unwieldy and academic to serve as the basis for a postwar plan, the study highlighted the magnitude of the issues the United States might face.[77] Colin Powell, concerned that CENTCOM had given too little attention to postwar matters, met with the president on August 5, 2002, to caution that the United States would claim ownership of a country of 24 million and needed to be better prepared for the responsibility.[78] Analysis by other agencies warned that regime loyalists might organize resistance against invading forces, the Iraqi economic infrastructure might be badly frayed by years of sanctions and neglect, and intra-communal tensions (Sunni versus Shiite versus Kurd) might erupt into violence. Sometimes the concerns became public, as in September 2002, when Lawrence Lindsay, the president's chief economic advisor, estimated that the war and its aftermath might cost $100–$200 billion. Many experts cautioned against the disruptive effects of disbanding the Iraqi military and against overzealous efforts to cleanse government institutions of Baathist influence.[79]

Rumsfeld had no intention of sharing any of the responsibility for postwar planning with other agencies. For the State Department, in particular, the defense secretary showed utter disdain, convinced that it had bungled its share of postwar responsibility in Afghanistan. Condoleezza Rice tried to orchestrate an interagency process to overcome Pentagon resistance, but her efforts were no match for Rumsfeld's willful opposition.[80] Bush unwittingly abetted his defense secretary's obstructionism by frowning on internal dissent over his Iraq agenda. Those who called attention to potential problems or anticipated a more difficult and costly postwar phase were seen as disloyal. Thus Lindsay's high figure for the price of the invasion and its follow-up earned him the scorn of other officials, and he was forced out before the end of 2002.[81]

The president remained largely detached from the internal debates over postwar Iraq. He refused to intervene to force Rumsfeld to cooperate with the other players. As time passed with no semblance of a usable plan in fall 2002, concern mounted among senior military officers at all levels.[82] Eventually, rumblings about the insufficiency of the preparation for a postwar occupation reached Bush's ears. He responded by formalizing the Pentagon's authority over postwar planning on January 20, 2003, while raising some specific concerns. For example, the president realized that a humanitarian crisis in the wake of the invasion, which might result if the fighting forced many Iraqis to flee their homes, would both disrupt the return to stability and become a public relations disaster for the United States. He insisted on adequate preparations for emergency relief supplies. Otherwise the president asked few questions and accepted vague answers to the ones he did pose.[83]

Having won the bureaucratic war, Rumsfeld finally woke up to the fact that his department needed to be ready for what would happen the day after Baghdad fell. He made it clear that the United States would not embark on another Balkans-style operation but instead would follow the Afghanistan model in which the Afghans had been left alone to build their own country.[84] In January 2003 he picked Douglas Feith, who worked for Wolfowitz, to oversee the postwar planning process.[85] Rumsfeld and Feith then selected retired Lieutenant General Jay Garner to head a temporary planning organization, the Office of Reconstruction and Humanitarian Assistance (ORHA), to prepare the civilian side of a postwar occupation. (Having led an earlier relief effort among the Kurds in 1991, Garner had some familiarity with Iraq.)[86] Franks assumed the military would exercise full authority in Iraq for several months following the end of hostilities. This meant Garner and his team, mostly former and current military personnel, should have sufficient time to organize their work. An exercise conducted in late February 2003 at Garner's behest to identify potential problems and clarify agencies' responsibilities revealed a host of unanswered questions. But too little time remained to remedy the situation.[87] Answers would have to be cobbled together on the fly. Concern over possible postwar security problems did result in a decision, later confirmed by the president, that the Iraqi Army would be retained under non-Baathist commanders to help preserve order.[88]

Meanwhile, Rumsfeld and his senior civilian aides showed no greater tolerance for questions about their postwar plan from within the military than they had from other agencies. One celebrated episode illustrated the mind-set at the top of the Pentagon. When asked during a February 2002 congressional hearing what might happen if unrest followed a U.S. invasion of Iraq, General Eric Shinseki, the army chief of staff, replied that it could require 400,000 troops to secure the country. Shinseki, who had headed the stability operation in Bosnia, was in a position to know.[89] Worded as a contingent possibility, his answer reflected unease at the decision to depart from the doctrine of overwhelming force that had characterized American military operations before Rumsfeld. A massive presence on the ground offered a comforting margin of error and would help preempt the very possibility—a violent insurgency—that Shinseki had been asked to consider.[90]

Wolfowitz promptly struck back, insisting that American troops would be greeted as liberators and that fears of sectarian tensions were very much overblown. Moreover, it was absurd to think that more troops would be needed for occupation duties than were required for the invasion itself, and no one doubted that the force agreed upon by Rumsfeld and Franks was sufficient to take down the Iraqi regime. Wolfowitz confidently predicted that other nations, even those opposed to an American-led invasion, would pitch in with postwar stability operations once it became clear how little risk was involved.[91] Shinseki became persona non grata in the Pentagon, marginalized for the remainder of his tenure.

Although Rumsfeld and his civilian subordinates later became the objects of widespread scorn for the Pentagon's failure to anticipate the insurgency that followed the invasion, the responsibility for postwar planning remains the president's. For a president facing what is expected to be a long war, the task can be postponed, though often it has been put off until too late. In the case of the planned invasion of Iraq, however, everyone on the American side looked to a brief conflict and quick victory. Thus, even before the campaign started, postwar planning had to be completed, which meant it should have been an early priority. Bush needed to make certain that careful postwar planning happened and to hold accountable those responsible for it.[92] He could not plead ignorance of the poor state of the postwar preparations: at a February 28, 2003, briefing Garner identified several key tasks, including dealing with terrorists and reshaping the Iraqi military, which lay beyond the capacity of his small team. But the president did not make sure other agencies would fill the gaps.[93]

Even more, Bush did not grasp the implications of his vision of post-Saddam Iraq and the broader region for the American postwar role. To accomplish such ambitious aims required the most thorough attention to the difficulties that can derail the establishment of a liberal, market-oriented society. It may well be, as Bush often insisted, that people yearn for liberty. Yet to get there they must still navigate a hazardous road if their point of departure is the Iraq of Saddam Hussein— fearful, sectarian, divided, impoverished, and, in a word, broken. What the president envisioned, in short, would require nation building, contrary to his supposition as a presidential candidate. Rumsfeld remained wedded to that earlier outlook, and Bush never instructed him otherwise.[94]

The entire prewar planning process, moreover, suffered from a lack of presidential leadership. By delegating so much responsibility and not scrutinizing the decisions made by key subordinates, Bush let slip from his hands much of the freedom of action that had been bestowed on him by the post-9/11 combination of circumstances. Important choices, such as the size of the force to be used in the invasion, would have far-reaching consequences that could not be reversed.[95] With very limited "boots on the ground," American field commanders could not secure Baghdad, other major Iraqi cities, all the potential WMD sites, critical facilities such as oil wells and the electrical grid, and Iraq's long borders, across which Baathist leaders might flee and find safe havens. CENTCOM and the generals leading the operation would be compelled to make difficult choices, and do so based on poor information from within Iraq. Also, because the small force meant much of Iraq would not see American troops, Rumsfeld's plan assured that postwar security would be precarious. This would invite Iraqis to settle old scores and ignite feuds; displaced Baathists and sectarian factions would find themselves with openings to organize resistance to whatever political authority eventually emerged in Baghdad.

Consider what might be termed the "Shinseki alternative." A much larger initial force could have covered all of the important locations and closed the borders, and could then have been withdrawn if the security situation did not necessitate an ongoing massive American military presence. It would certainly cost far less to prevent an insurgency than to fight against one. Although it can never be proven, observers such as Larry Diamond, who would later serve as a civilian advisor in Iraq, believe that had the United States invaded with overwhelming strength, no serious insurgency would have erupted.[96] Nor would it be easy after American troops seized Baghdad to increase the force level to the numbers Shinseki had recommended. After all, doing so would mean the administration had gotten the whole thing wrong, an admission that might have painful political repercussions.

"Mission Accomplished"

As a military operation, the invasion of Iraq that began on March 18, 2003, succeeded in achieving its immediate objective, ousting Saddam Hussein from power. Things did not go exactly as expected—we will see that initial Iraqi resistance assumed an irregular form few had anticipated—but in warfare they rarely do. In less than a month, American troops had entered Baghdad, and Saddam and the rest of the regime's senior leadership fled or went into hiding. American audiences were treated to television scenes of joyous Iraqis toppling statues and defacing images of their former ruler. Rumsfeld's vision of a new U.S. military that moved light and fast seemed to be vindicated, and the president basked in the public acclaim that follows a sweeping battlefield triumph.

Saddam had agreed to readmit UN weapons inspectors in January 2003, but a profound lack of mutual understanding precluded peaceful resolution of the crisis. Each side regarded the inspections process primarily as a political gambit aimed at an international audience. By agreeing to inspections, Saddam hoped split the international community and turn certain key nations against the United States. He was never prepared to comply fully and readily with the inspectors' demands, however, because he still sought to maintain some doubt about his WMD capability to deter his internal and regional enemies.[97] To the last minute, he seems to have questioned whether the United States seriously intended to invade. For his part, Bush was prepared to avoid a military showdown only if the Iraqis came clean about their WMD program. Because the administration believed Saddam understood that the United States was his most important adversary, he would see it as in his interest to comply with the weapons inspectors. His foot-dragging, then, invited but one interpretation. "The only logical conclusion," writes Bush, "was that he had something to hide, something so important that he was willing to go to war for it."[98] The UN inspectors and the United States established as the standard of compliance that Iraq would have to prove affirmatively that it had no WMD. But the Iraqi leader refused to meet this standard, lest his weakness be exposed to the foes he actually feared most. On the other side, the administration could not find the proverbial smoking gun that might have made it possible to overcome division within the UN Security Council. Despite Powell's attempts, it did not approve a resolution authorizing the use of force against Iraq.

The American invasion plan ultimately rested on a single main line of attack from Kuwait to Baghdad. Throughout the planning process, the United States had hoped to strike as well from the north, but the Turkish government held off granting approval. As the Army's 4th Infantry Division waited on ships in the Mediterranean, American diplomatic overtures to Ankara were rebuffed. Turkey refused even to permit American overflights, complicating the air campaign.[99] The entire ground effort would be mounted by the equivalent of a single American corps, under the command of Lieutenant General David McKiernan. A British division would be committed in the south of Iraq, to secure Basra and the surrounding area. All told, some 145,000 American and coalition troops would be used in the initial invasion.[100] CENTCOM commander Franks and McKiernan expected Saddam Hussein to concentrate his best troops, the Republican Guard, for a street-by-street defense of Baghdad, where close-quarters combat would neutralize American technological advantages. Through rapid movement and effective use of air power, the American command intended to prevent the Iraqis from regrouping in the capital and to destroy the Iraqi command and control system so enemy forces would be reduced to a disorganized, effectively headless mass.[101]

Iraqi plans continued to reflect Saddam's sensitivity to both external and internal threats. He wanted to meet a conventional attack much as the American plan anticipated: by forcing the United States into a costly fight for Baghdad. He still believed the Americans had no stomach for casualties and would either avoid such a contest or quit when their losses mounted, letting him remain in power.[102] Further, urban combat meant high civilian casualties, which would turn international opinion against the United States. At the same time, fearing a loss of control within Iraq once loyal troops withdrew to the capital, the regime decided shortly before the invasion to distribute arms to Baath Party headquarters across the country. These weapons would in turn be given to party cadres to repress any insurrections.[103] Although a few U.S. planners raised the possibility of attacks by Baathist fedayeen irregulars against the long, exposed lines of communication behind the troops heading toward Baghdad, senior officers and Pentagon planners paid little attention. In their defense, it is not clear that Saddam Hussein and his top commanders expected the fedayeen to play a significant part in the Iraqi defense scheme.

As the invasion commenced, McKiernan's corps moved northwest rapidly from Kuwait toward Baghdad, skirting densely settled areas where possible. Intelligence estimates predicted mass Iraqi military surrenders, even defections of entire units, but most Iraqi soldiers simply threw away their uniforms and blended into the population. Still, at points the advancing Americans encountered fierce resistance they had not anticipated from irregulars dressed in civilian clothes. Too lightly armed to block the armored thrust, many fedayeen sacrificed their lives in futile attacks. The resistance was more deadly to the follow-on transportation units trying to supply the forward combat elements. Despite this opposition, American commanders succeeded in preventing their Iraqi counterparts from regrouping major units in Baghdad. U.S. troops reached the outskirts of the capital within three weeks.[104]

The Stalingrad-style battle for Baghdad that Saddam Hussein sought never came. Upon their arrival in the Baghdad vicinity, American units captured several strategic locations such as the international airport. These served as launch points for a few armored thrusts into downtown Baghdad. The U.S. troops encountered determined opposition from fedayeen, but Iraqi command and control had already evaporated and the surviving fighters soon melted away. Saddam went into hiding, while other regime leaders sought sanctuary in the Tikrit area, the dictator's birthplace and base of political support, or escaped across the unsecured Syrian border.[105] With the effective end of any coherent defense, the victorious American soldiers and Marines occupied key points in the city. Too few U.S. troops were on hand, though, to establish real order in Baghdad, and massive looting occurred at ministries, museums, hospitals, and other public sites. American soldiers did protect the Iraqi oil ministry, which unfortunately suggested to the Iraqi people an ulterior motive behind the invasion.[106]

Saddam's departure marked the accomplishment of the first major objective—regime change—that Bush had established. Organized fighting by Iraqi army units petered out as the soldiers disappeared into the population. Most Iraqi officials likewise chose to lay low; government ministries, utilities, and more ceased to operate. In many places American and coalition forces received the kind of welcome that Wolfowitz had predicted in his response to Shinseki. Rumsfeld, with his invasion plan evidently vindicated by the results, believed he had demonstrated the validity of the doctrinal revolution he had been struggling to impose on a recalcitrant military. Reluctantly, he agreed to the request by McKiernan to commit the unused 4th Infantry Division to support Phase IV operations, but another reserve division would not be deployed.[107] That the unsettled security situation in Iraq did not trouble the defense secretary became clear when he dismissed the outbreak of large-scale looting with his famous "Stuff happens" retort. His attitude signaled to the troops on the ground that the looting was not their concern.[108]

As for a second purpose for invading Iraq, eliminating the WMD threat, the arriving troops turned up nothing, and despite vigorous search efforts in the following months no such weapons were ever found.[109] The administration subsequently trumpeted fragments of evidence to suggest that Saddam had preserved the capacity to reconstitute his programs at some future date. Even this was a stretch: facilities for producing chemical agents that might be converted into weapons also had benign civilian uses. Over time, the administration would insist it had acted in good faith, that Saddam refused to prove he did not have WMD and was still a danger, but damage was done to the president's credibility.[110] It took time for the information about the lack of unconventional weapons to sink in back home, but at least half the public later said it would be less likely to believe such claims by Bush in the future.[111]

The unraveling of the WMD story, though, would come later. For the moment, the administration reveled in the scenes of happy Iraqis. Rumsfeld's boss also took a victory lap, though in time he would rue how it was staged. Bush was flown out to the returning aircraft carrier *USS Abraham Lincoln* on May 1, 2003, where he announced the end of major combat operations and praised the troops.[112] An early draft of the speech had included the phrase "mission accomplished," but Rumsfeld judged it premature and struck it from the text. Unfortunately, no one thought to change the large banner in front of which the president spoke to the ship's crew. The photographs that appeared across the globe the following day all featured "Mission Accomplished," and it would be the only thing people remembered about the event. For the moment the banner seemed to do no harm. Later the words would haunt the president.

Success Unwound

For the next three-plus years, from mid-2003 until late 2006, George W. Bush vainly pursued his other war goals as Iraq plunged into deepening violence. American civilian officials in Baghdad and Washington committed monumental blunders, while military commanders stumbled as they tried to respond to a rising insurgency. Initial sporadic attacks on American and other coalition occupying forces became more widespread and increasingly lethal. Once so determined to control every aspect of Iraq war policy, Rumsfeld soon distanced himself from responsibility for the worsening postwar conditions. The president, wedded to his particular management style and convinced that wartime leadership demanded unwavering commitment, declined for too long to grab the reins. By 2006 his central peace-building goal of a democratic Iraq lay in tatters.

Signs that creating a new Iraq would be a greater challenge than the Pentagon optimists had admitted emerged even before the initial fighting ended. The widespread looting suggested a general erosion or absence of restraining social norms, while the failure by American troops to clamp down sent a dangerous signal of indifference about what would happen next. Harassing attacks on American supply convoys continued, an indication that Baathist hard-liners were not reconciled to defeat. Meanwhile, sporadic clashes erupted between U.S. troops and Iraqis protesting a lack of services or jobs, and the former, not prepared to cope with civil disturbances, sometimes responded with excessive force.[113]

As word of the problems reached Jay Garner in Kuwait, he persuaded Franks to allow his Office of Reconstruction and Humanitarian Assistance to move to Baghdad ahead of CENTCOM's timetable. But the arrival of the small ORHA staff resolved little: it was better suited to meet a humanitarian emergency that never arose than to restore a functioning infrastructure, while the division of responsibility between the military command and Garner's group remained murky.[114] Dissatisfied, Rumsfeld accelerated his own schedule for establishing a full-fledged occupation authority. Garner learned just a few weeks after he set up shop in Baghdad that he would be replaced by L. Paul "Jerry" Bremer III, who would head up a new Coalition Provisional Authority (CPA).[115]

Bremer regarded himself in the role of proconsul, like Douglas MacArthur in post–World War II Japan, with a broad mandate to remake Iraq into a liberal, democratic society.[116] Although he knew little about Iraq, he would make up for it through forceful leadership. He swiftly issued several momentous orders. Recall that the American plan for postwar Iraq, which Bush had approved, called for continuity in governing institutions. Thus, ministry personnel, apart from the most senior officials, would be retained to assure ongoing operations.[117] Military and civilian planners had likewise decided to keep much of the Iraqi military to assist in restoring order quickly.[118] Within days of his arrival in Baghdad, Bremer discarded this framework. He concluded that Baathist influence had to be eradicated root and branch, which entailed removing any official or soldier tainted by a party connection. In his first CPA order, he banned the top three layers of officials in every ministry from future government employment, an exclusion that covered as many as 85,000 people. Unfortunately, this approach did away not just with regime loyalists but also with many experts and technical specialists, for whom, as is often the case in one-party dictatorships, party membership had been a prerequisite for holding a position of responsibility.[119]

Worse soon followed. Bremer's next order disbanded the Iraqi Army and security services. In a single stroke, he destroyed the central pillar of the postwar security plan. With so few troops on hand, American commanders had only two alternative sources of trained military personnel: friendly nations that had held back from the coalition during the invasion phase and Iraqi military and police forces. As violence continued and then began to rise, any prospect for broadening coalition participation evaporated. That left only the Iraqis. Bremer claimed that the military and security services already had disappeared, which was true enough, but planners had expected as much and intended to recall troops. Overnight, the CPA head left 300,000 Iraqi men, many still armed, unemployed and angry with the United States, a pool from which groups opposed to the American occupation could recruit followers.[120]

Faced with a decision that begged for presidential intervention, indeed, one that contravened his own policy, Bush nonetheless declined to intervene. Bremer notified Washington of his intentions just before issuing his order, both in writing and in a video teleconference with the president. The president, faithful to his management philosophy of delegating responsibility and not interfering in the actions of subordinates, deferred to the official on the scene. Some in the administration were uneasy about the policy reversal, but the presumption prevailed that Bremer better knew the local situation. Other key officials, including Colin Powell, were not informed of the new policy, while the Joint Chiefs were never asked for a recommendation.[121] Delegation may have its place, but Bush's decision to defer to a man who had just arrived in Iraq verged on an abdication of responsibility.

Bremer also short-circuited the early steps Garner had taken to establish a transitional Iraqi government. Where Garner had moved immediately to gather Iraqi secular and religious leaders to chart a path to self-rule, Bremer instead declared the CPA the acting sovereign authority for Iraq.[122] Many Iraqis, who had been told the United States had come to deliver them from dictatorship, resented the idea of an external occupation, especially by a Western power. Without clearance from Washington, Bremer also announced plans to draft a new Iraqi constitution and then hold an election. The sequence predictably offended Iraqis, who rejected the idea of a constitution written by a non-elected body. Bremer sought to improve matters by establishing an Iraqi Governing Council, which included a number of prominent

Iraqis, to help prepare for the return of Iraqi sovereignty, and he announced (again without approval from the administration) that the occupation would end on June 15, 2004.[123] But the council operated too much under his thumb to claim popular legitimacy, while the interim constitution drafted by the council and the CPA vested most power in the hands of the Shia and Kurds, leaving the Sunnis marginalized and discontented.[124]

If the CPA claimed authority to govern Iraq, moreover, it needed to be prepared to do so effectively. Bremer's organization lacked the capacity to restore Iraq's infrastructure and services. Throughout its existence, the CPA remained woefully understaffed. American government rules preclude assigning civilian personnel in high-risk areas without their consent, so the CPA was forced to rely on federal agency volunteers. And with Iraq becoming more dangerous over time, these were in short supply.[125] Further, by comparison with many other governments, American foreign policy personnel are disproportionately militarized—that is, the ratio of troops to civilian diplomats and development staff is very high.[126] The CPA found itself depending on political appointees, often young former Republican campaign workers who did not speak Arabic and lacked the technical skills needed to help run Iraq. Many of them remained ensconced in the tight security and relative comfort of Baghdad's Green Zone. Widely criticized for such hires, Bremer and the CPA really had no better option.[127] The authority certainly tried, and it did register some accomplishments, but far too few to meet Iraqis' expectations.[128]

Replacement at the top of the military hierarchy likewise compromised the effectiveness of the military response to ongoing violence. Franks, scheduled to retire shortly after the invasion, showed little interest in its aftermath.[129] McKiernan, too, rotated out. In a peculiar selection that probably reflected the conviction of the Pentagon civilian leadership that little remained to be done in Iraq, his successor was Lieutenant General Ricardo Sanchez, the least senior "three-star" in the entire U.S. Army and an officer who had never commanded anything larger than a division.[130] Sanchez would prove to be a singularly poor choice, someone who never managed to grasp the changing situation in Iraq as the scattered violence increased in intensity. He never articulated a coherent strategy for meeting the incipient insurgency, either, and often clashed with Bremer.[131] But when a key commander falters, the responsibility for correcting his actions or finding another officer who can do better rests with those above him. Despite multiple indicators that conditions in Iraq were deteriorating, Sanchez stayed in his post for a year.[132]

Violence in Iraq rose in fits and starts from summer 2003 onward. Initially, before the overall upward trend became clear, the Bush administration dismissed the attacks as the work of Baathist diehards who refused to admit defeat. When Franks's successor at CENTCOM, General John Abizaid, referred to a classic guerilla-style adversary, the Pentagon immediately disavowed his comment. The president went so far as to challenge the extremists, saying, "Bring 'em on," words that were widely reported in Iraq and helped incite passions against the occupiers.[133] Once it became clear that Iraq was on the path toward a stable democracy, administration officials believed, the "bitter-enders" would give up. Each dip in the violence was taken as evidence that the corner had been turned in Iraq. Invariably, though, attacks would spike, though Rumsfeld sometimes maintained that the figures reflected more complete reporting than any actual change on the ground. Even the capture of Saddam Hussein in December 2003 did nothing to curb the spreading violence. American troops became the target of more insidious weapons, too. The first improvised explosive devices (IEDs) were used against American convoys and patrols, initiating a deadly cycle that saw U.S. forces developing countermeasures only to encounter ever more sophisticated roadside weapons.[134]

Reluctant though the administration was to acknowledge the state of affairs, the conflict assumed a very different nature from the one the Pentagon had planned. U.S. and coalition forces found themselves fighting a "war amongst the people," in British general Rupert Smith's formulation. For the American troops, it was the first such conflict since Vietnam. So much had the U.S. Army wanted to put that unhappy experience behind it that it had largely ceased to study counterinsurgency methods during the intervening generation.[135] Not surprisingly, then, the ill-prepared soldiers and Marines responded clumsily, using excessive force at times and alienating the very people whose support the United States sought. American patrols, intended to establish a "presence," instead reminded Iraqis their country had been occupied by a Western power.[136] The Iraqi population quickly became much cooler toward their erstwhile liberators, and, as in Vietnam, U.S. troops found it difficult to distinguish friend from enemy. In turn this led American units conducting operations, especially in Sunni areas, to sweep up large numbers of Iraqi men suspected of being insurgents or aiding them. As the influx swamped the available detention facilities and military police, the overcrowded conditions precipitated the inevitable scandal: photographs from Abu Ghraib prison that showed American guards mistreating Iraqis appeared widely across the Middle East and further tarnished the liberators' sagging image.[137]

Beneath the violence, the United States faced a complex, multisided conflict. The minority Sunni Muslims, who had dominated Iraq under Saddam Hussein, feared and resented the shift in power to the Shiite majority that any democratic system implied. In support of Sunni resistance, jihadist fighters from around the region flooded across the still-unsecured borders, establishing a terrorist organization called al-Qaeda in Iraq (AQI) that attacked coalition forces and Shia indiscriminately.[138] Armed Shiite factions, notably one led by the young cleric Muqtada al Sadr, formed their own militia groups to retaliate. The Shiite militia sometimes stood down from attacking the occupying forces but refused to disarm and periodically reopened campaigns against them.[139] Finally, in northern Iraq, the non-Arab Kurds, well organized and with their own militia, threatened to declare independence. They clashed with local Arabs that Saddam Hussein had moved into the region in his effort to secure control.

American efforts to find a political solution foundered on the deep sectarian rifts. Recognizing that formal U.S. occupation stoked Iraqi resentment, Bremer looked to restore Iraqi sovereignty at an early date and encouraged the writing of a new constitution. In June 2004, he turned over authority to an interim government under Prime Minister Ayad Allawi and departed. Nonetheless, the end of the CPA did not hasten a return of political stability. Iraqi leaders could not agree on an acceptable power-sharing formula. The Bush administration put great stock in the first free elections in modern Iraqi history in January 2005, but Sunnis organized a boycott rather than accept results that would confirm their minority status.[140] Absent their participation, the new government lacked legitimacy, and it remained under the influence of

Shiite leaders who evinced little interest in national reconciliation. After the voting, the violence spiked yet again, signaling that Sunni rejectionists would not trust their fate to any political process that curbed their dominant status. Later elections failed to yield political progress, even when Sunni participation increased. Weak Shiite prime ministers—first Allawi, then Ibrahim al-Jafari after the 2005 election, and finally Jawad al-Maliki in April 2006—lacked their own independent power base and were reluctant to antagonize Shiite figures such as Sadr who controlled their own militias. It was a formula for political deadlock and governance failure, which together fed popular frustration and contributed to the incessant violence.

On the military side, senior American field commanders could find no effective response to the bloodshed. Sanchez gave way to General George Casey, with Abizaid continuing at CENTCOM. American commanders, turning back to lessons learned during Creighton Abrams's tenure in Vietnam, began to introduce counterinsurgency (COIN) techniques that aimed to win over the population.[141] For the foot soldiers, though, frustration mounted: many were on their second tour in Iraq, and despite their sacrifices, they could see no evidence of progress.[142] Indeed, if anything, conditions grew worse, the number of violent incidents increasing over time, IEDs becoming more lethal, areas cleared once having to be swept yet again as the insurgents returned. Occasionally an American commander achieved a notable local success, such as in early 2005 when Colonel H. R. McMaster and his 3rd Armored Cavalry Regiment decided not merely to clear Tal Afar but to remain in place and forge relationships with the local Sunni community.[143] But Casey and Abizaid did not see how to reconcile such episodes with their larger operational design and so did not build on the results. The American commanders instead concluded that the best path lay in training a new Iraqi army to take over security responsibilities as the United States drew down its force in Iraq.[144]

Rumsfeld embraced the Abizaid-Casey approach, a practical expression of his oft-stated view that the United States ought to leave the Iraqis to work out their own future. From the planning of the invasion through the mounting insurgency, the defense secretary never wavered in his conviction that the U.S. military ought not to be used for nation building. After the invasion, he began to distance himself from what happened in Iraq.[145] Amid the escalating violence, Rumsfeld said repeatedly (in his favorite metaphor) that the United States needed to take its hand off the bicycle seat and let the Iraqis ride on their own, with all the risks that implied. Otherwise, their dependency on the United States would persist, and they would never learn to resolve their differences and find political solutions.[146] He also said it might take several decades for a viable democracy to emerge there, a more sober and realistic assessment than the scenario that guided the original postwar planning.[147] From Rumsfeld's perspective, Casey had it right when he emphasized the American training mission and prepared to disengage U.S. troops from active combat.

Deteriorating conditions in Iraq did not dislodge the secretary of defense from his dominance of American policy. Within the military, rumblings of discontent could be heard, but the Joint Chiefs remained docile. Rumsfeld's successive choices as JCS chairman, Generals Richard Myers and Peter Pace, proved compliant agents of his will and rarely pushed back against his edicts or policies.[148] Military leaders worried that the armed forces were being worn down by repeated deployments, a concern that led them to embrace the Abizaid-Casey plan for Iraqi training and American disengagement rather than focus on other ways to bring the war to a successful conclusion. Condoleezza Rice, who replaced Colin Powell as secretary of state soon after Bush won reelection in 2004, saw the indicators of a downward spiral and searched for ways to reverse the trend. When she learned about the positive results the army had achieved in Tal Afar in 2005, she declared in a congressional hearing that "clear, hold, and build" was now the administration's policy. Rumsfeld immediately countered that the policy was still to shift responsibility to the Iraqis as soon as possible, which meant that any holding of ground would have to be done by them. Although the president seemed to endorse the Tal Afar model, he evidently did not appreciate that it was an exception to the operational approach favored by his field commanders. He never used the example to call for a reconsideration of the Rumsfeld commitment to training and transition to Iraqi control, and Rice backed down.[149]

Bush opted not to challenge or question the policies established by Rumsfeld, Bremer, or the generals. Partly his refusal may have been an expression of an innate stubbornness and a refusal to admit that the initial invasion planning had been flawed. He preferred to emphasize the occasional good news, such as the strong turnout among non-Sunnis in Iraqi elections, over the mounting evidence of a failing policy.[150] Understandable though it is for a wartime leader to want to believe all goes well, it suggests a dangerous complacency. The numbers in Iraq told a grim story: total attacks rose from 26,500 in 2004 to 34,000 in 2005. Bush's declarations of firmness and optimism increasingly made him appear out of touch with reality. Thus in a May 2006 speech he asserted yet again that Iraq had reached a turning point and was demonstrating that democracy was the hope of the region. The claim of progress flew in the face of the 3,500 insurgent attacks that month, which equaled the one-month record.[151]

More than just a character trait seems to have been at work. Bush believed strongly that as a wartime president he needed to set a positive tone in difficult times, that he could not show doubt or lead anyone to question his will to persevere.[152] This was how he understood Winston Churchill to have acted in Britain's darkest days early in the Second World War. The president's attitude also stifled questions within the administration about whether the war was being fought correctly and discouraged any effort to find alternatives, while reducing senior officials to the role of cheerleaders and marketers for current policy.[153] At times, boosterism reached a point of absurdity, as when the vice president declared in mid-2005 that the insurgency was in its last throes.[154] Further, although familiar with arguments in favor of active political direction of military affairs, Bush still adhered to the notion that Johnson had erred in micromanaging during the Vietnam War. No matter that this was a misreading of the historical record. Bush believed the generals and officials on the ground needed to be given latitude, and he continued to practice leadership through delegation.[155]

Ironically, in his determination to avoid Johnson's approach, Bush brought himself closer to his failed predecessor's fate. Lincoln, not Churchill, would have been a more suitable model. The former took a hard look at his policies and his generals and never hesitated to make changes, something of which Eliot Cohen apparently reminded Bush in two face-to-face meetings in 2006. Churchill's doggedness, by contrast, owed more to his lack of options. Vastly overmatched by German power until the Soviet Union and the United States entered the war, the prime minister really had nothing more to offer than declarations of will. Bush, with exponentially greater resources at his disposal, should have been leading a search for political and military alternatives in Iraq from the earliest signs of a budding insurgency. The Johnson precedent echoed in another disturbing way, too, when Bush started to ask his military commanders for the body count of how many insurgents had been killed.[156]

Delegation also requires accountability, of which there seems to have been virtually none between 2003 and 2006. Retaining Rumsfeld was an inexcusable error. Each time the defense secretary came under criticism, Bush rushed to his defense. The president refused Rumsfeld's offer to resign after Abu Ghraib became public, and in the end only low-ranking soldiers suffered any punishment for a situation that grew out of a much broader policy failure. Following the 2004 election Bush again considered replacing Rumsfeld, but was talked out of it by Cheney lest the action raise questions about the conduct of the war— precisely what needed to be done.[157] More fundamentally, the secretary of defense was never on the same page as the president about the main peace-building objective in Iraq, establishing a democratic Iraq within a short time frame.[158] Certainly jettisoning Rumsfeld would have been an admission that the war was not going well, but his replacement would also have made clear that the president recognized what most observers were reporting and demanded better from the people around him.

The Diminishing Returns of Fear

The Bush administration decided to invade Iraq and fight the ensuing insurgency without first seeking broad popular mobilization back home. A limited war always poses a political challenge for leaders who need to sustain popular support, precisely because the conflict does not present a direct threat to national survival. Absent an existential peril to inspire sacrifice, rhetoric must be used to generate popular commitment. Yet this in turn makes likely a mismatch between the overheated language leaders use to inflate the stakes in the war and their reluctance to ask citizens to give up anything of value. Historically, major conflicts have imposed two burdens on a population, one human and the other monetary. The Bush administration shunned both, however, by rejecting either a major expansion of the armed forces or higher taxes to pay for the war. Eventually the president, by not calling for popular sacrifice, saw political support for the war evaporate.

Much as 9/11 created conditions that gave the Bush administration a free hand to pursue military intervention abroad, the global dominance enjoyed by the United States encouraged the president and his key advisors to believe they could do so without disrupting life back home. Theirs was a risky calculation. The president envisioned a struggle against terrorism that might last a generation or longer—what he and those around him called "the long war," even if the individual campaigns within it, such as Afghanistan and Iraq, were expected to be brief. Only a nation that enjoyed remarkable military, technological, and economic advantages over its adversaries could afford to embark on a struggle of indeterminate length and scope without asking its citizenry to bear real obligations. In the early 2000s the United States appeared to be in just such a position. The president urged Americans just weeks after 9/11 to continue to live as they had before, to "get down to Disney World."[159] Administration policy would reflect the confidence that wars like the one in Iraq need not inconvenience the American people.

At no point did civilian leaders weigh, or military commanders request, measures to increase dramatically the size of the American military. Unlike Vietnam, when the JCS pressed Johnson again and again to mobilize for large-scale war, the Chiefs under Bush and Rumsfeld never contemplated a return to the draft. They remembered the unpopularity of conscription during the Vietnam era. The president agreed at the start of the war to limit deployments to one year, a constraint that seemed unimportant at the time because the Pentagon expected a short war and quick exit. Of course, things turned out differently, forcing not just repeated tours in Iraq but extensive use of Reserves and National Guard units. Military personnel and their families endured with remarkable stoicism. To Rumsfeld, a larger ground army was anathema, the very antithesis of his intended revolution in war-fighting and an invitation to inappropriate use of American troops (e.g., for nation building). Pressure from multiple deployments finally compelled the administration to undertake modest steps to increase the active-duty force. Even so, the limited size of the military continued to place heavy stress on the U.S. Army and the Marine Corps in particular.

Initial administration expectations that the Iraq War would not have a significant budget impact also turned out to be unduly optimistic. Yet, despite the rising cost of the war, the Bush administration still did not seek additional funds in the regular annual budget process. In June 2001, Congress had approved the president's signature domestic policy initiative, a $1.35 trillion, ten-year tax cut that represented a key Republican Party objective.[160] The president refused to undo this, even though every previous American war had been financed by a combination of new taxes and borrowing. Two factors made it possible to defer paying for the war and instead to increase the federal deficit. First, much as Republicans were loath to raise taxes, Democrats did not want to cut spending on their preferred domestic programs. Rather than make hard choices, both sides cooperated in financing the war through various temporary spending measures that did not trigger existing deficit-reduction statutes. Second, broader global economic trends worked to the administration's advantage. Lyndon Johnson had sought to avoid picking between guns and butter during the Vietnam War, but inflation eventually forced him to accept a tax surcharge and cuts in domestic spending. In contrast, favorable international economic circumstances during the Iraq conflict, such as the willingness of creditors to fund a growing federal deficit at low interest rates, made it possible for the Bush administration to evade the same kind of reckoning.

As violence in Iraq increased after the initial success, the administration discovered that public support for the war was soft. People who had signed on for the expected quick victory showed much less patience for the rising casualties inflicted by IEDs and ambushes by a faceless enemy. Moreover, letting the nation off the hook for paying made for easy politics but did nothing to link the citizenry to the war. Public opinion on Iraq began to polarize along party lines.[161] Most Republicans continued to back the president and the war, showing a lingering faith in its original rationale—polls found that they had become more likely to believe that Saddam Hussein had possessed WMD, despite the post-invasion failure to actually find any stockpiles.[162] Less enthusiastic from the start, Democrats soon turned against the war. To Bush's political good fortune, overall public disenchantment came gradually and, unlike Vietnam, did not spread widely before he faced reelection. It also helped Bush in 2004 that leading Democratic politicians, including the eventual presidential nominee Senator John Kerry, had endorsed the initial October 2002 resolution authorizing military action. On Iraq, Kerry failed to offer a coherent alternative policy, one factor that contributed to his narrow defeat.[163]

Bush's reelection bought some time to redeem the situation in Iraq, but second-term missteps contributed to deepening public disaffection. Whatever momentum the president gained from his electoral victory soon dissipated in a failed attempt to dismantle Social Security, the most popular social program, and in the administration's bungled response to Hurricane Katrina in August–September 2005. The latter also fueled a damaging new narrative about the administration—that it was incompetent at handling major challenges.[164] Iraq came to be viewed through this lens, a story line fed by restive news media whose reports increasingly resembled the ones filed from Vietnam. When the administration complained that the media ignored progress in Iraq in areas such as reconstruction and focused instead only on the ongoing violence, journalists retorted that terror bombing attacks that killed dozens would be the lead story in any country. As for the president himself, his refusal to step in and assert firm direction after Hurricane Katrina struck New Orleans appeared to confirm his detachment from the reality on the ground in Iraq.

Under mounting criticism for their handling of the war, Bush and his senior officials reminded the domestic audience that Iraq fit into a larger struggle against terrorism. A retreat from Iraq, the president warned, would hand victory to Islamic extremists, especially al-Qaeda, and embolden them to follow with attacks on the homeland. To Bush, 9/11 always remained a fresh scar that highlighted the stakes in Iraq, and he expected his fellow Americans to react the same way. Further, if the United States quit the war, America's allies in the Middle East would lose confidence in the value of American pledges, and their will to resist Islamic fundamentalism would collapse. Opponents of the war and advocates of American withdrawal were accused of being naive about the extremist menace and encouraging enemy morale.[165] These arguments echoed ones heard a generation earlier when dominoes seemed destined to fall across Southeast Asia and American credibility was at stake.[166]

But warnings of future terror attacks worked only for a time before repetition numbed the audience. The very effectiveness of security countermeasures put in place after 9/11 lessened any sense of urgency, while frequent alarms and the absence of follow-up attacks made it appear that the administration was crying wolf about terrorist threats. Besides, as terrorist networks took root elsewhere in Asia, Africa, and the Middle East and cells of violent extremists launched attacks in Europe or were exposed in the United States itself, a war going badly in Iraq did not seem an effective antidote to the danger. Antiwar activists began to gain significant mainstream support, too, when Democratic Representative John Murtha, a Vietnam veteran, urged a prompt withdrawal from Iraq in November 2005.[167]

With the war at a stalemate by the end of 2005 and the administration unable to articulate a clear plan to bring it to a successful conclusion, public opinion turned against the president and his handling of the war, and he struggled to retain backing among key Republican leaders. Here, too, Bush looked more and more like Johnson. Support dipped to 40 percent or below, numbers that paralleled Johnson's from mid-1967 onward. An August 2006 poll found that 56 percent of Americans viewed the war as a mistake.[168] Although Bush did not need to think about reelection, the same could not be said for Republicans in Congress. By early 2006 they feared loss of their majority status, and growing numbers of those facing tough battles for their seats broke with the president over the war—much as Johnson had suffered mounting defections among Democratic lawmakers.[169]

Nearly three years into the insurgency, control over public debate about the war threatened to slip from the administration's hands. One GOP lawmaker expecting a hard reelection contest, Representative Frank Wolf, came up with the idea of a bipartisan commission to prod the administration to reexamine its Iraq policy. After Vice President Cheney rebuffed him, Wolf used intermediaries to persuade Rice instead, and she in turn got the president to sign off on a commission before Cheney, Rumsfeld, or others could object. Bush held out for James Baker, who had overseen the Bush campaign's successful legal challenge to the 2000 Florida recount process, to co-chair the commission with former Democratic Representative Lee Hamilton. The Iraq Study Group (ISG) would review the state of the war and issue its recommendation shortly after the 2006 elections.[170]

Bush's Lincoln Moment

Events both on the battlefield and at home in 2006 finally forced Bush to permit a long-overdue reassessment of Iraq policy and ultimately drove him to shift course. In Iraq the violence took a turn for the worse; in Washington pressure mounted to reconsider a situation that even backers of the war agreed was slipping out of control. The president received a stinging rebuke in the midterm elections that cost his party control of both houses of Congress. Soon afterward, the bipartisan Iraq Study Group issued its report, which in effect acknowledged the failure of the American war effort. Bush dug in his heels, however. Against the advice of both the ISG and the Joint Chiefs, he embraced a proposal to increase temporarily the number of American troops in Iraq to tamp down the violence. The decision marked his single hands-on intervention in the direction of the conflict.

A terrorist bomb attack on February 22, 2006, that destroyed the Askariya Mosque in Samarra, one of the holiest Shiite shrines, led to reprisal attacks on Sunni mosques in Baghdad and triggered an escalation in sectarian conflict across Iraq. In the months that followed, attacks reached an all-time high, surpassing 3,000 per week. Each morning in Baghdad bodies turned up by the dozens, victims of militias, gangs, or—worse from the American perspective—government security forces. American officials reported that the killers had been "dressed in police uniforms," but Sunni neighborhoods knew better: the killers *were* the police. Mixed Sunni-Shia neighborhoods experienced a process that resembled the Balkan "ethnic cleansing" of the previous decade.[171] Meanwhile, the Iraqi government under Prime Minister Maliki refused to move against Shiite militias, ignoring American calls for even-handedness.[172] Hope for political reconciliation evaporated. U.S. troops, often assaulted by both sides, suffered mounting casualties.

In the face of the epic tide of violence in Iraq, unease spread among senior Bush administration officials. Although some contended that the insurgency had been contained until the mosque bombing, Iraq policy had stalled much earlier. The bombing and its aftermath served instead as a much-needed wake-up call—much like the Tet Offensive in Vietnam in 1968[173]—that forced a long-overdue reconsideration of the American approach. Not everyone saw it that way: Rumsfeld continued to insist on the need to take the hand off the bicycle seat. But increasingly he sounded as though he had washed his hands of responsibility for the war he had once been so determined to control. An American departure now seemed likely to leave in its wake chaos and perhaps the fragmentation of Iraq into separate and warring Shiite, Sunni, and Kurdish entities.[174]

General Casey, though still wedded to drawing down the American force level, conceded that the withdrawal ought to be delayed.[175] By this point, however, the president finally had lost confidence in his commanders, Casey in Iraq and Abizaid at CENTCOM.[176] Sensing an opening in which new ideas might be considered, some of the president's key advisors (including Secretary of State Rice and Stephen J. Hadley, her successor as national security advisor) began a quiet search for alternatives.

Within the ranks of current and former military officers, too, the worsening situation in Iraq provoked criticism of the American approach. Rumsfeld had been the target of unusually public attacks by several former generals, whom he dismissed as a handful of malcontents.[177] As it became evident that conditions in Iraq were deteriorating, the questions mounted. At issue was whether the Abizaid-Casey project to transfer responsibility to the Iraqis as quickly as feasible made sense. The effort to frame a new counterinsurgency doctrine, pushed by Lieutenant General David Petraeus and others, recognized that an external power such as the United States needed to cede control over military operations to the local government at some point. But the precondition for political success in a counterinsurgency campaign was population security. Absent that, the government could not meet other needs or promote economic development, and its authority would erode. Achieving security in turn required that troops live among the people, use minimal force to safeguard civilians, and earn their trust—"winning hearts and minds."[178] It was a mode of warfare that looked nothing like the high-tech military transformation Rumsfeld had promoted, calling instead for ample numbers and ample patience.

Through summer and fall 2006, the search for an approach that might reverse the drift toward disaster in Iraq proceeded out of sight in Washington. If word of a strategy review leaked amid the midterm congressional campaigns, it would be perceived as an admission of failure by the administration and dishearten Republicans who still backed the president. On the surface, then, nothing changed: Bush offered the same defense of his policy and his commanders as before, grasping at straws, such as the killing of the vicious Abu Musab al-Zarqawi, head of al-Qaeda in Iraq.[179] Behind the scenes critical reassessment and consideration of alternatives gained impetus. Several groups, civilian and military, explored whether counterinsurgency methods modeled on earlier military operations such as Tal Afar might become the foundation for a broader operational initiative to "seize, hold, and build." If enough American troops could be made available to secure Baghdad, success there could create a breathing space in which Iraqi leaders representing the different sectarian factions could finally reach an acceptable political outcome.[180]

In time, this alternative approach would become known by the force commitment involved—a temporary increase of 20,000 to 30,000 U.S. troops—as "the surge." With the military overstretched by the war and needing to give units time to recover between deployments, no more than five brigades could be made available.[181] This, too, was a consequence of the decision not to mobilize for a long conflict.

Proponents of a troop surge swam upstream against powerful political currents within and beyond the Bush administration. Although influential former officers such as retired Army General Jack Keane and a cohort of counterinsurgency enthusiasts at the middle ranks of the military hierarchy promoted the surge and "seize, hold, and build" tactics,[182] the Joint Chiefs did not agree. These senior officers worried that Iraq had damaged the military, especially the army, and saw disengagement as a vital step toward restoring it. They doubted whether a modest temporary increase to 160,000 troops could accomplish what 130,000 had not been able to do in more than three years. Instead the JCS concluded that it would be best to continue gradual withdrawal coupled with an effort to prepare the Iraqi military to take over—essentially a continuation of the current Abizaid-Casey policy.[183] Similarly, the administration's unpublicized interagency review concluded on November 26, 2006, that an accelerated version of the current policy made the most sense. Only a minority, mostly National Security Council staffers, backed the surge.[184] Among policy experts and informed politicians generally, it seemed time to look for a graceful exit. Some recommended a "soft partitioning" of Iraq that would turn it into a loose federation of states, each dominated by its main ethno-sectarian group, effectively ratifying the sorting process already under way.[185]

With the public showing less patience for the war, moreover, it would be hard to sell a troop surge. The magnitude of public disenchantment became clear on election day when voters handed control of Congress to the Democrats. As is usually the case with elections, a number of factors contributed to Republican losses, but disapproval of the president's Iraq policy figured high on the list—only 29 percent approved of his handling of the war.[186] The day after the voters had spoken, Bush accepted Rumsfeld's resignation, too long delayed whether measured by results or political value. Incoming Democratic leaders Representative Nancy Pelosi (soon to become Speaker of the House) and Senator Harry Reid (the next Majority Leader) made plain that bringing home the American troops would be one of their top priorities. From the new congressional majority, the notion of sending additional brigades to Iraq could expect little support.

Pressure for a gradual troop withdrawal increased when the Iraq Study Group made public its recommendations in early December. Pronouncing the current U.S. policy to have run its course without yielding success, the ISG proposed that American combat troops (other than those needed for force protection) be withdrawn from Iraq by early 2008. They might remain in the region to continue to combat extremist forces and help police a political resolution. Further, the ISG urged diplomatic overtures to Syria and Iran to enlist their support for a stable Iraq. At the insistence of one ISG member, former Democratic Senator Chuck Robb, the report included a temporary troop increase among its list of options.[187]

The thrust of the report's recommendation, though, ran in the opposite direction, and the commission aligned itself with the swelling chorus of critics who wanted the United States to cut its losses and seek an exit strategy. For a president under siege, the ISG provided useful political cover, a withdrawal timetable with bipartisan sanction. Public opinion strongly favored the withdrawal timetable, too, with 71 percent in favor; only 9 percent responded that victory was still possible.[188]

The president faced a pivotal juncture. Having left too much in the hands of others for too long, he recognized the imperative to assert himself. The war had run off course, with a military strategy no longer connected to the national political objectives he had established at the outset. Determined not to be Lyndon Johnson, he had also not heeded Eliot Cohen's advice that he be Abraham Lincoln. In December 2006 and January 2007, with the war in Iraq at a turning point, Bush had his Lincoln moment. He finally claimed ownership of his war.

Rejecting the popular ISG proposal for a withdrawal timetable, Bush opted instead to augment U.S. troop strength temporarily. He saw disengagement as an admission of defeat that he was not prepared to make. To those around the president, such as Hadley and Cheney, or to anyone who had followed Bush's statements on the war, it was clear that the president had invested far too much to accept such an outcome.[189] He reiterated the apocalyptic implications of leaving Iraq to its fate in his January 7, 2007, speech announcing his choice:

> Radical Islamic extremists would grow in strength and gain new recruits. They would be in a better position to topple moderate governments, create chaos in the region, and use oil revenues to fund their ambitions. . . . Our enemies would have a safe haven from which to plan and launch attacks on the American people. On September 11th, 2001, we saw what a refuge for extremists on the other side of the world could bring to the streets of our own cities. For the safety of our people, America must succeed in Iraq.[190]

Withdrawal, then, was out of the question. But so, too, was massive, sustained escalation. The skeptical Democratic congressional majority would not authorize or fund force expansion on the scale that would be required. With no other options at hand, Bush seized on the surge concept. The prospects for success were not promising, either: the additional forces would create only a brief window in which to reverse the trends in Iraq, while COIN doctrine emphasized that the "seize, hold, and build" formula worked only if given time.

The president also put in place a new team to implement the surge policy. Robert Gates, a well-respected member of the Iraq Study Group but an agnostic about whether the new approach could work, replaced Rumsfeld as secretary of defense.[191] On the ground in Iraq, Petraeus replaced Casey, who would be given the Westmoreland treatment— kicked upstairs to serve as army chief of staff.[192]

Staying the Course Redux

Having chosen the troop surge option and picked a new commander, Bush again stepped back and let his subordinates run the Iraq War. Many critical choices had yet to be made, and presidential delegation meant they would be left to Petraeus and those around him. For a time the issue remained in doubt: violence in Iraq continued to increase and American casualties mounted. However, by fall 2007, insurgent attacks declined, the result of both new American tactics and other developments on the ground, notably the polarization between Sunni tribal leaders and foreign jihadists. Some Democrats tried to impose a deadline for American troop withdrawals, but the president and his allies easily forestalled these attempts. Bush thus staved off both the worst in Iraq and his opponents at home. Nonetheless, set against his initial war goals, the results fell far short of expectations. The American people responded in turn by distancing themselves from the war.

As we've seen, other presidents have relinquished hands-on direction of military affairs in the later stages of a war. Lincoln deferred to Grant after picking him as the overall Union commanding general in early 1864, going so far as to decline to inquire into the details of the general's plans. By that point in the Civil War, though, Grant had a demonstrated record of battlefield success, and he and Lincoln agreed on the need for a "hard war" against the South. It would be a stretch to claim that Petraeus had a comparable track record as an effective battlefield commander when he ascended to the top slot in Iraq in 2007. His previous assignment, developing the new COIN doctrine and codifying it in an official Army manual, had been seen within the service as derailing his rise to the top level of command. Roosevelt also left most operational decisions to his military commanders in the latter stages of the Second World War. Not only had they proven their capacity, they had shown that they understood the president's grand strategy and how to connect lesser choices to it. Petraeus, by contrast, would be asked to implement the still-unproven "seize, hold, and build" operational approach in Iraq and to gain the cooperation of hostile Iraqi factions.[193]

Still, Bush bestowed broad operational latitude and freedom from political oversight on the new American commander. Just where and how to use the additional troops rested with Petraeus and his subordinates.[194] They decided to disperse U.S. troops in contested areas of Baghdad, where they would live among the people. This tactic sought to make security visible to strife-torn neighborhoods and gradually build the residents' confidence that they would be protected from attacks by the various Iraqi factions. In time, such confidence would translate into better intelligence about insurgent activities, planned attacks, and membership, though in the short run U.S. troops would face local hostility and be more vulnerable to attack.

Initial returns were discouraging. As expected, the troops sent to stay in Baghdad's most dangerous areas came under frequent attack and suffered high casualties. Back home, where ordinary citizens knew little of the logic behind the tactics, the figures—more attacks, more Americans dying—suggested that nothing had changed for the better.

Iraqi politics, too, continued to bedevil American efforts to improve security. American commanders soon came to understand that Prime Minister Maliki's government was widely seen among Sunnis as a pro-Shiite actor in the sectarian violence rather than as a neutral broker.[195] That the Sunni perception had a sound foundation became evident when Maliki insisted on his right to approve any U.S. operation that targeted Shiite militias. Sunnis also complained about killings by the Iraqi army, which had been penetrated by Shiite extremists.[196] In cooperation with various American civilian officials, including the president, Petraeus pressured the Iraqi leader to be more even-handed and to distance himself from his hard-line Shiite backers. But as the Americans had discovered decades earlier in Saigon, an external power deeply invested in the success of a client regime exercises little leverage.

Nevertheless, some developments held promise, and Petraeus moved quickly to capitalize on these. Among Iraqi Sunnis, a number of tribal leaders had become disenchanted with al-Qaeda in Iraq, which had emerged as a powerful and brutal rival to their authority within their community. Beginning in Anbar Province (hence, termed the "Anbar Awakening") as early as September 2006, the increasing friction between the indigenous leaders and the foreign-led AQI took a violent turn, adding another layer of complexity to the sectarian strife ripping apart the country. Some tribal leaders, at great risk to themselves and their families, decided to seek ties with the U.S. military. Interestingly, they did so because they believed they had already defeated the American forces, which would soon begin to withdraw. In the time the U.S. troops remained, they could be useful allies in taking down AQI. The tribal leaders proposed a quid pro quo: arm us and we will help expose AQI so you can destroy it, while we also protect our communities against Shia depredations. Over objections from the Iraqi government, Petraeus agreed to give weapons to the Sunni groups, many of whom until recently had been fighting American troops.[197] The move soon paid dividends in improved intelligence that could be used against AQI leaders and in lessened violence in Sunni neighborhoods.[198] Through the confluence of COIN tactics and the shift in Sunni priorities, then, insurgent attacks began to decline in the latter half of 2007.

Moreover, the Iraqi government started to move at last to curb Shiite militia power. In southern Iraq, an area of British responsibility, forces aligned with Moqtada al-Sadr had largely taken over Basra. Sadr himself maintained close connections with Iran, and American officials were keenly sensitive to the prospect of expanding Iranian influence. Prime Minister Maliki decided unilaterally in early 2008 to mount a military operation with Iraqi troops against the Sadrist forces to restore government control. To the surprise of many, including U.S. commanders, Iraqi units demonstrated new effectiveness against the militia. Facing likely defeat, Sadr ordered his forces to stand down, permitting the reestablishment of government control over Basra.[199] The government finally showed it was not entirely the captive of Shiite factions.

Small signs of political progress could also be discerned, though not in the form the Bush administration had expected when the president approved the troop surge. Notwithstanding American urging, no political reconciliation occurred at the top of the Iraqi political system. Neither Shia nor Kurds nor Sunnis displayed willingness to compromise on power sharing, control of oil revenues, or other disputed issues.[200] Instead, the Awakening led local Sunni tribal leaders to make deals with the U.S. military, the first step toward incorporating them into the Iraqi political system.[201] By arranging to put 100,000 armed Sunni irregulars on the U.S. payroll, Petraeus took the first step in establishing a bond between erstwhile insurgents and the Maliki government. Better security brought in its wake the restoration of some public services and the beginning of small reconstruction projects. Left unresolved was whether these low-level steps could be parlayed into a broader political settlement.[202]

With Petraeus setting the direction for the war, the president limited himself to giving firm White House support. The original surge decision left open the total number of additional troops to be sent to Iraq. Some in the military hierarchy sought to hold down the increment to as few as two brigades. These senior officers included Admiral William J. "Fox" Fallon, the choice to run CENTCOM in tandem with Petraeus in Iraq. Fallon, who perceived himself as an expert on Iraq and COIN methods, adopted Rumsfeld-style skepticism toward each request for additional forces. When Petraeus indicated that he needed the full allotment, Bush overruled the resistance within the chain of command.[203] He assured Petraeus, moreover, that he need not worry about having enough time to complete his mission.

Paradoxically, time was a commodity that Bush had gained as a consequence of his recent policy and political setbacks. He had dissipated his second-term political capital in his quixotic effort to dismantle Social Security. With no significant domestic agenda left to fulfill, he did not need to think about political strategies that would let him assemble majority coalitions to support legislative initiatives. The Republican defeat in the 2006 midterm contests confirmed that the remaining two years of the president's second term would be spent in a holding pattern. This freed him to focus on preserving the policies he had earlier established. Whether his political foes could force him to bend on his timetable for Iraq was the only question.

With the help of his diminished cohort of congressional allies, Bush easily beat back attempts by the now-Democratic Congress to impose a deadline for withdrawing American troops from Iraq. Despite their majority status in both chambers, Democrats could not translate the antiwar sentiment that helped bring them to power into concrete measures to end American involvement. They tried repeatedly during their first months as a majority to force an end to the war through legislative action. Each attempt failed, either by falling short of sufficient votes in the Senate, by a Republican fili-buster in the Senate, or by a presidential veto that Democrats lacked sufficient votes to override. Even when measures did not require an extraordinary majority, as with the supplemental spending bills used to keep the war off-budget, Democrats could not muster the votes to block passage.[204] As was the case during the Vietnam War, lawmakers simply would not refuse funding for American troops in combat. Congress passed a measure that required the administration to report on eighteen benchmarks of progress in Iraq, but the legislation did not tie war funding or aid to Iraq on meeting the standards.[205] The situation frustrated antiwar activists outside Congress, who railed against legislative timidity. But for lawmakers, it sufficed to cast sym-bolic votes against the president's policy without being shackled with the political responsibility for the outcome of the war that would have accompanied a successful measure to set a fixed withdrawal timetable.[206]

Had lawmakers engaged in serious oversight of the war, they might have uncovered one of the more significant changes that occurred under Petraeus. The core national objective that Bush had framed in going to war in Iraq was quietly shelved. No longer did American military com-manders and civilian officials in Iraq expect to establish a pluralist, liberal democracy within the foreseeable future. Petraeus and company defined success down. At best, the United States might leave behind a stable government with some representation for the three main ethno-sectarian groups and a level of violence not so extreme as to disrupt the precarious political order.[207] As for transforming the Middle East, the Iraqi solution would hold little appeal, especially given the enormous price Iraqis had paid. Yet no one in the American leadership in Iraq ever explicitly declared the original goal unachievable.[208] The president continued to express his vision of an Iraq that would become a beacon of hope across the region.

Nothing Bush said about Iraq by this point registered with the American people. Throughout his last two years, the president's approval ratings remained below 40 percent. The public had soured on its limited investment in Iraq; even the continuing signs of progress in curbing violence and the sharp reduction in American casualties did not improve the citizenry's view.[209] For a time it appeared the war might again be an issue in the 2008 election. Republican John McCain, who had been an early and outspoken advocate of increasing the number of U.S. troops in Iraq, hoped to convert the good news into political gain. Voters did not respond, however, leaving his opponent, Senator Barack Obama (an early foe of the war) free to focus on other issues. The financial crisis that struck in September 2008 turned the contest decisively into a referendum on domestic issues.

Final Reckoning

Three-plus years after George W. Bush left office, the fate of Iraq still hangs in the balance. The American combat role has concluded, the last troops departing at the end of 2011. But Iraq continues to suffer from endemic, low-level violence that periodically threatens to escalate. For example, in March 2011 a possible clash between Kurds and Arabs in Kirkuk resulted in a deployment of U.S. troops to calm tensions. Henceforth it will be up to the Iraqis to resolve such disputes. Many Iraqis fear the American departure will open the floodgates to new sectarian violence.[210]

Elsewhere across the Arab world, early 2011 saw widespread popular uprisings, with dictators toppled in Tunisia and Egypt and massive demonstrations in Libya, Syria, Jordan, Bahrain, Yemen, and elsewhere. In none of these places did the protestors evoke Iraq as a model for the political and social reforms they sought. Ironically, during Bush's last years, American military leaders and policy makers admitted privately they would be relieved to see the emergence of an American-leaning Iraqi strongman along the lines of Hosni Mubarak, Egypt's now-deposed dictator. Prime Minister Maliki may yet fit the bill: in 2011 his security forces repressed youthful Iraqi protestors seeking to bring the spirit of reform to their country. Events plainly have bypassed any vision of a democratic Iraq ushering in a new era in the Middle East.[211]

The outcome in Iraq exemplifies the consequences of misguided wartime leadership. Bush mishandled nearly all of the tasks a wartime president faces. He permitted a drift into war rather than encouraging a rigorous, balanced assessment of the intelligence about the threat from Iraqi WMD, Saddam Hussein's alleged ties to terrorists, and the long-term risks of going to war. To boost public support for possible military action, the administration hyped the potential danger that Saddam might transfer WMD to extremists. All this produced deceptively high approval ratings for invading Iraq. By comparison with the 1991 Gulf War, the president and his key aides achieved disappointing diplomatic results both before and after the invasion. Few potential allies, for example, contributed troops to assist in the postwar occupation. (And other than Great Britain, many that did attached such tight restrictions on their forces that they were largely useless in fighting the insurgency.) The president also failed to tend closely enough to the planning for the invasion, which left no margin for error if the optimistic assumptions guiding Pentagon leaders turned out to be mistaken. Here he did not take care to make certain his war goals, especially his sweeping vision for postwar Iraq, were reflected in the preparations for postwar stability operations. When things went askew after the capture of Baghdad, Bush persisted in his version of a corporate management style. Secretary of Defense Rumsfeld continued to disdain nation building in Iraq, even though nothing else could assure accomplishment of the president's peace-building agenda. Further, in asking no sacrifice of the American people, the president saw to it that they would not be invested in the war's success.[212] They turned against the conflict just as it became evident that achieving anything like what the president wanted would entail a protracted counterinsurgency effort.

Even Bush's finest moment—the troop-surge decision—raises questions about his leadership. It took considerable boldness to reject the key ISG recommendations and disregard the advice of the Joint Chiefs. The president did not accept the surge proposal, though, because of its soundness. At that point in the war, little solid evidence supported the belief that counterinsurgency methods might be successful in Iraq. The decision reflected Bush's innate stubbornness, his willingness to grasp at anything rather than admit defeat.[213] Had the surge option not been on the table, the president's record suggests he would have simply stayed the course through the end of his second term.

This in turn highlights Bush's inability to recognize the endemic problem of wartime presidential leadership: how early choices compromise freedom of action. By the time he acknowledged that Iraq was slipping into chaos, most policy options were off the table; his own rhetorical commitment made withdrawal impossible (notwithstanding the political cover provided by the ISG report), while the troops needed for a dramatic escalation were unavailable and any attempt at a major military expansion would have failed in Congress.

On the other hand, Iraq also demonstrates that war sometimes creates new possibilities for exercising presidential agency, if only on a limited scale. U.S. commanders on the ground received no direction from Washington as the insurgency gained momentum. Left to their own devices to deal with a conflict for which they had not prepared, these officers initially stumbled. But over time, midlevel military leaders used their freedom to experiment to rediscover and invent more effective counterinsurgency methods. Concepts such as "seize, hold, and build" and an emphasis on population security percolated up from the field. Had it not been for this frontline innovation and the thinking it stimulated in higher military circles, the operational foundation on which the surge rested would never have existed. In this way, the war itself yielded an operational alternative without which Bush's belated intervention would have been meaningless.

Finally, after the president committed the additional troops in early 2007, he returned to the method of leadership by delegation. He stood back, moreover, despite the fact that he had banked everything on an unproven commander pursuing an untested operational approach.

Unexpected events play a large role in warfare, and they ultimately worked to the president's advantage in Iraq. The Sunni Anbar Awakening took American military commanders and diplomats in Iraq by surprise. Although various American actions contributed to the willingness of tribal leaders to reach out to the U.S. military, the Awakening owed more to their fear of the foreign jihadists in AQI who had overplayed their hand and overstayed their welcome. Analysts will continue to debate the relative importance of the Awakening and the troop surge in stemming the violence beginning in summer 2007.[214] But there seems no question that absent the willingness of Sunni tribal leaders to shift roles from insurgents to partners with the U.S. troops, the additional five brigades that Petraeus received could not have turned the tide. The insurgents could simply have bided their time, because the American military was too overextended to sustain the force level needed for population security. (General Shinseki turned out to be close to the mark: in the end, when the 160,000 U.S. troops were added to the Iraqi Army and the legitimized Sunni self-defense forces, the total number of soldiers and security personnel policing Iraq in late 2007 exceeded 400,000.) Nor could Bush have anticipated Prime Minister Maliki's decision to crack down on the Sadrist militia, though the president and his diplomats consistently encouraged the Iraqi leader to do so. Thanks to fortuitous developments, the disaster that seemed to be unfolding in 2006 was averted. The president deserves some credit for the reversal of fortune, but it does not balance the ledger on his overall record as a wartime leader.

Iraq reminds us of the limitations of wartime presidential power. This claim seems to fly in the face of the evidence. The Bush administration used the 9/11 attacks to justify a dramatic expansion of presidential authority, especially encroachments on civil liberties and on established protections for captured enemy combatants (recall the administration's defense of "waterboarding" and "enhanced interrogation techniques"). Yet despite the extraordinary military, intelligence, and police means at its disposal, despite the loosening of restraints made possible by 9/11, despite the effective exploitation of popular fears to sweep aside questions, the administration found itself unable to control the course of events in Iraq. The iconic weapon of this war turned out to be not some high-tech marvel of Rumsfeld's transformed military but the lowly IED. Much like his predecessors, Bush saw his early choices (and those he let others make) cramp his options, depriving him of the power to change direction.[215] He briefly held in his hands complete freedom of action, and then it vanished.

6

Inheriting a Bad Hand

Barack Obama

PRESIDENTS OFTEN HAVE A KEEN sense of history. In wartime, they are attuned to the real or perceived mistakes of their predecessors. Wilson thought Lincoln had interfered too much in how his generals fought; from Wilson's League of Nations debacle, Roosevelt recognized the need to put in place the framework of a postwar collective security system before World War II ended; Bush thought Johnson had meddled excessively in military decisions in Vietnam. When Barack Obama weighed what course to follow in Afghanistan, he feared a reprise of the incremental drift into war that had characterized Johnson's approach to Vietnam in 1964–1965. He thought that Johnson had failed to ask hard questions about the recommendations he was given from the military and that Bush had made the same error in planning the Iraq invasion.[1]

In thinking about Vietnam, Obama may have had the right war in mind, but his situation more closely resembled that faced by Richard Nixon in 1969 than Johnson four years earlier. Nixon, too, had inherited a war that had become a stalemate for his predecessor. Nixon's challenge had been finding a way out that did not look like defeat, as he played a weakening military hand during the gradual withdrawal of American forces. Obama actually came into office with two wars on his hands, one in Afghanistan and the other in Iraq. Fortunately, the

American combat role in Iraq was clearly winding down. Afghanistan claimed most of his attention.

The Nixon parallel suggests that when a president takes over a war he enjoys a limited and short-lived revival of flexibility. Nixon could not pursue all-out war or immediate disengagement, but the American people gave him more time than they would have granted Johnson, and he felt less bound by the self-imposed military restrictions that had governed the conduct of the war up to 1969. So it was with Obama: he had more options than did Bush, though all were unattractive. As an added complication, Obama, unlike Nixon, had committed himself while running for office in ways that foreclosed some possibilities.

I treat Obama's leadership of the Afghanistan War more briefly than the other presidents I have discussed. This more limited treatment reflects two considerations. First, Obama did not face some of the important tasks that confront presidents at the start of a military conflict. He did not have to decide whether war was necessary; nor did he need to prepare the American people for it, define an initial set of war aims, or create the military means to carry the war to the enemy. Second, since the war continues at full fury as this is written, I do not have the advantage of complete historical evidence or the perspective gained in hindsight to offer a fully developed account. But I think it important to offer a partial analysis that places Obama in the framework I have developed. His experience clearly confirms how difficult it is for presidents to control what happens in war.

Beyond that, Obama's Afghanistan policy lets us consider another argument about wartime presidential decision making—that the process by which a president reaches his decisions influences the results he will achieve. In the belief that poor decision processes had led Johnson into the Vietnam quagmire and contributed to Bush's problems in Iraq, Obama and his close advisors took pains to make his policy review deliberate, structured, and highly rational. The president also harbored suspicions about the military advice he received, so he subjected it to unusually close scrutiny. Despite the attention to process, however, he found himself with only one real option—for a troop surge of the same magnitude as the one Bush had ordered in Iraq. Process awareness may have value, but it cannot give a president freedom of action where prior choices, whether made by him or by others, have circumscribed his agency.[2]

The Price of a Light Footprint

The insurgency against which the United States and its NATO allies fought in Afghanistan had widened as an indirect consequence of Bush administration policies. After sweeping the Taliban from power using very modest forces, the United States committed fewer than 10,000 troops to hunt Taliban and al-Qaeda leaders. The light footprint approach, as it came to be known, contributed to the collapse of governance in Afghanistan. U.S. and NATO forces could clear territory occupied by the Taliban or other insurgents but not hold it. Nor did Western nations provide adequate rural development aid, though Bush in 2002 spoke of a large-scale assistance program to restore the war-ravaged country. In the years that followed, with the Bush administration heavily committed in Iraq, the United States and its allies deployed only 1.6 soldiers per thousand Afghans, a figure similar to that which has marked some of the least successful modern military interventions, such as the ill-fated Somalia effort in the early 1990s.

By 2005 the Taliban had recovered, thanks also to safe havens in neighboring Pakistan, and violence spread across large parts of Afghanistan. In a manner that recalled Vietnam, the insurgents undermined government control in rural areas through assassination and intimidation, then set up their own shadow government. The Afghan government in Kabul under President Hamid Karzai suffered from massive corruption and failed to deliver vital services, while government military and police performed poorly. Although the Bush administration finally became alarmed enough to add troops, by 2008, insurgents had expanded their area of control and American military commanders voiced worries that without substantial U.S. and NATO reinforcements the Karzai government might collapse.[3] At the time of Obama's inauguration, the situation bore an eerie and uncomfortable similarity to the one Johnson faced in 1964–1965.

Obama might have pursued military alternatives no longer available to his predecessor. In the abstract, a president who inherits an ongoing conflict can choose to withdraw (effectively accepting defeat), stay the course (leaving open whether to alter the military approach within the existing force commitment), or escalate American involvement. The options actually available in a particular war, though, may be more limited, as was the case in Afghanistan. Withdrawal had been removed from the table by Obama himself during his campaign: he had stressed that Afghanistan, not Iraq, was the war on which the United States should focus because al-Qaeda remained directly active in the Afghanistan-Pakistan region. He had gone so far as to suggest that he would consider sending additional troops to Afghanistan. (Here he had tied his hands to a greater degree than had Nixon when he ran for president in 1968.) At the other extreme, he could not undertake a major escalation of the American war effort for the same reasons Bush could not in Iraq—too few available troops, due to an overstretched military, and the political obstacles to a large-scale expansion of the U.S. armed forces. Effectively, then, Obama only had room in the middle to maneuver. Because Obama had not committed himself to any particular operational approach to fighting the war, he might embrace one that differed from his predecessor's—in this case, an implicit repudiation of the Bush-Rumsfeld way. A new president has that luxury when his predecessor has led the war to a stalemate.

Most important, Obama would be given some additional time, the precious commodity without which presidents can do little to shape the outcome of a conflict. The American people showed little enthusiasm for the Afghanistan conflict, but it also attracted limited domestic attention because the United States was beset by the massive financial collapse that began in fall 2008. If public patience for Bush's wars was exhausted, Obama could count on a breathing space, both to figure out how better to achieve the goals he defined and to execute any new policies he chose. Democrats in Congress, moreover, would give their party leader longer to find a way out of the stalemate before renewing demands for prompt withdrawal.

Just the same, as Obama and his advisors understood, they could not start from scratch—the Afghanistan War had been going on since late 2001 and Americans would not grant even a new president an indefinite extension to bring it to a conclusion.[4] The ticking political clock meant the president needed to define an approach that would yield positive results soon, and certainly before he faced reelection.[5]

The Price of Buying Time

Obama moved quickly to establish firm White House control over Afghanistan policy, and in doing so he began to set a course toward an increased American role in the conflict. At the time of the 2008 election, 38,000 American troops fought in Afghanistan (along with nearly 30,000 NATO and allied forces, plus Afghan security forces). General David McKiernan, the American commander on the ground (who had earlier led the invasion of Iraq), had asked for 30,000 reinforcements. At Bush's request, a strategy review had been started in summer 2008. It pointed to a host of problems—too few troops, poor cooperation between American military commanders and civilian officials in Kabul, corruption, ineffective performance by the Afghan Army—and concluded the United States was neither winning nor losing.

Obama received the results, as well as a report from Vice President Joe Biden, who visited Afghanistan and found U.S. troops and senior officers uncertain and divided about what they were trying to accomplish. General David Petraeus, now elevated to command CENTCOM and thus also responsible for Afghanistan, chimed in with a recommendation that the president meet the request for more troops while he weighed options.[6] Obama naturally preferred not to send reinforcements until he completed his own evaluation, but events forced his hand. The Afghan election scheduled for August 2009 might be disrupted by insurgent violence unless order could be improved, which might in turn fracture the country. In mid-February 2009, less than a month after taking office, Obama decided to send 17,000 more troops to Afghanistan. As Bob Woodward notes, the president really had only one option, because he could not afford to see the election swamped by chaos and bloodshed.[7] From that point onward, disengagement in the short run would never be on the table.[8]

The president took a second early step to put his stamp on the war. In May he replaced McKiernan with General Stanley McChrystal. Although the decision reflected a recommendation from defense secretary Robert Gates (who continued in the position to which he had been appointed by Bush at the time of the Iraq surge) and Admiral Mike Mullen, chairman of the Joint Chiefs of Staff, the initial impetus for the move came from retired U.S. Army General Jack Keane. Keane had been a forceful advocate for the Iraq surge and strongly urged that the counterinsurgency methods introduced there be extended to Afghanistan. To him, McKiernan was the wrong officer to conduct a COIN campaign, too old-school, too wedded to killing Taliban fighters rather than securing the population. McChrystal would be a better choice for the operational approach Keane and Petraeus believed was required.

In picking McChrystal, Obama set the stage for a dispute with the military over what kind of war the United States would fight in Afghanistan. The president did not meet his new Afghanistan commander before announcing the decision and had as yet not committed himself to a counterinsurgency effort.[9] But the military plainly had its own ideas about the war. In his confirmation hearing before the Senate Armed Services Committee, McChrystal said he might need an additional 20,000-plus troops, an indication that the military had started its push for the forces that a protracted COIN campaign would require.[10] The president would find himself challenged to make sure that the Pentagon, CENTCOM, and the military leadership in Afghanistan would execute faithfully his ultimate policy decisions, and he would go to unusual lengths to make certain of compliance.

Obama Claims Ownership

Over the following months and into late 2009, the administration engaged in a thorough evaluation of its options for the war. Besides culminating in a decision to commit roughly 30,000 additional troops in 2010 and to begin drawing down the force in mid-2011, the process also led to the president to redefine American war objectives. The striking feature of the Afghanistan policy assessment is just how limited the president's choices were. These constraints would push the president to frame new and deeply problematic war goals. Obama would not explain them clearly to the American people, either, because doing so would risk damaging political fallout.

Much has been made of the painstaking decision process that the president pursued before settling on his policy, but the attention misses a more important point. Many meetings were devoted to weighing the relative merits of a counterterrorism focus versus a COIN campaign and whether to send the 40,000 troops McChrystal wanted or perhaps only 20,000. Yet the sobering truth is that Obama and his advisors haggled over issues—small variations in troop numbers and questions of how best to use the few additional troops—that could not possibly make a decisive difference on the ground. It hardly mattered whether the United States deployed 100,000 or 110,000 troops in a country of more than 20 million people. Likewise, neither counterterrorism nor COIN could yield victory, defined as peace and stability in Afghanistan and the elimination of the al-Qaeda threat in the region. The military alternatives, moreover, failed to touch what all saw as the heart of the problem—the deficiencies of the Karzai government and the two-faced role of Pakistan, a supposed ally in the war on terror that permitted its territory to be used as a haven for the Taliban and al-Qaeda.

The policy reassessment was triggered by McChrystal's request for an additional 40,000 troops, accompanied by a warning that anything less invited a Taliban victory. He and Petraeus envisioned a kind of Baghdad II, a troop surge of indefinite duration in which American forces and their NATO and Afghan allies would practice "seize, hold, and build" tactics to bring population security and economic development to rural Afghanistan.[11] Obama and those around him had a keen sense of history, and they saw the request as similar to the one Westmoreland made in early 1965 when he asked for enough troops to initiate offensive operations in South Vietnam. The president feared slipping unwittingly into the same kind of open-ended commitment. He wanted a full debate as a defense against a repeat of the Vietnam tragedy. To make certain the risks received a full airing, he encouraged Biden, an avowed COIN skeptic, to push hard for his preferred counterterrorism alternative.[12]

If we step back from the sequence of the meetings (already chronicled by Bob Woodward and others)[13] to consider the main choices placed before the president, the first point that stands out is that he was presented with a menu of losing propositions. Both counterterrorism and counterinsurgency seemed plausible on the surface. On close inspection, though, each suffered from insurmountable weaknesses given the actual constraints presented by Afghanistan.

Counterterrorism had a superficial allure that masked its military limits and political costs. Over the previous year, counterterrorism conducted through aerial drone attacks and a 3,000-man CIA-directed force based in Afghanistan had inflicted a severe toll on Taliban and al-Qaeda leadership.[14] (This has continued, culminating in the killing of Osama bin Laden in Pakistan on April 30, 2011.) Yet decapitation strikes alone have never stopped an insurgency, and they depend on excellent information from the local population that in turn requires a significant military presence on the ground. Collateral civilian losses from mis-aimed attacks also have inflamed both Afghan and Pakistani hostility toward the United States, helping recruit new insurgents.[15]

The operational alternative, counterinsurgency, had come back into fashion, but presumed conditions that did not exist in Afghanistan. During Petraeus's command tenure in Iraq, COIN methods had con-tributed to lessened violence. Much of the gain, though, was due to the Anbar Awakening that saw Iraqi Sunnis reach out to the occupying Americans as allies against the foreign jihadists. In Afghanistan, as McKiernan had reported and Petraeus later conceded, nothing suggested that the Taliban was open to political reconciliation.[16] Numbers and the political clock also worked against the prospects for effective counterinsurgency. Even COIN advocates admitted that a suc-cessful counterinsurgency campaign requires a much greater density of troops in relation to the population than the United States could achieve in Afghanistan and far more time than the American public would tolerate. The cost would also be prohibitive, perhaps $1 trillion for ten years, as much as the president's health care initiative.[17] What might have been done with a larger U.S.-NATO presence in 2002 or even 2005 could not be accomplished after 2009. At best, counterinsur-gency might, by improving population security in key areas of Taliban influence, create an opening in which the Kabul government could demonstrate improved effectiveness, and some insurgents could be enticed to lay down their arms.

Diplomatic obstacles that had hampered the war effort under Bush continued to vex the Obama administration, rendering both counterter-rorism and COIN unworkable. The Karzai government ignored repeated American pleas to fight corruption among its own official ranks and to improve governance for the Afghan people. So long as the regime failed to generate economic development in impoverished rural regions, discontent would swell the ranks of the Taliban. Afghans also turned to its shadow institutions for protection, to resolve disputes, for permission

to keep schools open, and more.[18] American diplomats had tried everything from soothing words to blunt threats to influence the Afghan
president, all to no avail. As in Saigon a generation earlier or Baghdad
more recently, the head of the client regime has his own interests and
pursues them doggedly. Karzai sought to shore up his political base,
appointing governors and other officials whose loyalty he purchased by
letting them enrich themselves without interference. COIN tactics
depend on the capacity of the local government to meet the needs of the
populace, and nothing suggested that the regime in Kabul would do so
any better than it had in the past. The American ambassador in Kabul,
General Karl Eikenberry (a former commander of U.S. forces in
Afghanistan), concluded that Karzai was a hopeless case.[19]

Relations with Pakistan were no better, and indeed these seemed to
lie at the heart of the problem. Certain border regions of Pakistan, especially the Federally Administered Tribal Areas (FATA), have never been
under effective control by the Islamabad government. Populated by the
same ethnic group (Pashtun) that constitutes the core of the Taliban,
the FATA offered a haven to retreating Taliban and al-Qaeda leaders
after 2001. They continued to operate from the FATA and other friendly
territory just inside Pakistan, despite the increased tempo of U.S. drone
attacks and CIA raids. As the United States learned in Vietnam, it is
almost impossible to defeat insurgents who can choose when to enter
and exit the battle zone and can recover in relative safety. With Pakistan
a notional ally in the war on terror and the recipient of substantial military assistance since 9/11, the United States had to respect Pakistani
sovereignty. Pakistan might ignore drone strikes, contenting itself with
a diplomatic protest when these caused civilian deaths, but American
and Afghan forces could not carry the war onto Pakistani soil. Most
disturbing, the United States amassed evidence that the Pakistani intelligence service, the Inter-Services Intelligence Directorate (ISI),
continued to give important logistical support to both the Taliban and
al-Qaeda. So far as some elements within the Pakistani state were
concerned, Pakistan had its own security interests in Afghanistan, in
particular that of offsetting the rise in Indian influence in Kabul. American
officials believed that current and/or former senior Pakistani military
and ISI leaders were alerting Taliban and al-Qaeda operatives to
pending U.S. attacks.[20] Absent a change in Pakistani behavior, which

American officials admitted that they lacked leverage to secure, no military campaign in Afghanistan could achieve long-term success.

The diplomatic barriers and unpromising military choices frustrated Obama, who resented what he saw as efforts by the Pentagon and military to box him into a policy he did not support. The military tried to stack the deck in favor of the McChrystal request. A memo from the general, leaked to the press in September 2009, advised against either early disengagement or a narrow focus on killing terrorist leaders. If Obama decided against escalation in some form, he could be criticized for rejecting the advice of his military leadership.[21]

In the course of the White House deliberations over Afghanistan in late 2009, three alternatives were placed on the table. Obama might pick from among a fully resourced counterinsurgency approach requiring an additional 85,000 troops; the 40,000 increment; or adding just 10,000 troops to focus on counterterrorism. It seemed, then, that the president had options. But as we have seen in the case of Johnson and the Vietnam escalation decision, when a president receives three war options, only the middle one will meet the test of military and political plausibility. Johnson could not have selected all-out war or disengagement at an acceptable political cost. Likewise, Obama saw that only the middle option was a realistic possibility.[22] Biden advocated a focus on counterterrorism, but Gates, Secretary of State Hillary Clinton, and the military outweighed him. Toward the end, discussion narrowed to whether to give McChrystal all the troops he wanted or hold the increase to 30,000.[23] The numbers debate was more symbolic than substantive, though: at issue was whether the president would flex his muscles to show he was in charge. Obama settled on the 30,000 figure, then made sure to deny the Pentagon any latitude by spelling out precisely in writing what the number meant.[24]

Far more important than the number, though, the president shifted American wartime objectives. In framing his troop request, McChrystal spoke of defeating the insurgency, a trope that recurred in reports and statements by Petraeus, Gates, and others on the military side.[25] But the president and some of his advisors appreciated that conditions in Afghanistan and Pakistan, coupled with the real limits on available military resources, made victory impossible. To seek to defeat the Taliban, moreover, invited the kind of open-ended commitment Obama refused to make. The president instead settled for a lesser goal: the United States would seek merely to *degrade* the Taliban. In concrete terms, this meant the insurgents would not be in a position to defeat the Kabul government and its military when the United States and other external participants withdrew their combat forces.

The timetable that the president established reflected this new war goal. Obama insisted on a schedule for the troop surge different from the one the military proposed. Where the military had recommended a gradual deployment that would not be completed until well into 2011 and that would then extend into a potential Obama second term, he chose to "move the curve" by putting all the additional troops in place by mid-2010 and beginning the drawdown in summer 2011. Although the pace of withdrawals would depend on conditions in Afghanistan, he made clear that the starting date for disengagement would not be negotiated with the military and the duration of the American commitment was bounded. The tight time limit also meant that this troop surge, unlike the one in Iraq, precluded any serious counterinsurgency program.[26]

By deciding to eschew defeating the Taliban, Obama adopted a bold and very risky political objective. He gave up on *winning* the war in favor of *managing* it. When the United States and NATO disengaged from the conflict, it was hoped, the government in Kabul should have sufficient trained forces to preserve its grip on power. But Obama did not expect the violence to end by that point.[27] What he proposed might be seen as the Afghan equivalent of Nixon's Vietnamization program. In one vital respect, though, the two policies differed: where Nixon failed to set in place the political foundation for ongoing support for South Vietnamese security after the American departure, Obama intended a long-term security commitment to both the Afghan and Pakistani governments. He hoped that, despite rising war weariness in the public and on Capitol Hill, invoking 9/11 would continue to resonate at home, and Americans would agree to maintain a reduced yet still significant economic, military, and political presence in the region. As in South Korea, some American troops might remain indefinitely. But with no truce agreement in the offing in Afghanistan they would remain targets for extremist attacks.

Obama understood that it would be hard to sell a war that aimed for something less than victory. This became evident when he explained his decision to deploy the additional 30,000 troops to the American people on December 1, 2009. The president glossed over the diminished objective.[28] Even as the United States still sought "to disrupt, dismantle, and defeat al-Qaeda in Afghanistan and Pakistan," he said, the new military strategy aimed to "break the Taliban's momentum." Only the most careful listener would note the distinction, critical though it was. Dropped as well was all reference to Afghanistan as a "war of necessity," a phrase the president had used as recently as the previous September.[29] He was more forthright about his determination not to redo the Iraq surge. By insisting on a time frame for the transition to Afghan responsibility, he rejected "a nation-building project of up to a decade" as something "beyond what can be achieved at a reasonable cost."[30] The strongest advocates for that kind of counterinsurgency enterprise were his own military commanders. Obama went on record as rejecting their recipe for victory. Whether the public would grant him the time to pursue a military campaign that could not yield victory remained an open question.

As with his predecessors, Obama's decisions about troop increases and timetables eliminated most of his freedom of action. From that point forward, absent some dramatic change in the international setting, he could no longer alter the purpose of the war. He also could not increase troop levels without provoking a sharp political reaction among his core supporters and congressional allies. Lost, too, was a measure of diplomatic leverage over Kabul and Islamabad. Both the Afghan and Pakistani governments would calculate their best interests based on their assessment of the consequences of the pending American-NATO troop departures. Even with a pledge of long-term assistance, any real combat with insurgents by either government would have to be done by their own forces. Although Obama retained control over the pace of withdrawal, moreover, domestic political considerations—such as his reelection bid—would push him toward an earlier exit.[31]

Playing Out the String

The war has proceeded since December 2009 largely as might have been expected. American, NATO, and Afghan forces have improved security in the places they hold, but there are far too few troops to pacify most of such a vast country. McChrystal's command imploded when members of his staff were quoted disparaging the vice president and others, and Obama replaced him with Petraeus. The latter (now retired and appointed to head the CIA) was still not given the time to fight the counterinsurgency campaign he preferred. Despite heavy losses, the Taliban continues to fight, and it has returned to parts of Afghanistan from which it had been absent since the early 2000s. Reports suggest that some Afghan army units have improved to the point that they can operate independently, but these are few in number.[32] As for the Afghan people, their behavior mirrors that of civilians caught up in any "war amongst the people": to survive, they hedge their bets, aligning themselves cautiously with whichever side has the upper hand locally at the moment.[33] American troop withdrawals will occur, then, with the fate of Afghanistan still much in doubt.

On the diplomatic side, too, there have been few surprises. Hamid Karzai has looked to secure his political future among neighboring regional powers (Pakistan, India, Iran, and perhaps China) eager to shape Afghanistan to their own purposes. After public attempts to push him to combat corruption proved futile, American officials resorted to a more low-key approach, but the ongoing reality of limited leverage has continued to undercut American appeals. He has sent mixed signals about his willingness to seek a political accommodation with the Taliban, too. While he refers to the insurgents as his "brothers," some reports claim he has done his utmost to scuttle American efforts to negotiate with Taliban leaders.[34] At the same time, he still seeks long-term security guarantees from Washington. Karzai's stance evokes South Vietnamese President Thieu's desperate bids to thwart a peace deal between the United States and Hanoi. Plainly, far from being an American puppet, the Afghan president marches to the beat of his own drum.

Nor has the United States altered Pakistani behavior significantly. When Osama bin Laden was killed in Abbottabad, Pakistan, within a mile of an army base, the Pakistanis voiced more anger at the raid than dismay that the world's most wanted terrorist had found shelter in relative comfort within their borders.[35] The Pakistanis have also sought to curtail drone strikes and CIA activities in their border areas. At least some elements within the Pakistani military and intelligence service evidently continue to see the Taliban has a useful instrument for influencing political developments in Afghanistan.[36] Admiral Mullen, at the end of his tenure as JCS chairman, gave voice to American frustrations when he declared before Congress that Pakistani intelligence operatives assisted extremist attacks on Kabul, including the U.S. embassy.[37]

Like his wartime predecessors, Obama has seen his window of agency close. He began with a narrow scope for action—essentially, he could choose the speed of an American exit and how best to use U.S. forces for the remainder of the period when they would be engaged in active combat. Having made the decisions in late 2009, he has been reduced largely to the role of a spectator. As the United States draws down its forces in Afghanistan, Kabul and Islamabad seem less likely to respond to American appeals. The situation recalls Le Duc Tho's words to Henry Kissinger: if the United States could not prevail in Vietnam with a half million troops, why would it expect to have its way with far fewer? Obama is but the most recent president to discover that victory can be elusive.

Conclusion

Past and Future

WARS TEST PRESIDENTS, PERHAPS MORE severely than any other responsibility they face. A wartime president bears the burden of life and death. With the decision to go to war, moreover, comes a series of challenges that can overwhelm a chief executive. Abraham Lincoln and Franklin Roosevelt rank among our most accomplished presidents, two leaders of extraordinary skill and vision. Of the presidents I have examined in these pages, they came closest to fulfilling the full range of responsibilities that confront a political leader in wartime. Their performances merit deep respect. Yet they were still flawed.

And what of the other war presidents, the "mere mortals"? They were accomplished politicians in their own right, often with an enviable record on the domestic side. Nevertheless, when thrust into the role of wartime leader, whether by their own decisions or because they inherited an ongoing conflict, they came up short by a wider margin. Though it may be tempting to judge them harshly, their record says more about the impossibility of the challenges than about their personal limitations. Usually they approached the problems of wartime leadership with an appreciation of how hard it would be to achieve anything that looked like victory. And as control slipped from their grasp, their wars haunted them. This is the legacy we weigh as we look toward the future.

Revisiting the Puzzles

In the introduction, I framed several puzzles involving wartime presidential leadership. The seven presidents I have examined closely suggest that, in intellectual terms, the puzzles can be explained. But they also point to momentous political problems for American leaders and citizens. On this level, alas, effective solutions may not exist. That is deeply troubling, for at stake is the fate of each wartime presidency and its broadest consequences.

The first puzzle involves the broad latitude a president exercises to send American armed forces into battle nearly anywhere in the world with no effective political restraint. Presidents have capitalized on their constitutional powers and military resources to create situations in which military conflict is virtually inevitable. As commander in chief of the armed forces, a president can deploy troops in a way likely to provoke an attack. This may be intentional, as in the case of Abraham Lincoln in 1861 when he sent reinforcements to Fort Sumter, knowing this would precipitate a clash with rebels in Charleston Harbor. Or the provocation may be inadvertent: Franklin Roosevelt meant to deter a Japanese offensive in the Pacific when he reinforced Hawaii and the Philippines in 1941. Although Congress may not yet have authorized the use of force, once American troops are poised on the edge of combat, the political pressure on the legislative branch to acquiesce in the exercise of presidential war-making initiative has been too strong to resist. Lyndon Johnson demonstrated this in 1964 after the Tonkin Gulf incident, as did George W. Bush in 2002 when he sought approval to take military action against Saddam Hussein and Iraq. Diplomatic powers vested in the president also give him means to make war more likely. Roosevelt aligned the United States closely with Great Britain before the Second World War in ways certain to antagonize Hitler. On balance, the power to go to war has come to rest entirely in the hands of the president, hardly the situation envisioned by the Framers of the Constitution.

No effective check on presidential power to engage the nation in military conflict seems in the offing. From time to time, Congress bestirs itself and makes gestures to rein in presidential discretion over the use of force. But these have proven ineffective because they do not touch the core power of the president as commander in chief to position American forces. In the wake of Vietnam, Congress passed the War Powers Resolution, but the increased frequency of significant military operations in the past two decades demonstrates the ineffectiveness of the measure. Presidents have never acknowledged its constitutionality, instead preferring the prudent course of securing congressional approval in advance of most military interventions. Even when they do not, however, Congress has been unable or unwilling to act. To take a recent example, Barack Obama in March 2011 ordered American forces to participate in a multinational campaign to protect Libyan rebels against attacks by the Libyan regime. He did so without seeking congressional approval, and his action drew only feeble legislative protest.

The second puzzle is why presidents, in their role as military commander in chief, still struggle to find an effective approach to achieve the national objectives they have established in going to war. The historical record makes clear that there is no one right way to direct the military during wartime. I identified two contending schools of thought: one (objective control) that argues political leaders ought to leave military operations in the hands of the military; another (active direction) that counters that because war seeks political goals, no neat line can be drawn between political matters and military ones. Presidents have achieved some of their political goals using either approach. Lincoln and Roosevelt came closest to meeting their objectives, securing clear military success and fulfilling some of their core national political objectives. Both combined hands-on control with periods during which they left the fighting to their uniformed commanders. Interestingly, the two presidents followed a similar pattern: an initial phase of very active direction, followed later in the war by more detached guidance when they were confident that their military leaders had developed and would pursue effective strategies. Wilson, though, accomplished exactly what he sought—a demonstration of the indispensability of American military intervention to give him a strong hand at the peace table—despite giving Pershing virtually no direction in how best to use the American Expeditionary Force in France.

Wartime presidents have also tried different methods of overseeing military operations. Notwithstanding his fixation on certain battles (for example, Khe Sanh), Johnson never exercised a firm grip over ground operations in Vietnam. These yielded casualties for no gain. He was much more deeply involved in supervising air operations, with no better results. Nixon involved himself episodically (one might say, impulsively) in military matters when he wanted to demonstrate his toughness to the North Vietnamese, interventions that failed to produce the diplomatic breakthroughs he desired. American forces pursued a coherent and effective counterinsurgency campaign during the Nixon years, but this was done with minimal White House intervention, other than occasional directives to pursue ill-considered operations such as the Cambodia (1970) and Laos (1971) incursions. George W. Bush delegated responsibility for the Iraq invasion and its aftermath to his secretary of defense. Rumsfeld played a very active role in planning the invasion, then left it to generals at CENTCOM and in Iraq to deal with the worsening insurgency. Rumsfeld's detachment represented a variation on the objective control approach that disdains micromanaging military operations. When disaster loomed in late 2006, Bush himself briefly exercised active direction of the war effort. He then returned to his preferred style of leadership-via-delegation, this time entrusting full responsibility to his military commander in Iraq with better results.

Two conclusions emerge from this very mixed record of wartime military leadership. First, presidents seek to avoid the errors they believe their wartime predecessors have committed but often draw questionable conclusions. Convinced that Lincoln had been too meddlesome, Wilson went to the opposite extreme. But he had misread Lincoln's record, ignoring the last eighteen months of the Civil War; even where the earlier years of that conflict are concerned, it is hard to maintain that Lincoln would have done better by leaving McClellan and company to their own devices. Similarly, Bush felt Johnson had been overly involved in Vietnam military decisions and decided to refrain from questioning how his military commanders were addressing the worsening insurgency in Iraq. Here, too, a president misconstrued the historical record. Johnson had practiced minimal direction of the ground war with results that should have sobered any later president facing a serious counterinsurgency military challenge.

Second, focusing on how actively a president oversees military matters seems misplaced. No approach ensures that a president will achieve the national political objectives he set in going to war. To put it another way, there is no wartime president's "user's manual" that can serve as a guide—and there certainly isn't a 24/7 help desk a president can call when a war goes badly. Active direction by a president is by itself neither necessary nor sufficient for successful wartime leadership.

On balance, hands-on engagement seems the wiser course because an involved president is more likely to learn quickly when military operations have deviated from his broader political purposes. Johnson could have pressed Westmoreland more closely about the mismatch between his optimistic assessments and intelligence reports that showed communist strength steady or increasing. Likewise, Bush could have reconsidered his administration's repeated assertions that the Iraqi insurgency was on its last legs or found a defense secretary who shared his commitment to building Iraqi democracy. Recognizing failure earlier matters because, for wartime presidents, time is precious. Yet a president who attends closely to military matters may also have to pay an opportunity cost in the neglect of other critical wartime leadership tasks. It would be a serious, possibly fatal, error for a wartime chief executive to approach his role as though it consisted solely of acting as commander in chief of the armed forces.

A third puzzle is why wartime presidents regularly struggle to meet their non-military leadership challenges, especially planning for the aftermath of the conflict. Leading a nation at war involves far more than seeing to it that military operations reflect a president's war goals. On the home front, where presidents face the vital task of sustaining popular backing for the war effort, they have achieved mixed results. When a conflict poses an existential threat to national survival, presidents can tap a willingness to sacrifice, at least at the outset. Even with that, though, public support cannot be taken for granted, especially as the human cost of the war rises. Lincoln tended carefully to popular opinion, with cogent public letters explaining his policies and deft metaphors that resonated in the everyday lives of the men and women at home. Less admirably, his partisan allies went to great lengths to intimidate opponents, a lesson several of his successors have emulated. Roosevelt fought the Second World War in a way that minimized American casualties while also producing rapid economic growth, a formula that helped to neutralize criticism of the war effort. But he also did his best to avoid frank discussion of subjects that might alienate significant constituencies, such as the reality of postwar Soviet hegemony in Eastern Europe.

Wars in which the fate of the nation does not hang in the balance present a greater domestic political challenge to a president. Because of the brief duration of American involvement in the First World War and the relatively modest casualties incurred, Wilson did not face the difficulty of dealing with a war-weary public as did the heads of other nations. But he did suffer from self-inflicted political wounds, especially through a highly partisan approach that backfired and helped cost his party control of Congress. The most serious challenges in retaining public support arise in protracted limited wars. Johnson and Bush both discovered that a decision not to mobilize the nation for war becomes a double-edged sword. Although most citizens are not directly discomfited, especially in the absence of a draft, they also do not feel they have a direct stake in the outcome. As public support erodes, presidents then tend to resort to overheated rhetoric, likening a limited conflict to an existential one. Bush in particular fell back on alarmist warnings about how retreat from Iraq would invite future 9/11-style attacks in the United States. Apart from among core supporters, though, the language wears thin over time, as a growing percentage of the public wonders why, if so much is at stake, Americans have not been asked to make sacrifices.

In a number of wars, presidents have faced vocal opposition that they have treated as unpatriotic. Their reaction is understandable. From the perspective of a wartime president and his civilian and military advisors, antiwar critics encourage the enemy to resist. This view has some foundation. In modern "war amongst the people," the "people" include the external power's domestic audience, whose morale is one key target for insurgents. Thus, during the Vietnam War, Hanoi's diplomats encouraged dissent in the United States and cultivated ties with leading antiwar activists and journalists seen as critical of American policy. But antiwar opposition also serves the essential purpose of calling attention to a war policy that is failing and forces a president to respond. Protests against the Vietnam War gained traction in the political mainstream because it became evident that Johnson's approach had produced nothing better than a stalemate; later, Nixon's decision to expand the war into Cambodia in spring 1970 revived the antiwar movement because the military operation violated public expectations of a steady disengagement from the war. The Iraq War likewise became a quagmire to which Bush reacted far too slowly, until mounting criticism and the electoral backlash against his party forced his hand. Much as it is difficult for presidents to admit, opposition to their war policy may be constructive, raising a red flag that the policy itself is badly conceived and/or conducted.

Wartime presidents also have compiled a mixed record in their diplomatic efforts. Lincoln faced a diplomatic challenge unlike that of his modern successors: his main objective was to keep other nations out of his war, where later presidents have usually sought to enlist allies. He managed to convince Great Britain and France not to recognize the Confederacy. Roosevelt excelled as a wartime diplomat, capitalizing on the leverage that American economic and military power gave him. Johnson, Nixon, Bush, and Obama did not achieve critical wartime diplomatic goals. The first two met with extraordinary frustration in their dealings with the Vietnamese governments in Hanoi and Saigon, unable to bludgeon the former or buy off the latter to accept a peace agreement on American terms. In the end Nixon abandoned the Thieu government as the price for extricating the United States from a war in which it had ceased to have a meaningful stake. Bush, unlike his father, failed to secure UN backing for military action against Saddam Hussein or to put together a broad-based multinational coalition either for the invasion or the occupation that followed. As with Johnson and Nixon in their dealings with Saigon, moreover, Bush discovered that the United States exercised little leverage over client regimes in which it invests its prestige. Successive Iraqi prime ministers operated on their own political calculus, which assigned little weight to an American president's wishes or timetable. Obama has encountered similar obstructionism in Kabul and Islamabad.

Of all their non-military responsibilities, presidents have done worst in preparing for peace, the most vexing of all wartime tasks. Important though battlefield success may be as a step toward achieving the political goals that a president has framed, military triumph alone has never been enough. Presidents usually have expansive political goals that require steps beyond an enemy's surrender or his acceptance of peace terms. For Lincoln, peace-building meant measures to lift the freedmen from their position of racial subordination; for Wilson, a generous peace for Germany, an international organization to prevent future catastrophic conflict, and self-determination for the former subjects of collapsed empires; for Roosevelt, a stable international order policed by great powers and an end to colonialism; for Bush, a democratic Iraq that would trigger a broad movement for political liberalization across the Middle East and the Islamic world. By contrast, Johnson, Nixon, and Obama have pursued relatively limited objectives: the first two sought an independent South Vietnam that could determine its own political future;[1] the last has tried to reduce the violence in Afghanistan to a level that will not undermine the Kabul government and to neutralize the threat of future terror attacks.

Although a president might claim victory even without accomplishing his full set of peace-building objectives, some triumphs would be barren without them, and certainly Americans would doubt the cost to be justified by lesser returns. Consider Wilson: precisely because going to war for the principle of freedom of navigation in wartime meant so little to him or his domestic public, battlefield success would be hollow without a durable peace. Despite the stakes, though, all wartime presidents, including Lincoln, have devoted too little attention to realizing their vision for a postwar order, and they waited too long to prepare for the world they intended to fashion after the fighting ended.

Disappointing peace-building efforts result from a number of elements. Some scholars stress the check imposed by the changing international environment, and my analysis supports their finding.[2] Once the glue of wartime necessity no longer binds allies, a president will find himself with reduced leverage to advance his agenda. Wilson missed his chance to persuade Entente leaders to sign on to his design for collective security through an international organization by waiting for the armistice to secure their approval. Roosevelt, learning from his predecessor's failure, pushed ahead with the formation of the United Nations before the Second World War ended and the differences between the Western powers and the Soviet Union hardened. Even so, he exercised limited control over international developments and was powerless to draw the Soviet Union into a liberal international order or shape the political future in either China or Indochina.

Other forces also limit the control a president can exercise at the end of a conflict. Domestic politics quickly resumes its peacetime form, as Congress reasserts its role and the public turns its attention back to matters closer at hand. Nowhere was this demonstrated more vividly than when Wilson sought approval for the League of Nations. Wilson represents but the extreme case of a common pattern: every wartime president has faced the same dynamic. Thus, after the signing of the Paris Peace Accords in early 1973, Congress moved to bar the future use of American forces in Southeast Asia without explicit congressional approval, which the lack of public concern guaranteed would not be forthcoming. Domestic pressures have also compelled rapid demobilization following major wars, leaving presidents with fewer troops to police peace arrangements.

The window of opportunity for a president to shape postwar outcomes opens only briefly. Johnson could not miss the point, given that peace talks with Hanoi did not begin until he had announced his decision not to seek reelection. Others have deferred peace-building preparations in the mistaken belief that they would have ample time after the guns fell silent or because they underestimated the complexities of their postwar aspirations. Wilson misjudged how much pull he would retain after an armistice, so he postponed seeking Entente agreement with his agenda instead of exploiting the desperate British and French need for American help in early 1918. More recently, in the mistaken confidence that Iraq could be easily remodeled into a liberal democratic society, Bush paid minimal attention before the invasion to the plans for the postwar occupation. Nixon missed his moment to enlist domestic, especially congressional, support for a long-term security relationship with South Vietnam because he placed undue faith in his diplomatic abilities and his capacity to use demonstrations of brute force to influence communist behavior. As the exception, Roosevelt showed the keenest sensitivity to the limited time in which he could exercise broad influence over the postwar order. His administration orchestrated domestic backing for a new international organization at the most opportune moment, while his most critical military decision—the invasion of Northwest Europe—balanced the risks of military failure with the gain from checking the advance of the Red Army across Central Europe.

A fourth puzzle is why wartime presidents, even those elected by huge margins, suffer the defeat of their domestic agenda and the undoing of their reform aspirations. Johnson entered the Vietnam War with the most sweeping program, intending through his Great Society to outdo even the New Deal, only to see his program derailed by late 1967. An argument can be made that both Wilson and Roosevelt had finished their domestic projects before embarking on war, but certainly their supporters believed otherwise. Most Progressives enthusiastically participated in the mobilization effort in 1917–1918 because they regarded their activities as of a piece with earlier social reforms, and Wilson did nothing to disabuse them of this notion. Roosevelt continued to speak the language of the New Deal during the Second World War. Notwithstanding his claim that Dr. New Deal had passed the torch to Dr. Win-the-War, his Four Freedoms invoked New Deal themes and his 1944 opening campaign speech promised to take government promotion of economic prosperity and security to new lengths. New Dealers expected reform to define the postwar era and used agencies such as the National Resources Planning Board to set the stage accordingly. Bush sought to pursue his agenda of reducing the scale of government while the United States fought wars in Afghanistan and Iraq.

Yet presidents have seen their domestic initiatives unravel amid military conflict. One partial explanation lies in the cost of war and the competition for scarce resources. Lincoln capitalized on fiscal circumstances that did not recur under his wartime successors. Key elements of the Civil War Republican program, such as the homesteading law, called for no direct federal expenditures, so they did not compete for funding with the war. Where presidential domestic agendas come with a price tag, however, programs may be crowded out by military outlays. Yet cost alone does not suffice to account for the exhaustion of reform energy. Several conflicts have occurred in periods of rapid economic growth; indeed, the wars themselves have stimulated that economic expansion. World War II stands out because military expenditures finally lifted the economy out of the Great Depression, but the wars in Vietnam and Iraq were also accompanied by a robust economy. In the latter case, the American economy was sufficiently strong that policy makers decided they could afford to retain the massive tax cuts that had been approved shortly before 9/11: the widening federal deficit (largely a product of the cut and war-related expenditures) would have no serious economic consequences.

It is not so much the cost as it is wartime political calculation and contestation that drain the impetus from a president's reform agenda. In market-oriented societies, major wars tend to empower conservative economic elites, on whose cooperation governments depend to meet their urgent need for military output. Wilson and Roosevelt tapped leaders in the private sector to help steer economic mobilization, while in the Second World War especially the federal government offered generous incentives to large corporations to induce them to supply the vast production of war materiel needed by the U.S. armed forces and by the Allies. Even where a conflict does not require a broad shift in economic activity, presidents see a need to tend to the concerns of business leaders, particularly to their fear that wartime federal expenditures may create inflationary pressures. Wartime presidents also crave broad political support at home. Lincoln's incessant clashes with his Democratic foes were not lost on his successors. For liberal presidents, the quest for political unity has meant reaching a political accommodation with their conservative adversaries in Congress. These presidents also have seen conservatives command greater leverage after they gained seats in wartime midterm elections. Wilson lost control of Congress in 1918, while both Roosevelt after 1942 and Johnson after 1966 governed with reduced majorities.

Even as wars strengthen the hand of a liberal president's political foes, his natural allies find themselves weakened. The social reform movements in the eras of Wilson, Roosevelt, and Johnson drew their energy from the political left. In wartime, this cohort often generates the first voices of antiwar dissent and in turn becomes the target of mainstream opprobrium. Radical and liberal activists face attacks on their patriotism, a process that can delegitimize both them and the ideas they represent. The Wilson administration's relentless assault on those who objected to the war, coupled with the efforts of the American Protective League and other forms of political persecution, inflicted a fatal wound on the Progressive movement. Much the same might have happened during the Vietnam era, except the peace movement gained sufficient backing from mainstream Democrats to forestall marginalization.

Here, though, the war so deeply divided the party's ranks as to doom any prospect that Democrats might cooperate to protect the Great Society from conservative demands for retrenchment.[3]

The record of the Bush administration suggests that the same dynamic may not operate when a conservative president pursues a reform agenda during a war. Although the 2001 Bush tax cut created a federal deficit and the Iraq War made it larger, the budget gap occasioned minimal political discussion. In contrast to the conservative response to wartime deficits in earlier conflicts, the political right did not demand fiscal discipline as the price for supporting the war. Not until Obama became president did conservatives voice alarm about the size of the federal deficit. In part, the indifference to wartime deficit spending may have reflected the lack of inflation, an unusual wartime condition not enjoyed by Roosevelt or Johnson. Yet, given that inflation has not shown itself under Obama either, it seems reasonable to conclude that conservatives will hold one of their own in the White House to a different standard. Economic circumstances during the Iraq War made it possible to put off any fiscal reckoning and let both the Bush administration and the Democratic opposition carry on business as usual, something each preferred to the more painful alternatives. Bush tried to continue his program of downsizing the federal government after he won reelection in 2004, taking aim at Social Security with a proposal to privatize the system over time. The scheme went nowhere, but his political failure does not seem to be connected to the war.

In sum, it appears that during wartime a reformist conservative president, because he already enjoys the backing of business elites and does not depend on activists who will be marginalized by their antiwar dissent, can escape some of the anti-reform political pressures that weaken his liberal counterparts. That said, when a war becomes unpopular, any president, liberal or conservative, will find policy victories scarce for the remainder of his term.

The fifth puzzle is the most daunting of all. We have seen repeatedly that presidents find themselves bereft of strategic options, with little latitude to alter the course of the war they initiated. Debates about presidential war powers have obscured this central dynamic of wartime presidential leadership. On one side, liberals have complained that presidents have amassed enormous military power and exploited national security crises to increase their executive authority. My analysis suggests, however, that presidents have *too little power*, not too much. Lest conservatives draw from this the wrong conclusion—that presidents should be given even broader unilateral executive authority—I would emphasize that the power deficiency cannot be solved by giving the occupant of the Oval Office greater resources. No increase in the size of the military, no new weapons system, no assertion of a new executive prerogative can alter the wartime power paradox. It boils down to this: the kind of power that presidents command does nothing to preserve their freedom of action over time. This is not a matter of how a president approaches his role as military commander in chief. Whether he adopts the objective control approach or the hands-on style, his freedom of action will diminish over the course of a war.

In war, time is a president's true enemy. At the beginning of a conflict, he exercises agency over a broad range of choices. He defines national objectives including the kind of peace he seeks, chooses his military commanders, decides how many troops to commit, defines or approves strategy, and forges international coalitions. But each choice necessarily forecloses other possible paths and each one makes it more costly and perhaps impossible to reverse direction. For Bush, the decision to invade Iraq with a small force left too few troops on hand to cope with the disorder and insurgency that followed. Decisions made by subordinates also constrain a president's freedom of action. Roosevelt discovered how low-level officials could skew his plans before the United States entered World War II when the bureaucracy imposed its own interpretation of a strategic embargo on Japan. Bush had too few troops to cope with an Iraqi insurgency because Rumsfeld insisted on a light invasion force.

By the end of a war, a president tries to lead with his hands tied. If he has not yet set in place the elements of a postwar settlement, he will find his path blocked, with the American people demanding attention to domestic concerns, Congress reasserting its role and denying him the resources he seeks for postwar commitments, and allies pursing their own national interests. Time, then, is the one foe he cannot defeat by military prowess, artful diplomacy, or forceful rhetoric.

On occasion, circumstances may briefly grant a president greater latitude. When the nature of a conflict changes, a president can revisit some of his initial decisions. Lincoln did so when he decided to turn the Civil War into a struggle against slavery in the South—the shift opened an opportunity to pursue a hard war against the social and economic foundation of the Confederacy. Even then, however, the loss of agency resumes, and a president becomes bound by his second round of core decisions. Recall that in 1864, at a low ebb in Union fortunes, Lincoln considered a compromise peace with the South, one that would have forced him to revoke the Emancipation Proclamation. To do such a thing, he realized, would undermine the moral foundation of the North's cause and shatter his political coalition. Emancipation remained his policy. Sometimes, too, battlefield developments will place new tools in a president's hands. Military commanders on the ground in Iraq devised counterinsurgency methods unknown at the time of the 2003 invasion. But the gain conferred by an operational or tactical innovation does not reverse the broader trend toward reduced agency, as evident in the narrow scope of choice available to Bush by late 2006.

A new president who inherits an ongoing war also may regain discretion, at least if he has avoided committing himself to a policy before reaching the White House. Nixon, who pledged to seek "peace with honor" in Vietnam, had wider (but not unlimited) options in 1969 than Johnson did at the end of his term. Obama found himself with an opportunity to redefine the goal of military intervention in Afghanistan. Here, too, an incoming president discovers that his window to shape the war opens for just a few moments, because his choices will quickly limit his subsequent options. In Vietnam and Afghanistan alike, the decision to begin disengagement served as a clear signal to other governments that the U.S. military would depart sooner rather than later, with a concomitant decline in the president's capacity to shape their behavior.

The Next Wars

In time certain trends seem likely to impose restraints on the capacity of presidents to initiate a war. The United States for the moment enjoys a rare position of global military supremacy. This will not persist indefinitely. Other powers will eventually emerge—China, for example—to alter the international system in ways that deny the United States the kind of free hand it has claimed since the collapse of the Soviet Union. In addition, the extraordinary cost of American defense outlays cannot be sustained. Budget pressures will compel reductions in defense spending, which in time will limit the freedom of presidents to flex their military muscles as they see fit.

Nevertheless, for the foreseeable future, American presidents will continue to lead the nation into military conflicts. The hegemonic position the United States enjoys encourages American leaders to assume responsibility for sustaining the international order and responding to threats against it. Of course, presidents have some latitude in deciding which dangers require a military answer. But it seems inevitable that the actions of some rogue state or an insurgency in some strategically vital region will provoke military intervention. So long as the Oval Office sees itself engaged in an open-ended and loosely defined global war on terror, moreover, military force may be used against shadowy extremist organizations and their protectors or in so-called failed states where a power vacuum invites such groups to set up branch operations.

Domestic political factors will also contribute to the proclivity to wage war. Although the costly and disappointing expeditions in Iraq and Afghanistan may cool the enthusiasm for martial adventures in the short run, the post-Vietnam experience suggests that this popular reluctance will be short-lived. Republicans, partial to American unilateralism and muscle-flexing, will identify enemies who understand only force; Democrats, fearful of seeming too soft, will look for the opportunity to demonstrate their toughness. Either camp may heed the clarion call to intervene in the name of human rights. And American leaders will continue to find that their constituents can be easily frightened, whether by a successful terror attack on the homeland or by distant threats.

The wars to come will most likely take the form of "war amongst the people," as have most recent conflicts. With the United States enjoying commanding technological advantages, no adversary can meet American armed forces on even terms. Rather, an enemy will seek to draw U.S. troops into a protracted struggle, with the support of the populace the ultimate prize. Unlike the Vietnam aftermath, when the military turned its back on low-intensity conflicts and counterinsurgency, today COIN methods have thoughtful and dedicated proponents within the armed services. Whether counterinsurgency can produce the political goals presidents establish in going to war remains unproven. But the COIN approach does seem to add a politico-military tool to the repertoire of military instruments available to a commander in chief, and thus may encourage presidents to embark upon the kinds of conflict for which other weapons are unsuited.

On the other hand, if military intervention leads the United States into another protracted conflict, the president will again face the problem of domestic support. The American people can be readily primed to back a war at the start; getting them to stay with it is another matter. Presidents have generated public approval for military action by using their bully pulpit. They can appeal to both fear and the nation's instinct to improve the world, particularly in its own image. Over time, though, popular backing gives way to indifference or, worse, disillusionment and apathy. George W. Bush and senior administration officials believed that the 9/11 terror attacks inaugurated a "long war" against Islamic extremism—a struggle they concluded might continue for a generation. Nothing indicates, though, that the American people are prepared to fight long wars within this "long war." Put another way, the United States has adopted global policing responsibilities, of the sort associated in the past with great imperial powers, yet the American people have not adopted the imperial mind-set that translates into support for the extended conflicts that such an international posture presupposes.

The cases I have examined point to certain recommendations that a president might consider when weighing the prospect of war. First and foremost, there is the obvious: exhaust every alternative to military intervention. Wars are instruments of national policy with political objectives, and some of those goals can be achieved by other means ranging from diplomacy to economic sanctions. Although the gains may be incomplete and a threat to peace and stability remains, the cost—human, economic, and political—will likely be far less than war. It would help if the United States could call upon more effective nonmilitary tools to influence foreign policy outcomes; as it stands, the disproportionate allocation of resources toward the military encourages presidents to opt for military solutions. Moreover, should all other policy tools fail, the use of force still remains an option.

Second, when war cannot be avoided, aim low. That is, establish modest goals. Presidents who have embarked on a war with transformative objectives have fallen far short, spurring a political backlash that stimulates isolationist inclinations that have always been a part of the American sensibility. Many consequences of military conflict are unplanned; often these are the result of actions taken by leaders who placed excessive faith in their ability to control outcomes. If modest objectives seem insufficient to justify recourse to arms, military action is not worth the asking price. Transformative ambitions also tempt leaders to persist in supporting failing military ventures beyond the point of diminishing returns.

Third, when preparing for war, plan backward. Gideon Rose advises political and military leaders to jump ahead to the ultimate goal rather than to focus on the first step. The place to begin, he says, is with the desired political outcome. Then planners should consider each step that must be accomplished to get there.[4] To this I would add that in seeking a political outcome, presidents and those around them need a heavy dose of realism and rigorous external scrutiny. Those in the Bush administration who envisioned a democratic post-invasion Iraq knew what they wanted to achieve. They also convinced themselves that things would fall neatly into place once Saddam Hussein and his henchmen were ousted. In short, they thought they had planned realistically. Presidents need independent (and skeptical) assessments of their designs for postwar settlement. The more ambitious the objective—that is, the more profoundly the end state differs from the status quo ante bellum—the more searching should be the review of war plans and the links between military action and the desired outcome.

Fourth, recognize that freedom of action declines. The inescapable dynamic of wartime presidential leadership—as I have argued, emphasized, and highlighted—is the loss of control or discretion. The initial decisions therefore require the closest scrutiny, calling for hands-on direction by the commander in chief. Unless a president gets it right up front, he stands little chance of accomplishing the objectives he has established. With this suggestion, though, comes an important caveat, drawn from the historical cases we've considered: even deep engagement at the top in the lead-up to war and in its early stages does not guarantee success.

Last, from the outset, focus attention on peace-building. Given the inexorable decline in freedom of action, presidents must move quickly—even prematurely—on plans for peace, including building political support at home when the design of a postwar settlement rests on long-term American commitments. Sometimes this means the work needs to be done even before the fighting begins; always, the ground-work needs to be laid before combat ends. Both domestic and international political circumstances will strip away presidential leverage immediately upon the cessation of hostilities. Further, since battlefield success may be empty of value if what follows is bungled, peace-building demands as much active presidential direction as the choice of military commanders and strategy.

This asks a great deal of a president. Good intentions alone won't cut it. To anticipate conditions at the end of the war calls for broad vision and keen foresight, tempered by a cold appreciation of the limits of American military power and political influence. Certainly, a president should enlist the best minds. But if hands-on leadership is needed anywhere, it is here. The stakes are too high for the task to be delegated and the plans given cursory review.

War imposes responsibilities on citizens, not just on their leaders. As citizens, we need to be deeply skeptical about claims of what can be achieved by recourse to force. More than anything else, the record of wartime presidents underscores the limits of power: despite increasing capacity to inflict violence on a foe, no president has achieved all of his objectives. Some have accomplished none of them. Even the greatest wartime leaders, Lincoln and Roosevelt, while securing military victories vital to the country's survival, could not build the kind of postwar order they sought. We should note, too, a disturbing trend: even as the United States increases its military advantages over all other nations, effective presidential wartime leadership has been declining. This is due to the mismatch between the tools of war at a president's command and the kinds of wars the United States fights. If nothing else, this decline should feed healthy and justified popular doubt about the necessity of force and the viability of visionary goals.

At the same time, citizens' capacity to check presidential belligerency is very limited. I have argued that presidents can engineer circumstances to make military conflict unavoidable. This is not meant to imply that they act in bad faith. Quite the opposite: in every instance, they have believed sincerely that the national security of the United States requires military action, a decision none has taken lightly. Once persuaded of the need to go to war as a matter of national security, however, they also see it as essential to move the public to their position, an effort that does not encourage questions. Citizens typically lack the information that would let them challenge an administration's depiction of a national security crisis. After a conflict begins, moreover, citizens can do little in the short run to influence its course, even when the war goes badly. Congress has never shown itself willing to terminate a war when American troops are still fighting. Were Congress to dictate disengagement from an unpopular conflict by cutting off funds, the legislative branch would also acquire responsibility for what follows. "In war victory has a thousand fathers but defeat is an orphan."[5] Congress has no wish to become its adoptive parent.

Although popular opposition does not stop a war, challenges to presidential leadership remain critically important. Absent hard questions, presidents will stick doggedly to their chosen course, even if it has failed. Under pressure, presidents react defensively, accusing their domestic foes of giving aid and comfort to the enemy. Nonetheless, regardless of what presidents say in public, they cannot shield themselves from criticism of war policy that enters the political mainstream. At that point, protest compels the reexamination of policy and will likely yield new diplomatic and/or military initiatives. Skeptical citizens can overcome wartime inertia, a critical role that is in the interest of the nation and those who lead it.

Presidents often underestimate the American people. A president owes it to the nation to make plain the dangers of military action and ask all to share in the cost. Instead, however, presidents secure support by not asking for sacrifice—a Faustian bargain. They believe citizens will tolerate bloodletting only if the blood is not theirs. (The temptation to fight wars this way, moreover, increases when the troops are volunteers.) But when a nation goes to war, leaders and citizens depend on each other. Victory may not be swift, or easy, or cheap. And if things do not go well and the fighting continues, popular approval purchased on the cheap proves a weak link in the arsenal a president needs to bring the war to a successful conclusion. Once the public turns its back on the war, a commander in chief has been effectively disarmed. Victory will always be beyond his grasp.

AFTERWORD

The Story behind This Book

This book owes its origins to the decision by George W. Bush to invade Iraq and oust Saddam Hussein from power in 2003. I did not support his decision, though I thought it a close call. At the time I believed, as did most Americans, that Saddam continued to hoard unconventional weapons, and the memory of the terror attacks on September 11, 2001, remained fresh. But I found the administration's attempts to connect the Iraqi dictator to al-Qaeda and other known extremist organizations unpersuasive; I also regarded the attempt to track down Osama bin Laden as a vital piece of unfinished business. Two conflicts at one time risked overstretching the resources of the American military.

Although my work as a scholar focused in part on the presidency, I had written little on wartime leadership before the Iraq War. I was in good company. Few political scientists specializing in presidential politics directed much attention to the role of war. My colleagues and I were more interested in the relationship between the White House and other institutions (especially Congress and the political parties) or in presidential "leadership style" and character. A collection of essays widely used in college courses, including mine, did not contain a chapter on the presidency in wartime. This reflected a pre-9/11 sensibility that peace was the norm (even though the frequency of U.S. military interventions abroad had increased since the end of the Cold War a decade earlier).

When I began to examine the presidency at war in the years following the invasion of Iraq, I started from a familiar point. As I noted in Chapter 4, the distinguished historian Arthur Schlesinger Jr. had coined the term "Imperial Presidency" toward the end of the Vietnam War to characterize the long-term trend toward the concentration of military and police powers in the Oval Office. This theme seemed timely again in the wake of the Iraq invasion, especially when no evidence of weapons of mass destruction was uncovered. The Bush administration also defended an expansive interpretation of executive emergency powers to meet a national security crisis, echoing and amplifying claims to extraordinary presidential power asserted by earlier wartime leaders. It appeared, as administration critics on the political left (and a few on the right) charged, that a president could lead the nation into a military conflict with no effective restraint from Congress, the public, or other nations. My initial writing on the subject argued that presidents have a free hand to either start hostilities or position American troops in a way that makes conflict inevitable.

Events in Iraq and at home, however, suggested another dimension to the argument. Following the initial success of the American invasion, U.S. troops faced a widening insurgency for which they were poorly prepared. Casualties among Iraqi civilians and American forces increased, while American diplomats made no headway in resolving the differences among Iraqi sectarian leaders. Back in the United States, public opinion began to turn against the war, contributing to Republican defeats in the 2006 midterm elections that gave control of Congress to the Democrats. Rather than too much power, it now seemed Bush had too little—that is, he could no longer influence the course of the conflict to achieve the political objectives he had identified in going to war. Where he had framed a transformative mission in Iraq—to replace a brutal dictatorship with an open liberal society that would serve as a beacon of change across the Middle East—the United States by 2007 would settle for a reduction in the sectarian bloodletting. The reduced ambition never became official policy, but U.S. military and civilian officials in Iraq clearly understood the change.

Bush demonstrated what my research identified as a fundamental characteristic of wartime presidential power: presidents begin conflicts with extraordinary freedom of action, only to see it dissipate quickly. The initial choices a president makes necessarily constrain his discretion; subsequent decisions further narrow the field of possibilities. This loss of capacity becomes most acute when presidents turn to peace-building, their efforts to shape the postwar order they hope to establish. Often they wait too long to begin to plan for what will happen when the guns fall silent. Few wartime presidents have been alert to the inevitable decline in their capacity to alter direction, shape outcomes, or influence other key political actors. Even if they were, they could not escape the dynamic; at best (as in the case of Franklin Roosevelt), they could recognize it and adapt.

The book I have written, then, has taken a very different turn from the one I first conceived. Instead of taking its place on the bookshelf of liberal laments about excesses of executive authority, this volume has a distinctly conservative cast. It expresses a profound sense of the limits of power. Presidents enter wars believing they have in their hands the military instruments to accomplish their most ambitious political goals, sometimes on a truly visionary scale. Think of Woodrow Wilson banishing war and bestowing self-determination on oppressed peoples, Roosevelt establishing a benign liberal order that would encompass all the major powers (including Stalin's Soviet Union), or Bush remaking Iraq virtually overnight into the kind of society never seen before in the region. In each instance, they have fallen short, sometimes by a vast margin. Their power has misled them, and us, too.

ACKNOWLEDGMENTS

As an author, I have the pleasure of saving the best for last—thanking the many people who helped make this book possible. I begin with my students at Hunter College, an extraordinary public university that has been my academic home for more than two decades. Soon after the United States invaded Iraq in 2003, students organized a teach-in to protest the war and invited members of the Department of Political Science to speak briefly about the war. I offered some remarks about the expansion of presidential war powers and the lack of effective constraints on their use, which prompted me to begin thinking seriously about the subject of wartime presidential leadership. The rest, as we say, is history. Subsequently, I twice taught a special topics course, "The Presidency at War," which gave me an opportunity to explore some of the themes that ultimately coalesced in this volume. Many course discussions are reflected in these pages, and I owe a debt to all of the students who participated. Special thanks go to two outstanding Hunter students, Alex Neustein and Daniel Passentino, who did honors research projects under my supervision on topics connected to wartime presidents.

My appreciation extends to many others in the Hunter College community. I was chosen to present the 2006 TIAA-CREF Distinguished

Faculty Lecture, titled "The Presidency at War, 1787–2006: Unchecked Power and Political Risk," to the faculty and guests. For that opportunity and ongoing support that included a sabbatical in 2010–2011, during which I completed the manuscript, I thank Hunter President Jennifer Raab, Provost Vita Rabinowitz, and then Dean of Arts and Sciences Shirley Clay Scott. My colleagues in the Department of Political Science have been a consistent source of intellectual stimulation and fruitful conversation, plus a healthy dose of humor. This project took shape under three department chairs, Ken Sherrill, Walter Volkomer, and Charles Tien, who encouraged it in every way possible. I am grateful, too, to my other department colleagues (some of whom have since left Hunter), Eva Bellin, Ann Cohen, Jennifer Dwyer, Ken Erickson, Lennie Feldman, Rob Jenkins, Roger Karapin, Scott Lemieux, Robyn Marasco, Lina Newton, Ros Petchesky, Cynthia Roberts, Zachary Shirkey, Carolyn Somerville, Joan Tronto, John Wallach, and Emily Zackin.

As I became interested in writing about the presidency at war, I contacted Michael Nelson, a leading scholar on the presidency who has produced multiple editions of a sophisticated college reader on the presidency, *The Presidency and the Political System*, and proposed writing a chapter on the subject for the next edition. He readily agreed, and later showed himself to be a gifted editor, too. Some portions of that chapter have been adapted here in the introduction, and I thank CQ Press, publisher of his anthology, for permission. At the invitation of Ronald M. Peters, I wrote a piece, "Collective Inaction: Presidents, Congress, and Unpopular Wars," for the Spring 2008 issue of *Extensions*, published by the Carl Albert Congressional Research and Studies Center, University of Oklahoma. I thank Ron for his careful feedback and the Center for permission to incorporate some of the material into this book. Last, I explored the difficulties faced by Lyndon Johnson in Vietnam and George W. Bush in Iraq in an article, "Staying the Course: Presidential Leadership, Military Stalemate, and Strategic Inertia," which appeared in March 2010 in *Perspectives on Politics*. I am indebted to Jeffrey C. Isaac, who guided it through the review and editorial processes. With the permission of Cambridge University Press, I have adapted some of the material for inclusion here.

Over the past several years I have presented a number of lectures that helped me refine ideas for this book. On three occasions Jerry Mileur, professor emeritus of political science at the University of Massachusetts, invited me to present lectures on wartime presidential leadership to his summer cohort of international scholars. Nicole Mellow also gave me the opportunity to speak on the subject to her Williams College students. It was a privilege to deliver a series of four lectures on the theme, "Victory in the Balance: How Presidents Wage War," to the Smithsonian Resident Associate Program in Washington, D.C., on November 6, 2010. For that opportunity and the arrangements, my thanks go to Anna Lakovitch and Kristin Schmehl. Sid Milkis generously alerted the Smithsonian staff of my research and thus made my appearance there possible. He also spoke of my work to his University of Virginia colleague John Owen, which resulted in an invitation to a conference co-sponsored by the university's Miller Center and the journal *Security Studies* on the impact of recent American presidents on foreign policy. At that event I had the opportunity to present material drawn from chapters 5 and 6 of this book. Feedback from the participants, especially Ron Krebs, helped me refine my arguments.

A number of scholars offered constructive criticism of individual chapters of this book, based on their expertise in particular wartime presidencies and historical eras. I am deeply grateful for the generous help I received from James McPherson, Jon Rosenberg, Warren Kimball, Larry Berman, Jim Pfiffner, and Stephen Dyson. For comments and ideas on my earlier writings on presidential war powers and wartime leadership, I also thank William Adler, Don Anderson, MaryAnne Borrelli, John A. Garafano, Fred I. Greenstein, Joel Lefkowitz, Bruce Miroff, Stepen Pimpare, Stanley Renshon, and Brandon Rottinghaus. They all did their best to steer me in the right direction and correct mistakes. None of them shares responsibility for my interpretations or for any errors that may remain.

A book project is not a book, of course, until it finds a publisher. In helping me navigate the path into the world of commercial publishing, a tip of my hat goes to Phil Alcabes, Ruth O'Brien, Corey Robin, Rogan Kersh, and especially Jim Morone. When I went in search of a literary agent, I connected with Ted Weinstein, who combined realism and optimism in just the right amounts. He made the happy match with Tim Bent of Oxford University Press. Recognizing that as a recovering scholarly writer I still occasionally relapsed into dense academic prose, Tim has used his deft editorial touch to help me stay clean. We both know I have to take it one day at a time.

Others at Oxford have assisted in the editorial, production, and publicity phases of bringing this book project to completion. Patterson Lamb has been an attentive and effective copy editor. I am grateful for the help of Keely Latcham, Lana Goldsmith, Lora Friedenthal, and Tara Kennedy.

My greatest debt goes to my family. Even as an author writes, life goes on all around, sadness mixed with joy. I lost both of my parents as I was writing, but I spent many hours talking over my ideas with my father during his last year and he was able to read the conclusion before he passed. On the happier side, my wife and our two children joined in this project from the beginning. They have lived (that is, put up) with both the book and its author for several years, and done so with patience, humor, and many excellent suggestions. I thought I had mastered the fine art of appearing to pay attention to them while I was writing; in reality, they were not fooled, and they became accustomed to repeating themselves until I actually did tune in. My daughter Sara Polsky, a journalist and very talented wordsmith, read each chapter and gave me careful editorial comments. I discussed many of the military aspects of wartime leadership with my son Alex Polsky, who was recently commissioned a second lieutenant in the U.S. Army and is scheduled to be in training to become an infantry officer when this book appears. Through Alex I met a number of his fellow ROTC cadets from the Hoya Battalion in Washington, D.C. My respect for their dedication has increased my appreciation for the anxiety a president faces when he asks members of the armed forces to put their lives on the line. When I think of my wife Beth Morgenstern, my partner in all good things, I wish that I had the gifts of the poet or songwriter to express all she has meant to me, given me, and shared with me. Sadly, I don't. But I do know how blessed I have been to share life's ups and downs with a truly remarkable woman.

NOTES

———⟨∘⟩⟨∘⟩———

Introduction

1. Albert A. Nofi, *The Spanish American War, 1898* (Cambridge, MA: Da Capo Press, 1997).
2. Nofi, *Spanish American War*; Lewis L. Gould, *The Spanish American War and President McKinley* (Lawrence: University Press of Kansas, 1980, 1982), 70–71.
3. Nofi, *Spanish American War*, chap. 5; Gould, *Spanish American War and President McKinley*, 75–76.
4. This figure is larger than the total that eventually participated in the invasion because some units were withheld from the actual attack.
5. The United States committed 8,000 troops to counterterrorism operations in Afghanistan in 2002. Seth G. Jones, *In the Graveyard of Empires: America's War in Afghanistan* (New York: Norton, 2009, 2010), 115.
6. Among many published accounts of the Iraq invasion, see especially Thomas E. Ricks, *Fiasco: The American Military Adventure in Iraq* (New York: Penguin Books, 2006, 2007); Michael R. Gordon and General Bernard E. Trainor, *Cobra II: The Inside Story of the Invasion and Occupation of Iraq* (New York: Pantheon, 2006).
7. American naval forces launched a swift attack on the Spanish in Manila Bay and occupied the city of Manila. See Brian McAllister Linn, *The Philippine War, 1899–1902* (Lawrence: University Press of Kansas, 2000).
8. Early Bush administration discussions about Iraq are recounted in Bob Woodward, *Bush at War* (New York: Simon and Schuster, 2002).

9. Linn, *The Philippine War*; John M. Gates, "Philippine Guerillas, American Anti-Imperialists, and the Election of 1900," *Pacific Historical Review* 46 (1) (February 1977): 51–64.

10. Thucydides, *The Peloponnesian War* (New York: Modern Library, 1951).

11. Thucydides, *The Peloponnesian War*, 45.

12. Carl von Clausewitz, *On War*, Michael Howard and Peter Paret, eds. (Princeton: Princeton University Press, 1976, 1989).

13. See, for example, John Yoo, *Crisis and Command: A History of Executive Power from George Washington to George W. Bush* (New York: Kaplan, 2010).

14. Samuel P. Huntington, *The Soldier and the State: The Theory and Politics of Civil-Military Relations* (Cambridge: Belknap Press of Harvard University Press, 1957).

15. My analysis divides military affairs into three levels: the strategic, the operational, and the tactical. The first, strategy, addresses the larger plan behind a war; the intermediate or operational refers to particular campaigns within the larger strategic design; and the tactical covers actual methods of fighting an enemy. Although this distinction is common among military theorists and many writers on military matters, it is not universal. Some writers speak of grand strategy, to refer to the general approach a country adopts in pursuit of its national interest in the international arena. Journalists, on the other hand, often collapse the strategic/operational distinction.

16. Eliot A. Cohen, *Supreme Command: Soldiers, Statesmen, and Leadership in Wartime* (New York: Anchor Books/Random House, 2002).

17. Cohen, *Supreme Command*, chap. 6.

18. On the problems of planning for peace, see Gideon Rose, *How Wars End: Why We Always Fight the Last Battle* (New York: Simon and Schuster, 2010).

19. George C. Edwards III, *The Strategic President: Persuasion and Opportunity in Presidential Leadership* (Princeton: Princeton University Press, 2009).

20. Stephen Skowronek, *Presidential Leadership in Political Time: Reprise and Reappraisal* (Lawrence: University Press of Kansas, 2008), 162ff.

21. Joseph R. Avella, "The President, Congress, and Decisions to Employ Military Force," in *The Presidency Then and Now*, ed. Phillip G. Henderson (Lanham, MD: Rowman and Littlefield, 2000), 51–52.

22. Avella, "The President, Congress, and Decisions to Employ Military Force," 57.

23. Louis Fisher, "Congressional Checks on Military Initiatives," *Political Science Quarterly* 109 (1994–1995): 739–62.

24. It is more accurate in this context to speak of the Framers' mixed intentions. Alexander Hamilton stressed the need for an energetic chief executive who could act with dispatch in a crisis. For him, unilateral executive initiative in a national security emergency would

be essential. As noted earlier, however, Madison recognized the value of bringing multiple voices into deliberations on matters of such importance, and his own actions on the eve of the War of 1812 reflect in part this commitment.

25. That lawmakers would flinch before exercising the power of the purse during a war became evident early on. In mid-1847 the American war against Mexico was becoming increasingly unpopular back home. American forces had enjoyed brilliant successes on the battlefield that left them in control of Mexico City itself, but the Mexican government refused to negotiate an end to the war on terms acceptable to the administration of President James K. Polk. (These terms included cession of the Mexican provinces of Upper California and New Mexico to the United States and Mexican recognition of the Rio Grande as the border between Texas and Mexico.) With few good options at his disposal, the president asked Congress for additional military appropriations to increase pressure on the enemy. Just how that could be done short of occupying the entire country was not clear. Nevertheless, to the dismay of Polk's critics in the opposition Whig Party, Congress had little choice but to go along with his request. As one Whig writer put it in the party's leading journal, Congress "would never refuse to grant anything and everything necessary or proper for the support and succor of our brave troops, placed without any fault of their own, in the heart of a distant country, and struggling with every peril, discomfort and difficulty." See "The Whigs and the War," *American Review* 6 (October 1847): 343, as quoted in Norman Graebner, "Lessons of the Mexican War," *Pacific Historical Review* 47 (August 1978): 325–42.

26. John H. Schroeder, *Mr. Polk's War: American Opposition and Dissent, 1846–1848* (Madison: University of Wisconsin Press, 1973), chap. 1.

27. Edward Joseph Rhodes, "Sea Change: Interest-Based Vs. Cultural-Cognitive Accounts of Strategic Choice in the 1890s," *Security Studies* 5 (1996): 73–124; Mark R. Shulman, "Institutionalizing a Political Idea: Navalism and the Emergence of American Sea Power," in *The Politics of Strategic Adjustment: Ideas, Institutions, and Interests*, ed. Peter Trubowitz, Emily O. Goldman, and Edward Joseph Rhodes (New York: Columbia University Press, 1999), 79–104. My view of this development has been influenced by Douglas Haugen, *The Epistemic Origins of American Empire*, Ph.D. Dissertation, City University of New York, 2007.

28. On the pressure for rapid demobilization, see Michael S. Sherry, *In the Shadow of War: The United States since the 1930s* (New Haven: Yale University Press, 1995), 118.

29. Sherry, *In the Shadow of War*, 116ff.

30. Aaron L. Friedberg, *In the Shadow of the Garrison State: America's Anti-Statism and Its Cold War Strategy* (Princeton: Princeton University Press, 2000), chap. 2

31. Michael J. Hogan, *A Cross of Iron: Harry S. Truman and the Origins of the National Security State, 1945–1954* (Cambridge: Cambridge University Press, 1998).

32. American military expenditures dwarf those of any other nation, amounting to roughly half of the world's entire defense outlays.

33. Sherry, *In the Shadow of War*; Andrew D. Grossman, *Neither Dead Nor Red: Civilian Defense and American Political Development during the Early Cold War* (New York: Routledge, 2001).

34. Andrew J. Bacevich, *The New American Militarism: How Americans Are Seduced by War* (Oxford: Oxford University Press, 2005), 2.

35. Bacevich, *New American Militarism*, 22ff.

36. See Jane Mayer, "The Predator War," *The New Yorker*, October 26, 2009, http://www.newyorker.com/reporting/2009/10/26/091026fa_fact_mayer.

37. Robert F. Turner, "The War on Terrorism and the Modern Relevance of the Congressional Power to 'Declare War,'" *Harvard Journal of Law and Public Policy* 25 (Spring 2002): 519–37.

38. On the timing of these votes see Gary R. Hess, *Presidential Decisions for War: Korea, Vietnam, the Persian Gulf, and Iraq*, 2nd ed. (Baltimore: Johns Hopkins University Press, 2009), "Conclusion."

39. *United States v. Curtiss-Wright Export Corp.*, 299 U.S. 304 (1936).

40. The Supreme Court had suffered a loss of prestige from its *Dred Scott* (1857) decision, and Chief Justice Taney was in a particularly compromised position because of his role in that case—Lincoln had frequently condemned the ruling. Lincoln made clear early in the Civil War that he would disregard the judiciary if it interfered with his efforts to put down the rebellion.

41. Bacevich, *New American Militarism*, 40–54.

42. Bacevich, *New American Militarism*, 19.

43. Conventional wars settled by recourse to mechanized arms were fought primarily in the Middle East, including several conflicts between Israel and its Arab neighbors, the Iran-Iraq War of the 1980s, and the 1991 Persian Gulf War. India and Pakistan also fought wars on the same model.

44. On the general concept of revolutions in military affairs, see MacGregor Knox and Williamson Murray, eds., *The Dynamics of Military Revolution, 1300–2050* (Cambridge: Cambridge University Press, 2001).

45. General Rupert Smith, *The Utility of Force: The Art of War in the Modern World* (New York: Alfred A. Knopf, 2007).

46. In his influential book on the presidency, Stephen Skowronek suggests similarly that the three historical logics of continuity, change, and recurrence establish the framework for explaining presidential leadership across time. He identifies the Constitution as the source of continuity, describes broad modernizing trends in American politics as a key source of change, and sees the rise and decline of partisan governing coalitions and presidents' relationships to those coalitions as creating recurrent

leadership opportunity structures. See Stephen Skowronek, *The Politics Presidents Make: Leadership from John Adams to George Bush* (Cambridge, MA: Belknap Press of Harvard University Press, 1993).

47. For a particularly careful account of several presidential decisions to go to war, see Hess, *Presidential Decisions for War*.

48. James M. McPherson, *Abraham Lincoln and the Second American Revolution* (New York: Oxford University Press, 1991), chap. 4.

49. Presidents may choose not to issue orders, preferring instead to make suggestions to their military subordinates or to persuade through reasoned discussion. But behind these alternatives lies the possibility of command (and sanction for disobedience). Of course, orders are not necessarily obeyed by military subordinates, and we should note that some wartime presidents have been frustrated by compliance problems. Lincoln once complained, "I am as powerless as any private citizen to shape the military plans of the government." Geoffrey Perret, *Lincoln's War: The Untold Story of America's Greatest President as Commander in Chief* (New York: Random House, 2004), 340.

50. David R. Mayhew, "Wars and American Politics," *Perspectives on Politics* 3 (September 2005): 473–93.

51. Seth Jones finds that governments prevail more often in insurgencies than do rebels, but the longer a conflict drags on the less likely it is that the government side will prevail. See Jones, *In the Graveyard of Empires*, 153–54.

52. Only George H. W. Bush in 1990–1991 encountered strong legislative doubts about his plans to eject Hussein's troops from Kuwait. Antiwar legislators in 1991 displayed considerable backbone, questioning whether military action should be postponed until economic sanctions and diplomacy had been given every chance to compel Saddam Hussein to withdraw Iraqi troops from Kuwait. The congressional resolution supporting the use of force passed by only a narrow margin. Hess, *Presidential Decisions for War*, 190–94.

53. Rose, *How Wars End*, 4–5.

Chapter 1

1. Abraham Lincoln, "Address at Gettysburg Pennsylvania," in Lincoln, *Selected Speeches and Writings* (New York: Vintage/Library of America, 1992), 405.

2. For an enumeration of his mistakes by sympathetic scholars, see James M. McPherson, *Tried by War: Abraham Lincoln as Commander in Chief* (New York: Penguin, 2008), 266–67. Recent critics go further: they see Lincoln as reckless in his willingness to embrace war as a response to secession and stress the sheer destructiveness of the conflict. See William Marvel, *Mr. Lincoln Goes to War* (New York: Houghton Mifflin, 2006).

Such an outlook has a long lineage, as some earlier generations of historians regarded the war as a tragic and avoidable mistake.

3. See especially James M. McPherson, *Abraham Lincoln and the Second American Revolution* (New York: Oxford University Press, 1991), chap. 4; McPherson, *Tried by War*; Gabor S. Boritt, ed. *Lincoln's Generals* (New York: Oxford University Press, 1994); Eric Foner, *Reconstruction: America's Unfinished Revolution, 1863–1877* (1988; reprint ed., New York: Perennial Classics, 2002).

4. Eliot A. Cohen, *Supreme Command: Soldiers, Statesmen, and Leadership in Wartime* (New York: Anchor Books/Random House, 2002), chap. 2.

5. McPherson, *Tried by War*, 9.

6. Richard Franklin Bensel, *Yankee Leviathan: The Origins of Central State Authority in America, 1859–1877* (Cambridge: Cambridge University Press, 1990), 101, 103.

7. McPherson, *Tried by War*, 14.

8. Abraham Lincoln, "First Inaugural Address," in Lincoln, *Selected Speeches and Writings* (New York: Vintage/Library of America, 1992), 284–93.

9. Marvel, *Mr. Lincoln Goes to War*, 20.

10. McPherson, *Tried by War*, 9–10. By way of historical parallels, all modern states have suppressed secessionist movements, so any other choice by Lincoln would have been surprising. Bensel, *Yankee Leviathan*, 60.

11. McPherson, *Tried by War*, 14–21.

12. Marvel, *Mr. Lincoln Goes to War*, 50–56.

13. Marvel, *Mr. Lincoln Goes to War*, 30–31.

14. McPherson, *Tried by War*, 7–8; David Herbert Donald, *Lincoln* (New York: Simon and Schuster, 1995), 296.

15. McPherson, *Abraham Lincoln and the Second American Revolution*, 73.

16. McPherson, *Tried by War*, 35–36; McPherson, *Abraham Lincoln and the Second American Revolution*, 75–76.

17. McPherson, *Abraham Lincoln and the Second American Revolution*, 81–82.

18. McPherson, *Tried by War*, 58–59.

19. McPherson, *Tried by War*, 59–60.

20. McPherson, *Abraham Lincoln and the Second American Revolution*, 85.

21. McPherson, *Abraham Lincoln and the Second American Revolution*, 83–84.

22. McPherson, *Abraham Lincoln and the Second American Revolution*, 84–85.

23. McPherson, *Abraham Lincoln and the Second American Revolution*, 85.

24. McPherson, *Tried by War*, 86.

25. Herman Hattaway, "Lincoln's Presidential Example in Dealing with the Military," *Papers of the Abraham Lincoln Association* 7 (1985): 23–24.

26. McPherson, *Abraham Lincoln and the Second American Revolution*, 86–87.

27. Abraham Lincoln, "Second Inaugural Address," in Lincoln, *Selected Speeches and Writings* (New York: Vintage/Library of America, 1992), 450.

28. For a concise discussion of the Prussian General Staff as developed by Helmuth von Moltke, see General Rupert Smith, *The Utility of Force: The Art of War in the Modern World* (New York: Alfred A. Knopf, 2007), 95–100.

29. McPherson, *Tried by War*, 23.

30. McPherson, *Tried by War*, 42–43.

31. McPherson, *Tried by War*, 171–72.

32. Although dated and marred by a definite anti-Republican bias, Hesseltine's work treats these issues in depth. See William B. Hesseltine, *Lincoln and the War Governors* (New York: Alfred A. Knopf, 1948, 1955), chaps. 11–12.

33. Cohen, *Supreme Command*.

34. Andrew J. Polsky, "'Mr. Lincoln's Army' Revisited: Partisanship, Institutional Position, and Union Army Command, 1861–1865," *Studies in American Political Development* 16 (2) (Fall 2002): 176–207.

35. McPherson, *Tried by War*, 41–44. See similarly McPherson, *Abraham Lincoln and the Second American Revolution*, 70–71.

36. Richard Bruce Winders, *Mr. Polk's Army* (College Station: Texas A and M University Press, 1997), 36, 64–65.

37. Thomas J. Goss, *The War within the Union High Command: Politics and Generalship during the Civil War* (Lawrence: University Press of Kansas, 2003).

38. John Y. Simon, "Grant, Lincoln, and Unconditional Surrender," in *Lincoln's Generals*, ed. Gabor S. Boritt (New York: Oxford University Press, 1995), 171.

39. Ezra J. Warner, *Generals in Blue: Lives of the Union Commanders* (Baton Rouge: Louisiana State University Press, 1964, 1996), 234–35.

40. See Polsky, "'Mr. Lincoln's Army' Revisited," 189–91. Historians have long attributed partisanship to Union officers based on very loose standards of evidence, resulting in higher estimates of partisanship.

41. On McClellan's political ambitions, see Stephen W. Sears, *George B. McClellan: The Young Napoleon* (1988; reprint ed., New York: Da Capo Press, 1999), chaps. 5–6.

42. McPherson, *Tried by War*, 114–15, 137. Buell's biographer asserts that he held strong Democratic beliefs and had owned slaves until the very beginning of the war. Stephen D. Engle, *Don Carlos Buell: Most Promising of All* (Chapel Hill: University of North Carolina Press, 1999).

43. Polsky, "'Mr. Lincoln's Army' Revisited," 193–94.

44. McPherson, *Tried by War*, 268–69.

45. McPherson, *Tried by War*, 2–3, 69–71; Herman Hattaway and Archer Jones, "Lincoln as a Military Strategist," *Civil War History* 26 (1980): 293–303; Hattaway, "Lincoln's Presidential Example in Dealing with the Military," 18–20.

46. Cohen, *Supreme Command*, 23–29.

47. For revealing figures on the disparity in industrial resources, see James M. McPherson, *Battle Cry of Freedom: The Civil War Era* (Oxford: Oxford University Press, 1988), 318–19.

48. Hattaway, "Lincoln's Presidential Example in Dealing with the Military," 20–21.

49. McPherson, *Tried by War*, 34.

50. On the development of the Union's western strategy, see Hattaway, "Lincoln's Presidential Example in Dealing with the Military," 23.

51. McPherson, *Tried by War*, 199.

52. William J. Cooper Jr., *Jefferson Davis, American* (New York: Vintage, 2001), 488.

53. For a discussion of Lincoln's relations with each of these commanders, see Boritt, ed., *Lincoln's Generals*.

54. Until January 1863, the Army of the Cumberland was known as the Army of the Ohio. Its history is covered in detail in Larry J. Daniel, *Days of Glory: The Army of the Cumberland, 1861–1865* (Baton Rouge: Louisiana State University Press, 2004).

55. On the history of this formation, see Steven J. Woodworth, *Nothing but Victory: The Army of the Tennessee, 1861–1865* (New York: Vintage Civil War Library, 2006).

56. Peter Cozzens, *The Darkest Days of the War: The Battles of Iuka and Corinth* (Chapel Hill: University of North Carolina Press, 1997), 322

57. Herman Hattaway and Archer Jones, *How the North Won: A Military History of the Civil War* (Urbana: University of Illinois Press, 1983, 1991), 377, 391.

58. Hattaway, "Lincoln's Presidential Example in Dealing with the Military," 20.

59. See Kenneth P. Williams, *Lincoln Finds a General: A Military Study of the Civil War*, 5 volumes (New York: Macmillan, 1949–1959).

60. Cohen, *Supreme Command*, 49–50.

61. Cohen credits Lincoln with a striking capacity to act without illusions. Cohen, *Strategic Command*, 22. Although this was true in the main, there were glaring and costly exceptions,

62. McPherson, *Tried by War*, 34–35.

63. McPherson, *Tried by War*, 63.

64. McPherson, *Tried by War*, 187–89, 209–10, 216–17.

65. The fullest account of this campaign is Peter Cozzens, *Shenandoah 1862: Stonewall Jackson's Valley Campaign* (Chapel Hill: University of North Carolina Press, 2008).

66. Lincoln's effort to goad Meade into an attack remains a controversial subject to this day. On one side are those who maintain that, because a successful assault might have ended the war, it was worth the obvious risks; the counterargument holds that Meade would have thrown away the fruits of a great victory by sending his battered army (which itself

suffered losses in excess of 20 percent at Gettysburg) against an entrenched foe. As Hattaway points out, "Lincoln understood the power
of the defense and the futility of trying to destroy an enemy army in the
open field." Hattaway, "Lincoln's Presidential Example in Dealing with
the Military," 24. But the president seems to have forgotten this lesson
every time a Confederate force advanced onto northern soil. McPherson,
Tried by War, 268.

67. I consider here only Davis as a military commander in chief. Were the
discussion to extend to other aspects of his role as a wartime political
leader, such as laying a financial basis for the war or wartime international
diplomacy, he would fare even worse. For example, on Davis's failure
to understand the financial side of the war, see Cooper, *Jefferson Davis*,
377–78.

68. Historically, the British regarded a blockade to be in effect so long as a
navy patrolled outside a port and intercepted most ships seeking to enter
or leave. Although private blockade runners continued to penetrate the
U.S. Navy's cordon around southern ports, these examples did not suffice
to show that the blockade was ineffective. See Cooper, *Jefferson Davis,
American*, 394.

69. Smith, *Utility of Force*, 158–61.

70. Cooper, *Jefferson Davis, American*, 480–81.

71. Cooper, *Jefferson Davis, American*, 485–86.

72. Cooper, *Jefferson Davis, American*, 478–79.

73. Cooper, *Jefferson Davis, American*, 404.

74. Cooper, *Jefferson Davis, American*, 444, 448–49.

75. Cooper, *Jefferson Davis, American*, 429, 471, 474, 520.

76. Cooper, *Jefferson Davis, American*, 428.

77. Cooper, *Jefferson Davis, American*, 454–55, 472, 502.

78. Cooper, *Jefferson Davis, American*, 385, 440.

79. Cooper, *Jefferson Davis, American*, 382, 389–92, 467.

80. McPherson, *Tried by War*, 163–64. Although the incident has been widely
repeated in historical accounts, some question whether Hooker actually
did express support for a dictatorship. See Mark E. Neely Jr., "Wilderness
and the Cult of Manliness: Hooker, Lincoln, and Defeat," in *Lincoln's
Generals*, ed. Boritt, 56. Lincoln's tolerance for the human frailties of his
generals is noted by Cohen, *Supreme Command*, 20–21.

81. Cooper, *Jefferson Davis, American*, 491–93.

82. Cooper, *Jefferson Davis, American*, 518. It is not clear whether Davis
appreciated the need in 1864 to play for time with the northern elections
pending. Although Davis's best recent biographer contends that Johnston barely impeded Sherman, the fullest study of the campaign suggests
otherwise, crediting the Confederate general with deft maneuvering
that greatly hampered the northern advance. Compare Cooper, *Jefferson
Davis, American*, 521, with Albert E. Castel, *Decision in the West: The*

Atlanta Campaign of 1864 (Lawrence: University Press of Kansas, 1995). Others in the South seemed to have a better appreciation than did Davis that delaying Sherman fed popular discontent in the North before the election. McPherson, *Tried by War*, 233.

83. McPherson, *Tried by War*, 240.

84. Cooper, *Jefferson Davis, American*, 522, 525.

85. McPherson, *Tried by War*, 233–34, 240.

86. Foner, *Reconstruction*, 32. The three days of riots resulted in the deaths of as many as 500 persons and forced the Lincoln administration to send troops from the Army of the Potomac to assure order in the city. Some New York politicians, including Governor Horatio Seymour, contributed to the violence through their anti-draft statements. Hattaway and Jones, *How the North Won*, 440.

87. How much opposition Davis faced remains a matter of contention among historians. The most recent serious biography suggests that opposition was scattered and that he retained broad public backing. But draft resistance in the South was also serious, and some regions of the Confederacy, including East Tennessee and the mountainous western part of North Carolina, seem to have been barely under the control of the Confederate government. See Cooper, *Jefferson Davis, American*. Davis did not have to stand for reelection during the war because the Confederate constitution gave the president a six-year term.

88. Doris Kearns Goodwin, *Team of Rivals: The Political Genius of Abraham Lincoln* (New York: Simon and Schuster, 2005, 2006). See also Donald, *Lincoln*, 478–80.

89. Donald, *Lincoln*, 331–33.

90. On the constitutive role that skepticism toward executive power played in the Whig Party, see Michael F. Holt, *The Rise and Fall of the American Whig Party: Jacksonian Politics and the Onset of the Civil War* (Oxford: Oxford University Press, 1999), 29.

91. McPherson, *Tried by War*, 234–40.

92. Donald, *Lincoln*, 525–26.

93. Donald, *Lincoln*, 441–42.

94. Lincoln, "Address at Gettysburg, Pennsylvania," 405.

95. Abraham Lincoln to Albert G. Hodges, April 4, 1864, in Lincoln, *Selected Speeches and Writings* (New York: Vintage Books/Library of America, 1992), 419–21.

96. Abraham Lincoln to Horace Greeley, August 22, 1862, Lincoln, *Selected Speeches and Writings* (New York: Vintage Books/Library of America, 1992), 343.

97. Donald, *Lincoln*, 368–69.

98. Samuel Kernell, "Life before Polls: Ohio Politicians Predict the 1828 Presidential Vote," *PS: Political Science and Politics* 33 (3) (September 2000): 569–74.

99. Joel H. Silbey, *The American Political Nation, 1838–1893* (Stanford, CA: Stanford University Press, 1991), 54–55.

100. For a discussion of the Union Party that treats it as more independent of the Republicans, see Christopher Dell, *Lincoln and the War Democrats: The Grand Erosion of Conservative Tradition* (Rutherford, NJ: Fairleigh Dickinson University Press, 1975). The details in his account, however, support my claim that the new party functioned to advance Republican purposes.

101. Hesseltine, *Lincoln and the War Governors*, chaps. 9–10.

102. Hesseltine, *Lincoln and the War Governors*, 313–15; Mark E. Neely Jr., *The Union Divided: Party Conflict in the Civil War North* (Cambridge: Harvard University Press, 2002), 184.

103. Avram Fechter, "Lincoln and the Civil War State," in *A History of the U.S. Political System: Ideas, Interests, and Institutions*, volume 1, ed. Daniel J. Tichenor and Richard A. Harris (Boulder, CO: ABC-CLIO, 2010), 338.

104. McPherson, *Tried by War*, 174–75; Donald, *Lincoln*, 456–58.

105. Neely, *The Union Divided*, chap. 7.

106. Neely, *The Union Divided*, 191.

107. Neely, *The Union Divided*, 175, 186, 188–89.

108. Bensel, *Yankee Leviathan*, 98–99.

109. Donald, *Lincoln*, 331.

110. Fechter, "Lincoln and the Civil War State," 333–34.

111. Bensel, *Yankee Leviathan*, 170–74, 225; Donald, *Lincoln*, 424.

112. Bensel, *Yankee Leviathan*, 168–70.

113. Robert W. Johannsen, ed., *The Lincoln-Douglas Debates of 1858* (New York: Oxford University Press, 1965), 51–52.

114. Johannsen, *The Lincoln-Douglas Debates of 1858*.

115. Abraham Lincoln, "Address on Colonization to a Committee of Colored Men, Washington, D.C.," in Lincoln, *Selected Speeches and Writings* (New York: Vintage/Library of America, 1992), 338–42.

116. Foner, *Reconstruction*, 6.

117. Donald, *Lincoln*, 430–31.

118. Foner, *Reconstruction*, 61–62.

119. Foner, *Reconstruction*, chap. 2.

120. Foner, *Reconstruction*, 36, 61–62.

121. Fechter, "Lincoln and the Civil War State," 334.

122. Donald, *Lincoln*, 471–74.

123. Fonner, *Reconstruction*, 55–56, 60, 63–64.

124. Donald, *Lincoln*, 486–88.

125. Foner, *Reconstruction*, 61.

126. Donald, *Lincoln*, 552–54.

127. Abraham Lincoln, "Second Inaugural Address," in Lincoln, *Selected Speeches and Writings* (New York: Vintage/Library of America, 1992), 449–50.

128. His only public support for black suffrage came in the final speech he gave before his assassination. Foner, *Reconstruction*, 74.

129. Foner, *Reconstruction*, 68–70.

130. Donald, *Lincoln*, 564.
131. On the divisions within the Republican Party, see especially Bensel, *Yankee Leviathan*.
132. Bensel, *Yankee Leviathan*, 14, 238, 303–5.
133. James M. McPherson, *This Mighty Scourge: Perspectives on the Civil War* (Oxford: Oxford University Press, 2007), 216.
134. McPherson, *This Mighty Scourge*, 210–11.
135. McPherson, *This Mighty Scourge*, 211–12.
136. James McPherson contends that due to odd-year spring congressional elections in some northern states, July 1861 was the earliest that the new Congress could meet. See McPherson, *This Mighty Scourge*, 211. But this presumes there was more to be gained by having states such as Kentucky send representatives than by having Congress approve war measures through the established legislative process. Given that Congress would be incomplete anyway—the seceded states had withdrawn—the sacrifice of constitutional propriety seems too great.
137. McPherson, *This Mighty Scourge*, 214.
138. Cooper, *Jefferson Davis*, 415.
139. McPherson, *This Mighty Scourge*, 213. Although the Confederate government used its power to suspend habeas corpus more selectively, it does not follow that civil liberties were any more secure in the South. In areas of strong Unionist sentiment such as East Tennessee, extrajudicial repression of Unionists assumed savage form, including murders without trial.
140. McPherson, *This Mighty Scourge*, 216.
141. McPherson, *This Mighty Scourge*, 216.
142. Fechter, *Lincoln and the Civil War State*, 339.
143. McPherson, *This Mighty Scourge*, 215.
144. McPherson, *This Mighty Scourge*, 218–20.
145. McPherson, *This Mighty Scourge*, 209. Andrew Jackson earlier insisted that a president might veto a bill on policy grounds alone, but Whigs saw that as another example of an overreaching executive. Thus, although Lincoln plainly disagreed with Wade-Davis as policy, he felt it necessary to rationalize the veto on a constitutional basis.
146. McPherson, *This Mighty Scourge*, 214–15.
147. Fechter, *Lincoln and the Civil War State*, 333.
148. McPherson, *This Mighty Scourge*, 215.
149. Lincoln, *Second Inaugural Address*, 449.

Chapter 2

1. Robert H. Ferrell, "Woodrow Wilson: A Misfit in Office?" in *Commanders in Chief: Presidential Leadership in Modern Wars*, ed. Joseph G. Dawson III (Kansas: University Press of Kansas, 1993), 65–86. Among the strongly pro-Wilson accounts, see especially Arthur Link and John

W. Chambers, "Woodrow Wilson as Commander-in-Chief," in *The United States Military under the Constitution of the United States, 1789–1989*, ed. Richard Kohn (New York: NYU Press, 1991), 317–75. At the other extreme, the anti-Wilson polemics, see Jim Powell, *Wilson's War: How Woodrow Wilson's Greatest Blunder Led to Hitler, Lenin, Stalin and World War II* (New York: Crown Forum, 2005). Pulling no punches, Powell makes plain his view of Wilson on the first page of his book: "Wilson surely ranks as the worst president in American history."

2. Kendrick A. Clements, *The Presidency of Woodrow Wilson* (Lawrence: University Press of Kansas, 1992), xv. Clemenceau was not alone in his view. Sigmund Freud also concluded that the president identified himself with Jesus Christ. J. A. Thompson, "Woodrow Wilson and World War I: A Reappraisal," *Journal of American Studies* 19 (3) (1985): 326.

3. Other nations also joined the war on each side, including Italy and Japan with the Allies and Rumania with both at different times.

4. John Patrick Finnegan, *Against the Specter of a Dragon: The Campaign for American Military Preparedness, 1914–1917* (Westport, CT: Greenwood Press, 1974), 6.

5. David F. Trask, "The American Presidency, National Security, and Intervention from McKinley to Wilson," in *The United States Military under the Constitution of the United States, 1789–1989*, ed. Richard Kohn (New York: NYU Press, 1991), 292–93.

6. Trask, "American Presidency," 297–99.

7. Clements, *Presidency of Woodrow Wilson*, 116.

8. David Trask claims that Wilson saw a need to prevent German hegemony, but he is vague about just when the president did so. See Trask, "American Presidency," 300.

9. Clements, *Presidency of Woodrow Wilson*, 116.

10. There were notable exceptions. Radicals hoped defeat would topple the repressive regimes they had fled.

11. Finnegan, *Against the Specter of a Dragon*, 23.

12. David M. Esposito, "Political and Institutional Constraints on Wilson's Defense Policy," *Presidential Studies Quarterly* 26 (4) (Fall 1996): 1116.

13. Clements, *Presidency of Woodrow Wilson*, 119.

14. Arthur S. Link, *The Higher Realism of Woodrow Wilson and Other Essays* (Nashville: Vanderbilt University Press, 1971), 89.

15. Clements, *Presidency of Woodrow Wilson*, 120–22.

16. This policy would be adopted by Franklin Roosevelt early in the Second World War. Kendrick A. Clements, "Woodrow Wilson and World War I," *Presidential Studies Quarterly* 34 (1) (March 2004): 63.

17. Clements, *Presidency of Woodrow Wilson*, 127.

18. Clements, *Presidency of Woodrow Wilson*, 119.

19. Clements, *Presidency of Woodrow Wilson*, 129.

20. Clements, "Woodrow Wilson and World War I," 65–68, 70–71; Clements, *Presidency of Woodrow Wilson*, 117–18, 121–22.

21. Clements, "Woodrow Wilson and World War I," 62–63, 81; Clements, *Presidency of Woodrow Wilson*, 125.
22. Clements, "Woodrow Wilson and World War I," 73.
23. Clements, *Presidency of Woodrow Wilson*, 125–28.
24. Clements, "Woodrow Wilson and World War I," 62–63; Thompson, "Woodrow Wilson and World War I," 334, 336.
25. Clements, *Presidency of Woodrow Wilson*, 126.
26. Clements, *Presidency of Woodrow Wilson*, 131–32.
27. Ferrell, "Woodrow Wilson: Misfit in Office?" 65–66.
28. Clements, *Presidency of Woodrow Wilson*, 123–24. House's title was honorific. Wilson's emissaries did not always do his bidding, however. As House became more pro-Allied, he sought to commit the president to enter the war on the side of the Entente if Germany refused to negotiate a peace agreement. See Clements, *Presidency of Woodrow Wilson*, 129–30.
29. Clements, *Presidency of Woodrow Wilson*, 129–31; Thompson, "Woodrow Wilson and World War I," 336.
30. Trask, "American Presidency," 307.
31. Clements, *Presidency of Woodrow Wilson*, 137.
32. Trask, "American Presidency," 302. Trask adds that because the war represented a fundamental challenge to stability by German power, the issues could not be resolved by anything less than complete victory for one side.
33. Clements, *Presidency of Woodrow Wilson*, 124.
34. Margaret MacMillan, *Paris 1919: Six Months that Changed the World* (New York: Random House, 2001, 2003), chap. 22.
35. Link, *Higher Realism of Woodrow Wilson*, 97.
36. Clements, *Presidency of Woodrow Wilson*, 136.
37. Finnegan, *Against the Specter of a Dragon*, 25, 28.
38. Finnegan, *Against the Specter of a Dragon*, 56. More recent accounts suggest the incident may not have happened. Esposito, "Political and Institutional Constraints on Wilson's Defense Policy," 1115.
39. See Edward Coffman, "American Military and Strategic Policy in World War I," in *War Aims and Strategic Policy in the Great War, 1914–1918*, ed. Barry Hunt and Adrian Preston (Totowa, NJ: Rowman and Littlefield, 1977), 67–84.
40. Finnegan, *Against the Specter of a Dragon*, chap. 7.
41. Finnegan, *Against the Specter of a Dragon*, 38–39, chap. 6.
42. Finnegan, *Against the Specter of a Dragon*, 4.
43. Finnegan, *Against the Specter of a Dragon*, chap. 5, 157–58.
44. Finnegan, *Against the Specter of a Dragon*, chap. 9. Finnegan's detailed account makes it clear that Wilson took little active interest in army modernization in the prewar period, contrary to the claims of some historians. For an example of that view, see Arthur Link and John W. Chambers, "Woodrow Wilson as Commander-in-Chief," in *The United States Military under the Constitution of the United States, 1789–1989*, ed. Richard

Kohn (New York: NYU Press, 1991), 320–22. It is also clear that Wilson saw preparedness as a political issue and addressed it as such, not to deter Germany from pushing him too far. For that position, see Thompson, "Woodrow Wilson and World War I," 334.

45. Finnegan, *Against the Specter of a Dragon*, 161–63.
46. Esposito, "Political and Institutional Constraints on Wilson's Defense Policy," 1118.
47. Esposito, "Political and Institutional Constraints on Wilson's Defense Policy," 1120.
48. As Thompson points out, had Wilson backed down he would have been humiliated personally, suffered serious political damage, and lost all diplomatic credibility. Thompson, "Woodrow Wilson and World War I," 339.
49. Clements, *Presidency of Woodrow Wilson*, 102.
50. Thompson correctly notes that the problem of rallying broad popular support for the war "was aggravated by the apparent triviality of the issues at stake in the submarine dispute." Thompson, "Woodrow Wilson and World War I," 339.
51. Woodrow Wilson, "War Message to Congress," April 2, 1917, *War Messages*, 65th Cong., 1st Sess. Senate Doc. No. 5, Serial No. 7264, Washington, D.C., 1917, downloaded July 12, 2010 at http://wwi.lib.byu.edu/index.php/Wilson%27s_War_Message_to_Congress.
52. Wilson, "War Message to Congress."
53. Trask, "American Presidency," 310.
54. President Wilson's Message to Congress, January 8, 1918, Records of the United States Senate, Record Group 46, National Archives, http://wwi.lib.byu.edu/index.php/President_Wilson's_Fourteen_Points, accessed July 14, 2010.
55. Clements, *Presidency of Woodrow Wilson*, 164.
56. Soon after the Fourteen Points speech, Wilson for the first time used the expression "self-determination," which had been coined by Lenin and the Bolsheviks as a device for undercutting the multiethnic empires of Europe. Erez Manela argues persuasively that Wilson used "self-determination" as a synonym for "consent of the governed," a liberal ideal he had long espoused, rather than as shorthand for the kind of sweeping anti-imperialism and anticolonialism advocated by the Bolsheviks. See Erez Manela, *The Wilsonian Moment: Self-Determination and the International Origins of Anticolonial Nationalism* (Oxford: Oxford University Press, 2007), chap. 2.
57. MacMillan, *Paris 1919*, 10; Thompson, "Woodrow Wilson and World War I," 343–44.
58. Manela, *Wilsonian Moment*, chap. 2.
59. David Trask, *The AEF and Coalition Warmaking, 1917–1919* (Lawrence: University Press of Kansas, 1993), 3.
60. Finnegan, *Against the Specter of a Dragon*, 190–91.

61. Finnegan, *Against the Specter of a Dragon*, 189–90. Despite years of evidence of the terrible effectiveness of machine guns in the trenches of the Western Front, the army did not adopt a standard machine gun until May 1917. Esposito, "Political and Institutional Constraints on Wilson's Defense Policy," 1122.

62. Esposito, "Political and Institutional Constraints on Wilson's Defense Policy," 1115.

63. It had done so once, resulting in the inconclusive battle of Jutland in 1916.

64. Coffman, "American Military and Strategic Policy in World War I," 73.

65. Clements, *Presidency of Woodrow Wilson*, 148. Link and Chambers credit Wilson with the decision to introduce convoys, but it seems highly unlikely that a man who showed as little interest in military matters as the president had would be so astute as to recommend a major tactical innovation. Link and Chambers, "Woodrow Wilson as Commander-in-Chief," 324.

66. David M. Esposito, "Woodrow Wilson and the Origins of the AEF," *Presidential Studies Quarterly* 17 (2) (1987): 130–33.

67. Trask, *AEF and Coalition Warmaking*, 5, 8; John S. D. Eisenhower, *Yanks: The Epic Story of the American Army in World War I* (New York: Free Press, 2001), 16.

68. Esposito, "Woodrow Wilson and the Origins of the AEF," 133–35; Trask, *AEF and Coalition Warmaking*, 5–6.

69. Coffman, "American Military and Strategic Policy in World War I," 72–73.

70. Trask, *AEF and Coalition Warmaking*, 11–12.

71. Robert Ferrell contends that Pershing was actually chosen by Secretary of War Newton D. Baker. Ferrell, "Woodrow Wilson: Misfit in Office?" 76–77. Other accounts suggest a number of civilian and military leaders were involved in the selection process, which is more plausible. See Eisenhower, *Yanks*, chap. 3.

72. Trask, *AEF and Coalition Warmaking*, 11.

73. Eliot A. Cohen, *Supreme Command: Soldiers, Statesmen, and Leadership in Wartime* (New York: Anchor Books/Random House, 2002), 8–9.

74. Eisenhower, *Yanks*, 31.

75. Trask, *AEF and Coalition Warmaking*, 12.

76. Baker shared Wilson's view that political leaders should refrain from close oversight of their military commanders. Ferrell, "Woodrow Wilson: Misfit in Office?" 74–75. The secretary took this to an extreme, not meeting Pershing until after his selection as commander. Coffman, "American Military and Strategic Policy in World War I," 75. According to Pershing's later recollection, his written instructions from Baker arrived after the meeting with the president. Eisenhower, *Yanks*, 33–34. See also Trask, *AEF and Coalition Warmaking*, 12.

77. Just before Wilson asked for a declaration of war, the chief of ordnance for the army estimated it would take two and a half years to fully equip a one-million-man U.S. Army. Esposito, "Woodrow Wilson and the Origins of the AEF," 129–30.

78. Ferrell, "Woodrow Wilson: Misfit in Office?" 68–69.

79. Ferrell, "Woodrow Wilson: Misfit in Office?" 71–74.

80. Trask, *AEF and Coalition Warmaking*, 25–26.

81. Ferrell, "Woodrow Wilson: Misfit in Office?" 81–83; Link and Chambers, "Woodrow Wilson as Commander-in-Chief," 333.

82. Link and Chambers, "Woodrow Wilson as Commander-in-Chief," 326–27.

83. Link and Chambers, "Woodrow Wilson as Commander-in-Chief," 329–30. On Wilson's use of the Overman Act to reform procurement and transportation, see Trask, *AEF and Coalition Warmaking*, 26–27.

84. Link and Chambers, "Woodrow Wilson as Commander-in-Chief," 327; Clements, *Presidency of Woodrow Wilson*, 156.

85. Clements, *Presidency of Woodrow Wilson*, 156–58; Link and Chambers, "Woodrow Wilson as Commander-in-Chief," 331.

86. Ferrell, "Woodrow Wilson: Misfit in Office?" 84–85; Eisenhower, *Yanks*, 90–92.

87. Lyn Macdonald, *1915: The Death of Innocence* (Baltimore: Johns Hopkins University Press, 2000), chap. 22.

88. Clements, *Presidency of Woodrow Wilson*, 158.

89. Eisenhower, *Yanks*, 32.

90. Trask, *AEF and Coalition Warmaking*, 20.

91. Trask, *AEF and Coalition Warmaking*, 24.

92. Coffman, "American Military and Strategic Policy in World War I," 77; Trask, *AEF and Coalition Warmaking*, 29–30.

93. Determined to retain his freedom of action, Wilson refused to appoint a political delegate to the Council, in contrast to the Allies. The president appointed General Tasker Bliss as his permanent military representative. Trask, *AEF and Coalition Warmaking*, 31.

94. Coffman, "American Military and Strategic Policy in World War I," 77–79.

95. Trask, *AEF and Coalition Warmaking*, 38–39; Link and Chambers, "Woodrow Wilson as Commander-in-Chief," 339.

96. Trask, *AEF and Coalition Warmaking*, 29–30.

97. For an account of the offensives and the Allied response, see Trask, *AEF and Coalition Warmaking*, chap. 3.

98. Trask, *AEF and Coalition Warmaking*, 54–55.

99. Coffman, "American Military and Strategic Policy in World War I," 79; Trask, *AEF and Coalition Warmaking*, 64–65.

100. Coffman, "American Military and Strategic Policy in World War I," 79–80.

101. Coffman, "American Military and Strategic Policy in World War I," 81–82.
102. Trask, *AEF and Coalition Warmaking*, 74.
103. Trask, *AEF and Coalition Warmaking*, 83–85, 91–92.
104. Trask, *AEF and Coalition Warmaking*, 93–94.
105. Trask, *AEF and Coalition Warmaking*, 100–1.
106. Trask, *AEF and Coalition Warmaking*, chap. 6.
107. Figures from http://www.pbs.org/greatwar/resources/casdeath_pop.html, accessed July 16, 2010.
108. Trask, *AEF and Coalition Warmaking*, 98–99.
109. Trask, *AEF and Coalition Warmaking*, 131–34.
110. Trask, *AEF and Coalition Warmaking*, 134–36.
111. The record clearly does not support the contention by Link and Chambers that Wilson remained in control of all military matters and made the key decisions and that military professionals "were given comparatively little freedom of action." See Link and Chambers, "Woodrow Wilson as Commander-in-Chief," 319–21.
112. Clements, *Presidency of Woodrow Wilson*, 165–67.
113. Trask, *AEF and Coalition Warmaking*, 156, 173–74. Unconditional surrender also received some popular support in the United States, but Wilson refused to bow to the pressure. Gideon Rose, *How Wars End: Why We Always Fight the Last Battle* (New York: Simon and Schuster, 2010), 41–42.
114. Trask, *AEF and Coalition Warmaking*, 161–62.
115. Trask, *AEF and Coalition Warmaking*, 156–58.
116. Clements, *Presidency of Woodrow Wilson*, 167–68.
117. Trask, *AEF and Coalition Warmaking*, 158.
118. Link and Chambers, "Woodrow Wilson as Commander-in-Chief," 322–23; Clements, *Presidency of Woodrow Wilson*, 145.
119. Herbert Croly, *The Promise of American Life* (1909; reprint ed., Boston: Northeastern University Press, 1989). Although it is difficult to call particular texts representative of such a broad current, another influential volume in the period before the war was Walter Lippman, *Drift and Mastery* (1914; reprint ed., Madison: University of Wisconsin Press, 1985).
120. John F. McClymer, *War and Welfare: Social Engineering in America, 1890–1925* (Westport, CT: Greenwood Press, 1980), 154ff.; Andrew J. Polsky, *The Rise of the Therapeutic State* (Princeton: Princeton University Press, 1991), 90.
121. "Does not every American feel that assurance has been added to our hope for the future peace of the world by the wonderful and heartening things that have been happening within the last few weeks in Russia? Russia was known by those who knew it best to have been always in fact democratic at heart, in all the vital habits of her thought, in all the intimate relationships of her people that spoke their natural instinct, their habitual attitude towards life. The autocracy that crowned the summit of her

political structure, long as it had stood and terrible as was the reality of its power, was not in fact Russian in origin, character, or purpose; and now it has been shaken off and the great, generous Russian people have been added in all their naive majesty and might to the forces that are fighting for freedom in the world, for justice, and for peace. Here is a fit partner for a league of honor." Wilson, "War Message to Congress."

122. Clements, *Presidency of Woodrow Wilson*, 152, 155–56.
123. Polsky, *Rise of the Therapeutic State*, 87.
124. Clements, *Presidency of Woodrow Wilson*, 155–56.
125. Clements, *Presidency of Woodrow Wilson*, 152.
126. Eisenhower, *Yanks*, 24–25; Esposito, "Woodrow Wilson and the Origins of the AEF," 132.
127. Ferrell, "Woodrow Wilson: Misfit in Office?" 79.
128. Clements, *Presidency of Woodrow Wilson*, 161.
129. Clements, *Presidency of Woodrow Wilson*, 161.
130. Clements, *Presidency of Woodrow Wilson*, 153.
131. Clements, *Presidency of Woodrow Wilson*, 153–54; Link and Chambers, "Woodrow Wilson as Commander-in-Chief," 336.
132. Link and Chambers, "Woodrow Wilson as Commander-in-Chief," 334–36.
133. Clements, *Presidency of Woodrow Wilson*, 153–54.
134. Link and Chambers contend that Burleson felt he had enough political support in Congress to defy the president's request for moderation, but they also insist that Wilson remained in firm control over his administration. If the latter is true, then he surely had the power to force Burleson to back down. Link and Chambers, "Woodrow Wilson as Commander-in-Chief," 336.
135. David R. Mayhew, "Wars and American Politics," *Perspectives on Politics* 3 (September 2005): 473–93.
136. Clements, *Presidency of Woodrow Wilson*, 152–53.
137. Clements, *Presidency of Woodrow Wilson*, 158.
138. Link and Chambers, "Woodrow Wilson as Commander-in-Chief," 334–35.
139. Manela, *Wilsonian Moment*, 49–52.
140. MacMillan, *Paris 1919*, 55.
141. MacMillan, *Paris 1919*, 6.
142. For an excellent recent account, see MacMillan, *Paris 1919*. I have drawn heavily on her work. A useful complement that stresses how non-Western peoples saw and responded to the peace conference is Manela, *Wilsonian Moment*.
143. MacMillan, *Paris 1919*, chap. 7.
144. MacMillan, *Paris 1919*, 13.
145. MacMillan, *Paris 1919*, 96–97.
146. MacMillan, *Paris 1919*, 486–87.
147. MacMillan, *Paris 1919*, chap. 8.

148. MacMillan, *Paris 1919*, 471–72.
149. MacMillan, *Paris 1919*, 192–93.
150. MacMillan, *Paris 1919*, 461ff.
151. MacMillan, *Paris 1919*, 181, 466.
152. MacMillan, *Paris 1919*, 479–81.
153. MacMillan, *Paris 1919*, 160–61.
154. MacMillan, *Paris 1919*, 10ff.
155. See especially MacMillan, *Paris 1919*, Part Three.
156. MacMillan, *Paris 1919*, xxx, 54–55, 58–59.
157. MacMillan, *Paris 1919*, chap. 17.
158. MacMillan, *Paris 1919*, 22–24, 26–28, 31–32.
159. MacMillan, *Paris 1919*, 180–81.
160. MacMillan, *Paris 1919*, 160–61.
161. MacMillan, *Paris 1919*, 14–15, 287.
162. Clements, *Woodrow Wilson*, 172–73. This view was first expressed at the time by the press, but the warning was also self-serving—reporters wanted access to the meetings. See MacMillan, *Paris 1919*, 57.
163. For a discussion of how Wilson misread public opinion in Italy, see MacMillan, *Paris 1919*, 298–300.
164. The claim was first circulated widely by John Maynard Keynes, who had an axe to grind because his recommendation to eschew reparations had not been accepted. See MacMillan, *Paris 1919*, 478–79.
165. MacMillan, *Paris 1919*, 12–13.
166. See MacMillan's discussions of the Middle East, the Balkans, and Eastern Europe. MacMillan, *Paris 1919*.
167. MacMillan, *Paris 1919*, 9–10.
168. MacMillan, *Paris 1919*, 200–1.
169. MacMillan, *Paris 1919*, 187–89, 470–71.
170. Japan secured former German possessions in the Pacific as mandates and economic concessions in Shantung, China, over the strenuous objections of the Chinese delegation. On the other hand, the Japanese did not get everything they wanted: their proposed language on racial equality was not included in the League of Nations provisions.
171. MacMillan, *Paris 1919*, 96–97.
172. MacMillan, *Paris 1919*, 475.
173. Macmillan is more generous to Clemenceau, but concedes that his failure to build an alliance undermined all he gained at the conference. MacMillan, *Paris 1919*, 202–3.
174. MacMillan, *Paris 1919*, 151–52.
175. MacMillan reports that one journal poll found two-thirds of its readers supportive of the League. But such polls could yield misleading results. To cite the most notorious later example, the 1936 *Literary Digest* presidential poll predicted that Franklin Roosevelt would lose the presidential election, which he won by a landslide.

176. Clements, *Woodrow Wilson*, 178.

177. This summary is based upon Clements, *Woodrow Wilson*, chap. 10.

178. This is Clements's division. MacMillan suggests four groups, separating the Republicans who were not yet committed. MacMillan, *Paris 1919*, 487–88.

179. Clements, *Woodrow Wilson*, 190; MacMillan, *Paris 1919*, 152.

180. For a discussion of the various cultural, psychological, and medical explanations for Wilson's refusal to compromise, see John Milton Cooper Jr., *Breaking the Heart of the World: Woodrow Wilson and the Fight for the League of Nations* (Cambridge: Cambridge University Press, 2001), chap. 10.

181. Cooper, *Breaking the Heart of the World*, 418–19.

182. Clements, *Woodrow Wilson*, 194–95.

183. Cooper, *Breaking the Heart of the World*, 426.

184. Wilson, "War Message to Congress."

Chapter 3

1. Stephen Ambrose, "'Just Dumb Luck': American Entry into World War II," in *Americans at War* (Jackson: University of Mississippi Press, 1997), 57–66. Treasury Secretary Henry Morgenthau Jr. cautioned Roosevelt in August 1941 against continuing to rely on "dumb luck" to bring the United States into the war on favorable terms.

2. Mark M. Lowenthal, "Roosevelt and the Coming of the War: The Search for United States Policy 1937–42," *Journal of Contemporary History* 16 (3) (July 1981): 413–40, at 414.

3. See Thomas Ferguson, "Industrial Conflict and the Coming of the New Deal: The Triumph of Multinational Liberalism in America," in *The Rise and Fall of the New Deal Order, 1930–1980*, ed. Steve Fraser and Gary Gerstle (Princeton: Princeton University Press, 1989), 3–31.

4. Lowenthal, "Roosevelt and the Coming of the War," 417.

5. For the fullest account of the events leading to the outbreak of war in Europe in 1939, see Donald Cameron Watt, *How War Came: The Immediate Origins of the Second World War, 1938–1939* (New York: Pantheon Books, 1989).

6. Watt, *How War Came*, 556.

7. Lowenthal, "Roosevelt and the Coming of the War," 417–18.

8. Harold I. Gullan, "Expectations of Infamy: Roosevelt and Marshall Prepare for War, 1938–41," *Presidential Studies Quarterly* 28 (3) (Summer 1998): 510–22, at 514; Peter Trubowitz, *Politics and Strategy: Partisan Ambition and American Statecraft* (Princeton: Princeton University Press, 2011), 74.

9. Watt, *How War Came*, 129–30.

10. Watt, *How War Came*, 260.

11. Watt, *How War Came*, chap. 24.

12. This point is suggested by Eric Larrabee, *Commander in Chief: Franklin Delano Roosevelt, His Lieutenants, and Their War* (1987; reprint ed., Annapolis, MD: Naval Institute Press, 2004), 49–50.

13. In the mid-1930s, the U.S. Senate Special Committee on Investigation of the Munitions Industry, better known after its chairman as the Nye Committee, held a well-publicized series of hearings that suggested a tie between American arms manufacturers and other industries and the decision to enter the war. See David M. Kennedy, *Freedom from Fear: The American People in Depression and War, 1929–1945* (New York: Oxford University Press, 2005), 387–88.

14. Watt, *How War Came*, 612.

15. Watt, *How War Came*, 261.

16. Watt, *How War Came*, 268. See similarly, Ambrose, "'Just Dumb Luck,'" 59.

17. Jonathan G. Utley, *Going to War with Japan, 1937–1941* (1985; reprint ed. New York: Fordham University Press, 2005), 14.

18. Watt, *How War Came*, 134–36.

19. Watt, *How War Came*, 264–66.

20. Gullan, "Expectations of Infamy," 516–17.

21. Larrabee, *Commander in Chief*, 46–47.

22. Utley, *Going to War with Japan*, xiv–xv.

23. Utley, *Going to War with Japan*, 9–10, 19–21.

24. Utley, *Going to War with Japan*, 98–100.

25. Lowenthal, "Roosevelt and the Coming of the War," 418–19, 424–25.

26. Utley, *Going to War with Japan*, 112ff. For several decades, the United States had maintained a grandiosely titled Asiatic Fleet, based in the Philippines. Although headed by a full admiral, it lacked capital ships (aircraft carriers or battleships) and could offer scant resistance to a major Japanese move south of French Indochina toward Singapore, the Dutch East Indies (now Indonesia), or the Philippines. The Asiatic fleet was fought to virtual destruction in the four months following the start of war in the Pacific in December 1941. See W. G. Winslow, *The Fleet the Gods Forgot: The U.S. Asiatic Fleet in World War II* (Annapolis: Naval Institute Press, 1982, 1994).

27. Watt, *How War Came*, 266.

28. Ambrose, "'Just Dumb Luck,'" 59.

29. Lowenthal, "Roosevelt and the Coming of the War," 421–22; Larrabee, *Commander in Chief*, 46–47.

30. The incremental path toward an alliance with Great Britain began in summer 1940 when the president agreed to transfer a number of American World War I destroyers to the Royal Navy in exchange for bases that the U.S. Navy could use. Lowenthal, "Roosevelt and the Coming of the War," 422–23. The Roosevelt–Churchill relationship has been treated at length by several historians. See Warren F. Kimball, *Forged in War: Roosevelt, Churchill, and the Second World War* (New York: William Morrow, 1997).

31. Lowenthal, "Roosevelt and the Coming of the War," 425–26.

32. Kennedy, *Freedom from Fear*, 504–5. For a detailed analysis, see Christopher Thorne, *Allies of a Kind: The United States, Britain, and the War against Japan, 1941–1945* (New York: Oxford University Press, 1978).

33. Christopher Bayly and Tim Harper, *Forgotten Armies: The Fall of British Asia, 1941–1945* (Cambridge: Belknap/Harvard, 2004); Brian P. Farrell, *The Defense and Fall of Singapore 1940–1942* (Strould, Gloucestershire: Tempus, 2006).

34. Utley, *Going to War with Japan*, 100–1.

35. William Emerson, "Franklin Roosevelt as Commander-in-Chief in World War II," *Military Affairs* 22 (4) (Winter 1958–1959): 181–207, at 188–89.

36. Larrabee, *Commander in Chief*, 48–49.

37. Ambrose, "'Just Dumb Luck,'" 60–61.

38. Ambrose, "'Just Dumb Luck,'" 61.

39. Warren F. Kimball, "Franklin D. Roosevelt: 'Dr. Win-the-War,'" in *Commanders in Chief: Presidential Leadership in Modern Wars*, ed. Joseph G. Dawson III (Kansas: University Press of Kansas, 1993), 96. Anticipating the German invasion, the Roosevelt administration had defeated partisan effort by Republicans to deny Lend-Lease aid to the Soviet Union when the bill was being debated in early 1941. Kimball concludes that this preemptive move by the administration points up the president's "instinctive awareness of the importance of the Soviet Union in the overall international equation." Warren F. Kimball, *The Juggler: Franklin Roosevelt as Wartime Statesman* (Princeton: Princeton University Press, 1991), 23–24, 38–39.

40. Kennedy, *Freedom from Fear*, 509.

41. Larrabee, *Commander in Chief*, 74–80.

42. Lowenthal, "Roosevelt and the Coming of the War," 414; Emerson, "Franklin Roosevelt as Commander-in-Chief in World War II," 188–89.

43. Lowenthal, "Roosevelt and the Coming of the War," 418–19.

44. For a full discussion of the legislation and its effects, see Warren F. Kimball, *The Most Unsordid Act: Lend-Lease, 1939–1941* (Baltimore: Johns Hopkins University Press, 1969).

45. Lowenthal, "Roosevelt and the Coming of the War," 428.

46. Ambrose, "'Just Dumb Luck,'" 61–62.

47. Kennedy, *Freedom from Fear*, 479–81. See similarly Larrabee, *Commander in Chief*, 48–49.

48. Lowenthal, "Roosevelt and the Coming of the War," 426–27.

49. Ambrose, "'Just Dumb Luck,'" 60.

50. A number of historians have made this point. See Utley, *Going to War with Japan*, 180–81; Larrabee, *Commander in Chief*, 64; Kennedy, *Freedom from Fear*, 525.

51. Kennedy, *Freedom from Fear*, 510–11; Larrabee, *Commander in Chief*, 63–64.

52. Larrabee, *Commander in Chief*, 91.
53. Roosevelt's decision reversed long-standing American defense policy, which had regarded the Philippines as a strategic liability and so had rejected any steps to reinforce them. The prior plans had assumed the Philippines would be relieved or if necessary reconquered after the U.S. Navy regained control over the sea lanes across the Pacific.
54. Emerson, "Franklin Roosevelt as Commander-in-Chief in World War II," 189–90; Larrabee, *Commander in Chief*, 312–14.
55. Gullan, "Expectations of Infamy," 516; Larrabee, *Commander in Chief*, 114.
56. In addition, even before Japan announced its intention to exit the naval limitation regime, the Japanese navy started to build ships larger than permitted by treaty.
57. Emerson, "Franklin Roosevelt as Commander-in-Chief in World War II," 187. On the political economy of American mobilization in the Second World War, see Paul A. C. Koistinen, *Arsenal of World War II: The Political Economy of American Warfare, 1940–1945* (Lawrence: University Press of Kansas, 2004).
58. Gullan, "Expectations of Infamy," 512–16; Larrabee, *Commander in Chief*, 106–7.
59. Gullan, "Expectations of Infamy," 510.
60. Emerson, "Franklin Roosevelt as Commander-in-Chief in World War II," 183–85.
61. Gullan, "Expectations of Infamy," 518.
62. Larrabee, *Commander in Chief*, 117; John A. Thompson, "Conceptions of National Security and American Entry into World War II," *Diplomacy and Statecraft* 16 (2005): 671–97, at 678.
63. For a full discussion of the legislation and its effects, see J. Garry Clifford and Samuel R. Spencer, *The First Peacetime Draft* (Lawrence: University Press of Kansas, 1986).
64. When the war in Europe began in September 1939, unemployment in the United States was still more than 17 percent. Mark Allan Eisner, *The State in the American Political Economy: Public Policy and the Evolution of State Economy Relations* (Englewood Cliffs, NJ: Prentice Hall, 1995), 194–95.
65. Gullan, "Expectations of Infamy," 516.
66. Worried over the long-term return on investment in plants dedicated to defense production, business leaders were reluctant at first to build new facilities. But a combination of carrots (the federal government financed new factories) and sticks (the government could threaten the survival of non-cooperating firms) overcame business hesitation. Eisner, *State in the American Political Economy*, 198–99.
67. Gullan, "Expectations of Infamy," 520.
68. Robert Higgs, *Crisis and Leviathan: Critical Episodes in the Growth of American Government* (New York: Oxford University Press, 1987), 203.

69. Ambrose, "'Just Dumb Luck,'" 61.
70. For representative photographs, see the illustrations in Christopher R. Gabel, *The U.S. Army GHQ Maneuvers of 1941* (Washington, DC: U.S. Army Center of Military History, 1991).
71. Larrabee, *Commander in Chief*, 36.
72. Richard W. Steele, "Preparing the Public for War: Efforts to Establish a National Propaganda Agency, 1940–41," *American Historical Review* 75 (6) (October 1970): 1640–53, at 1642.
73. Steele, "Preparing the Public for War," 1646ff.
74. Larrabee, *Commander in Chief*, 117–18.
75. Steele, "Preparing the Public for War," 1650. The restriction did not prevent the president from sending U.S. Marines to Iceland, which he redefined as part of the Western Hemisphere.
76. Steele, "Preparing the Public for War," 1640n.
77. Ambrose, "'Just Dumb Luck,'" 61.
78. Historical counterfactuals are always open to challenge, and this one is no exception. As I discuss later, a successful invasion of northwest Europe hinged on a number of factors. Important though the buildup of American forces in England was, an argument could be made that Germany also needed to be weakened by ongoing losses on the Eastern Front and in the Mediterranean before an invasion could be mounted with a fair prospect of success.
79. Kimball, *Juggler*, 76–77; Brian L. Villa, "The U.S. Army, Unconditional Surrender, and the Potsdam Proclamation," *Journal of American History* 63 (1) (June 1976): 66–92, at 70.
80. Thomas Fleming, *The New Dealers' War: F.D.R. and the War within World War II* (New York: Basic Books, 2001), 174ff.; Villa, "U.S. Army, Unconditional Surrender, and Potsdam Proclamation," 70–71.
81. Larrabee, *Commander in Chief*, 504.
82. Eric Larrabee also comments on the difficulty of adjusting the goal of unconditional surrender as the fighting neared an end. See Larrabee, *Commander in Chief*, 10.
83. Kimball, *Juggler*, 7–8. Even Kimball, who argues for the larger coherence of Roosevelt's postwar vision, concedes, "What he did not want is much clearer than what he wanted." Kimball, *Juggler*, 103–4.
84. Kimball, *Juggler*, 96.
85. On Roosevelt's attitude, see Greg Robinson, *By Order of the President: FDR and the Internment of Japanese Americans* (Cambridge: Harvard University Press, 2001), chap. 3.
86. Kimball, *Juggler*, chaps. 3 and 5.
87. Kimball, *Juggler*, 86–87. Interestingly, Charles de Gaulle perceived that two of the four powers Roosevelt expected to sustain peace after the war would be beholden to the United States. Larrabee, *Commander in Chief*, 634.

88. Kimball, *Juggler*, 132–33.

89. On the differences between Churchill and Roosevelt over the future of colonialism, see Kimball, *Juggler*, 68–72. Churchill's statement followed the British triumph at El Alamein in November 1942. Andrew Roberts, *Masters and Commanders: How Four Titans Won the War in the West, 1941–1945* (New York: HarperCollins, 2009), 295.

90. Larrabee, *Commander in Chief*, 519–20.

91. Kimball, *Juggler*, 39–40, 84.

92. Kimball, *Juggler*, 87.

93. Larrabee, *Commander in Chief*, 543–44.

94. Quoted in Roberts, *Masters and Commanders*, 412.

95. The planners erred on the number of divisions the United States would field and other details, but as a starting point it served well for military leaders and civilian mobilization officials. From an initial figure of 215 divisions, the total was revised downward to the final tally of 90. Larrabee suggests there was too little margin for error because only two divisions had not been committed to combat by the end of the war. Larrabee, *Commander in Chief*, 145. On the other hand, as I point out below, the number was sufficient for a relatively extravagant approach in the Pacific with two lines of advance against Japan. Had manpower resources really been insufficient, the United States could have adapted by pursuing a single thrust against Japan.

96. Larrabee, *Commander in Chief*, 121–24.

97. Kennedy, *Freedom from Fear*, 623.

98. When disputes continued between Nelson and the services, the president, declining to be drawn directly into the fray, established the Office of War Mobilization under James Byrnes, an experienced political fixer, to oversee the entire mobilization effort and mediate disputes between the WPB and other agencies, including the military. Kennedy, *Freedom from Fear*, 622–23, 629; Eisner, *State in the American Political Economy*, 199–204.

99. Larrabee, *Commander in Chief*, 176–77, 198, 444–45.

100. Larrabee, *Commander in Chief*, 218.

101. Kennedy, *Freedom from Fear*, 619.

102. Kimball, *Juggler*, 189.

103. Kennedy, *Freedom from Fear*, 652–55.

104. The United States produced a total of 92 aircraft carriers between 1940 and 1945. Larrabee, *Commander in Chief*, 92.

105. Kennedy, *Freedom from Fear*, 624.

106. Eisner, *State in the American Political Economy*, 211–12. Eisner notes that the various wartime tax measures made the system more comprehensive (most workers paid income taxes for the first time) and progressive (the top rate applied to all income over $200,000).

107. Inflationary pressures mounted and were only partly contained by taxes and savings. After a decade of Depression-generated price deflation,

the initial war orders provided a welcome economic stimulus as prices recovered to their 1929 levels. By spring 1941, however, inflation worries spread. As with the first measures to coordinate production, the initial administration moves to stem inflation were insufficient. In 1942, the Office of Price Administration (OPA) received authority to set maximum prices based on 1941 levels, but important exclusions—it had limited power over agricultural prices because key political leaders realized the war could boost farm incomes—reduced its effectiveness. Price regulations were extended, first to consumer products in April 1942, later that year to wages and all commodities. Popular frustrations with OPA regulations contributed to large Republican gains in the 1942 congressional elections. Only when the president issued a directive in 1943 to all agencies to hold the line on prices was inflation finally checked. Eisner, *State in the American Political Economy*, 204–6; Kennedy, *Freedom from Fear*, 782.

108. Kennedy, *Freedom from Fear*, 641–42.
109. Eisner, *State in the American Political Economy*, 209–10.
110. Kennedy, *Freedom from Fear*, 782.
111. Eisner, *State in the American Political Economy*, 220–21.
112. Kennedy, *Freedom from Fear*, 782–87.
113. Kennedy, *Freedom from Fear*, 783.
114. Eisner, *State in the American Political Economy*, 210.
115. In this vein, the administration agreed before the 1940 presidential election to promote the first African American to general officer rank and appoint a senior black advisor to the War Department. Philip A. Klinkner with Rogers Smith, *The Unsteady March: The Rise and Decline of Racial Equality in America* (Chicago: University of Chicago Press, 1999), 153–54.
116. Klinkner with Smith, *Unsteady March*, 154–60; Kennedy, *Freedom from Fear*, 765–68.
117. Klinkner with Smith, *Unsteady March*, 168–70, 176–77.
118. Kennedy, *Freedom from Fear*, 769–71.
119. Klinkner with Smith, *Unsteady March*, 178–79, 191.
120. Klinkner with Smith, *Unsteady March*, 191.
121. Klinkner with Smith, *Unsteady March*, 186–90.
122. Klinkner with Smith, *Unsteady March*, 197–99; Kennedy, *Freedom from Fear*, 774.
123. Kennedy, *Freedom from Fear*, 784, 787–88.
124. Larrabee, *Commander in Chief*, 5–6.
125. Larrabee, *Commander in Chief*, 20–21.
126. Larrabee, *Commander in Chief*, chap. 2.
127. On King as a strategist and his commitment to defeating Germany first, see Larrabee, *Commander in Chief*, 153–54, 183. Admiral Harold Stark served for a time as another naval representative on the Joint Chiefs but soon resigned to avoid confusion and duplication. Larrabee, *Commander in Chief*, 20–21.

128. Larrabee, *Commander in Chief*, 20–21, 25–26.
129. Larrabee, *Commander in Chief*, 318. For a detailed account of MacArthur's role in the unsuccessful defense of the Philippines, see Richard Connaughton, *MacArthur and Defeat in the Philippines* (Woodstock: Woodstock Press, 2001).
130. Larrabee, *Commander in Chief*, 12, 321ff., esp. 351.
131. Larrabee, *Commander in Chief*, 176–78.
132. Roberts, *Masters and Commanders*, 68–69.
133. Larrabee, *Commander in Chief*, 173–74. The American emphasis on the European theater did not become clear in numerical terms until late 1943. Roberts, *Masters and Commanders*, 468.
134. See especially Roberts, *Masters and Commanders*.
135. Andrew Roberts, who relies heavily on the British record and is understandably influenced by the perspective of British participants, accepts the characterization of the American approach as one that favored a full frontal assault on the German army in France. He labels this the "Ulysses S. Grant" view of warfare, which reflects a further misunderstanding of American methods. Grant did not favor frontal attacks; his Vicksburg campaign was a brilliant example of maneuver warfare. Roberts, *Masters and Commanders*, 69–70.
136. Larrabee, *Commander in Chief*, 498–99.
137. Many historians and military analysts regard the *Wehrmacht* of the 1940s as the most proficient military of its day and accept the British view it could not be bested on even terms. The inexperienced American military leadership in 1942 failed to appreciate the qualitative advantages of the German Army. Larrabee, *Commander in Chief*, 137–38. For a contrasting view, see Keith E. Bonn, *When the Odds Were Even: The Vosges Mountains Campaign, October 1944–January 1945* (Novato, CA: Presidio Press, 1994, 2006). Even if one questions the superiority of the *Wehrmacht*, however, it is hard to see the U.S. Army achieving success without first ascending a learning curve. As Larrabee concisely frames it: "We needed a place to be lousy in." North Africa served as that place. Larrabee, *Commander in Chief*, 436.
138. Roberts, *Masters and Commanders*, 139, 223.
139. Roberts, *Masters and Commanders*, 215.
140. Roberts, *Masters and Commanders*, 138.
141. My view of the sequence of decisions follows that of Andrew Roberts. See Roberts, *Masters and Commanders*, 579ff.
142. Roberts, *Masters and Commanders*, 129.
143. Larrabee, *Commander in Chief*, 133–34, 138–39; Roberts, *Masters and Commanders*, 171–72, 232–33.
144. Roosevelt promised the Russians a second front in 1942 and felt obliged to offer some kind of action in the European theater at least as a sign of good faith. Roberts, *Masters and Commanders*, 174–75.
145. Roberts, *Masters and Commanders*, 290.

146. Larrabee, *Commander in Chief*, 135–36; Roberts, *Masters and Commanders*, 300.
147. Emerson, "Franklin Roosevelt as Commander-in-Chief in World War II," 198–99; Roberts, *Masters and Commanders*, 327–28.
148. Roberts, *Masters and Commanders*, 336.
149. Roberts, *Masters and Commanders*, 370.
150. Roberts, *Masters and Commanders*, 410–11, 428.
151. Roberts, *Masters and Commanders*, 411.
152. Roberts, *Masters and Commanders*, 492.
153. Roberts, *Masters and Commanders*, 359.
154. Roberts, *Masters and Commanders*, 359–60, 370–71; Kennedy, *Freedom from Fear*, 610–11.
155. Roberts, *Masters and Commanders*, 428.
156. Larrabee, *Commander in Chief*, 149; Roberts, *Masters and Commanders*, 453.
157. Roberts, *Masters and Commanders*, 401.
158. Roberts, *Masters and Commanders*, 451. The president's new hard line stung the prime minister. Rather abruptly, as the Anglo-American balance of power swung toward the United States, the relationship between Roosevelt and Churchill cooled. What had appeared an unusual personal friendship among leaders of two world powers stood revealed as a political marriage of convenience.
159. Emerson, "Franklin Roosevelt as Commander-in-Chief in World War II," 193–94; Larrabee, *Commander in Chief*, 16.
160. Larrabee, *Commander in Chief*, 240ff.
161. Larrabee, *Commander in Chief*, chap. 5.
162. The increased resources for the Pacific war reflected an inter-Allied agreement at the Casablanca Conference in January 1943 to allocate 30 percent of the American war effort to the struggle against Japan. This reflected King's belief that by devoting too little to the Pacific, the United States risked allowing the Japanese to consolidate their gains in a way that would make the cost of ejecting them prohibitive. Kennedy, *Freedom from Fear*, 587; Larrabee, *Commander in Chief*, 187.
163. King initiated the two-axis strategy, over MacArthur's objections; the general believed his should be the sole line of attack, with all military resources under his direction. Larrabee, *Commander in Chief*, 342.
164. Larrabee, *Commander in Chief*, 189ff.
165. Larrabee, *Commander in Chief*, 344.
166. Larrabee, *Commander in Chief*, 343–46.
167. Max Hastings, *Retribution: The Battle for Japan, 1944–45* (New York: Alfred A. Knopf, 2008), 24–31; Larrabee, *Commander in Chief*, 346.
168. Hastings, *Retribution*, 31; Larrabee, *Commander in Chief*, 348–50.
169. Hastings, *Retribution*, 219–21; Larrabee, *Commander in Chief*, 542.
170. Larrabee, *Commander in Chief*, 553.

171. Larrabee, *Commander in Chief*, 545–46, 572.
172. Larrabee, *Commander in Chief*, 541.
173. Kimball, *Juggler*, 140–43.
174. Kimball, *Juggler*, 141–42.
175. On the debates between the Roosevelt administration and the British government over the future of India, see Kimball, *Juggler*, 132–40.
176. Roberts, *Masters and Commanders*, 313. In pursuing campaigns in Burma, Churchill overrode the advice of his own military chiefs, who argued the British ought to join the main American counteroffensive across the Pacific. Roberts, *Masters and Commanders*, 468–69.
177. Andrew Roberts views Italy as an illustration of "mission creep," a concept of our own era that refers to operations that continue for reasons other than those for which they started. Roberts, *Masters and Commanders*, 346. Even analyses that argue for the merits of a Mediterranean strategy acknowledge that after mid-1944 it had reached a point of diminishing returns. See Douglas Porch, *The Path to Victory: The Mediterranean Theater in World War II* (New York: Farrar, Straus and Giroux, 2004).
178. Hastings, *Retribution*, 316, 318.
179. Villa, "U.S. Army, Unconditional Surrender, and Potsdam Proclamation," 70–72.
180. Gideon Rose, *How Wars End: Why We Always Fight the Last Battle* (New York: Simon and Schuster, 2010), 69.
181. Frank King, "Allied Negotiations and the Dismemberment of Germany," *Contemporary History* 16 (3) (July 1981): 585.
182. Kennedy, *Freedom from Fear*, 803.
183. King, "Allied Negotiations and Dismemberment of Germany," 592.
184. Kennedy, *Freedom from Fear*, 854.
185. Churchill fueled this narrative by claiming the president had been deceived at Yalta. But the prime minister had agreed to the Poland arrangement in his negotiations with Stalin the previous year. Kimball maintains that Churchill's post-Yalta posturing was designed to mask similarities between the Soviet quest for a sphere of influence in Eastern Europe and Great Britain's parallel efforts in the Mediterranean and Middle East. Kimball, *Juggler*, 172–75.
186. Roberts, *Masters and Commanders*, 485–86.
187. Kimball, *Juggler*, 100.
188. Kimball, *Juggler*, 160ff.
189. Press and public criticism of Churchill's agreement with Stalin about Poland, which left the London Poles in a weak position, led Roosevelt to withdraw even his tepid support for what the prime minister had negotiated. Kimball, *Juggler*, 167.
190. Larrabee, *Commander in Chief*, 202; Roberts, *Masters and Commanders*, 519–20.

191. Villa, "U.S. Army, Unconditional Surrender, and Potsdam Proclamation," 75–77.

192. Military opinion began to turn against the need for Soviet entry into the war against Japan after Yalta, with Admiral King advising Truman that the war could be won without Soviet help. Larrabee, *Commander in Chief,* 202.

193. Villa, "U.S. Army, Unconditional Surrender, and Potsdam Proclamation," 90–91.

194. Kimball, *Juggler,* 149, 152–53.

195. Larrabee, *Commander in Chief,* 577–78.

196. Lukas Haynes and Michael Ignatieff, "Mobilizing Public Support for the United Nations: A Case Study of State Department Leadership in Building Public and Congressional Support for a Leading U.S. Role in International Organization, 1944–1945," *Center for Public Leadership Working Papers,* Harvard University, 2003.

197. This is the term Kimball prefers. Kimball, *Juggler,* 93–94.

198. Haynes and Ignatieff, "Mobilizing Public Support for the United Nations."

199. Haynes and Ignatieff, "Mobilizing Public Support for the United Nations," 71.

200. Kennedy, *Freedom from Fear,* 854–55.

201. Roberts, *Masters and Commanders,* 346–47.

202. Eliot A. Cohen, *Supreme Command: Soldiers, Statesmen, and Leadership in Wartime* (New York: Anchor Books/Random House, 2002), chap. 4.

203. Roberts, *Masters and Commanders,* 411.

204. Larrabee, *Commander in Chief,* 635–36. For a full discussion of Churchill's responsibility for postwar British decline, see Peter Clarke, *The Last Thousand Days of the British Empire: Churchill, Roosevelt, and the Birth of Pax Americana* (New York: Bloomsbury Press, 2008).

205. Larrabee, *Commander in Chief,* 495–96.

206. Roberts, *Masters and Commanders,* 565–66. Churchill later claimed that had the Anglo-Americans advanced into the future Soviet zone and refused to withdraw according to the agreement, Stalin would have been forced to renegotiate the zone boundary. But the Soviets would have had no incentive to do so, particularly since the United States and Great Britain still wanted the Red Army to join the war against Japan. Larrabee, *Commander in Chief,* 496.

207. Larrabee, *Commander in Chief,* 3.

208. Roberts, *Masters and Commanders,* 410–11.

209. Importantly, too, Churchill and Roosevelt exercised different authority over their respective militaries. The president could issue an order and expect it to be obeyed, but the prime minister did not hold a position in the formal military chain of command. So he resorted to browbeating his military commanders. See Larrabee, *Commander in Chief,* 14–15.

210. Farrell, *Defense and Fall of Singapore 1940–1942*, 311. Interestingly, Hitler evinced an obsession with prestige, too, which led him to reject voluntary withdrawal from cities to which he attached symbolic importance. Hence the German disaster at Stalingrad, a pattern that was repeated time and again later in the war on the Eastern Front.

211. Roberts, *Masters and Commanders*, 283, 285.

212. The British military chiefs held Churchill's strategic judgment in low regard. Roberts, *Masters and Commanders*, 117.

213. Roberts, *Masters and Commanders*, 446.

214. Roberts, *Masters and Commanders*, 422–23. Even Brooke suspected Churchill wanted campaigns under British command for domestic political reasons, since the prime minister would face the voters as soon as the European war ended. Roberts, *Masters and Commanders*, 431–32. One has to wonder, though, whether the British people after four years of war would have shared Churchill's eagerness for British glory or instead preferred to let someone else take up the burden and cost.

215. Roberts, *Masters and Commanders*, 420–21, 498–99.

216. Larrabee, *Commander in Chief*, 496–97.

217. Roberts, *Masters and Commanders*, 556.

218. Larrabee, *Commander in Chief*, 579–80, 607–8.

219. Larrabee, *Commander in Chief*, 394.

220. Larrabee, *Commander in Chief*, 623–24.

221. For similar views, see Larrabee, *Commander in Chief*, 1–2; Roberts, *Masters and Commanders*, 77.

222. Kennedy, *Freedom from Fear*, 487–88. Publication of the details of the Victory Program, leaked by an isolationist senator, represented a grave security breach that gave German war planners key details about the American mobilization timetable and broad strategic plan. They might have used the information to impede the Anglo-American war effort if Hitler had been willing to listen to their recommendations. Since these would have involved going on the defensive on the Eastern Front and making operational withdrawals, however, he rejected their advice out-of-hand. Larrabee, *Commander in Chief*, 124–27.

223. Richard W. Steele, *Free Speech in the Good War* (New York: St. Martin's Press, 1999).

224. Kennedy, *Freedom from Fear*, 619.

225. Kennedy, *Freedom from Fear*, 793–94.

226. Kennedy, *Freedom from Fear*, 786–87. On the broad effects of the GI Bill, see especially Suzanne Mettler, *Soldiers to Citizens: The G.I. Bill and the Making of the Greatest Generation* (New York: Oxford University Press, 2005).

227. Personal consumption fell 22 percent in Great Britain during the war. Kennedy, *Freedom from Fear*, 646–47.

Chapter 4

1. Among many excellent accounts of the French war in Indochina (also often referred to as the First Vietnam War), see especially Martin Windrow, *The Last Valley: Dien Bien Phu and the French Defeat in Vietnam* (Cambridge, MA: De Capo Press, 2004). On the early days of the Vietminh and Giap, see A. J. Langguth, *Our Vietnam: The War 1954–1975* (New York: Simon and Schuster, 2000), 51ff.

2. Langguth, *Our Vietnam*, 79–80.

3. Langguth, *Our Vietnam*, 86.

4. Langguth, *Our Vietnam*, 86–87.

5. Herbert Y. Schandler, *America in Vietnam: The War that Couldn't Be Won* (Lanham, MD: Rowman and Littlefield, 2009), 18–19.

6. Langguth, *Our Vietnam*, 96–97, 99–100. The United States backed Diem's decision, and it was accepted by Great Britain and the Soviet Union, which acted as guarantors of the Geneva Agreement, in the interest of stability.

7. Langguth, *Our Vietnam*, 101–3. Langguth reports that nearly 700 village officials were assassinated by May 1958, more than a year before Hanoi authorized an uprising in the South. Langguth, *Our Vietnam*, 107.

8. Langguth, *Our Vietnam*, 116, 118–19, 143, 184–85.

9. For a vivid account of one such encounter, the battle of Ap Bac, see Neil Sheehan, *A Bright Shining Lie: John Paul Vann and America in Vietnam* (New York: Random House, 1988). Although, strictly speaking, not all South Vietnamese troops were part of the Army, I will use the acronym ARVN here as a generic term to encompass all regular forces under Saigon's control.

10. Schandler, *America in Vietnam*, 21.

11. Langguth, *Our Vietnam*, 211–15, 219–20.

12. Kennedy told Senator Mike Mansfield, a critic of American involvement in the war, that after he had been reelected president in 1964 he would withdraw from Vietnam, an idea he also shared with McNamara. But Kennedy did not suggest this to others and it seems unlikely, given the many pressures to prevent a communist triumph that any American leader at the time would have faced. Further, although it is true that he would no longer need to worry about reelection, he still needed to maintain his political credibility to accomplish other goals. He had spoken too often of the American commitment to preserve an independent South Vietnam to simply walk away after 1964. See Langguth, *Our Vietnam*, 208–9; Robert Dallek, "Lyndon Johnson and Vietnam: The Making of a Tragedy," *Diplomatic History* 20 (2) (Spring 1996): 147–62, at 148.

13. Langguth, *Our Vietnam*, 251ff.

14. Langguth, *Our Vietnam*, 279; Schandler, *America in Vietnam*, 43.

15. There is still dispute about when NVA formations (strictly speaking, People's Army of Vietnam or PAVN) began to join the fighting in South

Vietnam. Langguth says the Politburo in Hanoi, though hoping to overturn the Saigon government before decisive American intervention, still declined in December 1963 to send northern troops into combat. Langguth, *Our Vietnam*, 275. However, the Ninth Party Plenum in late 1963 approved the dispatch of northern troops to the South. Schandler, *America in Vietnam*, 43. Harry Summers dates the introduction of regular NVA troops to late summer 1964. Harry G. Summers Jr., *On Strategy: A Critical Analysis of the Vietnam War* (New York: Presidio, 1982, 1995), 87. Hanoi claimed after the war that none of its troops joined the struggle until after American forces arrived in large numbers, an assertion few Western observers then or later have accepted.

16. Hanoi clearly accelerated its efforts to achieve victory before the United States could intervene on a massive scale. Schandler, *America in Vietnam*, 43, 45.

17. H. W. Brands, *The Wages of Globalism: Lyndon Johnson and the Limits of American Power* (New York: Oxford University Press, 1995), 220.

18. Langguth, *Our Vietnam*, 266–67; Doris Kearns [Goodwin], *Lyndon Johnson and the American Dream* (New York: New American Library, 1976), 268. Not all scholars accept this view of an insecure Johnson on foreign policy. For contrasting assessments, see Gary R. Hess, *Presidential Decisions for War: Korea, Vietnam, and the Persian Gulf* (Baltimore: Johns Hopkins University Press, 2001), 80; Elizabeth H. Saunders, *Leaders at War: How Presidents Shape Military Interventions* (Ithaca: Cornell University Press, 2011), chap. 5.

19. Brands, *Wages of Globalism*, 235; Langguth, *Our Vietnam*, 118.

20. Hess, *Presidential Decisions for War*, 79.

21. Hess, *Presidential Decisions for War*, 107.

22. Dallek, "Lyndon Johnson and Vietnam," 148.

23. Former President Eisenhower advised Johnson in 1965 that if the Chinese entered the war the United States should use tactical nuclear weapons if necessary, and expressed confidence the Chinese would not retaliate. Langguth, *Our Vietnam*, 349. Others, fortunately, were not so sanguine about where the use of nuclear weapons might lead.

24. James S. Robbins, *This Time We Win: Revisiting the Tet Offensive* (New York: Encounter Books, 2010), 24. There was good reason for uncertainty about Chinese intentions. Mao Zedong in early 1965 signaled via the writer Edgar Snow that China would not intervene in the war unless attacked and added that Beijing expected to establish friendly relations with the United States at some point. But Mao also offered Ho Chi Minh support troops in April 1965 and pledged combat troops in the event of an American invasion of the DRV. As Johnson weighed sending major American ground units in summer 1965, General Harold Johnson, the army chief of staff, predicted that China would not send troops into the conflict, but could offer no answer when the president

pressed him on what to do if the Chinese intervened other than to admit "we have another ball game." Langguth, *Our Vietnam*, 348–49, 355–56, 379–80. Interestingly, the North Vietnamese also worried that the United States might push China into direct intervention. Hanoi feared that the Chinese, once in Vietnam, might not leave readily. Vietnam had a long history of resistance to Chinese control that remained much on the minds of DRV leaders, notwithstanding their ideological affinities with Chinese communism. Schandler, *America in Vietnam*, 104–5.

25. Robbins, *This Time We Win*, 25.

26. British Prime Minister Harold Wilson also regarded the American commitment in South Vietnam as misguided. When the United States began bombing the DRV in 1965, he tried to express his concern directly to Johnson, but the president refused a meeting. Langguth, *Our Vietnam*, 342.

27. Hess, *Presidential Decisions for War*, 93; Langguth, *Our Vietnam*, 317.

28. Hess, *Presidential Decisions for War*, 83.

29. For a description of the incident and how insignificant it seemed initially to leaders on both sides, see Langguth, *Our Vietnam*, 299–301.

30. Langguth, *Our Vietnam*, 305–7.

31. Hess, *Presidential Decisions for War*, 88; Langguth, *Our Vietnam*, 304. At the time of Tonkin Gulf, Americans saw Johnson as better able to handle the situation by nearly four-to-one over Goldwater if things got worse in Vietnam. Robbins, *This Time We Win*, 43.

32. Quoted in Herbert Y. Schandler, *Lyndon Johnson and Vietnam: The Unmaking of a President* (Princeton: Princeton University Press, 1977, 1983), 7.

33. Langguth, *Our Vietnam*, 323–32, 337, 340; Hess, *Presidential Decisions for War*, 91–92.

34. Langguth, *Our Vietnam*, 341–42.

35. Langguth maintains that Ball undercut his own objections by promising to support the president's decision. "With that concession, Ball guaranteed that he could always speak and could always be ignored." Langguth, *Our Vietnam*, 377–78. This is overly harsh. Ball's willingness to press his arguments in the face of strong opposition from his bureaucratic superiors reflects well on his integrity. There is no reason to assume that Johnson would have decided otherwise had Ball threatened to take his objections public or to resign.

36. Brands, *Wages of Globalism*, 240; Langguth, *Our Vietnam*, 382–83.

37. Hess, *Presidential Decisions for War*, 98–102.

38. Hess, *Presidential Decisions for War*, 104–5, 107.

39. Brands, *Wages of Globalism*, 239; Dallek, "Lyndon Johnson and Vietnam," 147; Dallek, "Lyndon Johnson and Vietnam," 149. However, Dallek adds that once the high cost of the war became clear, Kennedy would have found a way to extricate the United States.

40. Hess, *Presidential Decisions for War*, 107–8, 110; Dallek, "Lyndon Johnson and Vietnam," 150.

41. Dallek, "Lyndon Johnson and Vietnam," 151; Brands, *Wages of Globalism*, 242.

42. Schandler describes the beginning of sustained bombing as an effort "to broaden the reprisal concept . . . as gradually and imperceptibly as possible." *Lyndon Johnson and Vietnam*, 15.

43. Schandler, *Lyndon Johnson and Vietnam*, 21–22; Hess, *Presidential Decisions for War*, 106.

44. Hess, *Presidential Decisions for War*, 110; Brands, *Wages of Globalism*, 232–33; Dallek, "Lyndon Johnson and Vietnam," 152. On the risks of embarking on a protracted war without strong public support, see Summers, *On Strategy*, 12–13.

45. Hess, *Presidential Decisions for War*, 111.

46. For a detailed account of the process of writing the speech and testing some of its key themes in advance within the administration and with key press and congressional leaders, see Kathleen J. Turner, *Lyndon Johnson's Dual War: Vietnam and the Press* (Chicago: University of Chicago Press, 1985), chap. 5.

47. Lyndon B. Johnson, "Peace without Conquest," April 7, 1965, Johns Hopkins University, *Public Papers of the Presidents of the United States: Lyndon B. Johnson, 1965*, Book 1 (Washington, DC: Government Printing Office, 1966), 394–99.

48. Johnson, "Peace without Conquest."

49. Johnson, "Peace without Conquest."

50. Johnson, "Peace without Conquest."

51. Robbins, *This Time We Win*, 20.

52. For a discussion of the implications of the limits of American power in the 1960s, see Brands, *Wages of Globalism*.

53. Johnson, "Peace without Conquest."

54. General Westmoreland called for a staggered buildup of American forces from 1965 forward because South Vietnam simply could not accommodate the more rapid arrival of American troops. Schandler, *America in Vietnam*, 106–7.

55. Counterinsurgency methods went beyond military support to include assistance in political development and economic aid. Robbins, *This Time We Win*, 22; Summers, *On Strategy*, 72–73.

56. Lewis Sorley, *A Better War: The Unexamined Victories and Final Tragedy of America's Last Years in Vietnam* (Orlando, FL: Harvest/Harcourt, 1999), 2.

57. Summers, *On Strategy*, 43–44, 72–73. Decker reportedly assured Kennedy that "any good soldier can handle guerillas." Quoted in Schandler, *America in Vietnam*, 31.

58. Larry Berman, *Lyndon Johnson's War: The Road to Stalemate in Vietnam* (New York: W. W. Norton, 1989), 46.

59. Hess, *Presidential Decisions for War*, 117–18.

60. For example, at a November 10, 1965, meeting, Johnson told the chiefs they were naive and reckless, willing to bring on a world war. Robbins, *This Time We Win*, 30–31.

61. Schandler, *Lyndon Johnson and Vietnam*, 59–61; Langguth, *Our Vietnam*, 454–55.

62. For a full discussion and sharp critique of administration-JCS relations throughout this period, see H. R. McMaster, *Dereliction of Duty: Lyndon Johnson, Robert McNamara, the Joint Chiefs of Staff, and the Lies that Led to Vietnam* (New York: HarperCollins, 1997).

63. For example, he argued strongly in early 1967 for permission to extend ground combat operations into Laos and Cambodia. Langguth, *Our Vietnam*, 442.

64. The March–April 1967 discussion of Westmoreland's request to raise the 1967 troop ceiling from the approved 470,000 to at least 555,000 (he preferred 670,000) is recounted in Berman, *Lyndon Johnson's War*, 34–35.

65. For postwar criticisms of American strategy in Vietnam, see George C. Herring, "American Strategy in Vietnam: The Postwar Debate," *Military Affairs* 46 (2) (April 1982): 57–63, esp. 59 60.

66. Sorley, *Better War*, 6, 20–21.

67. Berman, *Lyndon Johnson's War*, 54–55.

68. Sorley, *Better War*, 15–16.

69. Hess, *Presidential Decisions for War*, 113. The administration's fear of Chinese involvement has been questioned, both during the war and later. Of note, however, notwithstanding American precautions, Beijing still sent thousands of military specialists to the DRV to assist in air defenses and engineering. Langguth, *Our Vietnam*, 374–75. Concern about the Chinese influenced American military leaders, too: among the reasons the JCS advocated reserve mobilization was a desire to deter Beijing, which was seen as less likely to send in its forces if it knew that the United States was prepared to meet them on equal terms. Schandler, *Lyndon Johnson and Vietnam*, 34.

70. The possibility that the United States would cut off the Laotian supply route deeply concerned communist military commanders. See Langguth, *Our Vietnam*, 439.

71. Schandler, *Lyndon Johnson and Vietnam*, 42.

72. In summer 1967, when U.S. officials pressed a number of Asian allies to increase their troop commitments, virtually all refused. They were untroubled by the prospect of a communist victory. Schandler, *Lyndon Johnson and Vietnam*, 53–54; Berman, *Lyndon Johnson's War*, 56.

73. Langguth, *Our Vietnam*, 409, 418; Berman, *Lyndon Johnson's War*, 23–24, 77–78.

74. Langguth, *Our Vietnam*, 438; Berman, *Lyndon Johnson's War*, 121–22. It is always possible to second-guess policy decisions that do not work, and

the bombing campaign is no different. Thus some revisionists have argued that the United States would have done better to wage a shorter, more intensive bombing campaign because it would have drawn less criticism. See Robbins, *This Time We Win*, 36. Such counterfactual speculation, though, requires that one accept a chain of implausible assumptions about how the government and people of the DRV would have responded, what China and the Soviet Union might have done, and how both world and domestic opinion would have reflected this.

75. Berman, *Lyndon Johnson's War*, 16.
76. Berman, *Lyndon Johnson's War*, 13–14.
77. Schandler, *Lyndon Johnson and Vietnam*, 65–66.
78. Sorley, *Better War*, 4–5, 20–21.
79. The relationship is discussed at length in Sorley, *Better War*.
80. Sorley, *Better War*, 61–62,
81. Schandler, *America in Vietnam*, 96–97.
82. Hess, *Presidential Decisions for War*, 116–17.
83. Westmoreland told Johnson at a meeting at Honolulu in March 1967 that the Vietcong could continue the war indefinitely. Langguth, *Our Vietnam*, 441. A number of plans were proposed to isolate the communist forces in South Vietnam by cutting off supply routes through Laos. These were rejected, as I note, for political reasons. See Summers, *On Strategy*, 119.
84. The CIA reported in early 1967 that Hanoi remained confident that American resolve would weaken first. Berman, *Lyndon Johnson's War*, 27–28. The problem extends beyond Vietnam. See Andrew Mack, "Why Big Nations Lose Small Wars: The Politics of Asymmetric Conflict," *World Politics* 27 (January 1975): 175–200.
85. Also at issue was where to stop: the communists could extend their supply lines westward into Thailand, increasing the risk of subversion there. Unlike Korea, then, no conventional defense line could be established across Southeast Asia that would make possible a quarantine of South Vietnam within the force limits set by the administration. (However, for a different view, see Summers, *On Strategy*.) In 1967, McNamara floated a proposal to create a barrier of electronic sensors across the 17th parallel westward through Laos to check infiltration, part of a scheme to stabilize the American troop commitment. The idea proved both impractical and very expensive, and it was eventually rejected.
86. Thus General Wheeler predicted in July 1965 that Hanoi, fearing an attack on the DRV, would not be willing to send more than one-quarter of its army into South Vietnam. Langguth, *Our Vietnam*, 378.
87. Schandler, *Lyndon Johnson and Vietnam*, 57–58; Berman, *Lyndon Johnson's War*, 94–95.
88. The president complained that his military commanders lacked imagination. Berman, *Lyndon Johnson's War*, 78.

89. Langguth, *Our Vietnam*, 446.
90. It should be noted that Johnson's key advisors, notably McNamara and Rusk, also refused to reconsider their initial assumptions about Soviet and Chinese intervention. Berman, *Lyndon Johnson's War*, 108–9. This suggests the danger in retaining for too long key aides who have invested so deeply in certain assumptions that they are beyond reassessment.
91. Berman, *Lyndon Johnson's War*, 41, 103, 25.
92. Turner, *Lyndon Johnson's Dual War*, 4–6.
93. Turner, *Lyndon Johnson's Dual War*, 140–41.
94. Johnson's own defensiveness and doubts about whether he as a southern president could ever get fair treatment from the elite media worked against his fitful efforts to improve press relations. Turner, *Lyndon Johnson's Dual War*, 117.
95. Turner, *Lyndon Johnson's Dual War*, 4.
96. Dallek, "Lyndon Johnson and Vietnam," 159–60.
97. These included several former senior military officers such as Generals James Gavin, Matthew Ridgeway, and David Shoup, whose arguments that the war was unwinnable and not in American interests gave considerable legitimacy to the antiwar movement. On the influence of retired officers who opposed the war, see Rob Buzzanco, "The American Military's Rationale against the Vietnam War," *Political Science Quarterly* 101 (4) (1986): 559–76.
98. He contended that Johnson had shifted war aims from those set by his brother, which he had helped establish. Robbins, *This Time We Win*, 53.
99. Schandler, *Lyndon Johnson and Vietnam*, 54–56; Berman, *Lyndon Johnson's War*, 73, 78. Even before the new targets were approved, the administration had authorized strikes on all but 39 of 242 targets recommended by the JCS. Berman, *Lyndon Johnson's War*, 71.
100. Schandler, *America in Vietnam*, 133–35.
101. Berman, *Lyndon Johnson's War*, 27, 60.
102. The president closely followed public opinion polls and tried to influence both question wording and, through the timing of his public statements and other actions, the results. Lawrence R. Jacobs and Robert Y. Shapiro, "Lyndon Johnson, Vietnam, and Public Opinion: Rethinking Realist Theory of Leadership," *Presidential Studies Quarterly* 29 (3) (September 1999): 592–616, esp. 606–7.
103. Berman, *Lyndon Johnson's War*, 60, 85–86. The administration sought to influence both the poll results and how they were interpreted by the media, with very little to show for its troubles. See Bruce E. Altschuler, "Lyndon Johnson and the Public Polls," *Public Opinion Quarterly* 50 (3) (1986): 285–99.
104. Robbins, *This Time We Win*, 44, 47–48. On the three-way split in opinion, see Jacobs and Shapiro, "Lyndon Johnson, Vietnam, and Public Opinion," 610.

105. Jacobs and Shapiro, "Lyndon Johnson, Vietnam, and Public Opinion," 600–602; Turner, *Lyndon Johnson's Dual War*, 192–93, 208.
106. Turner, *Lyndon Johnson's Dual War*, 164–65, 192–93, 208.
107. Historians continue to debate which side could better withstand a stalemate. The more established view holds that a stalemate played into communist hands because the American commitment was more vulnerable. Thus Larry Berman claims, "Hanoi could accept the conditions of a stalemate longer than the United States. Stalemate was tantamount to victory for Hanoi." Berman, *Lyndon Johnson's War*, 25. On the other hand, the revisionist school challenges the idea that insurgents win merely by not losing. See Robbins, *This Time We Win*. The response of both sides in early 1967 suggests deep frustration with the pace of the war, rather than confidence it could outlast its adversary.
108. Berman, *Lyndon Johnson's War*, 30–31, 33.
109. Robbins, *This Time We Win*, 39.
110. For a full account of the debate about the communist order of battle, see Berman, *Lyndon Johnson's War*.
111. Sorley, *Better War*, 21.
112. Robbins, *This Time We Win*, 37; Berman, *Lyndon Johnson's War*, 28–29, 38–39, 49–50, 74–75, 81–83, 110–11.
113. On the skepticism in the media about the new numbers, see Berman, *Lyndon Johnson's War*, 119. Years later Westmoreland would become involved in a lawsuit against CBS when a broadcast charged him with deliberately trying to deceive the president about actual truth strength. The dispute is discussed in detail by Berman, who concludes the deception was being foisted by the president and most of his senior officials, determined to create an impression of progress in the public mind. Johnson pressured MACV for evidence of military gains to suit his political needs at home. Berman, *Lyndon Johnson's War*, 111–13.
114. Berman, *Lyndon Johnson's War*, 113–17.
115. Robbins, *This Time We Win*, 90.
116. Berman, *Lyndon Johnson's War*, 119; Robbins, *This Time We Win*, 90.
117. Hess, *Presidential Decisions for War*, 139.
118. Robbins, *This Time We Win*, 67–68, 64, 75.
119. Giap understood the danger of premature efforts to launch the third phase of a Maoist people's war. In early 1951 he had attempted to inflict a decisive defeat on the French in the Red River region of what was then called Tonkin, the area that included Hanoi and Haiphong. His forces had suffered a stinging rebuff at the hands of the French, whose military assets were best suited to conventional warfare. For a vivid description of these failed attacks, see Bernard B. Fall, *Street without Joy* (New York: Shocken, 1972), chaps. 2–3. Now the Tet Offensive advocates proposed to leave their forces exposed to the firepower of an even more formidable adversary.

120. Robbins, *This Time We Win*, 76–77.
121. Robbins, *This Time We Win*, 86–88.
122. Berman, *Lyndon Johnson's War*, 141–42.
123. Robbins, *This Time We Win*, 115–16.
124. Robbins, *This Time We Win*, 121.
125. Berman, *Lyndon Johnson's War*, 145–46.
126. Berman, *Lyndon Johnson's War*, 146.
127. Johnson himself realized he had erred by conveying an unduly optimistic picture of the war back in November and by not calling attention to the expected major enemy attacks in his State of the Union address on January 17, 1968. Berman, *Lyndon Johnson's War*, 199. See also Robbins, *This Time We Win*, 122–23.
128. Langguth, *Our Vietnam*, 474–75.
129. Berman, *Lyndon Johnson's War*, 163–64; Langguth, *Our Vietnam*, 480, 490.
130. Berman, *Lyndon Johnson's War*, 166.
131. Berman, *Lyndon Johnson's War*, 175.
132. Berman, *Lyndon Johnson's War*, 186; Turner, *Lyndon Johnson's Dual War*, 7.
133. Berman, *Lyndon Johnson's War*, 160–62, 165, 171.
134. Berman, *Lyndon Johnson's War*, chap. 10.
135. Berman, *Lyndon Johnson's War*, 189–99.
136. Berman, *Lyndon Johnson's War*, 199–201.
137. Langguth, *Our Vietnam*, 354–55.
138. Langguth, *Our Vietnam*, 355.
139. Langguth, *Our Vietnam*, 361.
140. Langguth, *Our Vietnam*, 386, 408–9.
141. Berman, *Lyndon Johnson's War*, 83–84; Langguth, *Our Vietnam*, 451–53.
142. Berman, *Lyndon Johnson's War*, 79.
143. Langguth, *Our Vietnam*, 455–58.
144. Berman, *Lyndon Johnson's War*, 123; Robbins, *This Time We Win*, chap. 6.
145. Langguth, *Our Vietnam*, 510–11, 519–20, 521–22.
146. Langguth, *Our Vietnam*, 513, 523–27, 529; Hess, *Presidential Decisions for War*, 148.
147. Berman, *Lyndon Johnson's War*, 106–7; Robbins, *This Time We Win*, 72.
148. Johnson did no better when he sent a personal appeal to Ho because American terms remained unchanged. Hess, *Presidential Decisions for War*, 127–28. Many observers, then and later, have noted how Johnson underestimated Ho's commitment. See, for example, Robbins, *This Time We Win*, 29.
149. Larry Berman, *No Peace, No Honor: Nixon, Kissinger, and Betrayal in Vietnam* (New York: Free Press, 2001), 47.
150. Joan Hoff, *Nixon Reconsidered* (New York: Basic, 1994), 152.
151. Berman, *No Peace, No Honor*, 40.
152. Hoff, *Nixon Reconsidered*, 208–9; Berman, *No Peace, No Honor*, 44, 49.

153. Sorley, *Better War*, 38–40, 112–13, 115–16.
154. Hoff, *Nixon Reconsidered*, 163–65.
155. Hoff, *Nixon Reconsidered*, 212; Sorley, *Better War*, 128–29.
156. On the other hand, the Americans did claim that the North Vietnamese violated understandings dating back to the 1968 bombing halt not to take advantage of the situation to launch major offensive operations. Hanoi consistently denied that any such understandings existed.
157. Kissinger later acknowledged this conundrum. Berman, *No Peace, No Honor*, 80.
158. Sorley, *Better War*, 176–77. Sorley offers an excellent account of Abrams's tenure as MACV commander.
159. Langguth, *Our Vietnam*, 538.
160. Sorley, *Better War*.
161. Sorley, *Better War*, 160–61, 186–87, 331.
162. Sorley, *Better War*, 254ff.
163. Sorley, *Better War*, 321ff.
164. Sorley, *Better War*, 166. But on the matter of a residual American force, Laird evidently went back and forth. He suggested privately in late 1971 that some American troops would likely remain in Vietnam for decades. Sorley, *Better War*, 282.
165. Sorley, *Better War*, 117.
166. Berman, *No Peace, No Honor*, 55–58.
167. Later the president and others offered various rationales for the secrecy, such as a desire to avoid forcing Cambodia's head of state, Prince Norodom Sihanouk, to acknowledge the attacks. The record of internal administration discussions, though, makes it clear that domestic political considerations were the key factors.
168. Hoff, *Nixon Reconsidered*, 212–13, 217; Sorley, *Better War*, 117–19; Berman, *No Peace, No Honor*, 50–51.
169. Langguth, *Our Vietnam*, 557ff., 564.
170. Berman, *No Peace, No Honor*, 58–59; Sorley, *Better War*, 169; Hoff, *Nixon Reconsidered*, 229.
171. This interpretation is developed at length in Belma S. Steinberg, *Shame and Humiliation: Presidential Decision Making on Vietnam* (Pittsburgh: University of Pittsburgh Press, 1996), chap. 5. See also Langguth, *Our Vietnam*, 544–45.
172. Langguth, *Our Vietnam*, 566; Sorley, *Better War*, 116, 202.
173. Langguth, *Our Vietnam*, 568.
174. Sorley, *Better War*, 203–5.
175. Hoff, *Nixon Reconsidered*, 229; Sorley, *Better War*, 210; Langguth, *Our Vietnam*, 571.
176. Sorley, *Better War*, 213–14; Langguth, *Our Vietnam*, 568.
177. Sorley, *Better War*, 228, 230, 233, 262–63; Langguth, *Our Vietnam*, 578–79.

178. Sorley, *Better War*, chap. 20.
179. Abrams clearly understood that Saigon could not afford to keep so large an army in the field indefinitely with its own resources. Sorley, *Better War*, 215.
180. Sorley, *Better War*, 218–19.
181. Sorley, *Better War*, 276, 335.
182. Sorley, *Better War*, 282.
183. Sorley, *Better War*, 212–13.
184. Indeed, as long ago as 1847, Whig opponents of the Mexican War grudgingly conceded that they had no alternative but to support Democratic President James K. Polk's request for additional military appropriations. One Whig writer stated the political problem bluntly in the party's leading journal: "Congress would never refuse to grant anything and everything necessary or proper for the support and succor of our brave troops, placed without any fault of their own, in the heart of a distant country, and struggling with every peril, discomfort and difficulty." "The Whigs and the War," *American Review* 6 (October 1847): 343, as quoted in Norman Graebner, "Lessons of the Mexican War," *Pacific Historical Review* 47 (August 1978): 325–42.
185. Berman, *No Peace, No Honor*, 81.
186. Hoff, *Nixon Reconsidered*, 158.
187. Berman, *No Peace, No Honor*, 262.
188. Berman, *No Peace, No Honor*, 246.
189. Berman, *No Peace, No Honor*, 39–44.
190. Langguth, *Our Vietnam*, 554, 606.
191. Berman, *No Peace, No Honor*, 66, 70, 92–93.
192. Hoff, *Nixon Reconsidered*, 224–27.
193. Berman, *No Peace, No Honor*, 66, 69–70, 80.
194. Berman, *No Peace, No Honor*, chaps. 7–8.
195. Berman, *No Peace, No Honor*, 52, 68.
196. Berman, *No Peace, No Honor*, 112–17.
197. Berman, *No Peace, No Honor*, 164, 171–72, 189ff.
198. Berman, *No Peace, No Honor*, 184–87, 195, 199–202.
199. Berman, *No Peace, No Honor*, 177–79, 241–42, 253.
200. Sorley, *Better War*, 363, 365.
201. Berman, *No Peace, No Honor*, 255–58.
202. Sorley, *Better War*, 364; Berman, *No Peace, No Honor*, chap. 13.
203. Sorley, *Better War*, 367ff. In response to less American aid, South Vietnam reduced its military to just under 1 million troops, including paramilitary forces. This total greatly exceeded the estimated 280,000 NVA/VC troops in South Vietnam in late April 1975. Sorley, *Better War*, 370; Berman, *No Peace, No Honor*, 270.
204. Hoff, *Nixon Reconsidered*, 209.
205. Ever since the war ended, participants and historians have debated whether the United States and its Saigon allies might have won the conflict. Proponents of the view that the war was winnable tend to

focus on the military side of the equation, stressing the fact that American forces were never bested in combat and pointing to the improved effectiveness of the ARVN after 1969. See, for example, Sorley, *Better War*; Summers, *On Strategy*. From this perspective, blame for the ultimate collapse of South Vietnam rests with some combination of Congress, for failing to sustain aid to the Thieu government, and Watergate, which weakened Nixon to the point that he could not retaliate.

I reject this analysis. As I have explained, Nixon's key error lay in his failure to build domestic backing early in his administration for a durable commitment to support South Vietnam. Whether this was ever possible may be debated, of course, because it involves a historical counterfactual. But by the time of the peace agreement in 1973, it was foolish to believe the United States would punish violations over the long term based on Nixon's private pledges.

On the other side, skeptics contend that the war was always unwinnable by the United States because of the dedication demonstrated by the Vietnamese communists and the chronic weaknesses of the Saigon government. See, for example, Schandler, *America in Vietnam*. I do not question the fierce determination shown by the communists. To say they would have persisted indefinitely in the face of a permanent commitment by the United States along the Korean model, however, suggests they were simply unmindful of the costs of their struggle. This ignores evidence of their demoralization at various points in the war—possibly during the 1967 stalemate, after Tet, and in the wake of their setbacks in the post-1969 pacification campaign. The pacification gains also reflected significant reforms undertaken by the Saigon government that increased its popular support. Thieu proved to be his own worst enemy by his refusal to show any faith in his people—fearful they might reject him, he was unwilling to chance any political opposition.

I conclude that the United States might have achieved a different outcome in the war had presidents acted differently at critical junctures. But these windows of opportunity (pursuing a different approach to Westmoreland's misconceived search-and-destroy method, cultivating congressional support for a long-term commitment to South Vietnam rather than launching the 1970 Cambodia incursion) were short-lived. We also need to remember that in Vietnam, as in every war, both sides made significant mistakes. Hanoi might have fought a smarter war, too.

206. Arthur M. Schlesinger Jr., *The Imperial Presidency* (Boston: Houghton Mifflin 1973).

Chapter 5

1. Michael R. Gordon and General Bernard E. Trainor, *Cobra II: The Inside Story of the Invasion and Occupation of Iraq* (New York: Pantheon, 2006), xxxi. See similarly Richard N. Haass, *War of Necessity, War of Choice: A*

Memoir of Two Iraq Wars (New York: Simon and Schuster, 2009). Because few documents about the Iraq War have been declassified to date, analysts have relied heavily on several fine works by journalists as well as a number of memoirs by former members of the Bush administration. Both should be regarded with caution. Many insiders who speak to reporters seek favorable treatment in their books, while memoirs often have a self-exculpatory purpose, especially when the authors have become the target of criticism. Besides Gordon and Trainor, see Thomas E. Ricks, *Fiasco: The American Military Adventure in Iraq* (New York: Penguin Books, 2006, 2007); Thomas E. Ricks, *The Gamble: General David Petraeus and the American Military Adventure in Iraq, 2006–2008* (New York: Penguin, 2009); Bob Woodward, *Bush at War* (New York: Simon and Schuster, 2002, 2003); Bob Woodward, *State of Denial: Bush at War, Part III* (New York: Simon and Schuster, 2006); Bob Woodward, *The War Within: A Secret White House History, 2006–2008* (New York: Simon and Schuster, 2008).

2. For a detailed account of the diplomatic and military preparations that culminated in the Gulf War, see Gary R. Hess, *Presidential Decisions for War: Korea, Vietnam, and the Persian Gulf* (Baltimore: Johns Hopkins University Press, 2001), chap. 5.

3. Gordon and Trainor, *Cobra II*, 12.

4. Hess, *Presidential Decisions for War*, 202, 205–6.

5. The Guard's successful escape owed to several factors. One was the so-called fog of battle: American commanders believed they had engaged and destroyed a significant portion of the Republican Guard in Kuwait. Leaders in Washington also worried that ongoing attacks on retreating Iraqi troops would generate images of senseless slaughter of fleeing soldiers.

6. Hess, *Presidential Decisions for War*, chap. 6; Ricks, *Fiasco*, 4–6.

7. The belief that the dictator had retained WMD extended to members of his inner circle, who were later dismayed to learn on the eve of the American invasion in 2003 that no such weapons existed. Gordon and Trainor, *Cobra II*, 118.

8. Gordon and Trainor, *Cobra II*, 55.

9. Gideon Rose, *How Wars End: Why We Always Fight the Last Battle* (New York: Simon and Schuster, 2010), 241.

10. Ricks, *Fiasco*, 18–19; Gordon and Trainor, *Cobra II*, 13, 26.

11. Ricks, *Fiasco*, 15.

12. Gary R. Hess, *Presidential Decisions for War: Korea, Vietnam, the Persian Gulf, and Iraq*, 2nd ed. (Baltimore: Johns Hopkins University Press, 2009), 225–26; Dina Badie, "Groupthink, Iraq, and the War on Terror: Explaining US Policy Shift toward Iraq," *Foreign Policy Analysis* 6 (2010): 277–96, at 282.

13. Gordon and Trainor, *Cobra II*, 12–13.

14. Rose, *How Wars End*, 241–42.

15. Rose, *How Wars End*, 242. On the early warnings to the incoming Bush administration of the al-Qaeda threat, see Woodward, *Bush at War*, 34–35.
16. Ricks, *Fiasco*, 27–28.
17. Gordon and Trainor, *Cobra II*, 13; Rose, *How Wars End*, 257.
18. Gordon and Trainor, *Cobra II*, 16; Ricks, *Fiasco*, 30–31; Woodward, *Bush at War*, 60, 83–85.
19. Woodward, *Bush at War*, 99.
20. For a full account from the administration's perspective, see Woodward, *Bush at War*.
21. Rose, *How Wars End*, 268–69.
22. Rose, *How Wars End*, 270.
23. Ricks, *Fiasco*, 32–33; Rose, *How Wars End*, 243.
24. As journalist Thomas Ricks puts it, the decision to go to war with Iraq was made "more through drift than through any one meeting." Ricks, *Fiasco*, 58. See similarly John P. Burke, "Condoleezza Rice as NSC Advisor: A Case Study of the Honest Broker Role," *Presidential Studies Quarterly* 35 (3) (September 2005): 554–75, at 559; James P. Pfiffner, "Decision Making in the Bush White House," *Presidential Studies Quarterly* 39 (2) (June 2009): 363–84, at 375–76.
25. Ricks, *Fiasco*, 48–49; Rose, *How Wars End*, 243.
26. Burke, "Condoleezza Rice as NSC Advisor," 560, 563.
27. Even now, after multiple books and memoirs, the post-9/11 Bush administration fixation on Iraq remains "a bit mysterious." Rose, *How Wars End*, 252–53. On the heightened sensitivity to any and all possibilities of another terrorist attack, see Ron Suskind, *The One Percent Doctrine: Deep Inside America's Pursuit of Its Enemies Since 9/11* (New York: Simon and Schuster, 2006).
28. Gordon and Trainor, *Cobra II*, 72–73.
29. Rose, *How Wars End*, 270–71. Even those within the administration who had earlier espoused a realist perspective, such as Rice and Cheney, adapted to the new, more permissive setting. Hess, *Presidential Decisions for War*, 2nd ed., 223; Ricks, *Fiasco*, 47–48.
30. Peter W. Galbraith, *The End of Iraq: How American Incompetence Created a War without End* (New York: Simon and Schuster, 2006, 2007), 83–84.
31. Gordon and Trainor, *Cobra II*, 64.
32. James Dobbins, "Who Lost Iraq? Lessons from the Debacle," *Foreign Affairs* 86 (5) (September–October 2007): 61–74, at 66.
33. Burke, "Condoleezza Rice as NSC Advisor," 554–55, 560.
34. Many have commented on Cheney's important role and alleged he exercised undue influence over the president. It seems more reasonable to assume the vice president tended to echo and thus reinforce the president's own views. David Mitchell and Tansa George Massoud, "Anatomy of Failure: Bush's Decision-Making Process and the Iraq War," *Foreign Policy Analysis* 5 (2009): 265–86, at 274.

35. Badie, "Groupthink, Iraq, and the War on Terror."
36. One noteworthy exception was Marine Major General Gregory S. New-bold, who resigned in protest against the invasion but remained quiet about his decision.
37. Ricks, *Fiasco*, 22.
38. Among the Iraqi exiles touting information about Saddam Hussein's WMD and terrorist connections was Ahmed Chalabi, who would continue to find favor with Wolfowitz and other Defense Department officials until after the invasion. See Ricks, *Fiasco*, 56–57.
39. Gordon and Trainor, *Cobra II*, 127. On the general inflation of the Iraqi threat by the administration, see Chaim Kaufmann, "Threat Inflation and the Failure of the Marketplace of Ideas: The Selling of the Iraq War," *International Security* 29 (1) (Summer 2004): 5–48.
40. Kaufmann, "Threat Inflation and the Failure of the Marketplace of Ideas," 39–40; Badie, "Groupthink, Iraq, and the War on Terror," 287, 289. For an insider's perspective on the misuse of intelligence, see Paul R. Pillar, "Intelligence, Policy, and the War in Iraq," *Foreign Affairs* 85 (2) (March/April 2006): 15–27.
41. Hess, *Presidential Decisions for War*, 2nd ed., 232–33.
42. *New York Times*, June 1, 2002. For a discussion, see Hess, *Presidential Decisions for War*, 2nd ed., 232–33.
43. Ricks, *Fiasco*, 49, 51, 58–59, 61.
44. Kaufmann, "Threat Inflation and the Failure of the Marketplace of Ideas," 20–25, 37, 43–44.
45. In late 2002, polls showed 70 percent to 90 percent of Americans believed Saddam would attack the US with WMD at some point, and more than 95 percent believed he was stockpiling such weapons. Kaufmann, "Threat Inflation and the Failure of the Marketplace of Ideas," 30. On the impact of "one-sided information flow," see John R. Zaller, *The Nature and Origins of Mass Opinion* (New York: Cambridge University Press, 1992, 1995), chap. 6.
46. These were not declassified until after the 2003 invasion. Gordon and Trainor, *Cobra II*, 128–29; Kaufmann, "Threat Inflation and the Failure of the Marketplace of Ideas," 37–38; Ricks, *Fiasco*, 52–55, 61.
47. The House voted to authorize the use of force, 296 to 133, on October 10, 2002, and the Senate approved the resolution the following day, 77 to 23. Some of the Democratic presidential aspirants who supported the authorization resolution contended that they had done so only to enhance the president's diplomatic leverage at the United Nations. Gordon and Trainor, *Cobra II*, 130. But the congressional resolution explicitly empowered the president to use force if necessary. On the Democrats' concern about their vulnerability on national security issues and Bush's timing of the authorization vote, see Hess, *Presidential Decisions for War*, 2nd ed., 235–36, 239–43.

48. Gordon and Trainor, *Cobra II*, 41–43.
49. Gordon and Trainor, *Cobra II*, 71.
50. Hess, *Presidential Decisions for War*, 2nd ed., 243–44.
51. Hess, *Presidential Decisions for War*, 2nd ed., 245–46.
52. Gordon and Trainor, *Cobra II*, 133–34; Ricks, *Fiasco*, 90–93.
53. Michael C. Desch, "Bush and the Generals," *Foreign Affairs* (May/June 2007), http://www.foreignaffairs.org/20070501faessay86309/michael-c-desch/bush-and-the-generals; Mackubin Thomas Owens, "Rumsfeld, the Generals, and the State of U.S. Civil-Military Relations," *Naval War College Review* 59 (4) (Autumn 2006): 68–80, at 68–69, 78.
54. Ricks, *Fiasco*, 68; Gordon and Trainor, *Cobra II*, 5–6.
55. Gordon and Trainor, *Cobra II*, 3, 6–7.
56. Ricks, *Fiasco*, 68–69.
57. Risa A. Brooks, *Shaping Strategy: The Civil Military Politics of Strategic Assessment* (Princeton: Princeton University Press, 2008), 237–38.
58. A detailed account of the planning and the military operations may be found in Woodward, *Bush at War*. See also Seth G. Jones, *In the Graveyard of Empires: America's War in Afghanistan* (New York: Norton, 2009, 2010), chap. 6.
59. Ricks, *Fiasco*, 70.
60. Gordon and Trainor, *Cobra II*, 26; Ricks, *Fiasco*, 33–34.
61. Gordon and Trainor, *Cobra II*, 4, 21–22, 28–30, 48; Brooks, *Shaping Strategy*, 242–43; Rose, *How Wars End*, 267.
62. Gordon and Trainor, *Cobra II*, 34. Ricks gives a figure of 10,000. Ricks, *Fiasco*, 37–38.
63. Brooks, *Shaping Strategy*, 240–41. Further, unlike Operation Desert Storm in the 1991 Gulf War, this attack would not begin with a protracted bombing campaign. To catch the Iraqis off guard, the ground assault would occur almost as soon as the air strikes commenced. Gordon and Trainor, *Cobra II*, 88–89.
64. Gordon and Trainor, *Cobra II*, 53.
65. Ricks, *Fiasco*, 40–42.
66. Ricks, *Fiasco*, 73–76.
67. Gordon and Trainor, *Cobra II*, 80–83.
68. Gordon and Trainor, *Cobra II*, 95–98.
69. Ricks, *Fiasco*, 42.
70. Gordon and Trainor, *Cobra II*, 5.
71. Rose, *How Wars End*, 258–59.
72. Brooks, *Shaping Strategy*, 234, 242; Owens, "Rumsfeld, the Generals, and the State of U.S. Civil-Military Relations," 78.
73. Gordon and Trainor, *Cobra II*, 139; Brooks, *Shaping Strategy*, 248.
74. Gordon and Trainor, *Cobra II*, 139–40.
75. Gordon and Trainor, *Cobra II*, 73, 141–42; Ricks, *Fiasco*, 108–9.

76. Ricks, *Fiasco*, 109–10. Although critics blamed Iraqi exiles, especially Ahmed Chalabi and his Iraqi National Congress, for painting an overly optimistic portrait of post–Saddam Hussein Iraq for U.S. planners, Rose is correct when he suggests that this view just gave American leaders the excuse they sought for walking away from postwar Iraq and any problems that might arise. Rose, *How Wars End*, 260. Rumsfeld in particular showed enthusiasm during the planning process for any scheme that confirmed his assumptions about light, rapid military action with no lingering commitment.

77. Nora Bensahel, "Mission Not Accomplished: What Went Wrong with Iraqi Reconstruction," *Journal of Strategic Studies* 29 (3) (June 2006): 453–73, at 459.

78. Gordon and Trainor, *Cobra II*, 70–71.

79. Ricks, *Fiasco*, 64–66, 71–73; James P. Pfiffner, "The First MBA President: George W. Bush as a Public Administrator," *Public Administration Review* 67 (1) (January 2007): 6–20, at 10; Rose, *How Wars End*, 261–62.

80. Stephen Benedict Dyson, "'Stuff Happens': Donald Rumsfeld and the Iraq War," *Foreign Policy Analysis* 5 (2009): 327–47, at 333–35, 337–38.

81. Pfiffner, "First MBA President," 10.

82. Gordon and Trainor, *Cobra II*, 142–43.

83. Bensahel, "Mission Not Accomplished," 455–56; Gordon and Trainor, *Cobra II*, 160.

84. Gordon and Trainor, *Cobra II*, 151.

85. Rumsfeld directed Feith to begin postwar planning earlier, back in September 2002, but this does not seem to have been formalized and little was done until the lagging preparations were called to the attention of the secretary and the president in late 2002. Woodward, *State of Denial*, 91, 103.

86. Gordon and Trainor, *Cobra II*, 147–50; Ricks, *Fiasco*, 80.

87. Gordon and Trainor, *Cobra II*, 152–55, 159–60; Ricks, *Fiasco*, 101–2; Woodward, *State of Denial*, 124–25.

88. Gordon and Trainor, *Cobra II*, 105. As Garner rushed to put together his group, the bureaucratic pettiness and gamesmanship continued: Rumsfeld insisted that Garner drop several State Department Iraq experts in favor of less-qualified Defense Department officials. Rumsfeld claimed that the order to exclude State Department officials came from Cheney's office. Ricks, *Fiasco*, 102–3; Gordon and Trainor, *Cobra II*, 159.

89. Brooks, *Shaping Strategy*, 248–49.

90. Gordon and Trainor, *Cobra II*, 102. Shinseki had expressed his reservations about the sufficiency of the force at a meeting with the president on January 30, 2003. Some internal Army reviews advised an even larger force of a half million troops. Gordon and Trainor, *Cobra II*, 101–4. Some accounts suggest Shinseki intended to make his disagreements with the Rumsfeld-Franks plan public. Ricks, *Fiasco*, 96–97.

91. Eric Schmitt, "Pentagon Contradicts General on Iraq Occupation Force's Size," *New York Times*, February 28, 2003; Ricks, *Fiasco*, 97–98; Gordon and Trainor, *Cobra II*, 102–3.

92. Ricks faults General Franks for failing to connect the invasion plan to the larger objectives of the war. Ricks, *Fiasco*, 115–16. But this responsibility properly rests at the top, not with the general planning the operations. Woodward says Bush refused to crack down on Rumsfeld when he refused to cooperate with other principals and agencies. Woodward, *State of Denial*, 109–10.

93. Woodward, *State of Denial*, 132.

94. Dyson, "'Stuff Happens,'" 339.

95. For a similar analysis, see Burke, "Condoleezza Rice as NSC Advisor," 572–73. On Bush's leadership style and his reliance on delegation, see Pfiffner, "First MBA President."

96. The debate on this will likely never be resolved. On the other side, deep sectarian divisions might have erupted after the departure of the dictator, no matter how many troops were there to preserve order. For a discussion of the competing viewpoints, see Rose, *How Wars End*, 274–76.

97. Gordon and Trainor, *Cobra II*, 65.

98. George W. Bush, *Decision Points* (New York: Crown, 2010), 224.

99. Gordon and Trainor, *Cobra II*, 115.

100. Ricks, *Fiasco*, 117. Others give slightly lower totals, e.g., Rose says 130,000 troops. Rose, *How Wars End*, 246.

101. Gordon and Trainor, *Cobra II*, 51.

102. Gordon and Trainor, *Cobra II*, 65–66, 120–21. On the role of overconfidence in Saddam's approach, see Dominic D. P. Johnson, *Overconfidence and War: The Havoc and Glory of Positive Illusions* (Cambridge: Harvard University Press, 2004), 192, 194–95.

103. Gordon and Trainor, *Cobra II*, 62, 122.

104. For a detailed account, see Gordon and Trainor, *Cobra II*.

105. Baath officials took their families and money out of the country during the invasion and later used the funds to finance the insurgency. Ricks, *Fiasco*, 191.

106. Ricks, *Fiasco*, 134–35; Rose, *How Wars End*, 238.

107. Soon thereafter another division would be committed, but this corresponded to withdrawal of one from the invasion force, so there was no net increase in troop strength in Iraq. Ricks, *Fiasco*, 157.

108. Dyson, "'Stuff Happens,'" 341; Ricks, *Fiasco*, 136.

109. Ricks, *Fiasco*, 168.

110. Hess, *Presidential Decisions for War*, 2nd ed., 264.

111. Kaufmann, "Threat Inflation and the Failure of the Marketplace of Ideas," 31–32.

112. Ricks, *Fiasco*, 144.

113. Ricks, *Fiasco*, 138–44.

114. Bensahel, "Mission Not Accomplished," 461.
115. Ricks, *Fiasco*, 154–55.
116. Rose, *How Wars End*, 248–49.
117. Bensahel, "Mission Not Accomplished," 457–58.
118. For example, in March 2003, Douglas Feith presented to the president plans to reshape the Iraqi military as an apolitical and more representative force. Feith warned against dismantling the military completely, other than the Republican Guard. Gordon and Trainor, *Cobra II*, 162–63.
119. Ricks, *Fiasco*, 158–60; Pfiffner, "Decision Making in the Bush White House," 377. Later, when the consequences became clear, no one involved wanted to claim "ownership" of the order. Bremer and Feith blamed each other; Rumsfeld claimed the order came from above, while others maintained it originated in the Pentagon. Like so much else in the Bush administration Iraq policy, the order never went through a proper inter-agency process. Woodward, *State of Denial*, 194, 197–98.
120. Ricks, *Fiasco*, 161–64.
121. Pfiffner, "Decision Making in the Bush White House," 378–79.
122. Woodward, *State of Denial*, 197. Bremer's action may have been the correct step to establish the United States under law as an occupying power with certain responsibilities.
123. Ricks, *Fiasco*, 254–55.
124. Hess, *Presidential Decisions for War*, 2nd ed., 268–69.
125. Bensahel, "Mission Not Accomplished," 463–64. The problem was never remedied, either. In 2006, after Bush appealed to the cabinet to enlist personnel from all agencies to go to Iraq and assist, a total of forty eight volunteers stepped forward. Woodward, *War Within*, 53.
126. Where in Western democracies the military typically has eight to ten times the personnel of the combined personnel of ministries of foreign affairs and international development, in the United States government the ratio of personnel in the armed forces (1.8 million) to those in the State Department (6,000 Foreign Service Officers) and Agency for International Development (2,000 personnel) is 210:1. The mismatch in budgets is even larger, 350:1. Tore Nyhamar, "Accidental Vacuum or Counterinsurgency Logic? The Making of American Iraqi Surge Strategy 2007," paper prepared for the ECPR Stockholm, September 8–11, 2010, 21–22.
127. Ricks, *Fiasco*, 203–5, 207–8; Dobbins, "Who Lost Iraq?" 66–67. For a full account of the CPA experience, see Rajiv Chandrasekaran, *Imperial Life in the Emerald City: Inside Iraq's Green Zone* (New York: Alfred A. Knopf, 2006).
128. As an indicator, Iraqi confidence in the CPA declined from 47 percent expressing some confidence in it in November 2003 to a mere 14 percent in March 2004. Ricks, *Fiasco*, 326. For a somewhat more positive view of the CPA record, see Rose, *How Wars End*, 249–50.
129. Ricks, *Fiasco*, 155–56.

130. Rumsfeld said he had not been involved in or even aware of the decision to make Sanchez commander in Iraq. Woodward, *State of Denial*, 297–98. If so, it was a remarkable failure on his part to permit such a vital decision to be made without his approval—and likewise a failure by his boss, the president.
131. Ricks, *Fiasco*, 173–74.
132. Ricks, *Fiasco*, 324–25.
133. Ricks, *Fiasco*, 170, 172, 183–84; Woodward, *State of Denial*, 247; Hess, *Presidential Decisions for War*, 2nd ed., 262–63. Bush later acknowledged the comment to have been a mistake.
134. Woodward, *State of Denial*, 475; Ricks, *Fiasco*, 217–21, 262–64.
135. Ricks, *Fiasco*, 225–28.
136. Ricks, *Fiasco*, 192.
137. Ricks, *Fiasco*, 195, 197, 199–200, 270ff., 378–80; Hess, *Presidential Decisions for War*, 2nd ed., 267–68.
138. Ricks, *Fiasco*, 347–48.
139. Ricks, *Fiasco*, 358–59.
140. Hess, *Presidential Decisions for War*, 2nd ed., 271.
141. U.S. troops were cautioned against the indiscriminate use of firepower in populated areas, and Casey established a counterinsurgency school for newly arriving American officers. Ricks, *Fiasco*, 393–94, 414.
142. On problems of morale, see Ricks, *Fiasco*, 309–10.
143. Ricks, *Fiasco*, 420–21.
144. Bremer's reckless decision to disband the established Iraqi military meant starting over from scratch to reconstitute a functioning force. Time was lost, to no purpose—every officer and noncommissioned officer in the reconstituted army had served in its predecessor. Recruiting and training new units proved a slow, fitful process. Despite claims that Iraqi battalions were ready to assume security tasks, inspections by various American military and civil officials found that virtually none of the supposedly fully trained troops were considered sufficiently reliable to commit to combat on their own. They had to be partnered with American units, which did most of the heavy fighting. Further, despite claims of impressive numbers of Iraqi soldiers by 2006, no one knew how many actually remained under arms; the desertion rate was extraordinary, with entire units sometimes vanishing. All of it was eerily reminiscent of the ARVN during Westmoreland's days, which said little for what the Iraqi army would be capable of doing if left on its own.
    Abizaid and Casey, convinced that foreign troops were an irritant to Iraqi society, sought nevertheless to accelerate the transition to Iraqi military self-sufficiency. Thus, while paying lip service to COIN doctrine that stressed the importance of small unit tactics and population security (which implied dispersing forces among the people), Casey concentrated U.S. troops in large, cloistered Forward Operating Bases (FOB), lavishly

supplied with American comforts that helped boost morale. Woodward, *State of Denial*, 288, 336; Ricks, *Fiasco*, 338–41, 416–18; Woodward, *War Within*, 4–5; Stephen Benedict Dyson, "George W. Bush, the Surge, and Presidential Leadership," *Political Science Quarterly* 125 (4) (2010–2011): 557–85, at 560–61, 564.

145. Ricks, *Fiasco*, 167–68; Dyson, "'Stuff Happens,'" 339–40.

146. Ricks, *Gamble*, 58; Woodward, *State of Denial*, 393.

147. Dyson, "'Stuff Happens,'" 341.

148. Woodward, *State of Denial*, chap. 8; Dyson, "'Stuff Happens,'" 336.

149. Woodward, *State of Denial*, 418; Woodward, *War Within*, 31–33, 36–38; Dyson, "George W. Bush, the Surge, and Presidential Leadership," 563.

150. Ricks, *Fiasco*, 407–8; Dyson, "George W. Bush, the Surge, and Presidential Leadership," 560, 576.

151. Ricks, *Fiasco*, 413–14; Woodward, *State of Denial*, 471–72.

152. Woodward, *State of Denial*, 260, 326.

153. Woodward, *War Within*, 28.

154. Woodward, *State of Denial*, 397–98.

155. Woodward, *War Within*, 93–94. The White House had let it be known that Bush studied Cohen's book before the invasion of Iraq. Ricks, *Gamble*, 19.

156. Woodward, *State of Denial*, 319, 483; Woodward, *War Within*, 4.

157. Woodward, *State of Denial*, 306, 367–68.

158. Dyson, "'Stuff Happens,'" 342.

159. Andrew Bacevich, "He Told Us to Go Shopping. Now the Bill Is Due," *Washington Post*, October 5, 2008, http://www.washingtonpost.com/wp-dyn/content/article/2008/10/03/AR2008100301977.html.

160. John Frendreis and Raymond Tatalovich, "Riding the Tiger: Bush and the Economy," in *Ambition and Division: Legacies of the George W. Bush Presidency*, ed. Steven E. Schier (Pittsburgh: University of Pittsburgh Press, 2009), 224.

161. This was part of a broader post-9/11 partisan polarization on foreign policy. Jack Snyder, Robert Shapiro, and Yaeli Bloch-Elkon, "Free Hand Abroad, Divide and Rule at Home," paper presented at the 2007 Annual Meeting of the American Political Science Association, August 30–September 2, 2007, 15.

162. As late as 2005, 81 percent of Republicans believed Saddam Hussein had possessed WMD before the invasion. Snyder, Shapiro, and Bloch-Elkon, "Free Hand Abroad, Divide and Rule at Home," 21–22.

163. Hess, *Presidential Decisions for War*, 2nd ed., 270.

164. Ricks, *Gamble*, 13.

165. Woodward, *State of Denial*, 423.

166. The credibility parallel was not entirely coincidental: Bush met regularly to discuss the war with Henry Kissinger, who gave his particular—and misleading—spin on how the United States had failed in Vietnam. Woodward, *State of Denial*, 408–9.

167. Woodward, *State of Denial*, 424; Dyson, "George W. Bush, the Surge, and Presidential Leadership," 565.

168. Woodward, *War Within*, 89. By August 2005 Bush's approval rating fell to 38 percent, and only 34 percent approved of his handling of the war. Hess, *Presidential Decisions for War*, 2nd ed., 272–73. In November 2005, Bush's approval rating in an NBC News/*Wall Street Journal* poll was down to 38 percent favorable and 57 percent unfavorable. Woodward, *State of Denial*, 421.

169. Ricks, *Gamble*, 58–59.

170. Jordan Tama, "The Power and Limitations of Commissions: The Iraq Study Group, Bush, Obama, and Congress," *Presidential Studies Quarterly* 41 (1) (March 2011): 135–55.

171. Woodward, *State of Denial*, 481.

172. Woodward, *War Within*, 76.

173. Dyson, "George W. Bush, the Surge, and Presidential Leadership," 564–65.

174. Woodward, *War Within*, 81.

175. Woodward, *War Within*, 64, 72.

176. Woodward, *War Within*, 7.

177. Dobbins, "Who Lost Iraq?" 62–63; Owens, "Rumsfeld, the Generals, and the State of U.S. Civil-Military Relations," 70; Ricks, *Gamble*, 38–39.

178. Dyson, "George W. Bush, the Surge, and Presidential Leadership," 572–73.

179. Ricks, *Gamble*, 41–42; Dyson, "George W. Bush, the Surge, and Presidential Leadership," 572; Woodward, *War Within*, 71, 108, 189–90, 193.

180. Woodward, *War Within*; Dyson, "George W. Bush, the Surge, and Presidential Leadership," 571.

181. Woodward, *War Within*, 235.

182. Ricks, *Gamble*, chap. 3; Dyson, "George W. Bush, the Surge, and Presidential Leadership," 571; Woodward, *War Within*, 129ff.

183. Dyson, "George W. Bush, the Surge, and Presidential Leadership," 568.

184. Dyson, "George W. Bush, the Surge, and Presidential Leadership," 570.

185. This solution was promoted by Leslie Gelb, Peter Galbraith, and Democratic Senator Joe Biden, at the time also a presidential aspirant. Dyson, "George W. Bush, the Surge, and Presidential Leadership," 566. See also Galbraith, *End of Iraq*, chaps. 10–11; Woodward, *State of Denial*, 481.

186. Dyson, "George W. Bush, the Surge, and Presidential Leadership," 567.

187. Tama, "Power and Limitations of Commissions"; Dyson, "George W. Bush, the Surge, and Presidential Leadership," 573–74.

188. Dyson, "George W. Bush, the Surge, and Presidential Leadership," 566–68.

189. Woodward, *War Within*, 316.

190. George W. Bush, "President's Address to the Nation," January 7, 2007, http://georgewbush-whitehouse.archives.gov/news/releases/2007/01/20070110-7.html.

191. Dyson, "George W. Bush, the Surge, and Presidential Leadership," 581; Woodward, *War Within*, 202–3.

192. CENTCOM, at Petraeus's suggestion, would go to Admiral William J. "Fox" Fallon, an ill-considered choice because he neither understood the surge nor its underlying rationale. Fallon and Petraeus clashed often over the following months.

193. Ricks, *Gamble*, 123.

194. Nyhamar, "Accidental Vacuum or Counterinsurgency Logic?" 7; Woodward, *War Within*, 327. Petraeus brought with him as his deputy (and eventual successor) Lieutenant General Raymond Odierno and a number of the dissident colonels such as McMaster and Peter Mansoor who had advocated COIN methods.

195. Nyhamar, "Accidental Vacuum or Counterinsurgency Logic?" 9.

196. Nyhamar, "Accidental Vacuum or Counterinsurgency Logic?" 18–19.

197. For an excellent account of the Awakening and the motives of the tribal leaders that relies heavily on Arabic sources, see Marc Lynch, "Explaining the Awakening: Engagement, Publicity, and the Transformation of Iraqi Sunni Political Attitudes," *Security Studies* 20 (2011): 36–72. The decision to arm Sunni irregulars was made by Petraeus and Odierno in Iraq, with little or no discussion with administration officials in Washington. Ricks, *Gamble*, 217.

198. Woodward, *War Within*, 381.

199. Ricks, *Gamble*, chap. 10.

200. Ricks, *Gamble*, 261, 263.

201. Nyhamar, "Accidental Vacuum or Counterinsurgency Logic?" 6.

202. Ricks, *Gamble*, 264–65.

203. Ricks, *Gamble*, 236–37; Woodward, *War Within*, 307, 311, 342–43, 348–49.

204. For a fuller discussion of congressional efforts to set a withdrawal deadline, see Andrew J. Polsky, "Collective Inaction: Presidents, Congress, and Unpopular Wars," *Extensions* (Spring 2008): 4–8.

205. Tama, "Power and Limitations of Commissions," 149.

206. Ricks, *Gamble*, 244. Democrats looked forward to another opportunity to condemn the president's war policy when General Petraeus returned for a hearing before the Senate Foreign Relations Committee in fall 2007. By that point, however, insurgent attacks had abated and casualties had started to decline, so the Democratic narrative of "no progress in Iraq" no longer fit all the evidence. Democrats could still point up the lack of real political progress. Unfortunately for them, on the day of the hearing an antiwar organization published a large ad in the *New York Times* questioning Petraeus's patriotism, a remarkably maladroit swipe at a military commander in wartime. Republican senators had a field day condemning the ad and putting their Democratic colleagues on the defensive. Several Democratic would-be presidential candidates, including the eventual nominee, Senator Barack Obama, used the occasion to state their position against the war and the president's handling of it. The hearings otherwise shed little light on the actual situation in Iraq.

207. Ricks, *Gamble*, 155.
208. Nyhamar, "Accidental Vacuum or Counterinsurgency Logic?" 9.
209. Ricks, *Gamble*, 254.
210. Tim Arango, "Clashes Fuel Debate over U.S. Plan to Leave Iraq," *New York Times*, March 28, 2011. On Iraqi fears and expectations in the wake of the final American withdrawal, see Tim Arango, "U.S. Marks End to a Long War for an Uncertain Iraq," *New York Times*, December 16, 2011.
211. Tim Arango, "Iraqi Youths' Political Rise Is Stunted by Elites," *New York Times*, April 13, 2011.
212. On the failure to ask any sacrifice of the public, see Woodward, *War Within*, 436.
213. Dyson, "George W. Bush, the Surge, and Presidential Leadership," 578–79.
214. Ricks, *Gamble*, 217.
215. Gideon Rose arrives at the same conclusion. See Rose, *How Wars End*, 276.

Chapter 6

1. Bob Woodward, *Obama's Wars* (New York: Simon and Schuster, 2010), 158.
2. For an analytical assessment of the Afghanistan decision process, see James P. Pfiffner, "Decision Making in the Obama White House," *Presidential Studies Quarterly*, 41 (2) (June 2011): 244–62.
3. Seth G. Jones, *In the Graveyard of Empires: America's War in Afghanistan* (New York: Norton, 2009, 2010).
4. Woodward, *Obama's Wars*, 101–2.
5. Obama estimated that public patience with the war would be exhausted in two years. Woodward, *Obama's Wars*, 110.
6. Woodward, *Obama's Wars*, 41–44, 71, 73, 80–81.
7. Woodward, *Obama's Wars*, 96–97. My discussion of Obama's decision making on Afghanistan is based primarily on Woodward's account.
8. At a White House meeting of key security officials, including Petraeus, on October 3, 2009, Obama polled the group and found no one in favor of withdrawal. Woodward, *Obama's Wars*, 186.
9. Woodward, *Obama's Wars*, 82–86, 118–20.
10. Woodward, *Obama's Wars*, 82–86, 118–20, 123.
11. Woodward, *Obama's Wars*, 156, 158, 183–84.
12. Woodward, *Obama's Wars*, 160; Pfiffner, "Decision Making in the Obama White House," 257–58.
13. In addition to Woodward, *Obama's Wars*, see especially Peter Baker, "How Obama Came to Plan for 'Surge' in Afghanistan," *New York Times*, December 6, 2009.
14. Woodward, *Obama's Wars*, 8.
15. Woodward, *Obama's Wars*, 106–7, 190.
16. Woodward, *Obama's Wars*, 77, 214–43.

17. Woodward, *Obama's Wars*, 166, 213, 225; Baker, "How Obama Came to Plan for 'Surge' in Afghanistan."
18. Woodward, *Obama's Wars*, 177.
19. Woodward, *Obama's Wars*, 135–37, 147–48, 150–51, 218–21; Pfiffner, "Decision Making in the Obama White House," 257.
20. Woodward, *Obama's Wars*, 4.
21. Woodward, *Obama's Wars*, 195; Pfiffner, "Decision Making in the Obama White House," 256.
22. Mullen even tried to block the presentation to the president of the counterterrorism option, but Obama got wind of it and insisted on hearing the details. Woodward, *Obama's Wars*, 237–38.
23. Defense Secretary Gates hoped to make up the difference with contingents from NATO allies. Baker, "How Obama Came to Plan for 'Surge' in Afghanistan."
24. Woodward, *Obama's Wars*, 315–16.
25. Woodward, *Obama's Wars*, 145.
26. Woodward, *Obama's Wars*, 251ff., 270–71, 277–80, 290–91, 301–2, 304; Pfiffner, "Decision Making in the Obama White House," 258–59.
27. Woodward, *Obama's Wars*, 325.
28. Woodward, *Obama's Wars*, 331.
29. Baker, "How Obama Came to Plan for 'Surge' in Afghanistan."
30. "Obama's Address on the War in Afghanistan," *New York Times*, December 2, 2009.
31. Woodward, *Obama's Wars*, 230–31.
32. Carlotta Gall, "A Slice of Afghanistan Well Secured by Afghans," *New York Times*, May 23, 2011.
33. For a skeptical analysis of the American approach, see Bing West, *The Wrong War: Grit, Strategy, and the Way Out of Afghanistan* (New York: Random House, 2011).
34. Dominic Tierney, "Did Karzai Sabotage Peace Talks in Afghanistan?" *Atlantic*, September 5, 2011, http://www.theatlantic.com/international/archive/2011/09/did-karzai-sabotage-peace-talks-in-afghanistan/244511/.
35. See, for example, Jane Perlez, "Meeting with Pakistani Leaders, Kerry Seeks to Ease Anger over Bin Laden Raid," *New York Times*, May 16, 2011; Matthew Rosenberg, "Clinton Gets Cold Reception," *Wall Street Journal*, May 28–29, 2011.
36. Woodward, *Obama's Wars*, 356–57, 363–67.
37. Elisabeth Bumiller and Jane Perlez, "Pakistan's Spy Agency Is Tied to Attack on U.S. Embassy," *New York Times*, September 22, 2011.

Conclusion

1. Both presidents had other, more far-reaching goals, especially reaching an accommodation with the communist superpowers. These goals, though connected to Vietnam, did not depend on a particular outcome in the conflict.

2. Gideon Rose, *How Wars End: Why We Always Fight the Last Battle* (New York: Simon and Schuster, 2010).

3. Although wars have put an end to liberal presidents' efforts to expand the federal government, some groups have received expanded social benefits as a reward for their wartime sacrifices. Near the end of the Second World War, Congress approved the GI Bill of Rights, a package of education and housing benefits for those who served in the armed forces. As I noted, the British response to popular demands for increased social benefits covered the entire population, but the British people as a whole had suffered far more and for far longer than Americans had. Sometimes Americans who did not serve in uniform have pressed a claim that their wartime contributions be recognized. Women parlayed their efforts on behalf of mobilization in the First World War into approval of the constitutional amendment that granted them the right to vote. So long as the United States fights wars with a professional military and no broad social mobilization, however, it is unlikely that any other group will be able to build on the idea of wartime sacrifice as the basis for receiving social benefits.

4. Rose, *How Wars End*, 284–85.

5. John F. Kennedy popularized this phrase after the Bay of Pigs fiasco in 1961, but the quote has been attributed to several earlier public figures.

INDEX

Abizaid, John, 302, 304–5, 313, 315,
    420n144
Abrams, Creighton, 246, 255–57,
    259–62, 304, 411n179
Abu Ghraib, 303, 307
Afghanistan, 4, 6, 16–18, 22, 30, 278,
    286–87, 289–91, 308, 326–39, 347,
    349, 353–54, 369n5
Alabama, 33, 47, 55, 60
Alexander, Harold, 175
Algeria, 174
Alien Act of 1918, 116
Allawi, Ayad, 303–4
Allies, the (*see also* Great Britain,
    France)
    in World War I, 85–89, 91–92, 94,
        99, 101–2, 104, 106, 108–111, 113,
        121–24, 128, 381n3, 385n83
    in World War II, 135, 138–39,
        154–56, 171–72, 174–76, 178,
        183–86, 194, 350
Al-Qaeda, 7, 17, 22, 277–79, 281–84,
    310, 328–29, 332–34

Al-Qaeda in Iraq (AQI), 303, 314, 319,
    324
Ambrose, Stephen, 133, 154
American-British Conversations
    Number I (ABC-I), 147
American Civil War. *See* Civil War
American Expeditionary Force (AEF),
    101–3, 106–11
American Federation of Labor, 118, 164
American Inquiry, 120
American Protective League (APL), 116
Anaconda Plan, 46–47
Anbar Awakening, 319–20, 324–25, 333
Antietam, 38–39
Antiwar opposition, 24, 238, 345–46
    during Civil War, 61, 65, 74, 77, 79
    during Iraq War, 310–11, 321,
        423n206
    during Vietnam War, 237, 239–40,
        258–59, 263–64, 345–46
    during World War I, 116, 195–96, 237
    presidential responses to, 116,
        258–59, 310–11

Appomattox, 52, 79
Arkansas, 35, 58, 71
Army Appropriation Act of 1916, 105
Army of Northern Virginia
    (Confederate), 39, 49, 52, 56
Army of the Ohio/Cumberland
    (Union), 45, 50, 376n54
Army of the Potomac (Union), 44,
    49–50, 52, 56, 59, 378n86
Army of the Republic of Vietnam
    (ARVN), 206, 214, 225–26, 229,
    236, 244–45, 253–62, 267, 270,
    401n9, 411–12n205, 420n144
Army of Tennessee (Confederate), 59
Army of the Tennessee (Union), 44, 50
Army, United States. See United States
    Army
Arnett, Peter, 245
Arnold, Henry "Hap", 169
Askariya Mosque, 312
Asymmetric warfare, 21–22, 25, 29, 57
Atlanta campaign (1864), 51, 60, 62
Atlantic Charter, 158, 196
Atomic bomb, 159, 186. (See also
    nuclear weapons)
Australia, 144, 169–71, 177
Austria, 122, 194
Austria-Hungary, 86–87, 123
Austro-Hungarian Empire. See
    Austria-Hungary

B-17 bombers, 148, 154
B-29 bombers, 177, 185–86, 195
B-52 bombers, 268–69
Baath Party, 279, 290, 293, 296,
    298–99, 302, 418n105
Bacevich, Andrew, 17, 19
Bahrain, 322
Baker, James, 311–12
Baker, Newton, 103, 106, 109, 111,
    384n71, 384n76
Balfour, Arthur, 99
Balkans, the, 159, 172, 175, 184, 194,
    285, 290, 388n166

Ball, George, 208, 211, 214, 281, 403n35
Banks, Nathaniel, 55, 71
Baruch, Bernard M., 105, 152
Basra, 275, 295, 319
Bataan, 169
Beauregard, P. G. T., 35
Beijing (city), 135. See People's
    Republic of China
Berlin (city), 192. See also Germany
Berman, Larry, 266, 408n107, 408n113
Bethmann Hollweg, Theobald von, 89
Beveridge Report (Great Britain), 9
Bhagdad (city), 4, 276, 279, 287, 291,
    293–99, 301, 312, 314, 318, 323.
    See also Iraq
Biden, Joe, 330, 332, 335, 422n185
Bin Laden, Osama, 277–79, 333, 338
Bismarck, Otto von, 41
Bliss, Tasker, 108, 385n93
Bosnia, 20, 289, 292
Bragg, Braxton, 59
Bremer III, L. Paul "Jerry", 299–303,
    305, 419n119, 419n122,
    420–21n144
Bridges, George T. M., 102
British Army
    in World War I, 101–2, 106–10
British Navy, 86–88, 101, 137, 142–143,
    146, 149, 390n30
Brooke, Alan, 172–73, 175, 189, 191,
    400n214
Bryan , William Jennings, 88, 90
Buell, Don Carlos, 45, 50, 375n42
Bulgaria, 149, 183
Bundy McGeorge, 208, 215, 235
Bunker, Ellsworth, 267
Burleson, Albert S., 116–17
Burma, 143, 158–59, 170, 179–80, 186,
    194
Burma Road, 159
Burnside, Ambrose, 50
Bush Doctrine, 282, 284
Bush, George H.W., 8, 19–20, 24, 274,
    373n52

Bush, George W., 5, 10, 19, 23, 29, 273,
    277–78, 280–81, 294–95, 298,
    302, 323–25
    and allies, 279, 284, 323, 346
    and antiwar critics, 310–11, 346
    and Congress, 283, 309, 320–21,
        341
    decides on troop surge, 274, 316–17,
        323–24
    declines to mobilize nation for
        lengthy war, 308–9, 314, 345
    delegates responsibility to
        subordinates, 273, 298, 300,
        306–7, 317–18, 320, 323–24, 343
    discourages doubts or questions
        within administration about Iraq,
        281, 290, 305–6
    domestic agenda of, 309–10, 320,
        349, 351
    and expanded executive authority,
        278, 325
    fails to oversee invasion and postwar
        planning, 287–88, 290–92, 323,
        348, 356
    fails to respond assertively to
        insurgency, 274, 302, 305, 344
    lacks leverage over Iraqi
        government, 318, 346
    loses freedom of action in Iraq, 273,
        324–25, 352–53
    as a military commander in chief,
        287, 306–7, 312, 316–18, 320, 343
    and nation building, 288–89, 293,
        323
    and peace building, 273–74, 280,
        292–93, 298, 356
    and public opinion, 274, 279,
        282–83, 309–11, 315–17, 322, 345,
        415n45, 422n168
    and September 11, 2001 (9/11)
        terrorist attacks, 277–78, 280,
        293, 308, 310, 345, 355
    slides into Iraq invasion, 279–82
    and war goals, 288, 297, 321, 323, 347

Butler, Benjamin, 37, 72
Byrnes, James, 394n98

Cambodia, 209, 229, 232–33, 243–44,
    260–61, 264, 405n63
    secret bombing of, 7, 257–58, 261,
        410n167
    U.S. forces and ARVN incursion
        into, 257–61, 263, 343, 346,
        411–12n205
Caroline Islands, 177
Casablanca Conference (1943), 155,
    397n162
Casey, George, 304–5, 313, 315, 317,
    420n141, 420–21n144
Central Command, United States
    (CENTCOM), 274, 278, 286–88,
    290, 293, 295, 302, 304, 313, 320,
    330–31, 343, 423n192
Central Intelligence Agency (CIA), 16,
    281, 286, 334, 338
Central Office for South Vietnam
    (COSVN), 259
Central Pacific, 148, 169, 177
Central Powers (World War I), 86, 88,
    92, 98, 111, 123
Chalabi, Ahmed, 415n38, 417n76
Chamberlain, Neville, 135, 137
Chase, Salmon, 62
Chattanooga, battle of, 59
Cheney, Dick, 277, 280–81, 283, 307,
    311, 316, 414n29, 414n34, 417n88
Chiang Kai-shek, 136, 158–59, 170–71,
    178–79, 187, 190, 199. See also
    Nationalist China
Chickamauga, battle of, 54
Chicago Tribune, 196
China (Nationalist), 123, 125, 135–36,
    140–41, 149, 155, 157–59, 170–71,
    178–79, 191, 199, 347, 388n170.
    See also Chiang Kai-shek, People's
    Republic of China
China-Burma-India (CBI) theater,
    178–79, 186

Church, Frank, 263
Churchill, Winston, 143, 146, 155,
    158–59, 169, 171–73, 175–76,
    179–80, 182–85, 198, 306,
    397n158, 398n185, 398n189,
    399n206, 399n209
  as a military strategist, 190–95,
    400n212, 400n214
Civil War, 14, 18, 20, 24, 29, 32, 36, 38,
    45, 56, 58, 68, 113, 117–18, 150, 181,
    317, 343, 353
  anti-draft riots during, 61
  Border States in, 33, 35, 41–42, 64,
    66, 74–76, 81
  casualties influence public opinion,
    38, 61, 64
  frequent elections in North during,
    61
  as modern war, 20, 51–52
  role of slaves in, 36–38, 40, 42, 58,
    63, 68–74
Civilian Conservation Corps, 166
Clemenceau, George, 83, 109, 122, 124,
    126, 128, 132, 188, 388n173
Clausewitz, Carl von, 6, 23
Clifford, Clark, 208, 211, 214, 217,
    246–47, 250–51, 253
Clinton, Bill, 276–77, 285
Clinton, Hillary, 335
Coalition Provisional Authority,
    299–301, 303, 419n128
Cohen, Eliot A., 8, 32, 52, 103, 130, 191,
    285, 287, 376n61, 421n155
  advises George W. Bush, 306, 316
Cold War, 16–17, 20–21, 28, 202, 208,
    215, 278
Committee on Public Information
    (CPI). See Creel Committee
Confederacy (Civil War). See
    Confederate States of America
Confederate States of America, 33,
    36–37, 41, 45–47, 49, 53–54,
    57–59, 65, 70, 76, 81, 85, 87,
    346, 353

Geographic advantages of, 46
    trans-Mississippi region of, 47, 58
Confiscation Act of 1861, 38
Congress of Industrial Organizations,
    164
Congress Party (India), 179
Congress, United States. See United
    States Congress
Conscription, 16–17, 42, 58, 65, 76, 78,
    100, 113–14, 151–52, 154, 164, 221,
    263, 308, 345, 378n86, 378n87
Conscription Act of 1863, 42
Constitution, United States. See
    United States Constitution
Cooper-Church Amendment, 260, 264
Corregidor, 169
Council of National Defense (CND),
    94, 104
Counterinsurgency warfare (COIN),
    26, 206, 221, 223, 228, 231, 302,
    304, 313–14, 317, 319–20, 323–24,
    331–38, 343, 353, 355, 404n55,
    420n141, 420–21n144, 423n194
Counterterrorism, 331–33, 335, 369n5,
    425n22
Creel Committee, 114–116, 119–20, 153
Creel, George, 114
Crete, 172, 193
Croly, Herbert, 114
Cronkite, Walter, 246
Cuba, 3–4, 16, 208, 211
Cuban Missile Crisis, 208, 210
Czechoslovakia, 122, 135, 137

Daladier, Edouard, 137
Dallek, Robert, 403n39
Danang, 214
Davis, Jefferson, 32, 53, 56–57, 61, 377n67
  and civil liberties in the
    Confederacy, 75
  and selection of Confederate
    military commanders, 59–60
  pursues conventional strategy,
    57–59, 377n82

Debs, Eugene Victor, 117
Decker, George H., 222, 404n57
Defense Department. *See* United
     States Department of Defense
De Gaulle, Charles, 211, 393n87
Democratic Party, 136, 211–212, 354
     (*see also* War Democrats)
   during Afghanistan conflict, 329
   during Civil War, 36–39, 44–45, 61,
      64–65, 67, 77, 181–82, 350
   during Iraq War, 283, 309–12,
      315–17, 320–21, 329, 351, 415n47,
      422n185, 423n206
   during Vietnam War, 213, 237, 246,
      263–64, 266, 350–51
   during World War I, 93, 115, 118,
      127–29
   during World War II, 140, 165–67
Democratic Republic of Vietnam
     (DRV). *See* North Vietnam
Democrats. *See* Democratic Party
Detroit, 167
Dewey, Thomas E., 165
Diamond, Larry, 294
Diem, Ngo Dinh, 205–7, 401n6
Dien Bien Phu, siege of, 204, 244
Dodecanese, the, 159, 175
Domino theory, 209–10
Dong, Pham Van, 248
Doolittle raid, 176
Douglas, Stephen A., 69
Draft. *See* Conscription
Dred Scott (1857), 78, 372n50
Dresden, 230
Drones. *See* Predator drones
Dumbarton Oaks Proposals, 187
Dunkirk, British evacuation from, 143,
     191
Du Pont, 104

Early, Jubal, 52
Eastern Europe, 16, 28, 99, 122,
     183–84, 188, 192, 195, 208–209,
     345, 388n166, 398n185

Easter Offensive (1972), 256, 260, 267,
     270
Egypt, 126, 322
Eighteenth Amendment, passage of
     the, 115
Eikenberry, Karl, 334
Eisenhower, Dwight, 15, 211, 252,
     257–58, 285
   in World War II, 169, 175–76, 192
   and Vietnam, 202, 205, 209, 402n23
Eisner, Mark Allen, 394n106
Elections, U.S., 65
   1860 presidential, 33
   1861 spring congressional, 75
   1862 congressional, 39, 45, 65
   1863, 76
   1864, 52, 60–61, 71–73, 76
   1916 presidential, 91, 94
   1918 congressional, 85, 115, 121, 127,
      350
   1940 presidential, 142, 146, 153
   1942 congressional, 165, 174,
      394–95n107
   1944, 163, 167, 178
   1964 presidential, 206, 208, 213,
      403n31
   1972 presidential, 267
   2000 presidential, 277
   2004 presidential, 310
   2006 congressional, 5, 315, 320, 362
   2008 presidential, 322
Emancipation Proclamation, 40, 61,
      63, 69, 353
England. *See* Great Britain
Enola Gay (B-29 bomber), 186
Entente. *See* Allies
Espionage Act of 1917, 116

Fair Employment Practices
     Commission (FEPC), 166–67
Fallon, William J. "Fox", 320, 423n192
Far East, 138–39, 143–45, 147–49, 178
Federal Control Act of 1918, 104, 118
Federal Reserve System, 105

Federally Administered Tribal Areas
    (FATA), 334
Feith, Douglas, 282, 291, 417n85,
    419n118, 419n119
First World War. *See* World War I
Fisher, Louis, 13
Foch, Ferdinand, 108–9, 126
Foggia, 175
Foner, Eric, 32
Foreign Relations Committee, United
    States Senate, 237, 423n206
Formosa (Taiwan), 177–78, 187
Ford, Gerald R., 270–71
Fort Sumter, 33–35, 41–42, 75, 129–30,
    341
Four Freedoms, the, 196, 349
France, 16, 248, 284. *See* also Vichy
    regime
    in Civil War, 54
    in World War I, 86–87, 91, 96,
        99–100, 106–8, 110, 112, 118,
        121–22, 124–26
    in World War II, 137–40, 142–43,
        150, 171–72, 174–76, 187, 191
    in Indochina, 187, 204–205, 408n119
Franks, Tommy, 278–79, 286–89, 291–92,
    295, 299, 301–2, 417n90, 418n92
French Army
    in World War I, 101–2, 108–11
    in World War II, 142–43
Freedman's Bureau, 73
Frémont, John C., 37
Fulbright, J. William, 237

Galbraith, Peter, 422n185
Garner, Jay, 291–92, 299–300, 417n88
Gates, Robert, 317, 330, 335, 425n23
Gavin, James, 407n97
Gelb, Leslie, 422n185
Geneva accords, 205, 207, 248, 401n6
Geneva Conference (1954), 204–5, 248
Georgia, 47, 51
German Army
    in World War I, 107–10

    in World War II, 151, 173, 190,
        396n137
German Navy, 89, 101, 122, 149
    submarines (U-boats), 89–90, 94,
        101, 130, 143, 146, 170–71, 175, 194
Germany, 135–36, 181–83, 190
    and Treaty of Versailles, 122–24, 126
    in World War I, 86, 88–90, 92,
        94–96, 107, 112
    in World War II, 29, 36, 133–35,
        137–39, 141, 144–49, 154–56, 159,
        162, 171, 174–76, 191–93, 273, 282,
        393n78
"Germany First" strategy, 147, 149, 171,
    174
Gettysburg, battle of, 56, 376–77n66
Giap, Vo Nguyen, 204, 243, 245,
    408n119
GI Bill of Rights, 197, 426n3
Goebbels, Joseph, 155
Goldwater, Barry, 213, 403n31
Gompers, Samuel, 118
Grant, Ulysses S., 44, 50–53, 55–58, 60,
    72, 317, 396n135
Great Britain, 16, 86, 136, 140, 276,
    401n6, 426n3
    in Civil War, 57, 346
    in Iraq War, 287, 295, 319, 323
    in World War I, 85–89, 91–92, 94–96,
        99–101, 107, 112, 122, 124, 126
    in World War II, 140, 143–46, 148,
        152–53, 157–58, 160, 162, 171–72,
        175, 185–86, 189–93, 197, 199, 341,
        390n30, 398n185, 399n206,
        400n227
Great Depression, 136, 139, 162, 168,
    349, 395–96n107
Greece, 123, 172, 184, 191, 193–94
Greenland, 146
Gregory, Thomas W., 116
Guadalcanal, 174, 177, 192, 228
Guerilla warfare. *See* also asymmetric
    warfare, counterinsurgency
    in Civil War, 57–58, 377n68

Gulf War (1991), 6, 8, 17–21, 276, 285–86, 323, 372n43, 373n52, 413n2, 416n63

Hadley, Stephen J., 313, 316
Haig, Alexander, 257, 259–60, 268
Haiphong harbor, 229, 233, 261, 408n119
Hamilton, Alexander, 370–71n24
Hamilton, Lee, 312
Hanoi (city), 204, 268, 408n119. (*see also* North Vietnam)
Harding, Warren G., 129
Harriman, Averill, 250
Hastings, Max, 178
Hawaii, 142, 144, 177–78, 180, 341
High Seas Fleet. *See* German Navy
Himmler, Heinrich, 156
Hiroshima, 15, 186, 230
Hitler, Adolf, 123, 133–35, 137, 143, 146, 149, 155–56, 170, 172–73, 191, 199–200, 341, 400n210, 400n222
  view of Franklin Roosevelt, 137–38
  as a rigid strategist, 189–90
Ho Chi Minh, 204–5, 248, 251, 253, 402n24
Ho Chi Minh Trail, 207, 226, 229, 233
Hood, John Bell, 60
Hooker, Joseph, 44, 50, 59, 377n80
Hopkins, 151, 169
House, Edward M., 90, 92, 112–13, 120, 382n28
House of Representatives. *See* United States Congress
Howard, Oliver Otis, 44
Hue, 244–45
Hull, Cordell, 136, 140–41, 181–82
Humphrey, Hubert, 211, 214, 217
Hungary, 182
Huntington, Samuel, 7–8, 52
Hurricane Katrina, 310

Ia Drang Valley, 232
Iceland, 393n75

Illinois, 64
Imphal, 180, 194
Improvised Explosive Devices (IEDs), 17, 302, 304, 309, 325
India, 126, 143–44, 158, 178–80, 192, 334, 338, 372n43, 398n175
Indiana, 64
Indochina, 143, 148, 179, 186–87, 204, 255, 347, 390n26, 401n1. *See also* North Vietnam, South Vietnam, Thailand
Indonesia, 209, 234
Industrial Workers of the World (IWW), 116–17
International Monetary Fund, 188
Inter-Services Intelligence Directorate (ISI), 334
Iran, 276, 279–80, 282, 315, 319, 338
Iran-Iraq War, 372n43
Iraq, 4–6, 8, 16–19, 23, 25–29, 119, 273–331, 333, 336–37, 341, 343–49, 351–54, 356, 369n8, 412–13n1, 413n5, 414n24, 414n27, 415n38, 416n63, 417n76, 418n107, 419n118, 419n125, 419n128, 420n130, 420n144, 423n197, 423n206, 424n210
Iraqi Governing Council, 300–1
Iraqi National Congress, 417n76
Iraq Liberation Act of 1998, 277
Iraq Study Group (ISG), 312, 315–317, 323–24
Iraq War, 5, 24, 274, 309, 317, 346, 351, 412–13n1
Isolationism, 23, 93, 139, 185, 187–88, 196–97, 199, 212, 356
Israel, 277, 372n43
Italy, 91, 122–23, 126
  in World War II, 138, 144, 162, 172–73, 175–76, 180, 191, 193–94, 282, 398n177
Iwo Jima, 178, 180, 186

Jackson, Andrew, 62, 380n145

Jackson, Stonewall, 49, 55
Jafari, Ibrahim al, 304
Japan, 133, 135–138, 381n3, 392n56
    attacks China, 135–36, 140–141
    and Treaty of Versailles, 123, 125–26,
        388n170
    in World War II, 21–23, 29, 35–36,
        133, 135–36, 140–45, 147–49,
        154–59, 162, 1681–172, 174,
        177–82, 184–86, 189, 191–92, 194,
        197–200, 229, 273, 282, 299, 341,
        352, 390n26, 394n95, 397n162,
        399n192, 399n206
Johnson, Andrew, 64, 72–73
Johnson, Harold, 402–3n24
Johnson, Lyndon, 8–10, 27, 207–8,
        211–13, 242, 251, 271, 273, 341, 351,
        403n31, 407n94
    and allies, 219–20, 229, 403n26,
        405n72
    and antiwar movement, 237,
        239–40, 345
    commits to sustaining South
        Vietnam, 203, 210–11, 217–18
    and Congress, 213, 216, 228, 237–38,
        350
    and differences with Joint Chiefs of
        Staff, 216–17, 222–24, 230–31,
        233–34, 246–47
    escalates American involvement in
        Vietnam War, 214–17
    frames war goals, 217–19, 347
    and Great Society, 9, 212–13, 217,
        220, 228, 238, 271, 349–50
    lacks leverage over South
        Vietnamese government, 219,
        247, 249–51, 346
    limits bombing of North Vietnam,
        228–30
    loses freedom of action, 203, 215,
        228, 234–35, 353
    as military commander in chief,
        203, 220–21, 223–26, 228, 233–35,
        342–44

    and news media, 236–37
    and peace talks, 250, 348
    and public opinion, 203, 210,
        216–17, 220, 236–39, 242,
        246, 345, 407n102, 407n103,
        409n127
    recognizes need to limit Vietnam
        War, 210–12, 216, 219, 223–24
    seeks negotiations with Hanoi,
        247–49, 251–52, 346, 409n148
    speech at Johns Hopkins University,
        217, 248, 251–52
    and Tet Offensive, 203, 245–47
    views Vietnam War through Cold
        War framework, 208–11, 215,
        218
Johnston, Joseph E., 59–60, 377n82
Johnston, Albert Sidney, 58–59
Joint Chiefs of Staff (JCS). See United
    States Joint Chiefs of Staff
Joint Committee on the Conduct of
    the War, 62, 80
Jones, Seth, 373n51
Jordan, 322

Kabul (city), 286. See also Afghanistan
Karzai, Hamid, 328, 332–34, 338
Khanh, Nguyen, 207
Keane, Jack, 314, 330–31
Kennedy, David M., 161, 165
Kennedy, John F. 205–8, 217, 221–23,
        401n12, 403n35, 404n57, 426n5
Kennedy, Robert F., 208, 237, 246
Kentucky, 54, 58, 380n136
Kerry, John, 310
Keynes, John Maynard, 388n164
Khe Sanh, 235, 244, 342
Khmer Rouge, 260
Kimball, Warren F., 391n39, 393n83,
        398n185, 399n197
Kimmel, Husband E., 144
King, Ernest J., 168–69, 171, 176–78,
        185, 397n162, 397n163,
        399n192

Kissinger, Henry, 204, 249, 253–54, 257, 260–62, 264–70, 339, 410n157, 421n166

Kluge, Günther von, 156

Kohima, 180, 194

Komer, Robert, 232

Korean War, 15, 18–20, 29, 208, 210–11, 216–18, 220–21, 225, 252, 262, 406n85

Kosovo, 20, 289

Kosygin, Alexei, 234

Kurds, 275, 290–91, 301, 303, 313, 320, 322

Kuwait, 24, 274–75, 284, 288, 295–96, 299, 373n52

Ky, Nguyen Cao, 249

La Guardia, Fiorello, 153

Laird, Melvin, 253, 255–59, 261–62, 410n164

Lam Son 719, 256–57, 260–61

Langguth, A. J., 401n7, 401–2n15, 403n35

Lansing, Robert, 89–90, 92

Laos, 207, 209, 229, 232–33, 244, 256–57, 260, 264, 343, 405n63, 406n83, 406n85

Larrabee, Eric, 170, 390n12, 393n82, 394n95, 396n137

League of Nations, 99, 121–22, 126–28, 131, 187, 326, 348, 388n170

Lebanon, 193

Lee, Robert E., 39, 49–50, 52, 55–56, 72, 79

Lend-Lease, 146, 153, 159–60, 162, 391n39

Lewis, John L., 164

Leyte Gulf, battle of, 178

Liberty ships, 162

Libya, 170, 322, 342

Life magazine, 197

Lincoln, Abraham, 29, 31–32, 40–41, 79–82, 129–30, 135, 156, 182, 198, 200–201, 222, 225–26, 228, 237, 240, 263, 273–74, 306, 316–17, 326, 340, 344, 346–47, 349–50, 353, 357, 372n40, 373n49, 373n2, 374n10

and abolitionists, 35–36, 63

accepts need for war, 341

adjusts Union war goals, 36–41, 228, 353

and antiwar opposition, 32, 74, 76, 80, 344, 350

and Congress, 42–43, 62, 66–67, 71–78, 80, 82

curbs civil liberties, 33, 65, 74–79, 81–82

delays preparations for Reconstruction, 69–70, 72–73, 81, 182, 347

and diplomacy, 346

and emancipation, 32, 36–40, 44, 50–51, 53, 61–63, 65, 68–70, 72, 76–77, 156, 228, 353

establishes Union war strategy, 32, 45–50

exercises wartime emergency powers, 18–19, 33, 41–42, 63, 66, 74–77

faces secession crisis, 33–34

and freedmen, 40, 68–74, 347

as military commander in chief, 41–56, 342–43, 373–74n66

and Northern morale, 32, 39, 60–61, 80

and peace-building, 32, 68–71, 120, 263, 347, 357

and the press, 38, 49, 61, 64–65, 79

and Republican Party, 32, 34, 60–62, 66, 71, 80, 344, 349

and Reconstruction, 9, 69–73, 81, 380n145

sustains popular support for war, 32, 43, 62–63, 78

understands his constitutional responsibilities, 34, 63, 77–78, 380n145

Lindsay, Lawrence, 290
Lloyd George, David, 124, 126, 188
Lodge, Henry Cabot, 115, 121, 127–29, 132, 188
Lodge Jr., Henry Cabot, 235
London. *See* Great Britain
Louisiana, 55, 58, 70–71
Ludendorff, Erich von, 108–10
Lusitania, 89

MacArthur, Douglas, 20, 148, 177–78, 180, 193, 210, 220–21, 225, 299, 396n129, 397n163
    and Franklin Roosevelt, 148, 169–70, 177–78
Machiavelli, Niccolo, 6
MacMillan, Margaret, 123, 387n142, 388n173, 388n175, 389n179
Malaya, 143, 148, 159, 170, 180, 186, 193
Malaysia, 209
Maliki, Jawad al, 304, 312, 318–20, 322, 325
Manchuria, 135, 145, 186, 190
Manela, Erez, 383n56
Manhattan Project, 177, 186
Mansfield, Mike, 211, 215, 401n12
Mansoor, Peter, 412n194
Mao Zedong, 226, 402n24
March, Peyton, 106
Marion, Francis, 57–58
Mariana Islands, 177
Marshall Islands, 177
Marshall Jr., George C., 150–51, 154, 159, 168–69, 172–76, 180, 192, 200
Marshall Plan, 188
Maryland, 36, 49, 75
McAdoo, George, 105
McCarthy, Eugene, 237, 246
McClellan, George B., 39, 44–45, 49–50, 55, 225, 343, 375n41
McChrystal, Stanley, 330–332, 335, 338
McGovern, George, 264
McKiernan, David, 295–297, 301, 330–31, 333

McKinley, William, 4–5, 14
McMaster, H. R., 304, 423n194
McNamara, Robert S., 206, 208, 214–16, 222–26, 230, 233–34, 238, 246, 253, 284, 286, 401n12, 406n85, 407n90
Mills, Wilbur, 238
Military Assistance Command Vietnam (MACV), 207
McPherson, James, 23, 32, 36, 43, 380n136
McPherson, James B., 44
Meade, George, 50, 56, 376n66
Mediterranean, the, 159, 170, 173–76, 180, 184, 193–94, 198, 295, 393n78, 398n177, 398n185
Meuse-Argonne, 109
Mexican War, 13, 73
Mexican-American War. *See* Mexican War
Mexico, 54, 73, 92, 100, 102–3
Middle East, 24, 274–75, 280, 288, 303, 310–11, 321–22, 347, 362, 372n43, 388n166
    in World War II, 143–144, 170, 172, 193
Midway, battle of, 176
Military Assistance Command Vietnam (MACV), 233, 240–41, 245–46, 259–61, 408n113
Minh, Ho Chi. *See* Ho Chi Minh
Minh, Duong Van "Big", 207
Mississippi, 49–50
Mississippi River, 46–47, 50, 54–55, 70
Missouri, 37, 47, 58
Moltke, Helmuth von, 375n28
Montgomery, Alabama, 33
Morgenthau Jr., Henry, 136, 141–42, 151, 182, 389n1
Morgenthau Plan, 182
Morocco, 174
Morton, Oliver P., 64
Moscow, 145, 170. *See also* Soviet Union

Mubarak, Hosni, 322
Mullen, Mike, 330, 339, 425n22
Munich Pact, 1938, 135, 137–38, 145,
    150, 154, 209
Murtha, John, 311
Mussolini, Benito, 138–39, 175
Myers, Richard, 305

Nagasaki, 186
Napoleonic Wars, 6, 57, 87
National Defense Act of 1916, 93–94,
    101, 151
National Guard, 3, 93–94, 100, 259,
    308
National Labor Relations Board, 167
National Liberation Front (NLF), 205,
    231, 249, 265, 268
National Resources Planning Board
    (NRPB), 165–66, 349
National Security Act of 1948, 16
National Security Council (NSC), 16,
    257, 260, 315
National War Labor Board (NWLB),
    164
Nationalist China. See China
Navy, United States. See United States
    Navy
Neely Jr., Mark E., 65
Nelson, Donald M., 161, 394n98
Netherlands, the, 143, 147
Netherlands East Indies, 143–44,
    147–48, 170, 390n26
Nuclear weapons, 21, 200, 239, 279,
    402n23. (See also atomic bomb)
Neoconservatives, 276–77, 285
Neustadt, Richard, 10
Neutrality Act of 1937, 139–40, 142
Newbold, Gregory S., 415n36
New Britain, 170
New Deal, 136, 141, 152, 160, 163–66,
    181, 197
New Dealers, 165–66, 181, 196–97, 212,
    248, 349
New Guinea, Papua, 170, 174, 177

New Orleans, 55, 70–71, 310, 349
New York City anti-draft riots, 61,
    378n86
New York Times, 258
New Zealand, 144, 171
Nimitz, Chester, 169, 176–77
Nineteenth Amendment, passage of
    the, 117
Nixon, Richard M., 202–204, 250,
    259, 271, 326–27
    and antiwar movement, 258–59,
        263–64, 346–47
    and Congress, 253, 263–64, 270
    frames war goals, 252–53, 347
    loses freedom of action, 254, 264, 272
    and negotiations with North
        Vietnam, 253–54, 262, 265–69, 346
    and peace building, 254, 262–64,
        271–72, 348
    and public opinion, 254, 258–59,
        263–64, 266
    as military commander in chief,
        203, 254, 257–62, 343
    pursues Vietnamization, 203,
        253–55, 257, 259–63, 267, 336
    regains limited discretion as
        wartime leader on taking office,
        203, 252, 272, 353
    and relations with South
        Vietnamese government, 204,
        267–70, 346
    and return of American prisoners of
        war (POWs), 265–66, 270
    and Watergate, 270
    withdraws American troops over
        time, 254, 261
Nol, Lon, 258
Non-Aggression Pact (Germany and
    Soviet Union), 138
North Africa, 172–74, 180, 193–94,
    197, 228, 396n137
North Atlantic Treaty Organization
    (NATO), 16, 188, 229, 328, 330,
    332–33, 336–37, 425n23

North Carolina, 35, 47, 378n87
Northern Alliance (Afghanistan), 286
North Korea, 210, 282
North Vietnam, 8–9, 203–205, 207, 209–10, 212, 214–15, 218, 223, 228–30, 233–34, 237, 239–40, 242, 246–54, 257–58, 260–62, 264–70, 338, 343, 345–46, 348, 401n7, 401–402n15, 402n16, 402–3n24, 406n84, 406n86, 408n87, 410n156, 411–12n205
North Vietnamese Army (NVA), 207, 225–26, 232–33, 240–41, 244–45, 250, 255–58, 261–62, 265–71, 401–2n15, 411n203. (*see also* Vietcong)
Normandy, 175–6, 190, 194
Norway, 172, 194
Nye Committee, 390n13

Obama, Barack, 5, 30, 322, 326–27, 342, 351, 423n206
  and allies
  and Congress, 329
  decides on troop surge, 331–332, 336–37
  and decision making process on Afghanistan, 327–28, 331–32, 335
  frames limited war goals, 331, 335–36, 347
  loses freedom of action, 327–28, 337, 339
  as military commander in chief, 330–31, 335–36
  and peace building, 336
  and public opinion, 329, 333, 336–37, 424n5
  regains limited discretion as wartime leader on taking office, 327–29, 353
  and relations with Afghanistan government, 332–34, 337–39, 346
  and relations with Pakistan government, 332, 334–35, 337–39, 346
Odierno, Raymond, 423n194, 423n197
Office of Reconstruction and Humanitarian Assistance (ORHA), 291, 299
Office of Price Administration, 394–95n107
Office of War Mobilization, 394n98
Ohio, 65, 76
Okinawa, 178, 186
Operation Desert Fox, 276
Operation Desert Storm, 275, 416n63
Operation HUSKY, 174–75
Operation JUPITER, 194
Operation Linebacker, 257
Operation OVERLORD, 175
Operation Rolling Thunder, 214, 216, 229
Operation TORCH, 174, 197
Overman Act of 1918, 105
Ottoman Empire, 86, 122

Pace, Peter, 305
Pacification in Vietnam, 231, 255, 411–12n205
Pakistan, 17, 22, 328–29, 332–39, 372n43
Paris (city), 108, 120, 122–25, 127, 132, 250–51, 255, 258, 262, 265, 267. *See also* France
Paris Peace Accords, 265, 269, 348
Pashtun, 334
Patriot Act, USA, 278
Pearl Harbor, 15, 29, 134, 144, 148, 152–54, 171, 200
  attack on unifies American public opinion, 195–96, 217
  Japanese attack on, 22–23, 35, 133
Pelosi, Nancy, 315
Pemberton, John C., 59
Pentagon. *See* United States Department of Defense

People's Army of Vietnam (PAVN).
    See North Vietnamese Army
People's Republic of China, 17, 204,
    207–11, 218, 226, 229–30, 234,
    261, 264, 267, 338, 354, 402–3n24,
    405n69, 405–6n74. *See also*
    China (Nationalist)
Pershing, John J, 102–4, 106–12, 130,
    342, 384n71, 384n76
Persian Gulf War. *See* Gulf War
Petersburg, Virginia, siege of, 50, 72
Petraeus, David, 313, 317–21, 325,
    330–333, 335, 338, 423n192,
    423n194, 423n197, 423n206,
    424n8
Philippines, 5, 86, 133, 143, 148, 154,
    169–71, 177–78, 180, 194–95, 209,
    341, 369n7, 390n26, 392n53
Philippine Sea, battle of the, 177
Phoenix Program, 256
Plan Dog, 147
Ploesti raid, 176
Poland, 122, 124, 134, 137–39, 149, 151,
    154, 183–85, 192, 199, 398n185,
    398n189
Polk, James K., 13–14, 43, 73, 371n25
Pope, John, 39
Portugal, 149
Potsdam Proclamation, 186
Powell, Colin, 19, 277, 281, 284, 290,
    295, 300, 305
Predators drone, 17, 22, 332,
    334, 338
President of the United States
    and antiwar opposition, 113, 131,
        345–46, 358
    and assertions of wartime
        emergency powers, 6–7, 26, 33,
        42, 76–79, 81, 362
    can lead nation into war, 129–30,
        146, 341–42, 358
    constitutional war powers of, 11–12
    and domestic reform, 9–10, 66–67,
        117–18, 131, 349–51, 426n3

    encounters postwar obstacles, 85,
        120, 127, 129, 131–32, 182, 204,
        347–48, 352
    exercises broad discretion at outset
        of war, 26–27, 96, 352
    and "imperial presidency", 271–72
    loses freedom of action during war,
        26, 132, 134, 198, 272, 324, 351–52,
        356–57
    and future conflicts, 353–57
    loses leverage over allies at end of
        war, 123, 131–32, 182, 347
    media and press coverage of, 65
    as military commander in chief, 5,
        9, 11–12, 15, 23, 56, 71, 76–77,
        83–84, 341–44, 352,
        355–356, 359
    and mobilization for war, 104–6,
        149–50
    and peace building, 9, 26, 67–68,
        131, 182, 263, 292, 344, 346–48,
        356–57
    regains some flexibility when
        assuming war initiated by
        predecessor, 328–29, 353
    struggles to sustain morale and
        popular support, 67, 80, 118–19,
        197, 307–8, 344–45, 355, 358–59
    and wartime civil liberties, 7, 81–82
    and wartime diplomacy, 346
    wartime leadership tasks of, 5–6,
        22–25, 130–31, 149, 200, 271, 340,
        344
Progressivism, 90, 114, 117–18, 131
Prussia, 41, 155, 375n28

Quebec conference, 175

Rabaul, 170, 177
Radical Republicans, 70–72, 74,
    181–82
Railroads War Board, 105
Randolph, A. Phillip, 166
Reconstruction, 32, 69–73, 77, 81

Red Army (World War II), 15, 162, 172–73, 175, 183–84, 190, 192, 194–95, 198, 348, 399n206
Reid, Harry, 315
Republican Guard (Iraqi), 8, 275, 295, 413n5, 419n118
Republican Party, 136, 354 (see also Radical Republicans, Union Party)
  during Civil War, 32, 34, 39, 43, 60, 62, 64–66, 70–72, 74, 76, 80, 181–82, 349, 380n131
  during Vietnam War, 237–38
  during World War I, 93, 121, 127–29
  during World War II, 165, 187
  during Iraq War, 301, 309, 311, 314–15, 320–22, 362
Revenue Act of 1942, 163
Rice, Condoleeza, 281, 283, 290, 305, 311, 313, 414n29
Richardson, James O., 144
Richmond, 49, 55, 60
Ricks, Thomas, 414n24, 418n92
Ridgeway, Matthew, 407n97
Robb, Chuck, 315
Roberts, Andrew, 396n135, 398n177
Rome, 175
Rommel, Erwin, 156
Roosevelt, Franklin D., 9, 18–19, 22–23, 29, 35, 136–7, 141–42, 150–51, 157, 340, 346
  aids allies, 144, 148
  asserts broad wartime emergency powers, 146
  enjoys broad discretion when United States enters war, 199–200
  and conservatives, 135–36, 163–66, 181, 198–99, 350
  and cross-Channel invasion of France, 171–76, 194
  differs with allies over postwar order, 182–84
  and Douglas MacArthur, 148, 169–70, 177–78

  and failed plan to pack Supreme Court, 134, 136, 138–39
  and George C. Marshall, 150–51, 173, 175–176, 180, 192, 200
  identifies Hitler and Germany as primary threat, 133–34, 138, 148–49, 171
  and Josef Stalin, 159, 184–85, 188, 191, 198, 398n189
  learns from Wilson's mistakes, 136–37, 156–57, 181, 187–88
  loses freedom of action over course of war, 134, 156, 180–81, 186, 195, 198–200
  as military commander in chief, 134–35, 168, 171–80, 191, 194–95, 200, 318, 342
  and New Deal, 136, 168, 349–50
  and peace-building, 134–35, 176, 180, 182, 186–88, 191–92, 347, 357
  prepares for American entry into war, 134
  and public opinion, 23, 134, 139–40, 153–54, 184–85, 187–88, 192, 199, 344–45
  and race relations, 160, 166–67
  seeks to retain freedom of action, 134, 138–39, 142–43, 145–47, 149, 151, 180, 182, 195, 199–200, 348
  and social reform during and after the war, 163–64, 168, 350
  sustains support for the war, 195–98
  tries to deter Japan in Pacific, 137, 141–45, 147–50, 341, 352
  and unconditional surrender, 154–55, 185
  view of postwar order, 157, 178–79, 182, 187, 191–92, 347
  war goals of, 154, 156–59
  as wartime strategist, 135, 191–93
  war mobilization and finance under, 135, 150, 152, 154, 160–63, 173–74, 350–51
Roosevelt, Theodore, 86, 93, 102

Rose, Gideon, 28, 278, 356, 370n18, 417n76, 418n100, 419n128, 424n215
Rosecrans, William, 50
Royal Navy. *See* British Navy
Rumania, 176, 182
Rumsfeld, Donald, 4, 19, 273, 278–79, 285–94, 297–99, 302, 304–5, 307–8, 311, 313–315, 317, 323, 325, 329, 343, 352, 417n76, 417n85, 417n88, 417n90, 418n92, 419n119, 420n130
Russia, 86, 107, 114, 119, 124. *See also* Soviet Union
Russian Revolution, 107, 114, 119, 386n121
Rusk, Dean, 208, 407n90
Rwanda, 285

Saddam Hussein, 5, 8, 19, 23, 273–84, 289, 293–97, 302–303, 309, 323, 341, 346, 356, 373n52, 415n38, 415n45, 418n102, 421n162
Sadr, Muqtada al, 303–4, 319, 325
Saigon (city) 204, 236, 244, 250, 268, 271. *See also* South Vietnam
Saint-Mihiel, 109
Saipan, 177
Samarra, 312
Sanchez, Ricardo, 301–2, 304, 420n130
San Diego, 144
Schlesinger Jr., Arthur M., 271–72
Schwarzkopf, Norman, 8, 274–275, 285
Scott, Winfield, 35, 41, 45–47
Second Bull Run (Manassas), battle of, 38–39, 61
Second World War. *See* World War II
Security Council Resolution 1441 (2002), 284
Sedition Act of 1918, 116
Senate. *See* United States Congress

September 11, 2001 (9/11) terrorist attacks, 7, 19, 23, 273, 277–80, 283, 293, 308, 310–11, 316, 325, 334, 336, 345, 350, 355, 414n27, 421n161
Seven Days, battles of the, 38
Seward, William, 62
Seymour, Horatio, 378n86
Shenandoah Valley, 49, 52, 55, 60, 62
Sheridan, Phil, 45, 52, 62
Sherman, William Tecumseh, 45, 50–51, 60, 62, 72, 377–78n82
Shia, 275, 277, 290, 301, 303–4, 312–13, 318–20
Shiite. *See* Shia
Shiloh, battle of, 38
Shinseki, Eric, 19, 292, 294, 297, 325, 417n90
Shoup, David, 407n97
Sicily, 172, 174, 180, 194
Sihanouk, Norodom, 258, 410n167
Singapore, 137, 143, 148, 158–59, 170, 180, 186, 193, 390n26
Skowronek, Stephen, 372–73n46
Slim, William, 180
Smith-Connally Act, 166
Smith, Rupert, 22, 302
Social Security, 166, 310, 320, 351
Solomon Islands, 176
Somalia, 328
Sorley, Lewis, 410n158
South Carolina, 33, 35, 57, 70
South Korea, 209, 217–18, 229, 262, 336, 406n85, 411–12n205. *See also* Korean War
Southeast Asia, 179, 205, 210, 215, 218–21, 229, 248, 257, 263–64, 311, 348, 406n85
Southeast Asia Treaty Organization (SEATO), 205
South Vietnam (GVN), 202, 210–14, 218–20, 222, 228, 240, 242–43, 246–51, 254, 256, 263–65, 267–71,

South Vietnam (*continued*)
  318, 334, 346, 401n9, 401–2n15,
  411n179, 411–12n205. *See also*
  Army of the Republic of Vietnam
  (ARVN)
Soviet Army. *See* Red Army
Soviet Union, 15–16, 20, 133, 138, 157,
  160, 183–84, 278, 354, 363
  in World War II, 144–45, 148, 155,
    162, 170–72, 186, 189–91, 306,
    347, 391n39
  and Vietnam, 204, 209, 228–30,
    234, 264, 401n6, 405–406n74
Spanish-American War, 3–5, 14, 86
Spanish Civil War, 135
Speer, Albert, 162
Stanton, Edwin, 55–56, 80, 225
Stark, Harold, 147, 395n127
Stalin, Josef, 28, 138, 145, 155, 159, 169,
  172–73, 185–86, 188–90, 198, 208,
  398n185
  and pressure on Allies for Second
    Front, 171, 174–75
  and postwar Europe, 182–84, 188,
    190–92, 399n206
Stalingrad, 172, 190, 200, 296,
  400n210
State Department. *See* United States
  Department of State
Stennis, John, 237–38
Stimson, Henry, 151, 182
Sudetanland, 135
Summers Jr., Harry G., 401–2n15
Sunnis, 275, 290, 301, 303–4, 306, 312–13,
  317–20, 324–25, 333, 423n197. *See
  also* Anbar Awakening
Sun Tsu, 6
Supreme Court. *See* United States
  Supreme Court
Supreme War Council, 107
Syria, 193, 296, 315, 322

Taiwan, 209, 229. *See also* Formosa
Tal Afar, 304–5, 314

Taliban, 7, 17, 22, 278, 286, 289, 328,
  331–39
Taney, Roger, 75, 372n40
Taylor, Maxwell, 235
Teheran conference, 182
Tennessee, 35, 47, 49–50, 58, 71
Tennessee Valley Authority, 248
Tet Offensive, 225, 240, 243–46, 252,
  255, 313, 408n119, 411–12n205
Texas, 13, 46, 54–55, 58, 371n25
Terrorism, 17, 23, 274, 277, 308, 310
Thailand, 209, 406n85
Thanh, Nguyen Thich, 242–43
Thieu, Nguyen Van, 204, 244, 249–51,
  254, 256–57, 260–62, 265–72, 338,
  346, 411–12n205
Third Reich. *See* Germany
Tho, Le Duc, 250, 265–67, 269, 339
Thomas, George H., 54
Thompson, J. A., 383n48, 383n50
Thucydides, 6
Tikrit, 296
Tinian, 177
Tobruk, 191, 193
Tonkin Gulf incident, 212–13, 217, 341,
  403n31
Tonkin Gulf Resolution, 213, 216, 263
Trading with the Enemy Act of 1917,
  116
Trask, David, 381n5, 382n32
Treasury Department. *See* United States
  Department of the Treasury
Treaty of Versailles,
Truman, Harry, 10, 15
Tunisia, 156, 174, 322
Turkey, 123, 175, 191, 284, 295

Union Army, 41–44, 50–51. *See also*
  individual armies
Union Party, 64
United Mine Workers, 164
United Nations, 16, 18, 157, 187–88,
  199, 216, 263, 347
  and Iraq, 275–76, 284, 415n47

United States Agency for International
    Development, 419n126
United States Air Force, 160, 162, 176
United States Army Air Force. *See*
    United States Air Force
United States Army, 14–15, 33–35, 86,
    100, 137
  in Civil War. *See* Union Army
  in Iraq, 295–297, 301–4, 308–9
  in Vietnam, 221–22, 228–29, 232
  in World War I, 93, 100–101 (*see also*
    American Expeditionary Force)
  in World War II, 149, 151–3, 160
United States Central Command. *See*
    Central Command, United States
    (CENTCOM)
United States Congress, 13, 18, 130, 132,
    139, 275, 277, 309, 341
  during Afghanistan conflict, 329,
    331, 337, 339
  during Civil War, 37, 42–43, 62,
    66–67, 70–73, 75–78, 80, 82
  constitutional war powers of, 11–13, 75
  reasserts role at end of war, 67–68,
    73, 182
  supports president at outset of war, 25
  unable to end wars, 27, 260, 321, 358
  during Iraq War, 283, 292, 305,
    311–12, 315–16, 320–21, 324
  during Vietnam War, 211, 213, 216,
    237–38
  during World War I, 100–101, 105,
    118, 126–29
  during World War II, 133, 137, 140,
    146, 151–52, 154, 159–60, 163,
    165–66, 168, 186–88, 198, 200
United States Constitution, 5, 11–13,
    18, 33–34, 63, 74–75, 77–78, 130,
    372n46
  and presidential war powers, 5, 9, 11–12
United States Department of Defense,
    16, 21, 221–23, 256, 260, 273, 282,
    284–86, 301–2. (*See also* War
    Department)

and Iraq War planning, 286,
    288–92, 296, 298, 308, 323, 331,
    335, 419n119
United States Department of State, 89,
    142, 185, 187, 290, 417n88,
    419n126
United States Department of the
    Treasury, 163
United States Employment Service,
    167
United States House of Representatives.
    See United States Congress
United States Joint Chiefs of Staff
    (JCS), 19, 168–69, 178–79, 195,
    214, 216–17, 229, 238, 257–58,
    260, 339, 395n127, 407n99
  differ with Johnson over Vietnam,
    219–20, 222–24, 230, 233–34, 247,
    405n60
  and Iraq War, 300, 305, 308, 312,
    314, 323
United States Marines, 176, 180, 214,
    216, 228, 235, 244, 297, 302,
    393n75
United States Military Academy. *See*
    West Point
United States Military Assistance
    Command Vietnam. *See* Military
    Assistance Command Vietnam
    (MACV)
United States Navy, 5, 14, 86,
    390n26
  in Civil War, 46, 75, 377n68
  in Spanish American War, 3, 14
  in World War I, 15, 86, 92, 94, 101,
    144, 148, 169
  in World War II, 15, 137, 140, 142,
    144, 146, 149, 152, 168, 177–78,
    189, 390n30, 392n53
  in Vietnam, 212
United States Senate. *See* United States
    Congress
United States Special Forces (Green
    Berets), 206, 221

United States Supreme Court, 18, 78, 134, 136, 138, 372n40
USS *Abraham Lincoln*, 298
Utley, Jonathan G., 141

Vallandigham, Clement, 65, 74, 76
Vance, Cyrus, 250
Vandenburg, Arthur, 188
Vicksburg, 47, 49–51, 54, 56, 58, 59, 70, 396n135
Vichy regime, 143, 173, 193
Victory Program, 160, 173, 196, 400n222
Vienna, 194
Vietcong (VC), 206, 214–15, 225–26, 231–32, 240–41, 244–45, 255–56, 269, 406n83, 411n203. (*see also* North Vietnamese Army)
Vietnam. *See* Vietnam War. (*see also* South Vietnam)
Vietnam War, 6–9, 17, 19, 21, 202–3, 205, 210, 223, 234–35, 271, 306, 309, 321, 345, 362, 401n1
Villa, Pancho, 100, 102–3
Virginia, 37, 46, 49, 52, 54
    considers secession, 33, 35–36
    as key theatre in Civil War, 47

Wade-Davis Bill, 71–72, 380n145
Wake Island, 171
War Democrats, 36, 63–64
War Department, 73, 93, 104, 395n115. (*See also* Department of Defense)
War Industries Board (WIB), 105
War Labor Board, 167
War of 1812, 14, 24, 370–71n24
War Manpower Commission, 167
War Powers Resolution (1973), 18, 272, 342
War Production Board (WPB), 161, 394n98
Warsaw Uprising, 182, 184
Washburne, Elihu, 43–44

Washington, D.C. (city), 36, 49, 52, 55, 59–60, 128, 166, 236
Washington, George, 142
Washington Naval Treaty (1922), 149
Wavell, Archibald, 191, 193
Watergate, 270, 272
Watt, Donald Cameron, 138
Weapons of Mass Destruction (WMD), 5, 276–77, 279, 281, 283–84, 287, 293–95, 297–98, 309, 323, 413n7, 415n38, 415n45, 421n162
Wehrmacht. See German Army
Western Front (World War I), 51, 110, 138, 240
Western Hemisphere, 5, 86, 95, 142–44, 146, 151, 154
Westmoreland, William, 8, 207, 214, 216, 221, 224–26, 229, 231–32, 234–36, 240–46, 253, 255, 317, 332, 344, 404n54, 405n64, 406n83, 408n113, 411–12n205, 420n144
West Point, 43, 282
Wheeler, Earle "Bus", 223–24, 230, 246, 406n86
Whig Party, 43, 62, 371n25, 380n145, 411n184
Wilhelm II, Kaiser, 90, 121
Wilmington, 47
Wilmot, David, 73
Wilson, Harold, 403n26
Wilson, Woodrow, 9, 15, 18–19, 23, 25, 27, 29, 83, 86–87, 89, 94–95, 114, 119–20, 129–31, 133–34, 137, 139, 149, 152–53, 156–57, 161–62, 164, 181–82, 185, 187–88, 195–96, 199–201, 219, 222, 228, 273, 326, 345, 347–50, 385n93
    and antiwar critics, 116–17, 119, 131, 195–96, 237, 350, 386n134
    and Armistice, 85, 111–12
    cedes control over decision to go to war to Germany, 90, 94–96, 130

chooses neutrality at beginning of
World War I, 86–87
and Congress, 93–94, 96, 105, 118,
120, 127–29, 131–32, 345, 348, 350
differs with Allies over war goals,
99–100, 113, 123, 347–48
and end of Progressive reform
movement, 117–18, 131, 349
establishes ambitious war goals, 84,
91, 96–99, 121, 347
and League of Nations, 99, 121–22,
126–129, 131–32
as military commander in chief, 84,
101–4, 109, 111–12, 130, 342–43,
384n85, 386n111, 386n113
mishandles American neutrality,
83–84, 88–90, 91–92
negotiates Treaty of Versailles,
121–129, 132
and peace-building, 90–91, 98–99,
120, 131–32, 263, 347
and preparedness, 92–94, 382–83n44
proposes the Fourteen Points as
basis for peace, 98–99, 112–13
and Republicans, 84, 113, 115, 121,
350
seeks to sustain popular support for
war, 84, 113–15, 118–19, 130
selects Pershing to command AEF,
102–3, 130
and self-determination, 99–100,
121–24, 383n56
war mobilization under, 84, 104–6,
118, 130, 350, 385n77
Wingate, Ord, 194

Wolf, Frank, 311
Wolfowitz, Paul, 277, 282, 291–92,
297, 415n38
Wood, Leonard, 93, 102
Woodward, Bob, 330, 332, 418n92
Works Progress Administration,
166
World Bank, 188
World War I, 14, 18, 24–25, 28–29, 83,
118, 137, 139, 153, 161, 240
economic impact on United States,
87–88
effect of casualties on belligerents
and their populations, 91, 119,
125, 345
position of United States at
beginning of, 85–87
World War II, 14–16, 21, 25, 28–29, 36,
134, 200, 204, 208, 220–21, 223,
230, 236, 282
begins with German invasion of
Poland, 138
racial tensions in the United States
during, 160
spurs economic recovery in United
States, 135, 162, 165, 197, 349

Yalta conference, 183–85, 199, 398n185
Yalu River, 210
Yates, Richard, 64
Yemen, 322
Yugoslavia, 123, 183, 194

Zarqawi, Abu Musab al, 314
Zinni, Anthony, 286